THE ANNALS OF
THE KING'S ROYAL RIFLE CORPS

THE ANNALS OF THE
KING'S ROYAL RIFLE CORPS

Vol. I. 'The Royal Americans'
By Lt.-Col. Lewis Butler.

Vol. II. 'The Green Jacket'
By Lt.-Col. Lewis Butler.

Vol. III. 'The 60th: The K.R.R.C.'
By Lt.-Col. Lewis Butler.

APPENDIX, Dealing with Uniform, Armament and Equipment. By Maj.-Gen. Astley Terry and S. M. Milne.

KING'S ROYAL RIFLE CORPS
Regimental Chronicle for 1917.

ALL RIGHTS RESERVED

GENERAL THE RT. HON. SIR REDVERS BULLER, V.C., G.C.B., G.C.M.G.

[*Frontispiece*

THE ANNALS OF THE KING'S ROYAL RIFLE CORPS

BY
MAJOR-GENERAL SIR STEUART HARE,
K.C.M.G., C.B.

VOLUME IV

THE 60TH: THE K.R.R.C.

WITH ILLUSTRATIONS AND MAPS

LONDON
JOHN MURRAY, ALBEMARLE STREET, W.
1929

PREFACE

TO

THE FOURTH VOLUME

If the early part of the nineteenth century may be called one of the classic periods of the British Army, that from the Battle of Waterloo to the South African War may well be described as its Middle Ages. The nation, as regards the Army and its readiness for war, went to sleep. The Crimean War was only a nightmare. The sleeper woke up with a start, turned over, and went to sleep again. The much greater shock of the South African War, followed by the growing German menace, not only woke him afresh but kept him awake.

It is the history of our Regiment during the last twenty-five years of the Middle Ages, followed by the Renaissance period which prepared the nation to send to France in August 1914 the finest force that ever left these shores, which, in quality, could compare with anything the continental armies could produce, that this volume of our Annals aspires to tell.

There had been some signs of an awakening at the very beginning of our period. The successes of Prussia in the wars of 1864, 1866, and 1870 had made our authorities realise the necessity of Short Service and a Reserve; but the greater lessons, which now seem so obvious that it is hard to believe that they were not always of general acceptation, that an Army must be something more than a collection of independent units, that training and military education in peace is a necessary prelude to success in war, and that the formation of a properly organised General Staff was the first necessary step to the attainment of the desired reforms, were not learnt for another quarter of a century.

Cardwell's introduction of Short Service produced the men, but they were untrained except on the barrack square. The abolition of Purchase got rid of a certain number of Officers before they died of old age or were paid to make room for those who might be richer, but were not necessarily in any other respect but age more fitted for command than themselves. It did not ensure that the younger class of officer it produced should not suffer from cerebral atrophy owing to—in ninety-nine cases out of a hundred —the entire disuse of his brains from the moment he left school.

Certainly, all this time there was a leaven of more advanced ideas working in the lump. Wolseley and his school were engaged in a ceaseless struggle for reform; but the dead weight of the *vis inertiæ* of those who took the pious view that what was good enough for their fathers was good enough for them—generally backed by the controllers of national expenditure, who, when so-called experts differ, have a natural tendency to follow the cheapest advice—was too strong for them. Some rise in the dough there was, slight but persistent. Towards the end of the 'nineties' it was daily getting stronger. Perhaps a greater influence for good than that of Wolseley and all his followers was being produced by an obscure instructor at the Staff College, Major G. F. Henderson.

The reformers would never have got their way, for they would never have got the money, if the deficiencies of the Army had not been brought home to the nation at large by the South African War.

Of course, all this time there was the Army in India, which, although by its organisation and training it was hopelessly unsuited to take part in a European War—it had to wait for the Great War for its awakening—was adequate for the tasks contemplated for it, viz. preserving the peace in India, chastising any neighbours who might give trouble, or even conducting the long-expected war with such ' *be-bandobast wallahs* ' as the Russians, somewhere beyond the North-west Frontier.

For many years it had appeared that Russia was our only possible enemy on the grand scale. The small wars which might crop up from time to time could be dealt with, somehow, as they came along. India could look after Russia. The Army at home was nothing but a Depôt for supplying drafts for the Army in India. Of course we had fought on the Continent of Europe before, and we might have to do so again, but ' sufficient unto the day...'

Such was the state of ' pathetic contentment ' of the British public in matters of Defence during the closing years of the nineteenth century. The Boer has surely been the best friend and instructor the British Empire ever had.

For help in the production of this Fourth Volume of the Annals the thanks of the writer are due, firstly, to Lieut.-Colonel Lewis Butler, who has helped him in many ways, besides handing him over all the material he had already collected for this period ; secondly, to the Staff of the War Office Library, whose kindness to would-be military historians is immeasurable ; and, thirdly, to the few—very few—who have assisted with diaries, letters, and personal recollections, especially to the late Colonel

C. P. Cramer, Colonel Godfrey Astell, Lieut.-Colonel E. T. Thurlow, Colonel Sir Percival Marling, V.C., Brigadier-General L. F. Philips, C.B., and Mrs. C. R. R. McGrigor, for the loan of General McGrigor's diaries. The account of the capture of the Twin Peaks is borrowed from that by Sir Hereward Wake in the 'Chronicle' of 1908.

The thanks of the author are also due to the writers of Official Histories, on whose works he has chiefly relied for the groundwork of the accounts of the campaigns dealt with in this volume.

CONTENTS

	PAGE
PREFACE	v
LIST OF ILLUSTRATIONS	xiii
LISTS OF THE REGIMENT IN 1880, 1890, 1900, AND 1910 . .	xv
REGIMENTAL SUCCESSION OF COLONELS-IN-CHIEF, COLONELS COMMANDANT, AND LIEUTENANT-COLONELS, 1872–1914 .	xxxviii
SUCCESSION OF COMMANDING OFFICERS, 1873–1914 . .	xl

CHAPTER I

Third Battalion: The Zulu War, 1879—The First Boer War, 1881—Laing's Nek—The Action on the Ingogo River—Majuba—Sir G. P. Colley 1

CHAPTER II

Second Battalion: The Second Afghan War, 1878–1880—Northern Afghanistan—Advance on Kandahar—Yakub Khan—Mortality among Transport—Stewart's March North—Ahmad Khel—Roberts's March 36

CHAPTER III

Third Battalion: Ordered to Egypt—Egyptian Campaign of 1882 71

CHAPTER IV

Third Battalion: The Sudan, 1884—The Eastern Sudan . . 96

CHAPTER V

First Battalion: Ireland—The North-west Frontier, 1891-2-5—Hazara and Miranzai, 1891—Isazai Expedition, 1892—The Chitral Relief Expedition, 1895. 111

CONTENTS

CHAPTER VI

Fourth Battalion : Ireland and India—Burma—Manipur Expedition, 1891—Chin Hill, 1891-2 135

CHAPTER VII

Second Battalion : First Boer War, 1881—England—Ireland—Gibraltar—Malta—Cape of Good Hope 151

CHAPTER VIII

Third Battalion : Gibraltar—England—The First Battalion : The Wreck of the *Warren Hastings*—Mauritius 163

CHAPTER IX

The South African War, 1899-1902—Government's Difficulties—The Situation in Natal—Talana Hill—After Talana—The Retreat from Dundee—Ladysmith, before the Closing of the Door—Lombard's Kop 183

CHAPTER X

Arrival of Buller—The Situation in Natal—Colenso . . . 211

CHAPTER XI

The Twin Peaks 220

CHAPTER XII

Vaal Krantz 234

CHAPTER XIII

The Relief of Ladysmith 241

CHAPTER XIV

The Siege of Ladysmith 261

CONTENTS

CHAPTER XV

Northern Natal and Eastern Transvaal—End of South African War 280

CHAPTER XVI

The Drive and Blockhouse Period—Closing Stages of the South African War 300

CHAPTER XVII

First Battalion: End of the South African War to Outbreak of Great War—Mediterranean Stations—First Battalion at Home—Second Battalion: July 1900 to Outbreak of Great War—In India—Home Service—Third Battalion: South African War to Great War—Home Service—India—Fourth Battalion (1902–1914): Home Service—India . . . 305

CHAPTER XVIII

Mounted Infantry—The Zulu War of 1879 and Boer War of 1881—The Nile, 1885—Mashonaland, 1896—South African War, 1899–1902—Somaliland 331

APPENDIX I

PORTRAITS: Sir Redvers Buller—Lord Grenfell—Sir Edward Hutton—Donald Browne. 366

APPENDIX II

MARKSMANSHIP: Army Championship (at Home)—Queen Victoria Cup—Young Soldiers' Cup—The Company Match—The Army Sixty Cup—Company Match (Abroad)—Company Match (Home) 375

INDEX 378

LIST OF ILLUSTRATIONS

PORTRAITS

General The Rt. Hon. Sir Redvers Buller, V.C., G.C.B., G.C.M.G. . . . . *Frontispiece*

                                                                FACING PAGE

Field-Marshal The Rt. Hon. Francis Lord Grenfell, G.C.B., G.C.M.G. 100

Lieut.-General Sir Edward T. H. Hutton, K.C.B., K.C.M.G. 200

Colonel H. Donald Browne 300

MAPS

PLATE		PAGE
1.	Rough Sketch of the Zulu Attack on the Gingihlovo Laager	11
2.	Laing's Nek	19
3.	Ingogo	25
4.	View from Camp, Mount Prospect, of Inkwella and Amajuba Mountains	29
5.	Map of Southern Afghanistan	45
6.	Action at Ahmad Khel, April 19, 1880	55
7.	Battle of Kandahar, September 1, 1880	67
8.	Map to show Wolseley's Advance from Ismailia on Cairo	93
9.	Battle of El Teb, February 29, 1884	103
10.	Battle of Tamaai, March 13, 1884	109

LIST OF ILLUSTRATIONS

PLATE		PAGE
11.	Map to illustrate Action at the Malakhand Pass, April 3, 1895	131
12.	Map of Burma	141
13.	Talana, October 20, 1899	197
14.	Colenso, December 15, 1899. Relief of Ladysmith, February 14–28, 1900	215
15.	Spion Kop and Twin Peaks	239
16.	Defence of Ladysmith	*facing* 278
17	Map of Northern Natal	,, 298
18.	Map of Eastern Transvaal	,, 298
19.	View of Makoni's Kraal from the N.N.W.	349
20.	Action near Bakenlaagte, October 30, 1901	357

LISTS OF THE REGIMENT IN 1880, 1890, 1900, AND 1910

1880

COLONEL-IN-CHIEF

FIELD MARSHAL HIS ROYAL HIGHNESS
G. W. F. C., DUKE OF CAMBRIDGE,
K.G., G.C.B., K.P., G.C.S.I., G.C.M.G., s.   Mar. 3, 1869

COLONELS COMMANDANT

BATT.	NAME.	DATE OF APPOINTMENT.
1.	GENERAL SIR ART. AUG. THURLOW CUNYNGHAME, G.C.B.	Feb. 2, 1876.
2.	GENERAL FREEMAN MURRAY	Oct. 11, 1876.

LIEUTENANT-COLONELS

3.	W. LEIGH PEMBERTON, C.B.	Mar. 10, 1875.
4.	ROWLEY W. HINXMAN	June 5, 1875.
1.	JAS. D. DUNDAS	Dec. 19, 1877.
2.	JAS. JOSEPH COLLINS	Aug. 21, 1878.

MAJORS

2.	CROMER ASHBURNHAM	Oct. 18, 1873.
1.	K. G. HENDERSON	May 27, 1874.
4.	JAMES S. H. ALGAR	Mar. 10, 1875.
	GEO. HATCHELL, l.c., p.s.c., s.	Nov. 29, 1870.
1.	JAS. K. WATSON, d.	Dec. 19, 1877.
2.	WM. GERARD BYRON	June 29, 1878.
3.	W. L. K. OGILVY, p.s.c.	Aug. 21, 1878.
3.	ARTHUR TUFNELL, l.c.	April 7, 1879.
4.	JOHN CHARLEY	Sept. 12, 1879.

LISTS OF THE REGIMENT
CAPTAINS (40)

Batt.	Name.	Date of Appointment.
3.	Astley F. Terry	Dec. 18, 1867.
1.	John G. Crosbie	May 20, 1868.
2.	Geo. Hewitt Trotman	Jan. 11, 1869.
1.	Nesbit W. Wallace	Jan. 23, 1869.
3.	Arthur Morris, d.	April 24, 1869.
4.	Chas. M. Calderon	Feb. 9, 1870.
2.	V.C. Redvers H. Buller, C.B., C.M.G.	May 28, 1870.
3.	C. Pierson Cramer, d.	May 28, 1870.
4.	Jas. H. H. Croft	Aug. 9, 1871.
	Fra. W. Grenfell, l.c., s.	Oct. 28, 1871.
	Alex. A. A. Kinloch, m.s.	May 8, 1870.
3.	Aub. V. O'Brien	April 24, 1872.
2.	Chas. L. C. de Robeck	April 24, 1872.
1.	Geo. T. Whitaker, d.	Feb. 26, 1873.
1.	George Carpenter	April 30, 1873.
3.	Ric. C. Robinson	May 28, 1873.
2.	Geo. L. M. L. Farmer	July 5, 1873.
1.	Denis Bingham	July 5, 1873.
1.	John T. D. Crosbie, s.	Aug. 13, 1873.
1.	Hen. Donald Browne	Mar. 27, 1874.
1.	Edm. Lomax Fraser	April 1, 1874.
2.	Reginald Chalmer	April 2, 1874.
2.	Wm. Tilden, d.	Mar. 10, 1875.
	Hen. B. MacCall, s.	April 1, 1875.
4.	Benj. Frend	May 12, 1875.
3.	Ambrose H. Bircham	May 13, 1875.
4.	Hen. A. Houlton Ward	Dec. 1, 1875.
4.	A. F. H. Mitchell-Innes	Aug. 12, 1876.
4.	Philip A. Robinson, d.	May 17, 1876.
2.	Wm. Forster, d.	Nov. 29, 1876.
1.	Robt. Cradock Davies	Mar. 28, 1877.
	Hen. P. M. Wylie	June 30, 1877.
2.	Jas. N. Blackwood-Price	Dec. 8, 1877.
3.	Chas. Holled Smith	Dec. 19, 1877.
4.	Jas. John Mallandaine	Mar. 14, 1877.
2.	Hen. S. Marsham	Mar. 2, 1878.
2.	Thos. Sydenham Clarke	July 5, 1878.

LISTS OF THE REGIMENT xvii

CAPTAINS (40)—*continued*.

Batt.	Name.	Date of Appointment.
3.	Ernest H. Thurlow	Aug. 21, 1878.
3.	Hon. Keith Turnour	Oct. 30, 1878.
4.	Hen. S. Hutton Riddell	Nov. 30, 1878.
4.	H. J. Hope-Edwardes	Jan. 4, 1879.
4.	Thos. Prince Lloyd	Jan. 29, 1879.
3.	F. B. N. Dickenson	May 17, 1879.
1.	Edw. T. H. Hutton, s.c.	July 14, 1879.

LIEUTENANTS (LIEUTENANTS, 40; SECOND LIEUTENANTS, 28)

2.	F. Wright Archer	Aug. 9, 1871.
1.	Horace Walpole, d.	Oct. 27, 1871.
1.	John Dowling Howden	Nov. 30, 1870.
3.	Charles Michell, I. of M.	Oct. 28, 1871.
4.	Fra. Moore Ward	Oct. 28, 1871.
3.	Chas. R. B. Thorne	Oct. 28, 1871.
2.	Charles Hope, I. of M.	Oct. 28, 1871.
3.	R. S. R. Fetherstonhaugh	Oct. 28, 1871.
3.	Godfrey Astell	Oct. 28, 1871.
	Humphrey D. P. Okeden	Oct. 28, 1871.
1.	Nicholas E. de B. Fenwick	Oct. 28, 1871.
1.	Walter Hen. Holbech	Oct. 28, 1871.
2.	Wm. S. Anderson	Oct. 28, 1871.
3.	Henry Allfrey	Oct. 28, 1871.
3.	Corbet Stapleton Cotton	Oct. 28, 1871.
1.	Robt. Henley	Oct. 28, 1871.
1.	Mordaunt C. Boyle, I. of M.	Oct. 28, 1871.
2.	Horatio Reginald Mends	Dec. 30, 1871.
4.	M. C. B. Forestier Walker (Adjutant)	Mar. 6, 1872.
4.	Geoffrey G. Grimwood	July 24, 1872.
4.	Henry Vere	Oct. 5, 1872.
3.	Edwd. O. H. Wilkinson (Adjutant)	Aug. 9, 1873.
2.	Basil T. G. Montgomery	Oct. 5, 1872.
4.	Robert Story, d.	Nov. 12, 1873.
2.	Eugene A. Sanford	Nov. 12, 1873.
2.	Robt. Chas. D. Wilson	Oct. 19, 1872.
4.	Grenville H. Wells, d.	Feb. 28, 1874.
1.	Hon. A. H. Fulke Greville	Aug. 9, 1874.

LISTS OF THE REGIMENT

LIEUTENANTS—*continued*.

Batt.	Name.	Date of Appointment.
2.	Hubert Richd. Lovett	Aug. 9, 1874.
2.	Fred. S. Marsham (Adjutant)	Jan. 15, 1873.
3.	Rob. Hen. Gunning	Mar. 26, 1873.
1.	Edw. Wm. Herbert	Dec. 2, 1874.
2.	Gilbert S. Baynes	Feb. 11, 1875.
4.	Guy T. Campbell	Feb. 28, 1875.
4.	Rob. G. Buchanan-Riddell, I. of M.	Nov. 20, 1875.
4.	Hon. Conway S. G. Canning	Nov. 20, 1875.
2.	R. E. W. Copland-Crawford	Jan. 7, 1876.
4.	Gerald C. Kitson	Feb. 11, 1875.
3.	Archd. E. Miles	Feb. 11, 1876.
2.	Lord Fredk. FitzGerald	Feb. 11, 1876.
1.	Harold Gore-Browne (Adjutant)	Feb. 11, 1876.
1.	Wm. P. Campbell	Mar. 10, 1876.
2.	Arthur Davidson	Sept. 10, 1876.
1.	Lewis Wm. G. Butler	Sept. 10, 1876.
2.	Herb. Delamark Banks	Oct. 6, 1875.
	Harry J. Bolton (prob.)	July 17, 1872.
4.	Robt. C. A. B. Bewicke	Feb. 12, 1877.
2.	Robt. E. Golightly	April 28, 1877.
4.	Edgar W. Brodie	May 3, 1876.
2.	Hubert Cornwall Legh	Oct. 6, 1877.

SECOND LIEUTENANTS

Batt.	Name.	Date of Appointment.
4.	Edw. J. Stuart Wortley	Oct. 13, 1877.
2.	Daniel C. W. Lysons	Jan. 23, 1878.
3.	Horace John Nevill	Aug. 15, 1877.
4.	Chas. A. T. Boultbee	July 21, 1877.
3.	Archer P. Crawley	Oct. 13, 1877.
3.	Dudley G. R. Ryder	May 1, 1878.
3.	George C. B. Baker	Sept. 14, 1878.
1.	John Raymond Garrett	Jan. 30, 1878.
2.	Ramsay G. H. Couper	Sept. 14, 1878.
4.	Chas. Edw. Clowes	Dec. 4, 1878.
4.	Lee La T. Bateman	Jan. 22, 1879.
1.	Sir Thos. H. C. Troubridge, Bart.	Jan. 22, 1879.
4.	Lord Walter Fitzgerald	Jan. 22, 1879.
3.	William Joseph Myers	May 1, 1878.

LISTS OF THE REGIMENT

SECOND LIEUTENANTS—*continued*.

Batt.	Name.	Date of Appointment.
3.	Maurice O'Connell	Jan. 22, 1879.
4.	Edward T. Pakenham	Jan. 22, 1879.
3.	Warine Du V. Lysley	Jan. 22, 1879.
3.	Charles B. Pigott	Feb. 19, 1879.
2.	Geoffrey G. G., Lord Tewkesbury	June 21, 1879.
1.	Francis A. Fortescue	July 2, 1879.
1.	Edward S. St. Aubyn	July 2, 1879.
3.	Henry E. Buchanan-Riddell	Aug. 13, 1879.
3.	Thos. E. Milborne-Swinnerton-Pilkington	Aug. 13, 1879.
4.	Walpole S. Kays	Aug. 6, 1879.

PAYMASTERS

4.	Art. Gore Anderson, Hon. M. (Staff Paymaster, Army Pay Dept.)	
1.	A. J. Roberts, Hon. Captain (Paymaster, Army Pay Dept.)	
3.	E. C. Haynes, Hon. Captain (Paymaster, Army Pay Dept.)	

INSTRUCTORS OF MUSKETRY

3.	Chas. Michell, Lieutenant	July 15, 1876.
2.	Chas. Hope, Lieutenant	Jan. 5, 1877.
4.	R. G. Buchanan-Riddell, Lieutenant	Nov. 6, 1878.
1.	M. C. Boyle, Lieutenant	May 30, 1879.

ADJUTANTS

3.	E. O. H. Wilkinson, Lieutenant	Dec. 1, 1875.
4.	M. C. B. F. Walker, Lieutenant	May 29, 1877.
2.	F. S. Marsham, Lieutenant	Feb. 16, 1878.
1.	H. Gore-Browne, Lieutenant	May 30, 1879.

QUARTERMASTERS

2.	Wm. N. Holmes	April 17, 1867.
1.	Wm. Dixon	Jan. 19, 1876.
3.	Jas. Ireland	April 20, 1878.
4.	Eric J. Crane	Mar. 15, 1879.

Uniform, green; facings, scarlet.   Agents: Messrs. Cox & Co.

LISTS OF THE REGIMENT

1890
COLONEL-IN-CHIEF

Batt.	Name.	Date of Appointment.
	Field-Marshal H.R.H. G. W. F. C., Duke of Cambridge, K.G., K.T., K.P., G.C.B., G.C.S.I., G.C.M.G., G.C.I.E., Commander-in-Chief, A.D.C.	Mar. 3, 1869.

COLONEL COMMANDANT

	General Hon. Sir A. E. Hardinge, K.C.B., C.I.E., s. Eq.	Mar. 13, 1886.
		Nov. 20, 1881.

OFFICER COMMANDING RIFLE DEPÔT

	Colonel G. Hatchell, p.s.c.	Jan. 13, 1887.

PAYMASTER, RIFLE DEPÔT

	Staff Paym. W. D. Graham, Colonel	Nov. 22, 1883.
	Hon. Major	Feb. 8, 1888.

QUARTERMASTER, RIFLE DEPÔT

	T. Riley, Hon. Lieutenant	Sept. 27, 1882.

LIEUTENANT-COLONELS (4)

Batt.	Name	Date
4.	A. Morris	Oct. 9, 1885.
	Comdg. Battalion	Jan. 7, 1886.
	Colonel	Oct. 9, 1889.
1.	C. P. Cramer	Nov. 4, 1885.
	Comdg. Battalion	July 1, 1887.
	Colonel	Nov. 18, 1886.
2.	A. A. A. Kinloch	Jan. 7, 1886.
	Comdg. Battalion	July 1, 1887.
	Colonel	Mar. 2, 1885.
3.	G. T. Whitaker	April 21, 1886.
	Comdg. Battalion	July 1, 1887.

LISTS OF THE REGIMENT

MAJORS (16)

BATT.		NAME.	DATE OF APPOINTMENT.
	2.	G. L. Farmer	July 1, 1881.
	1.	H. D. Browne	July 1, 1881.
	3.	R. Chalmer	July 1, 1881.
			Mar. 2, 1881.
	4.	H. B. MacCall	July 1, 1881.
	3.	H. P. M. Wylie	Oct. 21, 1882.
e.a.		C. H. Smith	Dec. 20, 1882.
		Bt. Colonel	Dec. 28, 1888.
	1.	Hon. K. Turnour	Aug. 19, 1883.
v.		F. W. Archer	Oct. 27, 1883.
	4.	J. D. Howden	Sept. 9, 1884.
	3.	R. S. R. Fetherstonhaugh	April 18, 1885.
		Colonel	June 15, 1889.
d.	2.	G. Astell	June 10, 1885.
	3.	H. D. P. Parry-Okeden	June 10, 1885.
	1.	W. H. Holbech	June 10, 1885.
			Nov. 18, 1882.
	2.	H. R. Mends	Oct. 9, 1885.
d.	1.	M. C. B. F. Walker	Oct. 9, 1885.
	4.	G. G. Grimwood	Nov. 4, 1885.
	4.	H. Vere	Jan. 7, 1886.

CAPTAINS (24)

	3.	W. S. Anderson	July 21, 1880.
	1.	H. R. Lovett	Mar. 14, 1883.
m.		R. H. Gunning	Aug. 1, 1883.
v.		E. W. Herbert	Aug. 10, 1883.
		Bt. Major	May 21, 1884.
	2.	G. S. Baynes	Oct. 3, 1888.
			Oct. 27, 1883.
v.		Sir G. T. Campbell, Bart.	April 1, 1884.
	2.	R. G. Buchanan-Riddell	Sept. 9, 1884.
	1.	Hon. C. S. G. Canning	Nov. 26, 1884.
	4.	G. C. Kitson, p.s.c.	Jan. 1, 1885.
	2.	Lord F. Fitzgerald	Mar. 16, 1885.
		Bt. Major	June 15, 1885.
v.		H. Gore-Browne	April 18, 1885.

LISTS OF THE REGIMENT

CAPTAINS (24)—*continued.*

BATT.		NAME.	DATE OF APPOINTMENT.
v.		W. P. CAMPBELL	April 18, 1885.
	1.	A. DAVIDSON	April 23, 1885.
		Bt. Major	April 23, 1885.
	1.	L. W. G. BUTLER, p.s.c.	April 23, 1885.
v.		H. D. BANKS	June 10, 1885.
	1.	R. C. A. B. BEWICKE, p.s.c.	Oct. 9, 1885.
v.		E. W. BRODIE	Nov. 4, 1885.
	4.	R. E. GOLIGHTLY, D.S.O.	Jan. 7, 1886.
	4.	H. C. LEGH	Jan. 7, 1886.
s.c.	2.	E. J. MONTAGU-STUART WORTLEY, C.M.G.	Mar. 1, 1886.
		Bt. Major	Mar. 2, 1886.
	3.	D. C. W. LYSONS	April 21, 1886.
d.	4.	C. A. T. BOULTBEE	April 21, 1886.
	3.	D. G. R. RYDER	June 10, 1886.
d.	3.	W. J. MYERS	Mar. 14, 1888.
s.	2.	G. G. G., LORD TEWKESBURY	June 27, 1888.
	2.	F. A. FORTESCUE	July 1, 1888.
v.		HON. E. S. ST. AUBYN	Sept. 1, 1888.
	2.	H. E. BUCHANAN-RIDDELL (Adjutant)	Oct. 10, 1888.
	2.	T. E. MILBORNE-SWINNERTON-PILKINGTON	Dec. 19, 1888.
	4.	W. S. KAYS	Dec. 29, 1888.
	3.	C. R. R. McGRIGOR, p.s.c.	Mar. 11, 1889.
		Bt. Major	Mar. 12, 1889.
	4.	G. G. H. ALLGOOD (Adjutant)	Mar. 11, 1889.
	1.	A. D. PIXLEY	April 1, 1889.
s.	3.	H. A. KINLOCH	Sept. 11, 1889.
	4.	W. D. STUART	Nov. 13, 1889.

LIEUTENANTS (36)

		NAME	DATE
	2.	W. A. H. BEACH	July 1, 1881.
s.		F. M. BEAUMONT	July 1, 1881.
	1.	E. W. THISTLETHWAYTE	July 1, 1881.
d.	1.	R. S. BOWEN	July 1, 1881.
	1.	H. R. ADDINGTON	July 1, 1881.
d.	4.	A. J. B. ST. LEGER	July 1, 1881.

LISTS OF THE REGIMENT

LIEUTENANTS (36)—*continued.*

Batt.		Name.	Date of Appointment.
	2.	W. H. Kennedy	July 1, 1881.
		G. L. B. Killick	July 1, 1881.
s.	2.	R. L. Bower	July 1, 1881.
	1.	H. Newton	Sept. 27, 1882.
			Oct. 22, 1881.
s.		J. E. B. Martin	April 25, 1885.
			July 1, 1881.
	4.	C. J. Markham	Sept. 27, 1882.
		G. N. Prendergast	April 4, 1883.
			May 10, 1882.
	4.	O. S. W. Nugent	April 14, 1883.
			July 29, 1882.
e.a.		W. H. Salmon	April 14, 1883.
			Sept. 9, 1882.
	1.	F. B. M. Henniker	April 14, 1883.
			Jan. 27, 1883.
	4.	A. Blewitt	Aug. 1, 1883.
			Jan. 27, 1883.
	4.	E. J. Dewar	Dec. 5, 1883.
d.	3.	C. F. Sewell	Dec. 19, 1883.
s.		H. S. Rawlinson	Feb. 6, 1884.
	1.	H. F. Pakenham	Feb. 6, 1884.
	4.	G. C. Lister	Feb. 6, 1884.
	3.	C. J. Ryder	Mar. 26, 1884.
			Feb. 6, 1884.
d.	2.	G. H. Shakerley	May 21, 1884.
			May 14, 1884.
	4.	C. H. Fenwick	May 21, 1884.
			May 14, 1884.
	3.	C. E. H. Hobhouse	Aug. 23, 1884.
	4.	C. A. G. Clark	Aug. 23, 1884.
	4.	H. H. A. Walsh	Aug. 23, 1884.
	3.	T. L. N. Morland	Aug. 23, 1884.
	2.	F. A. Browning	Nov. 15, 1884.
			Aug. 23, 1884.
	4.	R. S. Oxley	Nov. 26, 1884.
			Aug. 23, 1884.

xxiv LISTS OF THE REGIMENT

LIEUTENANTS (36)—*continued*.

Batt.	Name.	Date of Appointment.
3.	H. C. Howard	Mar. 11, 1885.
		Nov. 12, 1884.
4.	J. K. Watson	April 25, 1885.
3.	Hon. St. L. H. Jervis	May 6, 1885.
2.	J. P. E. Gilmour	May 30, 1885.
		Feb. 7, 1885.
2.	C. S. Chaplin	May 30, 1885.
		May 6, 1885.
1.	N. N. Bedingfeld (Adjutant)	June 17, 1885.
		May 9, 1885.
3.	F. Douglas-Pennant	June 24, 1885.
	H. P. E. Parker (prob.).	Jan. 13, 1886.
		Aug. 29, 1885.
3.	C. Ashburnham (Adjutant)	Jan. 30, 1886.
1.	S. W. Hare	May 5, 1886.
3.	J. Curteis	May 12, 1886.
2.	St. J. D. T. Loftus	Aug. 25, 1886.
4.	Hon. S. H. R. L. Tollemache	Nov. 13, 1886.
4.	Hon. J. R. Brownlow	Dec. 4, 1886.

SECOND LIEUTENANTS (24)

2.	H. W. Christian	July 30, 1887.
3.	A. H. Terry	Sept. 10, 1887.
1.	H. C. Warre	Oct. 5, 1887.
3.	A. R. Montagu-Stuart-Wortley	Nov. 5, 1887.
3.	G. A. J. Soltau-Symons	Nov. 19, 1887.
3.	H. T. Peel	Feb. 15, 1888.
		May 4, 1887.
1.	E. Northey	Mar. 7, 1888.
3.	H. B. Nicholson	May 2, 1888.
		Feb. 11, 1888.
1.	M. H. K. Pechell	July 4, 1888.
		Feb. 11, 1888.
2.	J. H. G. Fielden	Aug. 1, 1888.
1.	H.H. Prince C. V. A. L. E. A. of Schleswig-Holstein	Aug. 27, 1888.
4.	R. P. Cobbold	Oct. 17, 1888.

LISTS OF THE REGIMENT

SECOND LIEUTENANTS (24)—*continued.*

Batt.	Name.	Date of Appointment.
1.	L. C. Maclachlan	Oct. 24, 1888.
3.	L. C. D. Jenner	Nov. 21, 1888.
2.	C. Gosling	Nov. 28, 1888.
		Aug. 22, 1888.
4.	R. J. Vernon	Jan. 16, 1889.
4.	C. L. E. Eustace	Jan. 30, 1889.
1.	H.S.H. Prince F. J. L. F. of Teck	April 17, 1889.
		Jan. 30, 1889.
2.	J. A. Hope	May 22, 1889.
2.	W. G. A. Orde-Powlett	July 24, 1889.
		Mar. 23, 1889.
3.	E. Pearce-Serocold	Oct. 9, 1889.
3.	H. A. W. Briscoe	Oct. 16, 1889.
3.	J. E. Rhodes	Oct. 30, 1889.
4.	C. J. Sackville-West	Dec. 18, 1889.

PAYMASTER

4. I. W. T. S. Smythe (ret. Major)

ADJUTANTS

4.	G. G. H. Allgood (Captain)	Nov. 1, 1887.
3.	C. Ashburnham (Lieutenant)	July 24, 1889.
1.	N. N. Bedingfeld (Lieutenant)	Oct. 1, 1889.
2.	H. E. Buchanan-Riddell (Captain)	Nov. 13, 1889.

QUARTERMASTERS

	J. Ireland	April 20, 1878.
	Hon. Captain	April 20, 1888.
4.	E. J. Crane	Mar. 15, 1879.
	Hon. Captain	Mar. 15, 1889.
3.	E. F. Overton (Hon. Lieutenant)	May 3, 1884.
2.	A. Wynn (Hon. Lieutenant)	Sept. 19, 1885.
	W. Holmes (Hon. Lieutenant)	April 14, 1886.
1.	J. W. Dwane (Hon. Lieutenant)	Feb. 15, 1888.

LISTS OF THE REGIMENT

1900
COLONEL-IN-CHIEF

BATT.	NAME.	DATE OF APPOINTMENT.
	FIELD-MARSHAL H.R.H. G. W. F. C., DUKE OF CAMBRIDGE, K.G., K.T., K.P., G.C.B., G.C.S.I., G.C.M.G., G.C.I.E., G.C.V.O., A.D.C., HON. COLONEL-IN-CHIEF TO THE FORCES	Mar. 3, 1869.

COLONELS COMMANDANT

	V.C. GENERAL THE RT. HON. SIR R. H. BULLER, G.C.B., K.C.M.G.	July 13, 1895.
	LIEUT.-GENERAL SIR F. W. GRENFELL, G.C.B., G.C.M.G.	Aug. 7, 1898.

OFFICER COMMANDING RIFLE DEPÔT

	COLONEL H. R. MENDS	May 25, 1899.
	Colonel	Oct. 15, 1898.

QUARTERMASTER, RIFLE DEPÔT

	T. RILEY	Feb. 8, 1888.
		Sept. 27, 1882.
	Hon. Capt.	Sept. 27, 1892.

LIEUTENANT-COLONELS (4)

2.	G. G. GRIMWOOD	Sept. 18, 1895.
	Bt. Colonel	Sept. 18, 1899.
4.	E. W. HERBERT	Oct. 15, 1898.
3.	R. G. BUCHANAN-RIDDELL	Dec. 29, 1898.
1.	H. GORE-BROWNE	Oct. 21, 1899.

MAJORS (4)
(SECOND-IN-COMMAND)

1.	W. P. CAMPBELL	April 16, 1898.
		April 5, 1893.
3.	R. C. A. B. BEWICKE-COPLEY, p.s.c.	Jan. 13, 1899.
		Jan. 15, 1894.
4.	E. J. MONTAGU-STUART-WORTLEY, C.M.G., D.S.O., p.s.c.	Jan. 24, 1899.
		April 4, 1894.
		Mar. 2, 1886.

LISTS OF THE REGIMENT

MAJORS (12)

BATT.		NAME.	DATE OF APPOINTMENT.
	1.	C. A. T. BOULTBEE.	April 16, 1894.
	3.	F. A. FORTESCUE, p.s.c.	July 1, 1895.
	2.	H. E. BUCHANAN-RIDDELL, p.s.c.	Sept. 18, 1895.
d.	3.	W. KAYS	June 10, 1896.
s.		C. R. R. MCGRIGOR, p.s.c.	July 1, 1896.
			Mar. 12, 1889.
s.		H. A. KINLOCH	Dec. 10, 1896.
	1.	F. M. BEAUMONT	Aug. 21, 1897.
	3.	E. W. THISTLETHWAYTE	Mar. 23, 1898.
	2.	R. S. BOWEN	April 16, 1898.
d.	3.	H. R. ADDINGTON	May 18, 1898.
s.		C. J. MARKHAM	Oct. 15, 1898.
	1.	G. N. PRENDERGAST	Dec. 29, 1898.
	1.	O. S. W. NUGENT, D.S.O., p.s.c.	Oct. 21, 1899.

CAPTAINS (24)

	4.	F. B. M. HENNIKER	Nov. 20, 1890.
	4.	W. H. SALMON	May 6, 1891.
e.a.		A. BLEWITT	May 6, 1891.
		Bt. Major	Nov. 16, 1898.
		E. J. DEWAR	July 1, 1891.
	1.	H. F. PAKENHAM	Nov. 10, 1891.
v.		G. C. LISTER	Dec. 20, 1891.
d.	4.	C. A. G. CLARK	Jan. 4, 1893.
		T. L. N. MORLAND, p.s.c.	April 5, 1893.
		Bt. Major	July 8, 1899.
s.		R. S. OXLEY, p.s.c.	Aug. 4, 1893.
	3.	H. C. HOWARD	Sept. 9, 1893.
s.		J. K. WATSON, D.S.O.	Sept. 23, 1893.
		Bt. Major	Nov. 16, 1898.
s.		HON. ST. L. H. JERVIS	Oct. 10, 1893.
v.		J. P. E. GILMOUR	Nov. 1, 1893.
m.		C. S. CHAPLIN	Jan. 15, 1894.
	2.	N. N. BEDINGFELD	Feb. 28, 1894.
	4.	F. DOUGLAS-PENNANT	Mar. 14, 1894.

LISTS OF THE REGIMENT

CAPTAINS (24)—*continued*.

BATT.		NAME.	DATE OF APPOINTMENT.
		C. Ashburnham	Mar. 14, 1894.
m.		S. W. Hare	April 4, 1894.
p.d.		J. Curteis	June 20, 1894.
m.		St. J. D. T. Loftus	Aug. 10, 1894.
m.		Hon. J. R. Brownlow	Jan. 3, 1895.
	3.	H. C. Warre	Jan. 23, 1895.
	1.	A. R. Montagu-Stuart-Wortley	Mar. 11, 1895.
v.		G. A. J. Soltau-Symons	May 15, 1895.
	1.	E. Northey	July 1, 1895.
	4.	J. H. G. Fielden	Nov. 9, 1896.
		H.H. Prince Christian V. A. L. E. A. of Schleswig-Holstein, G.C.B., G.C.V.O. (Spec. Ser. S. Africa)	Dec. 3, 1896.
		Bt. Major	Dec. 4, 1896.
v.		L. C. D. Jenner	Jan. 30, 1897.
	2.	C. Gosling	Feb. 5, 1897.
		R. J. Vernon (Spec. Ser. S. Africa)	May 19, 1897.
	2.	C. L. E. Eustace	May 19, 1897.
	4.	J. A. Hope	Aug. 21, 1897.
	2.	E. Pearce-Serocold	Dec. 11, 1897.
	3.	H. A. W. Briscoe	Dec. 21, 1897.
d.	2.	J. E. Rhodes	Jan. 3, 1898.
s.		C. J. Sackville-West	Jan. 27, 1898.
	3.	C. W. Wilson (Adjutant)	Jan. 27, 1898.
m.		R. Byron	Jan. 27, 1898.
	2.	A. J. Lainson	Feb. 18, 1898.
	3.	L. F. Philips	May 18, 1898.
	1.	H. R. Blore (Adjutant)	Sept. 14, 1898.
		G. C. Shakerley	Dec. 29, 1898.
	1.	L. B. Cumberland	Dec. 29, 1898.
s.		G. S. St. Aubyn	Mar. 8, 1899.
		W. H. L. Allgood (Spec. Ser. S. Africa)	Mar. 8, 1899.
	3.	R. H. Beaumont	Mar. 8, 1899.
	2.	W. Barnett	May 17, 1899.
	1.	Lord R. W. O. Manners	May 17, 1899.
	1.	W. J. Long	Oct. 21, 1899.
	4.	V. H. S. Scratchley	Oct. 22, 1899.

LISTS OF THE REGIMENT

LIEUTENANTS (37)

	Batt.	Name.	Date of Appointment.
	1.	G. V. Hordern	June 20, 1894.
d.	4.	C. C. Herbert-Stepney	Aug. 10, 1894.
	2.	H. C. R. Green (Adjutant)	Jan. 3, 1895.
	4.	Hon. R. Cathcart	Jan. 9, 1895.
s.	2.	W. F. G. Wyndham	Jan. 23, 1895.
	2.	M. L. Porter	Mar. 11, 1895.
	2.	E. F. Ward	Mar. 13, 1895.
	1.	F. M. Crum	July 26, 1895.
	2.	C. E. Balfour	Jan. 1, 1896.
s.		R. C. Master	Jan. 1, 1896.
	2.	S. F. Mott	Mar. 18, 1896.
	1.	R. G. Jelf	Mar. 28, 1896.
	3.	A. R. Mildmay	Nov. 9, 1896.
	3.	G. A. P. Rennie	Jan. 30, 1897.
	2.	B. F. Widdrington	Feb. 5, 1897.
	4.	D. H. Blundell-Hollinshead-Blundell	May 19, 1897.
	3.	C. B. Petre	July 7, 1887.
s.	4.	G. A. Armytage	Aug. 21, 1897.
d.	2.	G. F. B. Hankey	Dec. 11, 1897.
d.	3.	W. P. Lynes	Dec. 31, 1897.
		A. L. Paine	Dec. 31, 1897.
		C. E. de V. Beauclerk	Jan. 27, 1898.
	3.	H. F. F. B. Foljambe	Feb. 18, 1898.
	1.	R. Johnstone	April 12, 1898.
	2.	L. W. de Sausmarez	May 18, 1898.
	3.	M. Pratt	June 14, 1898.
	1.	B. J. Majendie	Aug. 1, 1898.
	4.	H. F. W. Bircham	Sept. 14, 1898.
	1.	J. H. Davidson	Oct. 15, 1898.
		W. A. I. Kay	Jan. 1, 1899.
	4.	A. E. Cathcart	Feb. 4, 1899.
	3.	R. J. Grant	Feb. 8, 1899.
	3.	H. Wake	Feb. 8, 1899.
	1.	H. C. Johnson	Mar. 8, 1899.
	2.	C. H. N. Seymour	Aug. 30, 1899.
	2.	L. A. E. Price-Davies	Oct. 21, 1899.
	3.	R. F. M. Sims	Oct. 21, 1899.

LISTS OF THE REGIMENT

LIEUTENANTS (37)—*continued*.

Batt.	Name.	Date of Appointment.
3.	G. K. Priaulx	Oct. 21, 1899.
	E. Perceval	Oct. 21, 1899.
4.	R. L. C. Hobson	Oct. 22, 1899.
1.	A. D. Legard	Oct. 22, 1899.
3.	G. H. Davenport	Oct. 31, 1899.
2.	G. Makins	Dec. 18, 1899.

SECOND LIEUTENANTS (24)

Batt.	Name.	Date of Appointment.
2.	F. H. Raikes	July 13, 1898.
4.	H. H. R. White	July 27, 1898.
1.	H. B. P. L. Kennedy	Oct. 12, 1898.
1.	G. H. Martin	Oct. 15, 1898.
1.	R. G. Stirling	Jan. 25, 1899.
4.	G. J. Acland-Troyte	Feb. 8, 1899.
2.	A. R. Leith	Feb. 15, 1899.
1.	C. F. Hawley	Feb. 25, 1899.
2.	Hon. A. F. W. Harris	Feb. 25, 1899.
4.	R. E. Crichton	Mar. 22, 1899.
4.	T. G. Dalby	April 5, 1899.
2.	F. G. Willan	Mar. 20, 1899.
3.	A. R. W. Spicer	May 27, 1899.
1.	R. E. Reade	Aug. 2, 1899.
2.	G. Culme-Seymour	Oct. 4, 1899.
3.	Sir R. Price, Bart.	Oct. 18, 1899.
3.	H. G. French-Brewster	Oct. 18, 1899.
3.	A. F. C. Maclachlan	Oct. 18, 1899.
1.	R. F. Dalrymple	Oct. 25, 1899.
1.	A. T. Hodgson	Oct. 25, 1899.
1.	W. S. W. Parker-Jervis	Oct. 25, 1899.
3.	E. A. Bradford	Oct. 25, 1899.
4.	G. H. Barnett	Oct. 25, 1899.
2.	T. H. Harker	Oct. 28, 1899.
2.	G. C. Kelly	Nov. 11, 1899.
4.	A. J. Fife	Nov. 11, 1899.
3.	B. J. Curling	Nov. 29, 1899.
	B. Seymour	Dec. 30, 1899.

LISTS OF THE REGIMENT

ADJUTANTS

BATT.	NAME.	DATE OF APPOINTMENT.
3.	C. W. WILSON (Captain)	July 26, 1895.
1.	H. R. BLORE (Captain)	Mar. 11, 1899.
2.	H. C. R. GREEN (Lieutenant)	Oct. 23, 1899.

QUARTERMASTERS

BATT.	NAME.	DATE OF APPOINTMENT.
	A. WYNN	Sept. 19, 1885.
	Hon. Captain	Sept. 19, 1895.
	W. HOLMES	April 14, 1886.
	Hon. Captain	April 14, 1896.
2.	J. W. DWANE	Feb. 15, 1888.
	Hon. Captain	Mar. 13, 1897.
4.	T. O'SHEA (Hon. Lieutenant)	Jan. 10, 1894.
3.	W. C. HARRINGTON (Hon. Lieutenant)	Nov. 26, 1898.
		Feb. 1, 1898.
1.	T. C. McNALLY (Hon. Lieutenant)	Mar. 22, 1899.

1910

COLONEL-IN-CHIEF

GENERAL H.R.H. GEORGE F. E. A., PRINCE OF WALES AND DUKE OF CORNWALL AND YORK, K.G., K.T., K.P., G.C.S.I., G.C.M.G., G.C.I.E., G.C.V.O., I.S.O., COLONEL-IN-CHIEF ROYAL FUSILIERS, ROYAL WELCH FUSILIERS, ROYAL MARINES, AND CAMERON HIGHLANDERS, PERSONAL A.D.C. TO THE KING . . . May 1, 1904.

COLONELS COMMANDANT

1. FIELD-MARSHAL RT. HON. F. W. LORD GRENFELL, G.C.B., G.C.M.G.
4. MAJOR-GENERAL W. L. PEMBERTON, C.B.
3. HON. MAJOR-GENERAL SIR C. ASHBURNHAM, K.C.B.
2. LIEUT.-GENERAL SIR E. T. H. HUTTON, K.C.M.G., C.B., p.s.c.

LISTS OF THE REGIMENT

OFFICER COMMANDING RIFLE DEPÔT (ALSO COLONEL IN CHARGE OF RIFLE RECORDS)

Batt.	Name.	Date of Appointment.
	Colonel A. E. Jenkins.	July 1, 1908.

ADJUTANT, RIFLE DEPÔT

	Lieutenant F. W. L. Edwards, K.R.R.C.	May 16, 1909.

QUARTERMASTER, RIFLE DEPÔT

	T. C. McNally	June 5, 1909.
		Mar. 22, 1899.
	Hon. Capt.	Mar. 22, 1909.

LIEUTENANT-COLONELS (4)

4.	O. S. W. Nugent, D.S.O., p.s.c., A.D.C.	Oct. 15, 1906.
	Bt. Colonel	June 23, 1909.
1.	R. S. Oxley, p.s.c.	Dec. 18, 1907.
3.	C. S. Chaplin	Mar. 18, 1908.
2.	S. W. Hare	Aug. 20, 1908.

MAJORS (16)

	1.	Hon. A. R. Montagu-Stuart-Wortley, D.S.O., p.s.c.	May 4, 1904.
	2.	Northey, E.	Aug. 3, 1904.
	3.	C. Gosling	Sept. 14, 1904.
	4.	E. Pearce-Serocold, p.s.c.	May 3, 1905.
s.		C. J. Sackville-West, p.s.c.	Aug. 2, 1905.
			Nov. 29, 1900.
s.		L. F. Philips, p.s.c.	Nov. 29, 1905.
			Aug. 22, 1902.
s.	3.	H. C. Warre, D.S.O., p.s.c., q.s.	Dec. 5, 1906.
s.		H. R. Blore, p.s.c.	Oct. 21, 1907.
			Nov. 29, 1900.
	1.	G. C. Shakerley, D.S.O., Rifle Sub Depôt	Dec. 18, 1907.
s.		W. H. L. Allgood	Feb. 13, 1908.
	2.	W. Barnett	Mar. 18, 1908.

LISTS OF THE REGIMENT xxxiii

MAJORS (16)—*continued*.

BATT.	NAME.	DATE OF APPOINTMENT.
1.	Lord R. W. O. Manners, D.S.O.	May 6, 1908.
3.	W. J. Long	May 6, 1908.
s.	G. V. Hordern, p.s.c.	Aug. 20, 1908.
		Nov. 29, 1900.
2.	H. C. R. Green	Sept. 1, 1908.
3.	W. F. G. Wyndham, M.V.O. (L.) (F.)	Oct. 5, 1908.

CAPTAINS (26)

		F. M. Crum	Jan. 1, 1901.
		Bt. Major	Aug. 22, 1902.
d.	3.	R. C. Chester-Master	Jan. 13, 1901.
		Bt. Major	Jan. 14, 1901.
		S. F. Mott	Jan. 13, 1901.
		Bt. Major	Aug. 22, 1902.
s.		R. G. Jelf	Jan. 13, 1901.
	2.	G. A. P. Rennie, D.S.O.	Feb. 25, 1901.
	4.	B. F. Widdrington	Mar. 10, 1901.
s.		D. H. Blundell-Hollinshead-Blundell, M.V.O., p.s.c. (L.)	Mar. 19, 1901.
r.		G. A. Armytage	June 26, 1901.
t.		G. F. B. Hankey	June 26, 1901.
		H. F. F. B. Foljambe	July 20, 1901.
		R. Johnstone	Sept. 18, 1901.
	1.	M. Pratt, D.S.O.	Sept. 24, 1901.
d.	4.	B. J. Majendie	Oct. 9, 1901.
t.		H. F. W. Bircham	Oct. 25, 1901.
s.		J. H. Davidson, D.S.O., p.s.c.	Oct. 25, 1901.
	4.	W. A. I. Kay	Dec. 11, 1901.
d.	2.	A. E. Cathcart	Jan. 7, 1902.
s.		H. Wake, D.S.O., p.s.c.	Jan. 7, 1902.
s.c.		H. C. Johnson, D.S.O.	Jan. 7, 1902.
	4.	C. H. N. Seymour	Jan. 7, 1902.
		V.C. L. A. E. Price-Davies, D.S.O.	Jan. 7, 1902.
	2.	G. K. Priaulx	Jan. 22, 1902.
	4.	G. R. Wake	June 24, 1908.
			May 3, 1902.
(5)	1.	A. D. Legard	June 14, 1902.

iv—3

xxxiv LISTS OF THE REGIMENT

CAPTAINS (26)—*continued*.

BATT.	NAME.	DATE OF APPOINTMENT.
2.	G. MAKINS, M.V.O.	Jan. 22, 1904.
2.	S. F. McI. LOMER	July 25, 1908.
		July 15, 1904.
1.	H. B. P. L. KENNEDY	Aug. 8, 1904.
1.	G. H. MARTIN	Jan. 23, 1905.
4.	G. J. ACLAND-TROYTE	Jan. 28, 1905.
t.	A. R. LEITH	April 25, 1905.
1.	C. F. HAWLEY	Nov. 23, 1905.
3.	HON. A. F. W. HARRIS	Nov. 23, 1905.
2.	R. E. CRICHTON (Adjutant)	Jan. 11, 1906.
1.	F. G. WILLAN	Feb. 2, 1906.
3.	G. CULME-SEYMOUR	Mar. 22, 1906.
3.	A. F. C. MACLACHLAN, D.S.O. (Adjutant)	Aug. 25, 1906.
4.	J. F. F. TATE	June 24, 1908.
		Jan. 1, 1907.
3.	W. S. W. PARKER-JERVIS	Feb. 10, 1907.
3.	E. A. BRADFORD	June 4, 1907.
r.	C. A. HOWARD	July 19, 1907.
4.	G. H. BARNETT	Oct. 9, 1907.
2.	T. H. HARKER	Jan. 22, 1908.
c.o.	G. C. KELLY	Jan. 22, 1908.
s.	A. J. FIFE	Jan. 22, 1908.
	B. J. CURLING	Jan. 22, 1908.
1.	B. SEYMOUR	Jan. 22, 1908.
2.	J. E. N. HESELTINE	Jan. 22, 1908.
1.	R. H. SEYMOUR (Adjutant)	Feb. 28, 1908.
3.	F. V. YEATS-BROWN	Mar. 31, 1908.
(6) 4.	G. T. LEE	April 24, 1908.
1.	F. L. PARDOE	Oct. 23, 1908.

LIEUTENANTS (39)

	1.	R. N. ABADIE	April 15, 1901.
		H. A. VERNON	May 9, 1901.
	4.	F. W. L. EDWARDS (Adjutant Depôt)	June 10, 1901.
	4.	C. V. L. POË (Adjutant)	June 24, 1901.
s.		H. W. M. WATSON	June 26, 1901.
d.	1.	C. D. EYRE	July 3, 1901.

LISTS OF THE REGIMENT

LIEUTENANTS (39)—continued.

BATT.	NAME.	DATE OF APPOINTMENT.
	G. T. BLEWITT	July 20, 1901.
2.	R. D. TEMPLE	Sept. 24, 1901.
c.o.	G. WYNNE-FINCH	Oct. 9, 1901.
d. 2.	E. B. DENISON	Dec. 20, 1901.
2.	G. A. H. BEAUMONT	April 23, 1904.
4.	C. J. T. R. WINGFIELD	Nov. 16, 1904.
4.	A. A. SOAMES	Jan. 23, 1905.
3.	G. J. JACKSON	June 24, 1905.
		April 5, 1908.
s.	A. J. HUNTER	April 22, 1905.
c.o.	W. D. BARBER	April 25, 1905.
4.	E. G. ST. AUBYN	April 25, 1905.
2.	M. L. S. CLEMENTS	May 6, 1905.
1.	H. C. M. PORTER	May 16, 1905.
	L. AYLMER	Jan. 22, 1906.
3.	W. H. DEEDES	Jan. 22, 1906.
t.	A. P. EVANS	Jan. 22, 1906.
3.	G. M. ATKINSON	Feb. 2, 1906.
2.	W. J. DAVIS	May 9, 1906.
d. 3.	J. WORMALD	June 27, 1906.
2.	R. H. WILLAN	Feb. 10, 1907.
2.	R. H. BOND	Mar. 27, 1907.
1.	J. F. R. HOPE	April 3, 1907.
1.	A. C. OPPENHEIM	June 4, 1907.
3.	H. J. FLOWER	July 19, 1907.
4.	W. L. CLINTON	Aug. 26, 1907.
4.	H. C. PONSONBY	Oct. 9, 1907.
d. 4.	J. S. MELLOR	Oct. 17, 1907.
2.	M. F. BLAKE	Jan. 22, 1908.
3.	J. F. B. PEARSE	Jan. 22, 1908.
(5) 1.	J. G. HARGREAVES	Jan. 22, 1908.
4.	C. K. HOWARD-BURY	Feb. 13, 1908.
2.	F. W. PARISH	Feb. 13, 1908.
c.o.	L. G. MOORE	June 25, 1908.
2.	HON. E. E. M. J. UPTON	Oct. 3, 1908.
1.	A. M. SAUNDERS	Oct. 21, 1908.
1.	R. H. WOODS	Oct. 23, 1908.
3.	W. A. C. SAUNDERS-KNOX-GORE	Dec. 29, 1908.

LISTS OF THE REGIMENT

LIEUTENANTS (39)—*continued*.

Batt.	Name.	Date of Appointment.
2.	C. F. Lee	Feb. 4, 1909.
4.	J. N. Bigge	Mar. 10, 1909.
4.	R. J. H. Purcell	June 27, 1909.
4.	J. F. P. Butler	Aug. 21, 1909.
1.	J. F. Franks	Oct. 16, 1909.

SECOND LIEUTENANTS (24)

	Batt.	Name.	Date of Appointment.
	1.	L. D. St. A. Salusbury-Trelawny	May 4, 1907.
	3.	A. L. Bonham-Carter	Oct. 9, 1907.
	1.	J. V. E. Lees	Oct. 9, 1907.
	1.	P. G. Chaworth-Musters	Oct. 9, 1907.
	1.	G. V. H. Gough	Feb. 8, 1908.
	4.	J. E. Pleydell-Bouverie	Feb. 8, 1908.
	3.	C. A. Grazebrook	Feb. 18, 1908.
	3.	A. D. Thursby	Feb. 8, 1908.
	3.	C. C. Grattan-Bellew	Feb. 22, 1908.
w.a.		J. H. S. Dimmer	May 6, 1908.
	2.	G. C. Campbell	May 27, 1908.
	3.	Hon. T. J. A. Cecil	Sept. 19, 1908.
	4.	S. H. Ferrand	Sept. 19, 1908.
	3.	E. V. Pringle	Sept. 19, 1908.
	4.	H. O. Curtis	Oct. 14, 1908.
	3.	H. M. B. de Sales La Terriere	Oct. 14, 1908.
	3.	F. W. Cavendish-Bentinck	Oct. 14, 1908.
	4.	L. Frewen	Dec. 16, 1908.
	4.	C. T. Ellison	Feb. 6, 1909.
	1.	E. G. W. Bourke	Feb. 6, 1909.
	2.	B. W. Jackson	Feb. 6, 1909.
	4.	A. E. Lawrence	Sept. 18, 1909.
	4.	A. C. P. Butler	Sept. 18, 1909.
	3.	E. D. Shafto	Nov. 6, 1909.
	4.	G. S. Oxley	Nov. 6, 1909.

ADJUTANTS

Batt.	Name	Date
3.	A. F. C. Maclachlan, D.S.O. (Captain)	Dec. 10, 1907.
2.	R. E. Crichton (Captain)	May 17, 1908.
1.	R. H. Seymour (Captain)	Sept. 3, 1908.
4.	C. V. L. Poë (Lieutenant)	June 27, 1909.

LISTS OF THE REGIMENT

QUARTERMASTERS

BATT.	NAME.	DATE OF APPOINTMENT.
r.	T. O'SHEA	Jan. 10, 1894.
	Hon. Major	Jan. 10, 1909.
r.	W. J. WILKINS (Hon. Lieutenant)	Feb. 7, 1900.
4.	W. JUDGE (Hon. Lieutenant)	Feb. 11, 1903.
3.	A. C. WATKINS (Hon. Lieutenant)	Feb. 5, 1908.
2.	W. SHERMAN (Hon. Lieutenant)	Oct. 3, 1908.
		May 3, 1902.
1.	A. HARMAN, Hon. Lieutenant	July 7, 1909.

REGIMENTAL SUCCESSION OF COLONELS-IN-CHIEF, COLONELS COMMANDANT, AND LIEUTENANT-COLONELS, 1872-1914

COLONELS-IN-CHIEF

FIELD-MARSHAL H.R.H. THE DUKE OF CAMBRIDGE, K.G., K.P., G.C.B., G.C.M.G., 1869–1904

GENERAL H.R.H. THE PRINCE OF WALES, DUKE OF CORNWALL AND YORK, K.G., K.T., K.P., G.C.M.G., G.C.V.O., 1904–

COLONELS COMMANDANT, 1874–1914

BATT.	NAME.	DATE OF APPOINTMENT.
2.	GENERAL GEORGE FREDERICK, VISCOUNT TEMPLETOWN, K.C.B. (Served in the Regiment as a Captain, February 13, 1827—June 7, 1830)	Oct. 24, 1862.
1.	GENERAL HENRY, VISCOUNT MELVILLE, G.C.B.	April 1, 1863.
1.	GENERAL SIR ARTHUR A. T. CUNYNGHAME, K.C.B. (Joined the Regiment as 2nd Lieutenant, November 2, 1830; transferred to 3rd Foot as Captain, December 3, 1841)	Feb. 2, 1876.
2.	GENERAL FREEMAN MURRAY. (Transferred to the Regiment as a Captain, July 11, 1834; transferred to the 17th Foot as a Major, April 23, 1847)	Oct. 11, 1876.

SUCCESSION OF LIEUTENANT-COLONELS xxxix

COLONELS COMMANDANT—*continued*.

BATT.	NAME.	DATE OF APPOINTMENT.
1.	GENERAL EDWARD ARTHUR SOMERSET, C.B. (Did all his regimental service in the Rifle Brigade)	Sept. 14, 1884.
	GENERAL THE HON. SIR ARTHUR E. HARDINGE, K.C.B., C.I.E. (Never served in the Regiment)	Mar. 13, 1886.
	MAJOR-GENERAL (HON. LIEUT.-GENERAL) R. B. HAWLEY, C.B.	Feb. 26, 1890.
1.	GENERAL THE RT. HON. SIR REDVERS BULLER, V.C., G.C.B.	July 13, 1895.
2, later 1.	FIELD-MARSHAL THE RT. HON. FRANCIS, LORD GRENFELL, G.C.B., G.C.M.G.	Aug. 7, 1898.
3.	LIEUT.-GENERAL HENRY FRANCIS WILLIAMS	July 29, 1903.
4.	MAJOR-GENERAL ROWLEY WILLES HINXMAN	July 29, 1903.
4.	MAJOR-GENERAL WYKEHAM LEIGH PEMBERTON, C.B.	July 3, 1906.
3.	MAJOR-GENERAL SIR CROMER ASHBURNHAM, K.C.B.	May 2, 1907.
2.	LIEUT.-GENERAL SIR EDWARD T. H. HUTTON, K.C.B., K.C.M.G.	June 3, 1908.

SUCCESSION OF COMMANDING OFFICERS
1873 to 1914

1st Battalion

C. A. B. Gordon
August 9, 1871.

J. D. Dundas
December 19, 1877.

G. Hatchell
July 1, 1881.

A. F. Terry
January 7, 1886.

C. P. Cramer
July 1, 1887.

H. B. MacCall
July 1, 1891.

M. C. B. F. Forestier-Walker
July 1, 1895.

R. H. Gunning
December 29, 1898.

* H. Gore-Browne
October 21, 1899.

R. C. A. B. Bewicke-Copley
March 18, 1900.

C. J. Markham
March 18, 1904.

R. S. Oxley
March 18, 1908.

E. Northey
December 18, 1911.

2nd Battalion

Gibbes Rigaud
April 24, 1872.

H. P. Montgomery
August 13, 1873.

J. J. Collins
August 21, 1878.

* J. S. H. Algar
October 9, 1880.

K. G. Henderson
November 22, 1882.

W. G. Byron
September 9, 1884.

W. L. K. Ogilvy
June 6, 1885.

* A. A. A. Kinloch
July 1, 1887.

G. L. McL. Farmer
January 7, 1890.

Hon. K. Turnour
January 7, 1894.

G. G. Grimwood
September 18, 1895.

H. Gore-Browne
March 18, 1900.

W. S. Kays
October 21, 1903.

Sir F. B. M. Henniker, Bart.
October 21, 1907.

S. W. Hare
August 20, 1908.

E. Pearce Serocold
August 20, 1912.

3rd Battalion

P. B. Roe
September 18, 1860.

W. Leigh Pemberton
March 10, 1875.

C. Ashburnham
March 10, 1880.

* W. L. K. Ogilvy
November 1, 1884.

J. Charley
June 6, 1885.

G. T. Whitaker
July 1, 1887.

H. D. Browne
April 16, 1890.

R. S. R. Fetherstonhaugh
April 16, 1894.

* R. H. Gunning
April 16, 1898.

R. G. Buchanan-Riddell
December 29, 1898.

W. P. Campbell
January 25, 1900.

C. R. R. McGrigor
January 25, 1904.

* R. S. Oxley
December 18, 1907.

C. S. Chaplin
March 18, 1908.

C. Gosling
March 18, 1912.

4th Battalion

R. B. Hawley
May 18, 1860.

C. Williamson
October 13, 1873.

R. W. Hinxman
June 5, 1875.

* K. G. Henderson
June 5, 1880.

J. S. H. Algar
November 22, 1882.

* A. F. Terry
October 9, 1885.

A. Morris
January 7, 1886.

A. A. A. Kinloch
October 15, 1890.

R. Chalmer
October 15, 1890.

H. R. Mends
October 15, 1894.

E. W. Herbert
October 15, 1898.

F. A. Fortescue
October 15, 1902.

O. S. W. Nugent
October 15, 1906.

Hon. A. R. Montagu-Stuart-Wortley
October 15, 1910.

Hon. C. J. Sackville-West
April 1, 1914.

* Exchanged.

THE KING'S ROYAL RIFLE CORPS

CHAPTER I

Third Battalion

THE Battalion had arrived at Shorncliffe from Aden in December 1872, and remained there till June 1875.

In spite of the introduction of Short Service, by Cardwell, in 1870, the average length of service in the Battalion at the end of 1873 was $9\frac{1}{2}$ years. The strength of the Battalion on the last day of the year 1873 was 586 of all ranks.

The valise equipment and short-lived lambskin busby were issued in January 1873. The Martini-Henry rifle was issued in October 1874. It was a very much better shooting weapon than the old Snider, which it replaced, and its ammunition was lighter—its calibre being ·450 to the ·500 of the Snider—but it was apt to jam on service and was a very hard kicker.

On March 10, 1875, Colonel P. B. Roe, who—as related in Vol. III—had commanded from 1864 to 1869 and again been brought in to command after the short and unfortunate régime of Colonel Kennedy, was succeeded by Lieut.-Colonel W. Leigh Pemberton.[1]

In June 1875 the Battalion went to Aldershot for the summer drills, sending a detachment to Chatham under Captain J. K. Watson. On leaving Aldershot at the end of July, the Battalion went to Chatham. Five Companies

[1] Major-General Sir Wykeham Leigh Pemberton, K.C.B., Colonel Commandant 4th Battalion, 1906–18.

were moved to Woolwich in June 1876, and from thence to Winchester in August. Headquarters and the remaining five Companies—there were ten Companies in the Battalion, as the two Depôt Companies had rejoined the Battalion from Winchester on its arrival from abroad—joined them there in November, detachments being sent to Portsmouth and Marchwood.

The Battalion moved to North Camp, Aldershot, in February 1877, and from thence to Colchester in September 1878.

The Zulu War, 1879

The Zulus, who are of Bantu stock—akin to the Matabili, the Basutos, and all the Kaffir tribes—had in the early years of the nineteenth century been welded by their national hero Tchaka into a great military nation. His armies had a discipline and power of manœuvre very unusual among savage races. His successors, in keeping up his military system, had also retained his tactics. Although all their warriors were armed with a throwing assegai, or javelin, and in recent years many had acquired firearms, they relied almost entirely on shock tactics. Their invariable formation for attack was a long, loose line, with flanks thrown forward, and their aim was, while charging right home in front, to wrap their wings round their enemy's flanks and attack him in flank and rear. The hand-to-hand weapon was a short, stabbing assegai, and as every warrior carried a cowhide shield, that covered his whole body, he made a difficult proposition for the infantry soldier to deal with if not kept out of reach by fire-power. In fact, a charge by a Zulu impi had the strength and weakness of a charge by the Highland clans in old days. If the charge got home, it swept away all opposition; if it failed, the impi broke up and dispersed for the time being. Fortunately, the Zulus seldom attacked at night, and, although they had a good many firearms—especially after Isandhlwana, where they captured many hundreds of Martini-Henry rifles and many thousands of rounds of ammunition—they never learnt to use them intelligently, so as to prepare for or cover their shock tactics.

The military strength and warlike spirit of the Zulu nation had been a constant threat to the existence of the Boer Republic of the Transvaal, which had been an independent State from 1852 to 1877. In the early part of the latter year, as the Republic was practically bankrupt and threatened by an invasion by the Zulus, which in its decrepit condition would probably have meant its annihilation, the British Government sent Sir Theophilus Shepstone, then Secretary for Native Affairs in Natal, on a mission to Pretoria, with full powers to annex the Republic to the British Crown if he considered such a course advisable. Shepstone, when on the spot, speedily arrived at the conclusion—if he had not done so before starting—that the Boers were incapable of self-government or self-defence, and that the continued existence of the Republic was ' dangerous to the welfare of H.M.'s subjects and possessions in South Africa.' He therefore declared the Transvaal annexed, and hoisted the British Flag in Pretoria in April 1877.

Although the annexation was accepted with a good grace by President Burgers and his Government, with the majority of the Boers it was exceedingly unpopular, and they never concealed their intention to recover their independence by force of arms should the opportunity offer. At the date of annexation, though there had been no open war between Boer and Zulu since the shattering defeat by the Boers of Dingaan's invasion in 1838—

the 16th of December had ever since been celebrated among them as Dingaan's Day—there was a question of a disputed frontier line which had caused frontier incidents and which would, it can hardly be doubted, before long have given Ketchwayo, the Zulu King, an excuse for letting loose his warriors and overrunning the Transvaal.

In taking over the Transvaal the British Government took over, in this new and doubtful frontier, a probable cause of war with the Zulus. Sir Bartle Frere, who came out as Governor of Cape Colony and High Commissioner in March 1877, soon recognised that so long as Ketchwayo maintained his standing army of 40,000 men, well disciplined, vainglorious, and burning to emulate the achievements of their forbears, a war with the Zulus was only a question of time. So long as the Transvaal remained a weak, independent State, the probability was that Ketchwayo would give vent to the military aspirations of himself and his warriors by attacking the Boers, he having so far always kept on very good terms with his British neighbours.

After the annexation, Ketchwayo's attitude underwent a considerable change. While a Commission was actually at work on the boundary question—which Commission in the end gave a decision very favourable to the Zulus—Ketchwayo forced all missionaries resident in Zululand to abandon their mission-stations and leave the country. There followed several acts of violence committed by Zulus on the Natal frontier. Natal, which marched with Zululand from the Transvaal border to the sea, had a white population of 20,000 and a coloured population of 300,000. An invasion by Zulus might easily be followed by a Kaffir rising and a massacre of the whites.

Sir Bartle Frere determined to remove this sword of Damocles. In communicating his award on the frontier question to the Zulu King—he was acting as Arbitrator on the report of a joint Commission of British Officials and Zulu Chiefs—he sent him an ultimatum, demanding not only reparation for various frontier outrages, but that the Zulu Army should be disbanded; not to be brought together again without the consent of the British Government. This ultimatum, together with the award on the boundary dispute, was handed to the Zulus on December 11, 1878. The Zulu deputation was informed that a definite reply was required by December 31, and that the reparation demanded must be made by January 10, 1879.

Sir Bartle Frere had meanwhile given orders to Lieut.-General the Hon. F. A. Thesiger (Lord Chelmsford from October 5, 1878), commanding the Forces in South Africa, to be ready to take action should Ketchwayo not accept the demands of the ultimatum. Lord Chelmsford appreciated that, with the small force at his command and the length of the frontier to be protected, his only way to prevent an invasion of Natal was an immediate offensive. The total force under Lord Chelmsford's command on January 11, 1879, consisted of 5,128 British Infantry; 1,193 white mounted troops (local corps and M.I.); 315 mounted natives; 9,035 Natal Native Contingent, and 20 guns (mostly 7-pounders) : total, 17,929 Officers and men. The nature of the country—lack of roads and of any possibility of local supply—compelled dispersion; he therefore planned to cross the frontier on a wide front in three Columns which were to converge on Ulundi, the Zulu capital, some sixty miles from the nearest point in Natal.

On January 10, 1879, the three Columns were concentrated at Fort Pearson on the Tugela River, Rorke's Drift on the Buffalo River, and Bemba's Kop on the

Blood River respectively—over 100 miles from right to left—ready to advance. There were two more Columns; one, a Reserve, was left in Natal to protect the frontier from raids; the other was located at Luneberg on the extreme left, near where the frontiers of Natal, the Transvaal, and Zululand met.

The centre Column, which began its advance on January 11, met with the disaster of Isandhlwana on the 22nd, losing 52 Officers, 806 white N.C.O.s and men, and 471 natives, killed. The result of this reverse was that the remnant of the centre Column retired behind the frontier, the right Column under Colonel Pearson of the Buffs, which had reached Etshowe, about forty miles over the frontier, on January 23, remained there blockaded by the Zulus, though not attacked, and all offensive operations were suspended pending the arrival of reinforcements. In those days there was no telegraphic communication with the Cape, the cable not going farther than St. Vincent, Cape Verde Islands, and Lord Chelmsford's report of Isandhlwana did not reach London till February 11. Reinforcements, including two regiments of Cavalry and six battalions of Infantry, were at once dispatched. Our 3rd Battalion was among these. The Battalion at this time, though it contained a fair proportion of old N.C.O.s and Riflemen, consisted for the greater part of men of from nineteen to twenty-three years of age, and was made up to war strength by the addition of a lot of untrained recruits. Except for two or three senior Officers and a N.C.O. or two who had served in the Mutiny or China, no one in the Battalion had seen any active service. As in those days war was almost the only training for war, this meant more than it did in 1914.

Battalion H.Q. and six Companies (21 Officers, 690 O.R.) embarked at Gravesend on the *Dublin Castle* on

February 19, disembarking at Durban on March 20; two Companies (9 Officers, 209 O.R.) embarked on the *Danube* at Southampton on February 27, disembarking at Durban on April 1. With H.Q. were Lieut.-Colonel W. L. Pemberton, commanding the Battalion; Lieut.-Colonel F. V. Northey; Major W. L. K. Ogilvy; Captains A. Tufnell, A. Morris, C. P. Cramer, A. V. O'Brien, A. H. Bircham, Hon. K. Turnour; Lieutenants E. T. H. Hutton,[1] C. Michell, G. Astell, H. Allfrey, E. O. H. Wilkinson; Lieutenant and Adjutant R. H. Gunning; 2nd Lieutenants A. C. B. Mynors, D. G. R. Ryder, G. C. B. Baker, A. P. Crawley; Lieutenant and Quartermaster J. Ireland; Captain and Paymaster E. C. Haynes. On disembarking at Durban the Battalion heard that they were to form part of the Column which Lord Chelmsford was assembling at Fort Pearson, on the Tugela River, for the relief of Etshowe. They marched on the 22nd, reaching Fort Pearson on the 27th.

The Column assembled at Fort Pearson consisted of the 57th and 91st Regiments, six Companies of the 3rd 60th, five Companies of the 99th, and two Companies of the Buffs, with a Naval Brigade formed of men from H.M.S. *Shah*, *Tenedos*, and *Boadicea*. There was also a proportion of M.I., some local Mounted Troops, and the 4th and 5th Battalions of the Natal Native Contingent; the total strength of the Column amounting to 3,390 whites and 2,280 natives, with two 9-pounder guns, four 24-pounder rocket-tubes, and two Gatlings. (The Gatling was the machine gun of the period, an indifferent weapon, very liable to jam.) Two Brigades were formed; one under Lieut.-Colonel F. T. A. Law, R.A., and the other under Lieut.-Colonel W. L. Pemberton, 60th Rifles; the

---

[1] Lieut.-General Sir Edward Hutton, K.C.B., K.C.M.G., Colonel Commandant 2nd Battalion, 1908–23.

Battalion therefore came under the command of Lieut.-Colonel F. Northey. The Battalions of the Natal Native Contingent were composed of Natal Kaffirs—of whom only one man in ten was armed with a rifle—and were not to be relied on for serious fighting. The transport consisted, for the most part, of wagons drawn by oxen and could not exceed two miles an hour on good going.

The advance began on March 29, the force having been assembled on the left bank of the Tugela the previous day. Marches of nine or ten miles were made on each of the following days without opposition. At the end of each day's march the wagons were parked in a hollow square or laager, with the animals, mounted troops, and non-combatants inside. The white infantry dug a trench about twenty yards outside the wagon line; bivouacking in the space between the trench and the wagons. The N.N.C. were kept in reserve inside the square for use in pursuit, which, with reconnoitring, was their special *métier*, in fact, their only use. On April 1 the Column only marched about six miles to Ginginhlovo, and laagered on a slight rising ground (see Plate 1). The surrounding country was fairly free from bush, but mostly clothed in long grass three or four feet high. During the day large parties of Zulus were reported in the distance by the mounted scouts, and during the night the numerous fires on the hills to the northward showed that a considerable force of the enemy was in the neighbourhood.

At dawn next morning the mounted troops went out to reconnoitre while the infantry stood to their arms. It was not intended to advance this day and the cattle were about to be sent out to graze when, shortly before 6 a.m., reports came in that a Zulu army was approaching. At 6 a.m. they appeared in sight of the laager. The square was occupied in the following order: front face (N.E.) 3rd 60th; right face, the 57th; left face, 99th and Buffs; rear face, 91st; with the guns, Gatlings, and rocket-tubes at the corners. Two Columns of Zulus first appeared on the other side of the Inyezane River, after crossing which they deployed and came on; one Column against the front face of the square, the other against the eastern corner. Two more Columns then appeared from the west and deployed opposite the left and rear faces of the laager. The enemy gradually worked up through the long grass to within about 150 yards of the square, where they opened fire in answer to the heavy fire of our infantry, which had been opened at a range of 800 yards. The Zulus' shooting must have been very poor, as our casualties were few. Very early in the action Lieut.-Colonel Northey, in command of the Battalion, who was walking over to the Gatling gun, which had just opened fire, to ask for the range, was hit by a bullet in the shoulder, which lodged in his spine. Soon tiring of the fire fight, which was not their trade, the Zulus made a few determined charges against different sides of the square, in some cases getting to within twenty yards. By 7.30 a.m. they had had enough of it and began to retire. The Mounted Troops and N.N.C. were promptly sent in pursuit, and did great execution.

The Zulu army was about 10,000 strong, and it was estimated that they lost about 1,200 killed. The British losses amounted to 9 N.C.O.s and men killed; 6 Officers and 46 O.R. wounded, of whom two officers died. The 3rd Battalion lost 1 man killed and 5 wounded, besides Lieut.-Colonel Northey, who died on April 6. Northey was a great loss to the Regiment, as he was a very promising soldier, a good comrade, and particularly distinguished as a cricketer. An obituary notice in the Press compares him to Adrian Hope, one of the most distinguished Riflemen of the preceding generation.

Next day Etshowe was relieved.

Colonel Evelyn Wood[1] had, on March 29, inflicted a severe defeat on the enemy who attacked his laager at Kambula, the Zulu loss being about 2,000. These two defeats broke the back of the Zulu resistance, and Lord Chelmsford made his arrangements for a final advance on the capital. These took some time, and it was not till July 4 that Ketchwayo made, at Ulundi, his final effort, the complete failure of which, with a loss of 1,500 men, finished the war. Ketchwayo took to the bush with a few followers, and Columns were sent out to round him up. It was with one of these Columns that the 3rd Battalion, who had done nothing since Ginginhlovo, next found employment.

On April 5 Etshowe had been evacuated, the garrison starting to march direct back to the Tugela, Lord Chelmsford's Column retiring on Ginginhlovo. An unpleasant incident occurred that night which did the 3rd Battalion undeservedly a lot of harm. A shot being fired in the night by a sentry of the 91st, some of the native scouts who were outside our piquet line bolted for the laager, sweeping right over a piquet of the 3rd Battalion posted 80 yards outside, falling over the sleeping men and overturning the piles of arms. The men in the laager opened fire and the Naval Detachment let off three rockets, one hitting the tree under which the piquet was posted, the other two going over them. The two Officers with the piquet did their best to restore order, but did not succeed in doing so before some of their men had joined in the stampede. Considerable damage was done among the native scouts, and one man of the 60th was killed and

[1] Field-Marshal Sir H. Evelyn Wood, V.C., G.C.B., G.C.M.G.

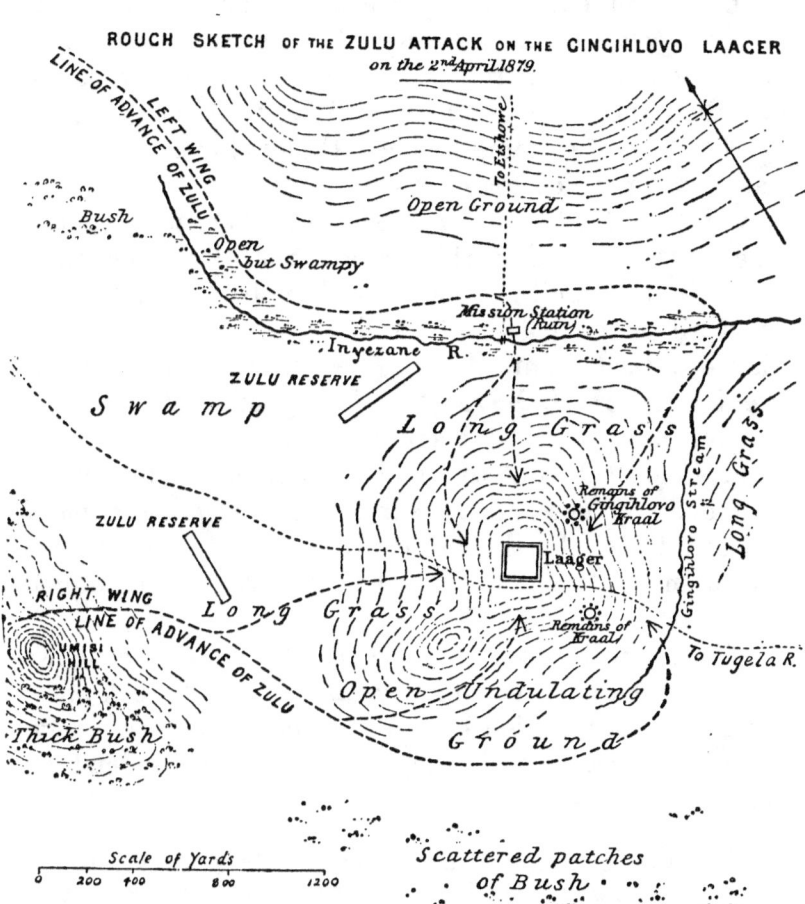

PLATE 1.

four wounded. It was a small incident and not an uncommon one in the British Force in Zululand—there is no doubt that after Isandhlwana the Zulu rather got on the nerves of the troops—but the story got about in various and exaggerated forms, with the result that entirely unfounded stories were spread about the conduct of the Battalion then and in the Boer War two years later.

Next day the force reached Ginginhlovo. Here the Battalion remained for nearly a month, after which they moved to a fresh camp named Fort Chelmsford, a few miles away. During this period the two Companies under Captain Smith,[1] which had disembarked at Durban on April 1, joined the Battalion, with Captain E. H. Thurlow, Lieutenants A. E. Miles, R. S. R. Fetherstonhaugh,[2] and H. J. Nevill, 2nd Lieutenants W. J. Myers and W. Du V. Lysley. There was a good deal of sickness. Lieut.-Colonel Pemberton and Lieutenant Mynors were invalided; Mynors, an exceedingly promising and popular Officer, dying shortly afterwards. Ogilvy and Morris had been left behind sick when the Battalion entered Zululand.

The following extract from an Officer's diary shows that even at this time, which we are inclined to look on as a period of occultation of the Staff of the British Army, there was at least one Intelligence Officer who understood his job :—

'A couple of Zulus were captured by the M.I. patrols and brought in to-day. With a view to extracting information from them regarding the enemy's movements, we adopted the following expedient. They were taken out of sight of each other and blindfolded. A shot was then fired and, on each prisoner, much frightened, asking what that was, they

[1] Major-General Sir Charles Holled Smith, K.C.M.G., C.B.
[2] Major-General R. S. R. Fetherstonhaugh, C.B., Colonel Commandant 3rd Battalion, 1917– .

were told, "Your companion has been shot for not speaking the truth in answer to our questions," and that he would meet the same fate if he replied falsely; whereupon they both protested with much earnestness they would speak truthfully if their lives were spared. They were then each questioned and, as their answers agreed, it was concluded that reliable information had been extracted from them.'

The following extract from 'Our Special Correspondent's' letter of May 6 possibly explains this unexpected subtlety: 'John Dunn has been gazetted to the Intelligence Department.' John Dunn was an Englishman who had lived nearly all his life among the Zulus and was a sort of chief among them. After the war he was put in charge of one of the districts into which the country was divided.

Towards the end of June the Battalion moved to Port Durnford, the nearest point on the coast to Ulundi, where a Division of two Brigades was being assembled.

On June 28 Sir Garnet Wolseley,[1] who had been sent out to supersede Lord Chelmsford, arrived at Durban and came on to Port Durnford, arriving there on July 7. All organised resistance having ceased after Ketchwayo's final defeat at Ulundi, Wolseley now began to reduce his force in the field, at the same time breaking up what was left of it into small Columns; our 3rd Battalion joining a Column under Lieut.-Colonel Clarke, 57th Foot,[2] which, leaving Port Durnford on July 24, trekked about the country till the end of August. The only event of any interest in this march was that two Companies, under Captain C. P. Cramer, were detailed to escort Ketchwayo— who had been captured by a squadron of the K.D.G.s under Major Marter, on August 28—a two days' march

[1] Field-Marshal the Rt. Hon. G. J., Viscount Wolseley, K.P., G.C.B., G.C.M.G., Commander-in-Chief, 1895–1900.
[2] General Sir Charles Mansfield Clarke, Bart., G.C.B., G.C.V.O.

into Ulundi. On September 2 the force was broken up, Colonel Clarke's Column starting on that day on its return march into Natal. The Battalion reached Pietermaritzburg on October 3, and settled down there to garrison duty with detachments at Greytown, Durban, and St. John's River.

The First Boer War, 1881

As has already been told in this chapter, the Transvaal Republic had been annexed to the British Crown in April 1877, against the wishes of the great majority of its inhabitants. Whether annexation saved the Transvaal Boers from annihilation by the Zulus or not, no one can say; but it is certain that the destruction of the Zulu power by the British in 1879 must have had the effect of removing the doubts of any half-hearted followers of those Boers who were clamouring for independence and meant to take it if it were not conceded to them. Deputations of Boer leaders to England, protesting against the annexation, had met with no success. A great national Boer meeting was held near Pretoria from December 10 to 17, 1879, where the republican flag was displayed and resolutions passed to regain independence by force of arms. The Boers had been much encouraged in their claim for independence by the accession of the Liberals to power in England after the general election of 1880, and were greatly disappointed to find that the new Government did not immediately grant it them. By December 1880 the whole nation was in arms, and on the 16th of that month the independence of the South African Republic was proclaimed. On the 20th a British force composed of the Headquarters of the 94th Regiment, about 250 of all ranks, was attacked by a superior force of Boers while on the march, at Bronkhorst Spruit, between Leydenberg and Pretoria, and surrendered after losing about 150 in killed and wounded. The small British garrisons scattered about the Transvaal were besieged and the First Transvaal War had begun.

Major-General Sir George Pomeroy-Colley, an Officer of distinguished reputation, who had seen a great deal of service in South Africa, and who was indeed looked upon as the coming man in the British Army, had succeeded Sir Garnet Wolseley as Governor and Commander-in-Chief in Natal and High Commissioner in South-east Africa in the previous July. On receipt of the news of the outbreak, Colley, having sent an ultimatum to the Boers, ordering them as insurgents to disperse, concentrated all the troops at his disposal at Newcastle in the north-west corner of Natal, with the purpose of invading the Transvaal and relieving the beleaguered garrisons, which could not be expected to hold out long enough for reinforcements to reach Colley from overseas and make up his force to one adequate to his purpose. On January 24, 1881, Colley marched out from Newcastle with the following force: two 9-pounder guns; two 7-pounder guns, and two more 7-pounders manned by volunteers from the 60th; five Companies 58th Regiment; five Companies 3/60th; 120 Mounted Troops (K.D.G.s and M.I.); about 100 of the Naval Brigade with two 24-lb. rocket-tubes and two Gatlings; one Company 21st Royal Scots Fusiliers and about 20 Natal Mounted Police. Three short marches took him to Mount Prospect, $3\frac{1}{2}$ miles from Laing's Nek, where the Boers had taken up a position which had to be forced before he could enter the Transvaal.

Our 3rd Battalion, since the Zulu War, had been scattered in detachments throughout Natal and Griqualand East. In the last-named country there had been a native rising which had been quelled by local forces before the regular troops, which included some of our 3rd Battalion under Major Astley Terry, could arrive. Headquarters had been all the time at Pietermaritzburg. On March 12, 1880, Lieut.-Colonel and Brevet Colonel W. Leigh Pemberton, C.B., had gone on half-pay and had been succeeded by Lieut.-Colonel Cromer Ashburnham,[1] an old Mutinyman, till recently serving with the 2nd Battalion in Afghanistan, who took over command on November 27. On December 21 two Companies, under Major Ogilvy, left Pietermaritzburg for Newcastle, followed on the 26th by two more under Captain Holled Smith, and by H.Q. and one Company on January 1, 1881; the five Companies being concentrated at Newcastle on the 18th.

LAING'S NEK (see Plate 2)

Colley had reached Mount Prospect on January 26. Rain and mist prevented all movement the next day, and on the 28th he moved out to attack and clear the Nek.

The Boer force, which was estimated pretty correctly as far as can be known at 2,000, was holding a line from the foot of Majuba to a point about 1,000 yards to the east of the road over the Nek, the spur marked A being occupied by a detached post of about 200 men.

After leaving 200 men and the Gatlings to protect the camp, Colley only had for his purpose 870 Infantry (5 Companies 58th and 4 Companies 60th), 140 mounted men, 6 guns, and 3 rocket tubes. Possibly he underestimated the fighting prowess of the Boers, and hoped to end the war at a blow, but he was urged to take the risk by the belief that the Garrison of Potchefstrom could not

[1] Major-General Sir Cromer Ashburnham, K.C.B., Colonel Commandant 3rd Battalion, 1907–17.

hold out till he was reinforced. He advanced as far as B—B, and then decided to make his main attack on C with the 58th, protecting their right flank by attacking A with his mounted troops. He brought his guns into action about B—B, sending his rocket battery of sailors, escorted by one Company 3/60th, under Lieutenant Dudley Ryder, to D, where, although under fire at pretty close range even for those days, they had good cover behind a stone wall and had few casualties, while the rockets searched the Boer position and their laagers behind it. The remaining three Companies of the 60th, with the Mounted Police, were in reserve with the guns.

The attack was a fiasco. As soon as the mounted troops and the 58th were launched against their several objectives, Major Brownlow, K.D.G.s, in command of the mounted troops, delivered a mounted charge up hill A. A few of the leaders actually got among the Boers on the top, but Brownlow's horse was shot, all his immediate followers were killed, wounded, or unhorsed, and in a few minutes what were left of his command were at the bottom of the hill again. Meanwhile the 58th were half-way up to C, and so far in dead ground, but after the repulse of the mounted troops the garrison of A were at liberty to take them in flank and rear. Colonel B. M. Deane, commanding the Natal Field Force under Colley and who was by ways of commanding the attack, finding his duties appropriated by the Commander-in-Chief, evidently thought he could not do better than take on those of the Officer Commanding 58th. He proceeded to lead that unfortunate Regiment up the hill in column at such a pace that they soon lost all formation. Giving them no time to halt and deploy while they were still in dead ground, he hustled them on and arrived at the top of the hill at the head of a panting and exhausted mob. Attempting a charge with the few pumped-out men near him, he was quickly shot down, together with his staff (including Lieutenant E. M. L. Inman, 3/60th, his Orderly Officer). It says a great deal for the discipline of the Battalion that, plastered at close range, from front, flank, and rear, they—to quote Colley's dispatch—'fell back without haste or confusion and re-formed at the foot of the hill.'

The Companies of the 60th, in reserve, were pushed out to cover the retreat, and the Boers made no effort to follow up their success.

The force then returned to camp with a loss of 194 killed and wounded and 2 prisoners, of which the loss of the 58th was: killed 3 Officers, 70 other ranks; wounded 2 Officers, 98 other ranks, and 1 prisoner. The loss of the 3/60th was 1 man slightly wounded, but the Mounted Infantry section from the Battalion lost 1 man killed and 4 wounded.

There was nothing for Colley to do after this reverse but to await the reinforcements now on the way to him. Of these the 15th Hussars, 2/60th, and a Battery of Artillery reached Durban, from India, on January 25. These were followed on the 30th by the 83rd and 92nd. The next day a further addition to the Naval Brigade, consisting of about 60 men with two Gatlings and two 24-lb. rocket tubes, were landed. These, with the exception of the 83rd, immediately started on their march to Newcastle. Colley, writing on February 4 to Brigadier-General Sir Evelyn Wood, gives his plans for the future :—

'I shall add the 15th Hussars, 2/60th and 92nd, to the field force under my personal command, giving me about 2,200 Infantry, 450 Cavalry, and 8 guns and Gatlings. From the troops remaining in Natal, viz. 83rd, 97th, 6th Inniskillings, and two Batteries of Artillery, I propose to form a second Column, under your command, to be assembled at

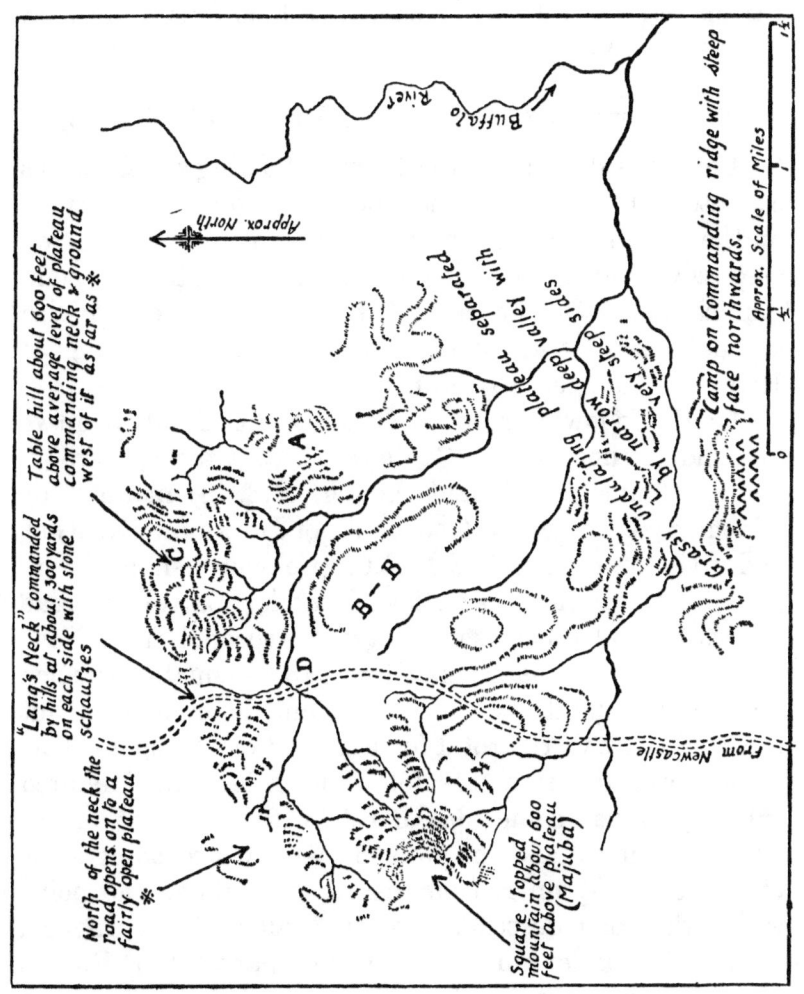

PLATE 2.

Newcastle and used either to co-operate by a flanking movement if the Boers mass such large forces here as to make that necessary, or to support and occupy and pacify Wakkerstrom, Utrecht, etc. . . . I hope to be in a position to move forward about the 20th.'

THE ACTION ON THE INGOGO RIVER (see Plate 3)

For some days after the failure at Laing's Nek it was expected, and hoped, that the Boers would make an attack on the entrenched camp at Mount Prospect, but their first aggressive move was directed against the British communications. On February 7 the mail from camp with a small escort was fired on just south of the Ingogo River and obliged to return.

On the following morning Colley marched out with two 9-pounder guns, R.A. (Captain C. R. Greer); two 7-pounder guns (Lieutenant Young, R.S.F.), manned by Riflemen; 38 mounted troops (Major Brownlow K.D.G.s), and five Companies 3/K.R.R.C. (Colonel Ashburnham), in order to, as he says in his dispatch, 'patrol the road and meet and escort some wagons expected from Newcastle.' This seems a small force and a small operation for the Commander-in-Chief to command in person, but it was about half the total force he had on the spot. The force marched out in the following order, viz. Mounted Infantry, 5 Companies 3/K.R.R.C. with one Company as advanced guard, and the guns in rear. On reaching some high ground $2\frac{1}{2}$ miles from camp, just above the point where the road descends into the valley of the Ingogo, the two 7-pounder guns (with one Company 3/K.R.R.C. as escort—Lieutenant D. G. R. Ryder and 2nd Lieutenant P. Marling[1]) were left in a position to sweep the ground to the west of the road, down to the river and beyond it.

---

[1] Colonel Sir P. S. Marling, Bart., V.C., C.B.

The remainder of the force then moved on and crossed the Ingogo, which was then not much more than ankle deep. The mounted troops went on to a plateau about 3,000 yards south of the river, the scene of the fight as shown in the sketch. They soon came into contact with the enemy, who were advancing from the south-west as if to occupy the plateau. As the Battalion reached the plateau, Companies were pushed out to the right and left and a line taken up round the edge of it, forming almost a complete circle. While the deployment was taking place, the guns opened on the advancing Boers and sent them to cover. The Boers were constantly reinforced till the occupants of the plateau were under fire from every side. A very stiff fire fight ensued which lasted all day, the Boers constantly pushing in with the evident intention of rushing the position, every part of the position being under fire at not more than 500 yards' range and in some places less than 100. The first shot was fired at 11.30 a.m., and soon after 12 noon the fire became very hot. Nearly all the horses of the mounted troops, artillery, and mounted Officers were very soon killed or wounded. Captain Greer, R.A., was killed at about 12.30 p.m.

About 2.30 p.m. Sir George Colley sent one of his Staff, Captain McGregor, R.E., to Colonel Ashburnham with a message that he was to send a company out to the left, as he thought the Boers were going to rush the position. Colonel Ashburnham sent I Company (Lieutenant Garrett), his only reserve. This side of the position was the one with least cover, being bare grass, while the rest of the position was mostly covered with rocks and boulders. Captain McGregor went with them, mounted, to show them where to go. He seems to have taken them farther than was intended. He was killed at once and Lieutenant Garrett very soon afterwards. Though the Boers got within 50 yards of them and the Company lost 23 men during the advance, they 'stuck it' well for the rest of the day. Colonel Ashburnham says in his account of the fight :—

'As the day wore on, things began to look serious. We had started after breakfast, but had taken no food with us ; neither had we a water-cart or any reserve ammunition. . . . Our ammunition, too, was going fast, but I passed an order to husband it, and the way in which the fire was afterwards controlled was beyond all praise. The conduct of the Battalion throughout the day was admirable ; the cool courage, the order and discipline that were maintained, and the devoted manner in which all ranks performed their duties left nothing to be desired.'

About 3 p.m. the fire began to slacken ; there was a certain 'liveliness' again between 4 p.m. and 5 p.m. on the arrival of Boer reinforcements, but the enemy had evidently given up hope of rushing the position and intended to finish the British off in the morning. Soon after 5 p.m., rain, which had been threatening for some hours, began to come down in torrents. A move was made about this time by a party of Boers towards the Ingogo Drift, as if to cut off any chance of retirement to camp, but this was stopped by the fire of the two 7-pounders from the other side of the river. As it got dark, fire ceased altogether. About 8 p.m. the General decided to make the attempt to retire to camp during the night. The troops were assembled, all available blankets, waterproof sheets, and great-coats were collected and the wounded made as comfortable as possible, in the charge of the Chaplain (the Rev. G. M. Ritchie), the M.O., Surgeon McCann, and his assistants, and at 9 p.m. the force moved off. The Battalion was formed in a hollow square with the M.I., the guns and the General and Staff inside. A patrol that had been sent on to the Drift reported it clear of the enemy and the force was got safely across, but with great difficulty as the river was rapidly rising. Again, to borrow from Colonel Ashburnham :—

'We now moved off up the gorge ; the night was as black as ink, and we were all drenched to the skin ; the road was so slippery that the horses could not stand. . . . When near the top of the hill the guns stuck altogether. I was obliged to pull them up the rest of the way with my men [about three miles]. When we arrived in camp at 5.30 a.m., it was quite daylight. Such was the night march after the action. Splendidly as the Battalion had behaved during the day, I think their conduct during this long and trying night march was even more creditable ; the order, regularity, and discipline maintained during the whole march was beyond all praise.'

The losses of the Battalion were :—

Killed : Lieutenant M. O'Connell, Lieutenant J. R. Garrett, 55 O.R.
Died of Wounds : 2nd Lieutenant W. S. S. Haworth.
Wounded : Lieutenants A. D. Pixley and E. W. Thistlethwayte, 53 O.R.
Drowned : Lieut.-Adjutant E. O. H. Wilkinson, 6 O.R.

A total of 120 casualties out of 217 actually engaged.

As soon as the Battalion had got back to camp ' Peter ' Wilkinson started back to help the wounded. He reached the battlefield, but on his return was swept off his pony crossing the drift and was drowned. He was an exceptionally promising Officer and a general favourite. Besides being devoted to his profession, he was very good at games, having been Captain of the Eleven at Eton, as was Colonel F. Northey, killed in Zululand. Sir George Colley in his dispatch says :

' The comparatively young soldiers of the 60th Rifles behaved with the steadiness and coolness of veterans. At all times perfectly in hand, they held or changed their ground as directed, without hurry or confusion; though under heavy fire themselves fired steadily, husbanding their ammunition, and at the end of the day, with sadly reduced numbers, formed and moved off the ground with most perfect steadiness and order; and finally, after eighteen hours of continuous fatigue, readily and cheerfully attached themselves to the guns and dragged them up the long hill from the Ingogo, when the horses were unable to do so.'

Among those specially mentioned was S. M. Wilkins, 60th Rifles :—

'who throughout the day was to be seen wherever the fire was hottest, setting an example to the men by his cool and steady shooting and cheerful gallantry.'

As usual, it is difficult to get at any accurate figures of the Boer forces engaged, but they were probably, towards the end of the day, not far short of 1,000. Their losses, from the numbers of wounded seen to be carried away, may be set down as considerable, if not severe.

Next day, under a flag of truce, the dead were buried and the wounded removed to Newcastle.

Whether or not the Boers at Ingogo got more than they liked, it is certain that they made no further serious effort to interfere with Colley's communications or with the advance up country of the reinforcements.

Sir George Colley rode back to Newcastle to meet Sir Evelyn Wood, and on February 21 inspected the Indian Column (one Squadron 15th Hussars, 2/60th and 92nd).

Next morning at 2 a.m. the Column marched out for Mount Prospect with a convoy of 150 wagons. The 2/60th were sent back to Newcastle with a convoy of empty wagons, so Colley's force was only reinforced by one Squadron of Cavalry and one Infantry Battalion.

On February 23 the following Officers joined the

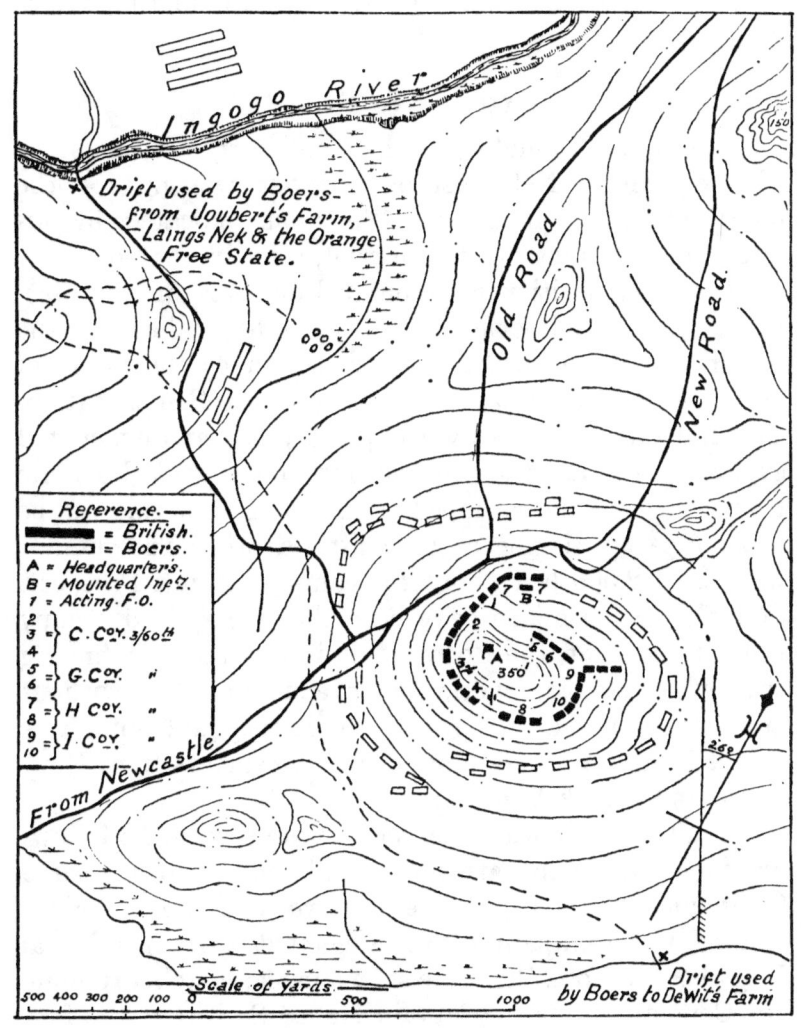

PLATE 3.
INGOGO.

Battalion: Major W. L. K. Ogilvy, Captain R. Henly, Lieutenants M. C. Boyle, T. E. M. S. Pilkington, H. E. Riddell.

MAJUBA (see Plate 4)

Colley now thought that he could turn the Boers out of the Laing's Nek position without waiting for the co-operation of Sir Evelyn Wood, as indicated by his letter to that Officer of February 4, already quoted.

The Boer position was bounded on its right by a flat-topped mountain with very steep sides, called by the Kaffirs Amajuba, which ever since, under the name of Majuba, has been a painful memory to the British nation. This hill was occupied by a piquet by day and evacuated every night. Its flat top was reported by local Kaffirs to be rather saucer-shaped, and water was said to be obtainable by digging at very little depth. The summit was about 2,500 feet above the camp at Mount Prospect. Colley's idea seems to have been that if he could occupy this hill by night, the Boers would in the morning, finding their whole position overlooked, evacuate the Nek without any further move on his part, or if they did not go he would bring up the rest of his reinforcements from Newcastle and attack them again.

At 10 p.m., February 26, he left camp with the following force, the men carrying three days' rations: three Companies 92nd Highlanders; two Companies 3/60th Rifles; two Companies 58th Regiment; 64 men Naval Brigade. He took the route shown in the sketch, dropping two Companies 3/60th (Captain Holled Smith) at the foot of Inkwella Mountain and one Company 92nd on the col between that mountain and Majuba. This Company was joined later by a Company of the 60th (Captain Thurlow). What happened on Majuba, so far as it concerns the Regiment, is best told in Captain Thurlow's own words in a letter to Colonel W. Leigh Pemberton, his late C.O. :—

'About 12 midnight I was sent out with 75 men . . . to escort 10 pack-mules with ammunition, and with me went two subalterns, Pigott and Howard Vyse, also a doctor called Cornish, with a pack-horse and medical comforts and a few stretchers. My orders were to make the best of my way to the ridge between the two mountains, about three miles distant, and join the Company of the 92nd Highlanders ; and I was told that I was only an escort, and should probably get orders to return to camp on handing over my ammunition, but that I was to await orders. We reached the ridge after a long climb in the dark and joined the 92nd Company, the Captain of which, being my senior, then became my C.O. I found him very busy entrenching himself, and of course set the men to work to help, and by daylight we had a very respectable little redoubt built, into which we put the reserve ammunition.

'When daylight broke, we could see our men on both the Inkwella and Amajuba Mountains ; and the Boers in numbers to the left of the Amajuba, from whence soon came firing. This went on all the morning ; we were, in the meantime, in communication with our camp and our two Companies on the Inkwella Hill to our rear, but I received no orders either to advance with my reserve ammunition or to retire to camp.

'About 12 noon, 27th, we were joined by a troop of the 15th Hussars, and soon after this the firing on the Amajuba became very heavy, and spent bullets began to drop all around us ; then we saw a redcoat running down the steep slopes in our direction, and then some bluejackets, and then a confused lot of men, Highlanders, sailors, and 58th, and soon the edge of the hill was occupied by the Boers, who poured a tremendous fire into our unfortunate men as they scrambled down the rocks on the mountain-side, knocking them over like rabbits ; those that escaped retired on our redoubt, giving their story of their repulse from the mountain and of the General's death. Soon after this we saw a great crowd of Boers on the top of the mountain, and could hear them cheering, and soon they began coming down from both sides, and it was plain enough that they intended to attack us in our redoubt ; they streamed down the dongas and ravines in large numbers. We signalled to camp for orders, but somehow or other the messages miscarried, and we made all preparations for defending our post, and ran up two shelter trenches near the redoubt, as the beggars soon got round us, which, owing to the nature of the ground, it was easy enough for them to do, and began firing at about 200 yards off, which we returned. Just then an orderly came in from the camp with an order for us to retire.'

Captain Thurlow goes on to say that in rear of his position was a precipitous ravine leading towards the camp. Down this were first dispatched the wounded, the Hussars, and the ammunition-mules, all of which got safely to camp except for two boxes of ammunition carried by one mule which was shot. The two Companies (92nd and 60th) then retired down the ravine under a hot fire and made the best of their way back to camp, covered, when half-way back, by artillery fire. The Boer fire cannot have been very accurate as our Company had only one man wounded, which is explained by the fact that the two Companies under Holled Smith advanced and by their fire prevented the Boers from following up the retreat. They then themselves withdrew to camp without loss. Captain Thurlow's company lost 10 O.R. prisoners. He says : ' These, I fancy, fell down exhausted on the line of our retreat, as the sun was frightfully hot,' but, as the Boers did not follow up, it seems unlikely that anyone falling out by the way would not somehow have made his way back to camp, and it appears more probable that they were left behind in the post.

Field-Marshal Lord Grenfell, who arrived just after Majuba as a Staff Officer with the reinforcements, wrote :

' I found, when I got there as a Q.M.G. just after the battle, that Smith was eulogised, as he was the only one that advanced towards the bottom of Majuba slopes and rallied the bolters. I don't remember the other Company, but as G.H.Q. recalled

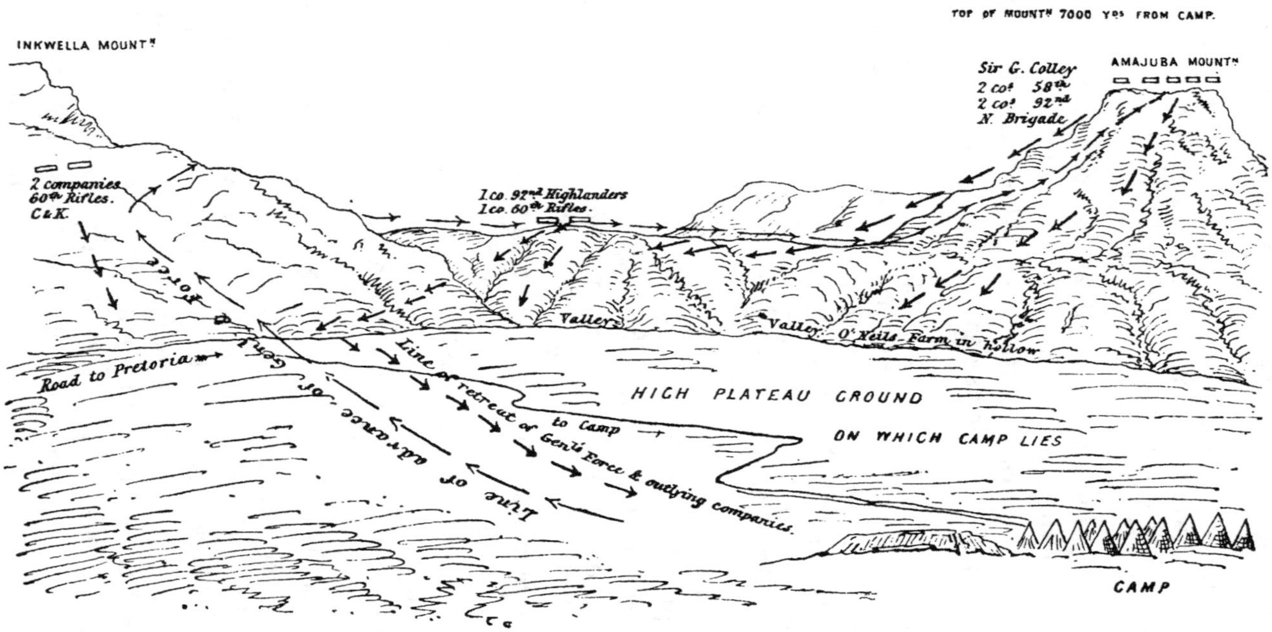

PLATE 4.

VIEW FROM CAMP, MOUNT PROSPECT, OF INKWELLA AND AMAJUBA MOUNTAINS LYING TO THE LEFT AND LEFT FRONT OF THE CAMP. CAMP FACING NORTH. HILLS LYING TO WEST AND CIRCLING ROUND TO FRONT AND RIGHT OF CAMP, NORTH AND EAST.

all outlying Companies, I fancy Smith (a real good fighting man as I saw afterwards) did not respond, and stuck it, by which he saved many stragglers.'

A story which was started at the time and actually appeared in the Press at home was satisfactorily refuted by a cable from Sir Evelyn Wood, who had succeeded to the command on Colley's death :

'Please contradict unfavourable reports of 3/60th on 28th February. None on Majuba. One Company sent out with spare ammunition to join supporting Company of 92nd, and retired with it by orders from Prospect Camp, bringing all the ammunition in. Two Companies posted three miles off covered retreat steadily. Am perfectly satisfied with their behaviour.'

Majuba was shortly followed by a truce, and peace was proclaimed on March 23.

Sergeant-Major J. Wilkins was recommended for the D.C.M. for gallantry at Ingogo. H.R.H. the Commander-in-Chief regretted that as he had since been promoted to Warrant Rank he was no longer eligible. He got his D.C.M. on October 2, 1882, when Quartermaster of the Battalion.

On July 1, 1881, on the introduction of the Territorial System, by which single-battalion regiments were united in pairs and the old numbers were abolished throughout the Infantry, our Regiment ceased to be The 60th (King's Royal Rifle Corps) and became The King's Royal Rifle Corps. There was a great deal of heart-burning over the loss of the old numbers, especially among those Regiments who with them lost their identity. In our own Regiment the number has survived for everyday use for convenience, if not from sentiment. It may interest anyone who at the time felt aggrieved at the loss of our numerical title to know that so recently as August 3, 1869, a request was made on behalf of the Regiment, and refused, that we might drop the number and be known as The King's Royal Rifle Corps.

The Battalion remained at Mount Prospect till December 31, 1881, when it marched for Pietermaritzburg, where it arrived on January 13, 1882. A and D Companies had rejoined from Detachment in June.

On February 22, 1882, H.Q. and half the Battalion embarked at Durban on H.M.S. *Orontes*, followed by the other half Battalion and the married families next day, and sailed for Malta via Zanzibar and the Suez Canal. The following Officers embarked with the Battalion :—

Lieut.-Colonel C. Ashburnham, C.B.,
Major C. P. Cramer,
„ E. L. Fraser,
Captain F. W. Archer,
„ W. S. Anderson,
„ R. Henley,
Lieutenant A. E. Miles,
„ D. G. R. Ryder,
„ G. C. B. Baker,
„ C. B. Pigott,
„ T. M. S. Pilkington,

Lieutenant H. G. L. Howard Vyse,
„ F. M. Beaumont,
„ P. S. Marling,
„ E. T. Scudamore-Stanhope,
„ W. H. Kennedy,
„ G. L. B. Killick,
„ R. L. Bower,
Lieutenant & Adjutant C. R. R. McGrigor,[1]
Lieutenant & Quartermaster J. Ireland,
Paymaster J. E. Orange.

It is impossible to leave the subject of the First Boer War without making some attempt to solve the enigma of Sir George Colley. What was it about the man who had so far succeeded in everything he touched, who was not only looked upon in the Army as the last word in knowledge of his profession and as possessing every quality which could be wanted to make a successful

[1] Major-General C. R. R. McGrigor, C.B.

soldier, but was recognised as a man of exceptional intellect by all with whom he had worked, soldiers and statesmen alike, which made him a total failure as soon as he got an independent command in the field? for a failure he undoubtedly was. Although he had an impossible task, if it be granted that it was his duty to try to relieve the beleaguered garrisons with the force immediately at his disposal, it cannot be claimed that he made the best, or anything like the best, of a bad job, or the best use of the very inadequate instrument in his hand.

Take, firstly, the attack on Laing's Nek: granted that the exigencies of the political and strategic situation justified the great tactical risk of attacking at all—and this is a very big concession, as it would appear that a repulse at Laing's Nek of the only striking force, under the Commander-in-Chief himself, would have a worse effect on the political situation than the surrender of all the garrisons in the Transvaal—and granted that he cannot be held responsible for poor Colonel Deane's eccentric methods, or Brownlow's ideas of handling Mounted Infantry, still, his attack was rendered much more of a gamble than it need have been by the fact that, not only its success, but the difference between success and disaster hinged on the success of the attack on the right by 120 mounted men against some 200 expert riflemen in a strong position. His main attack should never have been launched till the success of that on its right was assured, and yet, from his own reports of the action, it is evident that he meant the two to be simultaneous.

His plan for Majuba seems even more open to criticism. If his occupation of Majuba was to have the effect, both moral and material, which he hoped for—and it is doubtful if its possession was really a very great asset, as the troops when on the top only had the nearest part of the Boer position under very long range fire—it should have been immediately followed up by an attack with his whole available force. He should have brought every man he could collect from Newcastle the day before. It has been said in his defence that he did not want, by doing this, to give the Boers warning of an attack. But, surely, his occupation of Majuba was equally a warning. Moving his reinforcements up from Newcastle would have given the Boers only one day's notice. As he had made no previous arrangements for moving them up, should his night march prove successful—he signalled the following message from the top of Majuba about 9 a.m.: 'Order up 60th and 15th Hussars from Newcastle, to leave this afternoon, and try and get in to-morrow morning,' etc.—one can only conclude that he gambled on his occupation of Majuba having the effect of making the Boers quit their position, but intending, if they did not, then to make up his mind what to do next. One cannot acquit him of taking a wholly unnecessary risk in thus isolating himself, and a considerable portion of his force, out of all reach of support, and giving the Boer leader the opportunity—which he took—of calling his bluff and counter-attacking with any proportion he liked of his force without risking his own position.

To borrow a metaphor from the chess-board, Colley seems to have thought that to make a move and say 'Check' was as good as 'Check-mate,' forgetting that the best reply to 'Check' is to capture the attacking piece, and that the only way to convert 'Check' into 'Check-mate' in such a case is to have another piece ready, which will offer check from another direction should the enemy make his counter-attacking move.

If the rest of Colley's force had been ready to attack as soon as he was installed on Majuba, the Boers would have been far too busy to attack him, and the History of the British Army would have been spared one of its darkest blots. How was it that he who since his early days as a subaltern in Kaffraria had shown ability, intellect, nerve, self-confidence, judgment—his written views on every conceivable subject are full of sound common sense —should have failed so lamentably when put to the test of commanding troops in the field? It was not that he was a man who was past his best or one who had deteriorated from a long spell in an office chair—his life up to the last had been one of great physical activity. The only explanation seems to be that he was one of those men on whom command in the field, holding the lives of men in his hand, when judgment has to be turned into immediate action, has a paralysing effect, obscuring the vision and turning the practical man of action into a doctrinaire; seeing things not as they are but as he would wish them to be. He makes a gesture and mistakes it for a blow. He makes what he calls a 'demonstration,' which deceives no one, and is disappointed when the enemy refuses to be bluffed. He takes what he calls the 'key of the position' and finds that he has only got himself surrounded. He has lost the first quality of a general, hard common sense, and what military knowledge he retains in the back of his brain has congealed into the pedantry and formalism which have been the most certain cause of failure since wars first began.

Whatever the cause of Colley's failure may have been, it certainly had the worst possible effect on the British Army. At a time when a small band of thinking soldiers were trying to persuade the British Officer that he must qualify himself for war by thought and study, the failure of their prize pupil, the *white-headed boy* of the Staff College, gave a plausible argument to the reactionaries, who preached that there was nothing to be learnt about the theory of war, that theory meant dogmatism, and the study of it only produced a doctrinaire and a prig; who said that war was only common sense, and that that most indispensable gift would infallibly guide its possessor in the day of battle. Their case was a good deal strengthened by the fact that military study at that period was inclined to get into a wrong groove; there was more dogmatism than deep thought about it, and the Staff College did then turn out a considerable proportion of both doctrinaires and prigs. It was not till the teachings of G. F. Henderson had brought military education on to more practical lines and the South African War had shown them that inherent qualities alone will not turn out ready-made leaders, that the majority of British Officers began to realise that Napoleon and other great masters were right when they preached that the study of War as a Science is an indispensable prelude to practising it as an Art.

CHAPTER II

Second Battalion

THE Battalion had reached Rawal Pindi on February 16, 1873. It moved on April 15, 16, 17, and 18 to the Murree Hills, where it remained—except for coming by Companies to Rawal Pindi during the next cold weather for musketry, and one Company for a couple of months on detachment at Attock—till November 1874, when it returned to Rawal Pindi.

Colonel Rigaud was succeeded in command by Lieut.-Colonel H. P. Montgomery on August 13, 1873, the delay having been caused by Colonel Williamson being promoted to command the Battalion and then being transferred to the 4th Battalion without having joined.

In March 1875 the Battalion again went to the Murree Hills for the hot weather, being, as before, distributed over several different stations. This year the married families accompanied the Battalion to the hills for the first time. It is almost incredible that at such a recent date the women and children should have been the last to be considered, but perhaps in those days the Indian Government took the strictly business view that the health of the fighting man came first.

On return from the hills the Battalion set out on October 27 to march to Delhi for a Camp of Exercise, arriving there on December 15, where it was brigaded with the old Delhi friends of the 1st Battalion, the 2nd Gurkhas, and the 1st Punjab Infantry (Coke's Rifles).

The following is an extract from a General Order by

their Brigadier, Brigadier-General Sir Charles Brownlow, K.C.B., at the dispersal of the Camp :—

'The 2nd Battalion 60th Rifles, commanded by Lieut.-Colonel H. P. Montgomery, composed of men in the prime of life, with health, condition, and training to fill up the measure of their efficiency, is, in his opinion, the perfection of a Light Infantry Battalion. Admirably drilled, equipped, and cared for in every respect, the individual intelligence of the soldier developed to the highest extent, with a boundless *esprit de corps* pervading all ranks, it would be difficult to find its equal as an engine of war.'

After referring to the 2nd Gurkhas and Coke's Rifles, he goes on :

'The Brigadier-General never before has seen three such Regiments working together, and, in taking leave of them, would convey to every officer and man his high appreciation of their merits as good Riflemen and wish them all the success which they deserve as such.'

After the Delhi Camp of Exercise, the Battalion was distributed : H.Q. and five Companies at Meerut ; three Companies at Fatehgarh.

In December 1876 the Battalion marched to Delhi to take part in the great concentration of troops for the proclamation of Queen Victoria as Empress of India. The Battalion joined the 1st Division under General Sir James Brind, K.C.B., making up, together with the 2nd and 3rd Gurkhas, the 3rd Brigade under Brigadier-General Herbert Macpherson, V.C., C.B., an old 2nd Gurkha. On January 1, 1877, took place the proclamation parade, the infantry firing a *feu de joie*, followed by an artillery salute of 101 guns.

The Battalion left Delhi for Meerut and Fatehgarh on

January 17. It was inspected on February 28 by Major-General the Hon. A. E. Hardinge, C.B., the total of all ranks being 898.

The Battalion remained at Meerut throughout 1877 and was inspected by Lieut.-General the Hon. A. E. Hardinge, C.B., on March 4, 1878, the total strength of all ranks being 937.

Regimental Paymasters having been abolished many years ago, the following order by Major C. Ashburnham, commanding the Battalion in the absence of Colonel Montgomery, will bring home to the Officers of the present day how much in those days the Regimental Paymaster was a part of the Regiment :

'Paymaster F. Fitzpatrick being about to proceed to England, failing health having compelled him to seek a change of climate, Major C. Ashburnham cannot permit him to quit the Battalion without placing on record his high opinion of and expressing his thanks for the many and valuable services he has rendered during the lengthened period he has served in the Regiment.

'Paymaster F. Fitzpatrick entered the Service in the latter part of the year 1838, and ever since has served uninterruptedly in the 2nd Battalion, a period of well-nigh forty years. During this time he has served abroad in the Mediterranean, in the West Indies, at the Cape of Good Hope, in China, and he has twice accompanied the Battalion on a tour of Indian Service. For upwards of twenty-three years he has performed the duties of Paymaster to the Battalion, and of the admirable manner in which these duties have been conducted it is needless to speak ; suffice it to say that they have alike been performed in a manner as advantageous to the Battalion and as beneficial to Her Majesty's Service as it is hoped they have been satisfactory to himself.

'Major C. Ashburnham cannot refrain from remarking on the devoted nature of Major F. Fitzpatrick's service. For forty years, with the exception of a few days or perhaps a week at a time, he has never quitted the Battalion. Deeply as Major C. Ashburnham regrets the loss to the Battalion of the services of so valuable an Officer, he regrets still more that ill-health should have been the cause.

'In now bidding him farewell, and in wishing him a prosperous voyage and trusting that a change of climate may restore him to health, Major C. Ashburnham is aware that he is not only expressing his own sentiments, but those of his comrades of all ranks of the Battalion. Farewell.'

Lieut.-Colonel H. P. Montgomery completed his term of command on August 13, 1878, and was succeeded by Lieut.-Colonel J. J. Collins from the 3rd Battalion, who joined on February 18, 1879, but by that time the Battalion had been for some months on Active Service in Afghanistan.

The Second Afghan War, 1878—1880

On the death of the Amir Dost Muhammad, who, recognising that it was in his best interest to let bygones be bygones, had remained our firm friend ever since his unfortunate experience of helping our enemies in the Second Sikh War, the scramble for the vacant throne, usual when 'Amurath an Amurath succeeds,' had left one of his sons, Sher Ali Khan, in possession.

The attitude of the Indian Government during this family quarrel had been so entirely impartial that Sher Ali never forgave them. This ill-feeling, which various unfortunate differences had not lessened, culminated in his reception of a Russian Mission at Kabul in 1878 (a time when the danger of war between Britain and Russia over the Near Eastern question had not yet passed).

It was decided that a Mission from India should be sent to Kabul after due notice, and that a refusal to receive it would be treated as a hostile act. The Mission started in September 1878, and on the 21st of that month, after being formally refused admission to Afghanistan by

Afghan officials at Ali Musjid, in the Khyber Pass, it withdrew. The next two months were spent in preparations for the almost inevitable war, and in November an ultimatum was sent to the Amir with the warning that failing a satisfactory answer by the 20th *idem*, he would be treated as an enemy of the British Government.

The forces assembled, of which I and IV had orders to be ready to cross the frontier on the 21st, were:

I. The Kurram Valley Column (Major-General F.S. Roberts, V.C., C.B.[1]):

> One Cavalry Brigade.
> Two Infantry Brigades.
> 18 Guns.

The task before this Column was the invasion of Afghanistan by the Peiwar Kotal—Shutargardan route, one of the nearest ways to Kabul.

II. The Multan Division (subsequently 1st Division Kandahar Column) (Lieut.-General D. M. Stewart, C.B.[2]):

> One Cavalry Brigade.
> Two Infantry Brigades.
> 60 Guns.

In this force the 1st Infantry Brigade (Brigadier-General R. Barter) was made up of 2nd Battalion 60th Rifles, 15th Sikhs, 25th Punjab Infantry.

III. The Quetta Reinforcement (subsequently 2nd Division, Kandahar Column) (Major-General M. A. S. Biddulph, C.B.):

> One Cavalry Brigade.
> Two Infantry Brigades.
> 18 Guns.

---

[1] Field-Marshal the Rt. Hon. F. S., Earl Roberts, V.C., K.G., K.P., G.C.B., O.M., G.C.S.I., G.C.I.E., V.D., Commander-in-Chief 1901-4.
[2] Field-Marshal Sir Donald Stewart, Bart., G.C.B., G.C.S.I.

IV. The Peshawar Valley Field Force (Lieut.-General Sir Sam Browne, V.C., K.C.S.I., C.B.):

At Peshawar—One Cavalry Brigade.
Four Infantry Brigades.
At Hasan Abdal—One Cavalry Brigade.
One Infantry Brigade.
} 48 Guns.

The doings of the Kuram Valley and Peshawar Valley forces, the only ones to have any serious fighting during the first phase of the war, do not concern our story, but the result of the Afghan defeats by General Roberts and Sir Sam Browne was that Sher Ali abdicated and fled, leaving his son Yakub Khan as Amir. Negotiations were soon opened between Yakub and the British, and on May 26, 1879, a treaty was signed at Gandamak between Jalalabad and Kabul, the most important provisions of which were: that the Amir should in future conduct his relations with foreign states ' in accordance with the advice and wishes of the British Government'; that for the future a British representative should reside at Kabul with a suitable escort; and that, to assist the Amir to maintain his legitimate authority in his own country, the British Government should pay him an annual subsidy of six lakhs of rupees.

During October Column III had been pushed on to Quetta. General Biddulph arrived there on November 9, where he got a telegram ordering him to continue his advance to Peshin. He had already begun preparing for the reception of a large force at Quetta and reconnoitring the roads towards Kandahar.

He moved on November 19, improving the roads as he advanced.

General Donald Stewart had meanwhile been advancing from Multan up the Bolan Pass.

On September 23, 1878, our 2nd Battalion had received orders to hold itself in readiness for Active Service. The detachment at Fatehgarh was relieved on September 30 and joined H.Q. at Meerut on October 6. The Battalion was for the first time put into khaki; the scabbards of the officers' swords were bronzed and Sam Browne belts taken into wear. The Battalion left for Multan by train on October 18, arriving there on the 20th; strength, 21 Officers, 760 O.R.

The names of the Officers were as follows :

Major C. Ashburnham (Commanding).
Major W. G. Byron.

A Company.
Capt. C. de Robeck.
Lieut. H. D. Banks.

B Company.
Capt. H. S. Marsham.

C Company.
Capt. Blackwood-Price.
Sub-Lieut. D. Lysons.

D Company.
Lieut. H. Riddell.
Lieut. A. Davidson.

E Company.
Capt. G. H. Trotman.
Lieut. R. Golightly.

F Company.
Capt. J. Charley.
Lieut. B. Montgomery.
Lieut. H. C. Legh.

G Company.
Capt. O. Forster.
Lieut. G. S. Baynes.

H Company.
Capt. G. L. McL. Farmer.
Lieut. C. Hope.

Lieut. Lord F. FitzGerald (Acting Adjutant). Lieut. W. Holmes (Quartermaster). Captain T. P. Lloyd (Acting Paymaster).

On November 14 the Left Half Battalion entrained for Sukkar, arriving there the following day. H.Q. and the Right Half Battalion entrained on the 15th, but did not arrive till the 17th.

On November 18 H Company (Captain Farmer) was detailed as escort to Lieut.-General D. M. Stewart, C.B., commanding the Division, and commenced the march to Quetta on the 19th.

On November 22 the Battalion started its march to the front, reaching Jacobabad on the 26th.

On December 1, 2, and 3, G, E, and F Companies resumed the march to Quetta, escorting three Batteries of Artillery. On December 4 H.Q. and the Right Half Battalion started to march to Quetta, arriving there on the 23rd. One of the marches across the desert was thirty miles in length and was completed in eleven hours, including halts, no man falling out. The other Companies of the Battalion accomplished this march equally well.

On December 8 General Stewart had arrived at Quetta and assumed command of the Southern Afghanistan Field Force.

The first half of December was spent in improving the road over the Khojak Pass and in the occupation of Chaman.

On December 21 the main body of the 2nd Division (Biddulph's) began crossing the Khojak, and by the end of the month all the Division were over the Pass. By the same date the Gwajha Pass had been opened as an alternative route.

On Christmas Day the Right Half Battalion and F Company (still escorting its battery) marched for Gulistan Karez, arriving there on the 29th, where it joined the Headquarters Camp of the G.O.C. 1st Division (Stewart). On the 31st, A, B, C, and F Companies commenced the march over the Khojak Amran Range—D Company had relieved F Company as escort to the Artillery—by the Gwaja Pass, and encamped just below the crest that night, reaching Gwaja at the farther end of the Pass next day. On January 2, 1879, the march was continued towards Kandahar.

The force advanced in two Columns, the 2nd Division on the right, the 1st on the left.

On January 5 the enemy's Cavalry was encountered about Ghlo and Kurkora Kotals. There was a slight skirmish in which the hostile Cavalry were induced to expose themselves to the fire of our guns. Their loss was estimated at 100 killed and wounded; ours was under a dozen.

The enemy retired to Kandahar, which they left for Herat two days later. The two Columns joined at Abdur Rahman on January 6.

On January 7, at Khushab, seven miles from Kandahar, news arrived that the Governor of Kandahar had fled and a letter of surrender was received from his deputy.

The next day, at 3.30 p.m., Stewart entered Kandahar and marched through it at the head of the leading Brigades of the two Divisions.

The occupation was quite peaceable, the population appearing entirely uninterested.

The distance marched by the Battalion from Sukkar to Kandahar was 440 miles. The Battalion was encamped on the north side of the city and a week's halt was made here, during which the two Companies still escorting Artillery rejoined H.Q.

Lieut.-Colonel J. J. Collins joined and took over command of the Battalion on February 18.

On January 14 General Stewart, leaving a composite Brigade to garrison Kandahar, started on a reconnaissance-in-force towards Kalat-i-Ghilzai, the 2nd Division doing the same towards the Helmund River. The reason of these marches was that at this time, though Sher Ali had fled and his son Yakub Khan, who had succeeded him, was outwardly suing for peace, Yakub was behind our backs trying to stir up the country to further resistance. It was therefore necessary to march troops through

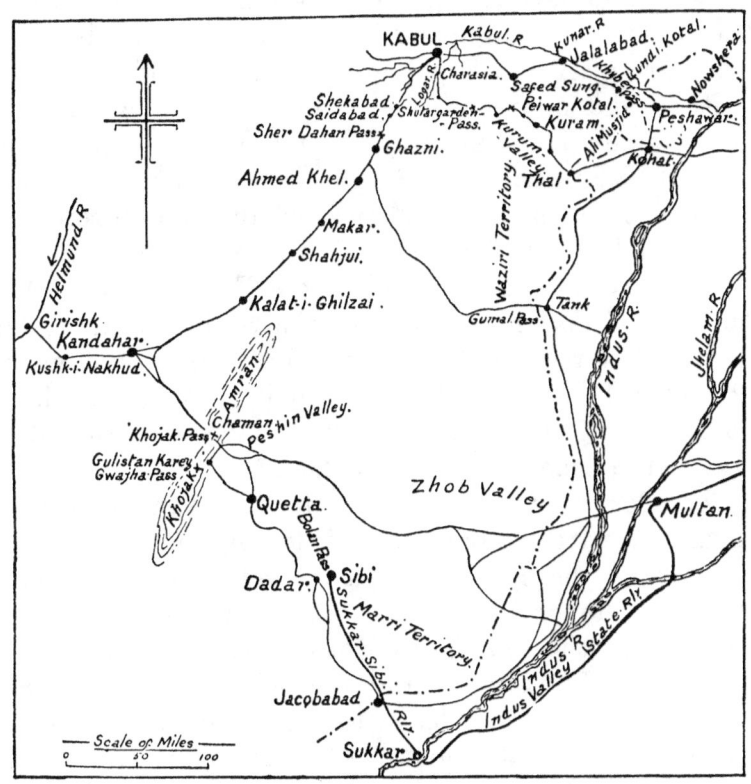

PLATE 5.

Southern Afghanistan to ascertain whether the country was really settling down or preparing for a prolonged war.

In this march the 1st Brigade, 1st Division, followed one day's march in rear of the main body. Local supplies at this time of year were almost unobtainable, and it was difficult to march large forces united.

The Advanced Guard reached Kalat-i-Ghilzai on January 20, the garrison, 500 or 600 Militia, having retired towards Ghazni. The main body of the Division arrived at Kalat-i-Ghilzai on the 22nd and remained there till February 2. The country seemed quite peaceful. The Ghilzais (the large and important tribe that inhabits that part of Afghanistan) were almost friendly in their attitude and all requisitions were complied with. The 1st Brigade did not get farther than Jellak, fifteen miles short of Kalat-i-Ghilzai. Stewart sent a few reconnoitring Columns through the neighbourhood and himself returned to Kandahar on February 11 without incident. The main body reached Kandahar on February 22. The 2nd Division had not found the country so peaceful to the west. They reached Abazai opposite Girishk on January 29, and on February 27 fought a small action at Khushk-i-Nakhud; our loss amounting to 25 killed and wounded, that of the enemy being about 200.

The losses in transport up to this time had been appalling, partly from lack of forage, but chiefly on account of the rigour of the climate. The transport animals were chiefly Indian camels, which were quite unable to withstand the cold of the Afghan winter. On November 28, before entering the Bolan Pass, Sir Donald Stewart mentions in a letter that the temperature in his tent is 90° in the afternoon and 40° at night. At Quetta on December 8 it was down to 10°. Writing from Kalat-i-Ghilzai on January 26 he says: 'I have never felt such cold. It is sometimes below zero and constantly down at 8° and 10°, with a cutting wind, which kills the Indian camels like flies.' Referring on March 9 to the march to Kalat-i-Ghilzai and back, he says: 'I asked Brigadier-General Hughes to count the skeletons of camels on the road from Kalat-i-Ghilzai to Kandahar, and the list was

1,924. This was what we lost out of a division transport of about 3,500. . . . We have already got a mortality return of over 9,000 camels.'

Early in March about half the force in Southern Afghanistan was sent back to India, a garrison for Kandahar being left, under Brigadier-General Hughes, consisting of one Cavalry Brigade and the 1st and 2nd Infantry Brigades. After the Treaty of Gandamak was signed, it was decided that, on account of the heat, the remainder of the troops would not return to India till autumn. A severe cholera epidemic raged throughout July and August in Kandahar and Quetta. In our 2nd Battalion nineteen men died out of twenty-six attacked.

Evacuation began on September 1.

Meanwhile, in accordance with the Treaty of Gandamak, Major Louis Cavagnari, the Political Officer who had signed that treaty, had been sent to Kabul as British Envoy. He was accompanied by a Secretary, a Medical Officer, and an escort of 25 Cavalry and 50 Infantry of The Guides, under Lieutenant W. H. P. Hamilton. The party reached Kabul on July 24.

On September 3 the Residency in Kabul was attacked by a mob of mutinous Afghan soldiers, and after a magnificent defence, all in it were killed. The Amir at this time was certainly not master in his own house, and how far he was responsible, by sins of commission or omission, for the attack on the Residency was never clearly determined. Whatever had been his attitude up to the time of the massacre—and Cavagnari seems to have believed in his good intentions—he came down decidedly, though secretly, on the anti-British side of the fence when the Indian Government made the inevitable reply to the outrage by ordering the immediate occupation of Kabul. Though he came and gave himself up to Roberts on the arrival of that General at Kushi, one march the Kabul side of the Shutargardan Pass, ostensibly for protection against his own people, he was working against us all the time.

The news reached Simla on September 4, and next day Brigadier-General Massy, commanding the Kuram force, during the absence in Simla of Sir F. Roberts, was ordered to occupy the Shutargardan Pass, at the head of the Kuram Valley and only fifty miles in a straight line from Kabul.

The same day the following plan was submitted by the C.-in-C. to the Viceroy, and was approved: Sir F. Roberts to advance over the Shutargardan Pass with one Cavalry and three Infantry Brigades and occupy Kabul; Major-General Bright to occupy Jellalabad with one Division; and Kandahar to be occupied by Sir Donald Stewart with all available troops.

On September 11 the Shutargardan was occupied, and on the 18th an Infantry Brigade had concentrated there under Brigadier-General T. Baker.

Sir F. Roberts, arriving at Kushi on September 28, found that the Amir Yakub Khan had arrived the day before. He remained with Sir F. Roberts during the advance on Kabul, and was dispatched to India as a prisoner on December 1.

There were delays from want of transport, but Sir F. Roberts, after heavily defeating the Afghans at Charasia on October 6, reached the outskirts of Kabul on the 8th and, meeting with little opposition, formally occupied the Bala Hissar, the citadel of Kabul, on the 12th. On the same day the Amir Yakub Khan resigned the Afghan throne. Roberts then occupied the fortified cantonment of Sherpur, one and a half miles north-east of Kabul, and his force settled down to spend the winter while the future of the country was being decided.

The religious leaders having got to work, at the instigation of Yakub Khan, and preached a Jehad, the fighting men of all Northern Afghanistan began closing on Kabul with the purpose of turning out the infidel. The outcome of this was the isolation of Roberts's force and a good deal of fighting which was not always in our favour, culminating in a determined attack on Sherpur on December 23, which was easily driven off.

The assembly of tribesmen then melted away.

At the time of the Kabul massacre the Kandahar Field Force was in process of withdrawal to Peshin, though H.Q. and a part of the force, including our 2nd Battalion, was still at Kandahar.

On September 5 Sir Donald Stewart received orders for all troops north of Peshin to return to Kandahar. Within ten days the whole Field Force was reassembled.

The 2nd Brigade was then sent out on a reconnaissance march similar to those of the previous winter. Leaving Kandahar on September 23, it reached Kalat-i-Ghilzai on the 30th. It fought a successful action near Shahjui on October 24, and returned to Kandahar on November 8, leaving a garrison in Kalat-i-Ghilzai.

Owing to the quiet condition of Southern Afghanistan during the ensuing months, it was the intention of the Indian Government to relieve all the Bengal troops in that area and march them as a Division back to India via Ghazni, under command of Sir Donald Stewart, leaving Major-General J. M. Primrose, C.S.I., in command at Kandahar.

On March 29, 1880, the 1st Brigade (Brigadier-General Barter)—1st Punjab Cavalry; 4 Mountain Guns R.A.; 2nd Battalion 60th Rifles (less one Company), 25th Punjab Infantry—began their march. On the 30th and 31st respectively there followed H.Q. with the Cavalry

Brigade (Brigadier-General Palliser) and the 2nd Infantry Brigade (Brigadier-General Hughes). By a process of redistribution each Column was now a Brigade of all arms. The strength of our 2nd Battalion on leaving Kandahar was 720 of all ranks.

On December 1, 1879, Captain R. Chalmer had taken over command of the General's escort, and on his appointment as Brigade Major, 1st Infantry Brigade, on March 3, 1880, he was succeeded by Lieutenant A. Davidson.

Kalat-i-Ghilzai was reached on April 6 and 7. On the 8th the march was resumed, H.Q., Barter's and Palliser's Brigades advancing on that day; Hughes's Brigade following one day's march behind. Shahjui was reached on April 11 and Makar on the 14th.

Since leaving Kalat-i-Ghilzai all villages passed had been found deserted, consequently the force which was, for the most part, living on the country found great difficulty in obtaining supplies. Considerable bodies of hostile Afghans were seen hovering on the flanks of the Column, and on April 22 Sir Donald reported to Simla that he expected opposition within the next few days. Shots were exchanged on the 15th and 16th and on the 17th the main body halted at Jan Murad to let the rear Brigade catch up.

The whole force moved on together on the 18th.

On this date a force estimated at from 8,000 to 10,000 Afghans was seen moving on a line parallel to General Stewart's advance, eight or ten miles distant from his right flank.

The supply difficulty was relieved at Jan Murad by the help of the Hazaras, a race of Mongol origin occupying Central Afghanistan and always at war with the Afghans till their final subjection by the Amir Abdurrahman in the 'nineties' of last century.

AHMAD KHEL

On the morning of April 19 the order of march of the 1st and 2nd Brigades was reversed, and the Division left camp at Mashaki in the following order:—

19th Bengal Lancers	300 lances	
A—B R.H.A.	6 (9-pdr.) guns	
19th Punjab Infantry	470 rifles	Advanced Guard:
Divisional H.Q., escorted by:		Brigadier-General Palliser.
2nd 60th Rifles	63 rifles	
25th Punjab Infantry	85 rifles	Total: 350 lances.
19th Bengal Lancers	50 lances	698 rifles.
Number 4 and 10 Companies, Bengal Sappers and Miners	80 rifles	6 guns.
59th Foot	436 rifles	Main body, 2nd
3rd Gurkhas	289 rifles	Infantry Brigade:
2nd Sikh Infantry	367 rifles	Brigadier-General
G—4 R.A.	6 (9-pdr.) guns	Hughes.
6—11 R.A.	2 (40-pdr.) ,,	
	2 (6·3-in.) howitzers	Total: 1,092 rifles. 349 sabres.
2nd Punjab Cavalry	349 sabres	10 guns.
Field Hospitals		
Ordnance and Engineer Field Parks		Baggage and Supply
Treasure		Train with detachments on the flanks.
Commissariat		
Baggage		
		Rear Guard,
2nd Batt. 60th Rifles	443 rifles	1st Infantry Brigade: Brigadier-General Barter.
15th Sikh Infantry	570 rifles	
25th Punjab Infantry	380 rifles	Total: 1,393 rifles.
11—11 R.A. (Mountain Battery)	6 (7-pdr.) guns	316 sabres. 6 mountain guns.
1st Punjab Cavalry	316 sabres	

The length of the entire Column when on the march was about six miles.

Divisional H.Q. and the main body had advanced about seven miles and were halted for a short rest when the Cavalry of the Advanced Guard reported bodies of the enemy in position three miles ahead. The nature of the country is seen from the attached rough sketch. The line of march was over a fairly level plain, stretching away to the right (E) to the Ghazni River. A line of low hills ran parallel to the line of march about one mile away to the west. This north and south ridge trended north-east and then east, crossing the Ghazni road at the point where the Cavalry had reported the enemy to be in position. Sir Donald ordered the Infantry of the 2nd Brigade to form on the left of the road, in line with the Horse Artillery. The 2nd Punjab Cavalry moved out to the right. The three Batteries were in column of route on the road. The 19th Punjab Infantry, H.Q. escort, and Sappers followed in reserve. An order was sent to Brigadier-General Barter to bring up half his Infantry and send 2 Squadrons 1st Punjab Cavalry to join the Cavalry, of which Brigadier-General Palliser took command. The advance being resumed, half a Squadron 19th Bengal Lancers were sent out to cover the left flank of the Infantry. It was now seen that the enemy's position across the British line of march was extended a long way to his right and forward, along the line of hills flanking our advance. When within one and a half miles of the enemy the Horse and Field Batteries took up positions to shell the ridge in front, the 2nd Punjab Cavalry finding the escort for the R.H.A. and a Company of 19th Punjab Infantry that for the Field Battery. The 2nd Infantry Brigade deployed in line of quarter columns, facing the enemy's right wing, i.e. west-north-west. $1\frac{1}{2}$ Squadrons 19th Bengal Lancers were now on the left flank of the Infantry. The 2nd Punjab Cavalry (3 Squadrons) were on the right of the Artillery. The Heavy Battery unlimbered just east of the road, beyond the extreme left of the line.

At 9 a.m. the British force had hardly assumed the formation in which they were about to advance to the attack, when the crest of the line of hills occupied by the enemy was seen to be swarming with men along a front of nearly two miles. Scarcely had the guns opened fire when waves of swordsmen, on foot, began to pour down from the enemy's position, spreading out to either flank as if to envelop the British force. At the same time, from their extreme right descended a mass of Afghan Horse which caught the 19th Bengal Lancers napping, charging them before they could get sufficient way on to meet their opponents fairly. The Lancers were driven back in disorder on to the 3rd Gurkhas—the left of three Infantry Battalions which by this time were in Company squares—causing some confusion. The Afghan Horse, having swept right through, disappeared into the plain to the east. The 2nd Brigade then deployed into line, the best formation in which to resist such a charge, as it gave cohesion together with the greatest fire power. The swordsmen charged right home, and the whole of the reserve had to be sent up into the front line. Half the 19th Punjab Infantry and the Sapper Companies came up on the left; the other half Battalion with the Companies of the H.Q. escort of the 60th and 25th Punjab Infantry were pushed in between the batteries. For a moment the situation was critical, as one Regiment was thrown into some confusion owing to a mistaken order reaching it to throw back its right flank. This was quickly righted, and the charge was soon brought to a halt by the deadly fire poured into it along the whole line. From check to defeat and from defeat to rout was a matter of a few minutes, and by 9.45 a.m. the enemy's force was broken up and dispersed all over the country. At the height of the enemy's advance the 2nd Punjab Cavalry brought off a most effective charge against their left flank. The number of Afghans engaged is estimated at about 15,000, and they left more than 1,000 dead in front of the British position. Our total losses were 17 killed and 124 wounded. The Company of the 60th on H.Q. escort lost 3 killed and 1 wounded, while the rest of the Battalion, which with some of Brigadier-General Barter's Brigade came in at the end of the action, had 1 man wounded. After a two hours' halt the Division moved on, completing a march of seventeen miles to Nani.

On the 21st the Division reached Ghazni (223 miles from Kandahar) and halted there for four days.

A reconnaissance sent out to the north-east of Ghazni reported a strong hostile force occupying two villages about five miles away, and at 3.30 a.m. on the 23rd the following force was sent out under Brigadier-General Palliser to disperse them :—

Cavalry, 6 Squadrons :
   1st Punjab Cavalry . 322 sabres.
   2nd Punjab Cavalry . 325 sabres.
Artillery :
   1 Battery R.H.A.
   1 Mountain Battery.
Infantry, 4 Battalions :
   2nd Batt. 60th Rifles . 525 rifles ⎫
   2nd Sikhs . . . 424 rifles ⎬ Brigadier-General
   15th Sikhs . . 578 rifles ⎪ Barter.
   25th Punjab Infantry . 458 rifles ⎭

After marching about three miles, the enemy was seen to be occupying a position between and including two

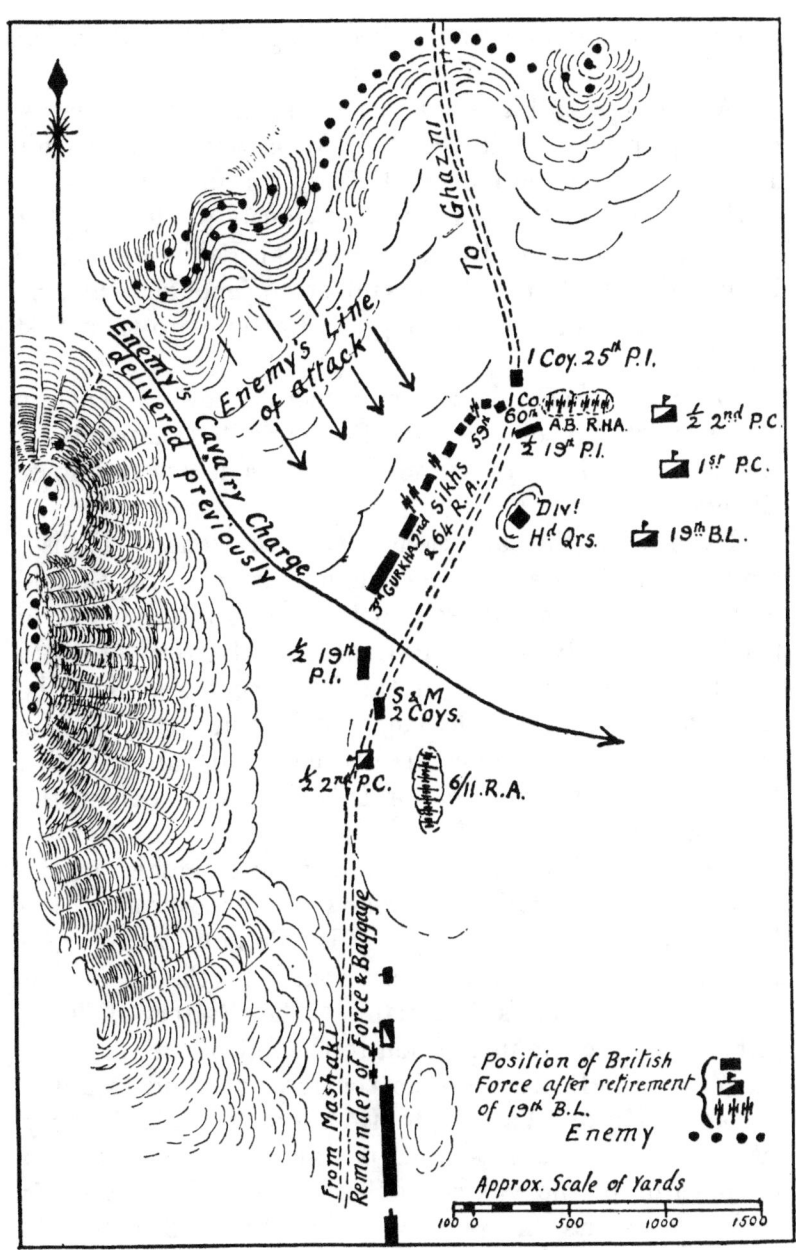

PLATE 6.

ACTION AT AHMAD KHEL, APRIL 19, 1880.

strongly enclosed and mud-walled villages, Arzu and Shalez, standing about half a mile apart.

At 5 a.m. both Batteries opened fire on the two villages, changing position till the R.H.A. Battery was within 1,600 yards, and Mountain Battery within 1,400 yards, of the villages. As the fire was obviously producing little effect, at 8.30 a.m. Brigadier-General Palliser signalled back to the G.O.C. that he was not strong enough to attack, at the same time withdrawing the Batteries to their first positions.

On receipt of this report General Stewart sent up half a Battalion of the 59th Foot and 6 Companies of the 3rd Gurkhas from the 2nd Brigade, to reinforce General Palliser.

Even with this additional strength General Palliser did not think himself strong enough to attack. Sir Donald Stewart then went himself, with almost all the rest of his force, viz. 19th Bengal Lancers, a Battery of Field Artillery, the remainder of the 59th Foot and half the 19th Punjab Infantry, leaving the Heavies, the Sappers and Miners, 2 Companies of Gurkhas, and half the 19th Punjab Infantry, under Major Tillard, R.A., to defend the camp and watch Ghazni.

Sir Donald Stewart at 11 a.m. took command of the operations and made the following dispositions: the Battery R.H.A., escorted by the 1st Punjab Cavalry and 19th Bengal Lancers, to work round to the right and enfilade the enemy's left flank. The Battery R.F.A., just come up, came into action to the left of the Infantry, the Mountain Battery in the centre of the 2nd Infantry Brigade. Major Warter, R.H.A., brought his Battery into action in a succession of positions till it was within 1,000 yards of the village of Shalez on the enemy's left flank, where its fire was very effective. The R.F.A.

Battery opened fire on the village of Arzu on the enemy's right. At 11.40 a.m. the Infantry moved forward to the attack, the Mountain Battery accompanying them. The position was rushed at a loss of 2 killed and 8 wounded; the losses of the enemy, who were pursued some way by the Cavalry and Artillery, being estimated at about 400 men.

On April 24, just after resuming his march from Ghazni, Sir Donald Stewart received orders from Simla telling him to go himself to Kabul and take over the chief command and not to go any farther with the withdrawal of the Ghazni force via the Kuram Valley to India until he had acquainted himself with the state of affairs at Kabul, as there was another gathering of tribes which might mean mischief. On April 28 the Ghazni Field Force H.Q. with Hughes's and Palliser's Brigades reached Saidabad, where was a force under General Ross, sent out from Kabul to gain touch with Stewart. On the same day General Barter's Brigade reached Shekhabad and General Stewart handed over command of the Ghazni Field Force to General Hughes.

On April 29 General Stewart set out for Kabul with Ross's force, and on May 5 assumed command of the forces in Afghanistan.

The force under the immediate command of Sir Donald Stewart, now known as the Northern Afghanistan Field Force—which name had hitherto covered only the 1st and 2nd Divisions under Sir F. Roberts—included:—

    I. The 1st and 2nd Divisions, which remained one group under command of Sir F. Roberts.

    II. The 3rd Division—late the Ghazni Field Force, under Major-General James Hills, V.C., C.B.

    III. The Khyber Line Force.

    IV. The Kuram Force;

the two latter being the forces keeping open the two lines

of communication to Northern India. Of these the 3rd Division was in the Logar Valley on account of the difficulty of supply anywhere nearer Kabul.

The position of affairs now was that although Afghanistan—except where occupied by British troops—was in a state of complete anarchy, the leaders were so far agreed that all wished to get rid of the invaders as quickly as possible, and, recognising that they could not hope to do so by force, were willing to unite in furthering the negotiations for establishing another Barakzai prince on the throne. Sirdar Abdurrahman Khan, the Amir-designate, was a shy bird and suspicious, and although he had accepted the throne, it took a long time to persuade him to come to Kabul and take over. He was on his way and within a few days' march of Kabul when, on July 29, news reached Sir Donald Stewart from Simla of the disaster at Maiwand, in which Ayub Khan, a younger brother of the late Amir Yakub, and a claimant to the throne, had, invading Southern Afghanistan from Herat, on the 27th, completely defeated a British force under Brigadier-General G. R. S. Burrows, sent from Kandahar to oppose him, but which had been left in the air on the banks of the Helmund by the mutiny of the Afghan troops under our ally Wali Sher Ali of Kandahar. This event seemed at the first glance to complicate the political situation considerably, but on reflection the authorities agreed that it should not be allowed to delay the accession of Abdurrahman and the evacuation of Northern Afghanistan. The solution was to send a force to destroy Ayub's power in the south—he was as much Abdurrahman's enemy as ours—and in the north to carry on as if nothing had happened. On July 31 Abdurrahman had arrived at Ak Sarai, eighteen miles north of Kabul, and near that place the first interview took place between him and Lepel

Griffin, the Chief Political Officer. From this date the arrangements for handing over to the new Amir and the evacuation of Northern Afghanistan went on without a hitch.

On the morning of August 11 Sir Donald Stewart held a Durbar outside the Sherpur Cantonments, where he received Abdurrahman and handed over to him his capital. On the same day the last of the British troops left for India.

To settle Ayub's affairs, while the rest of the Army of Occupation withdrew to India, a picked force of about one Division was to march direct to Kandahar, under the command of Sir Frederick Roberts.

This course, though it entailed a march through a hostile country, cut off from any base, with the prospect of meeting at the end of it an enemy elated by recent success, was thought preferable to the longer and more cautious process of relieving Kandahar by the Sind—Quetta line of communication which connected Southern Afghanistan with India.

Sanction for the adoption of this course, which was recommended to the Government of India by Sir Donald Stewart, reached Kabul on August 3, and on the same day the detail of the force, styled the Kabul—Kandahar Force, was published as follows :—

Cavalry.

9th Lancers.
3rd Bengal Cavalry.
3rd Punjab Cavalry.
Central India Horse

Brigadier-General Hugh Gough, V.C., C.B.

Artillery.

Three Mountain Batteries, R.A.
(two British, one Indian).

Infantry.

1st Infantry Brigade, Brigadier-General Herbert Macpherson, V.C., C.B.
 92nd Highlanders.
 23rd (Punjab) Pioneers.
 24th Punjab Infantry.
 2nd Gurkhas.
2nd Infantry Brigade, Brigadier-General T. D. Baker, C.B.
 72nd Highlanders.
 2nd Sikh Infantry.
 3rd Sikh Infantry.
 5th Gurkhas.
3rd Infantry Brigade, Brigadier-General C. M. MacGregor, C.B., etc.
 2/60th Rifles.
 15th Sikhs.
 4th Gurkhas.
 25th Punjab Infantry.

Strength.

British.		Native.
Officers.	Other Ranks.	All Ranks.
274	2,562	7,511

Followers, 7,000. Transport Animals, 6,000.

Following on the receipt of the news of Maiwand, the 3rd Division had been drawn in to near Kabul, and on August 6 Roberts's force was concentrated round Kabul with the exception of one Mountain Battery and the C.I.H., which were marching up to join him from the Khyber Line. The force was distributed as follows: The Cavalry Brigade on the Bimaru Plain; 1st Infantry Brigade between Siah Sang and Sherpur; 2nd Infantry Brigade in Sherpur Cantonments; 3rd Infantry Brigade close to the Bala Hissar.

On Sunday, August 8, the march began, the Cavalry Brigade moving to Chakarasia, the 1st and 3rd Infantry Brigades to Beni Hissar, and the 2nd Brigade to Indaki.

The march was uneventful so far as interference by the enemy is concerned, but it was a great physical feat on the part of man and beast and a triumph of organisation, especially as regards supply, which was almost entirely local, and had to be obtained and distributed daily in a far from prolific and distinctly hostile country. The success of the supply arrangements may be judged from the fact that throughout the march the British troops were seldom reduced to the humble chupatti instead of bread, and not a single instance was brought to notice of either a soldier or follower failing to receive his rations. Trees on the line of march were almost non-existent, and, except where the timber of the roofs of houses—always paid for and willingly sold by the villagers, at a price—could be obtained, the only firewood consisted of the roots of shrubs which had to be laboriously dug up. After the first few marches, water became a difficulty and was only found at considerable intervals, which made it difficult to keep to an average length for the day's march. The climate was very trying owing to the extreme variations of temperature, amounting to as much as 80° in twenty-four hours. The days were hot all the way and got hotter as the march progressed, Kandahar being about 3,500 feet above the sea and Kabul almost 6,000. On some nights the thermometer fell nearly to freezing-point and by day reached 110° in the shade. There were constant sandstorms, and of course suffocating dust raised by the column.

On August 15 the force reached Ghazni, 100 miles in seven days. As opposition was expected, the Sher Dahan Pass was occupied by a mixed Advance Guard. This was the only day till Kandahar was reached that the Cavalry did not perform the entire duties of the Advance Guard.

On August 23 Kalat-i-Ghilzai was reached (225 miles in fifteen days). His progress having been satisfactory and reports from Kandahar reassuring, Roberts decided to rest his troops here for twenty-four hours, and sent the following message to the Government of India, which reached Simla on the 30th :—

'KALAT-I-GHILZAI, *August* 23.

' The force under my command arrived here this morning. Authorities at Kandahar having stated on the 17th inst. that they have abundant supplies and can make forage last until September 1, I halt to-morrow to rest troops, and more especially the transport animals and camp followers.

' The force left Ghazni on the 16th, and has marched 136 miles during the last eight days. The troops are in good health and spirits. From this I purpose moving by regular stages, so that the men may arrive fresh at Kandahar.

' I hope to be in telegraphic communication with Kandahar from Robat, distance 20 miles, on the 29th. . . .

' We have met with no opposition during the march, and have been able to make satisfactory arrangements for supplies, especially forage, which at this season is plentiful. The Cavalry horses and Artillery mules are in excellent order. Our casualties to date are one soldier 72nd Highlanders, one sepoy 23rd Pioneers, one sepoy 2nd Sikhs, and two sepoys 3rd Sikhs, dead ; one sepoy 4th Gurkhas, two sepoys 24th P.N.I., and a daffadar 3rd Punjab Cavalry, missing ; six camp followers dead and five missing. The missing men have, I fear, been murdered.'

On advancing again on the 25th, Roberts took with him the garrison of Kalat-i-Ghilzai, consisting of 100 Sowars 3rd Sindh Horse, 2 guns R.A., 2 Companies 66th Foot, and the 29th Bombay Infantry (2nd Baluchis).

On August 26 a message was received from Kandahar that the siege had been raised on the 23rd and that Ayub on the 24th had retired to Mazra in the Arghandab Valley, about 4 miles north-west of Kandahar, where he was said to be entrenching his camp. On August 27 Brigadier-General Hugh Gough, with two Cavalry Regiments, marched 34 miles to Robat, 19 miles from Kandahar, and got into communication by telegraph with that place. Lieut.-Colonel St. John, the Resident, with Major F. J. S. Adams, A.Q.M.G., rode out to meet him, re-establishing direct connection between the garrison and the Relief Force. The main body reached Robat next day. Information received by General Roberts at Robat, from Kandahar and other sources, convinced him that Ayub intended to make a stand and was strengthening his position. He therefore resolved to halt at Robat on the 29th and divide the remaining distance into two easy marches. Fighting men, followers, and animals were all showing the effect of the continuous marching in the daily increasing heat. The health of the force was good, though Roberts himself was down with fever, but they had marched 280 miles in 20 days (19 marches). The transport animals had suffered very heavily, as the following table shows.

The total number of transport animals, actually employed during the march, and those which became ineffective from sickness, death, or loss, on or before arrival at Kandahar, are as follows :—

	Afghan Ponies.	Indian Ponies.	Mules.	Donkeys.	Camels.[1]
Total employed	1,651	1,303	4,510	1,163	177
Dead or missing	419	308	216	107	nil.
Sick	681	479	942	57	nil.
Total ineffective	1,090	787	1,158	164	nil.
Balance effective	561	516	3,352	999	177
Percentage effective on completion of march	34%	39%	73%	85%	100

[1] Six started from Kabul; 171 purchased on the march.

The heavy loss in camels by Sir Donald Stewart's force in the first months of the war has been already related. No doubt the few camels that Roberts had with him on the march from Kabul to Kandahar were of the Afghan breed—familiar to anyone who knows the North-west Frontier—which, though one-humped, have the cobby conformation and thick coat of the Bactrian camel.

On August 30 the force marched 7½ miles to Mohmand, and on the 31st they completed the march to Kandahar. The following is a list of the marches performed by the Kabul—Kandahar Force :—

Left Kabul August 9, 1880.

Arrived August	9,	Zaidabad	15	miles.
,,	,, 10,	Zarghunshahr	14	,,
,,	,, 11,	Padkao-Rogan	16	,,
,,	,, 12,	Amirkilla	10	,,
,,	,, 13,	Haidar Khel	14	,,
,,	,, 14,	Shashgao	18	,,
,,	,, 15,	Ghazni	13	,,
,,	,, 16,	Ahmadkhel	22	,,
,,	,, 17,	Chardeh Babud	12	,,
,,	,, 18,	Karez-i-Oba	18	,,
,,	,, 19,	Makar	14	,,
,,	,, 20,	Killa Andari	22	,,
,,	,, 21,	Shahjui	18	,,
,,	,, 22,	Babar Razai	17	,,
,,	,, 23,	Kalat-i-Ghilzai	17	,,
,,	,, 24,	Halt	—	
,,	,, 25,	Jaldak	15	miles.
,,	,, 26,	Tirandaz	16½	,,
,,	,, 27,	Shahr-i-Safa	14½	,,
,,	,, 28,	Robat	20	,,
,,	,, 29,	Halt	—	
,,	,, 30,	Mohmand	8	miles.
,,	,, 31,	Kandahar	12	,,
		Total	326	miles.

The position Roberts had selected was to the west of the town, his right on the old British Cantonments, his left on Old Kandahar. This position, though within range of Afghan guns on the Kotal-i-Babawali, was Hobson's choice, owing to difficulties of water-supply anywhere else. However, 3,600 yards was in those days a longish range, and the best use was made of the cover afforded by Karez Hill. By 3 p.m. the troops were camped, with tents pitched, and a line of piquets ran through Piquet Hill—Karez Hill to the northern spur of Dukhteran Hill. From what he could see of the enemy's position, Roberts came to the conclusion that a frontal attack on the Kotal-i-Babawali would be an expensive business, and he determined to turn it. He therefore sent out Brigadier-General Gough with the 3rd Bengal Cavalry, 15th Sikhs, and two guns to find out how far the enemy's position reached to his (the enemy's) right. Starting at 1 p.m., the Column first occupied the high ground overlooking Gundigan and Murghan unopposed. Leaving the Infantry and Artillery there, the Cavalry went on another couple of miles till they found the enemy strongly entrenched in front of Pir Paimal village. After drawing the enemy's fire along this line the Cavalry fell back. After a few rounds from the guns in order to check the enemy, who were seen rapidly passing into the gardens near Gundigan, the Infantry and Artillery were ordered to withdraw inside the piquet line. The enemy followed up so persistently that the 3rd Brigade and part of the 1st were ordered to fall in. Just before dark, part of the 3rd Brigade was sent out towards Kohkaran to cover the retirement, and by nightfall the troops were back in camp, the object of the reconnaissance having been successfully attained. The total casualties had been five killed and fifteen wounded. Sir Frederick Roberts, having got the information he wanted, decided to attack next morning.

His plan was to threaten the enemy's left on the Kotal-i-Babawali, while the main attack turned his right by Pir Paimal village. With this object the 3rd Brigade, which was to threaten the Kotal, was drawn up behind Piquet Hill; the 1st and 2nd Brigades, which were to make the main attack, were behind Karez Hill. The Cavalry Brigade of the Kabul Force was drawn up in rear of the left, their task being to pass by Gundigan to the bed of the Arghandab River, there to be ready to cut off Ayub's retreat either west towards Girisk or north-west towards Kharez. A battery R.H.A., 2 Companies Royal Fusiliers, and 4 Companies 28th Bombay Infantry, were placed at General Gough's disposal to occupy the village of Gundigan. To cover the assembly of the striking force and form a reserve a heavy battery (four 40-pounders), 4 Companies R.F., the 4th and 19th Bombay Infantry, and some Sappers, under Brigadier-General Burrows, took up a position to the right of Piquet Hill, while 4 Companies 66th Foot and 2 Companies each of 1st and 28th Bombay Infantry relieved the Kabul Force in the Piquet Line. The Bombay Cavalry Brigade (Brigadier-General Nuttall) were on the right of Burrows's detachment.

These dispositions were complete soon after 9 a.m., and before 9.30 the heavies opened fire on some guns on the Kotal which had been shelling the British Camp the previous afternoon. These guns replied till about noon, when they were turned against the troops attacking Pir Paimal. Meanwhile the enemy, who, by the retirement of Gough's force the previous afternoon had been led to congratulate themselves on another success, were also planning an attack, for which purpose they were occupying the villages of Gundigan and Gundi Mulla Sahibdad in

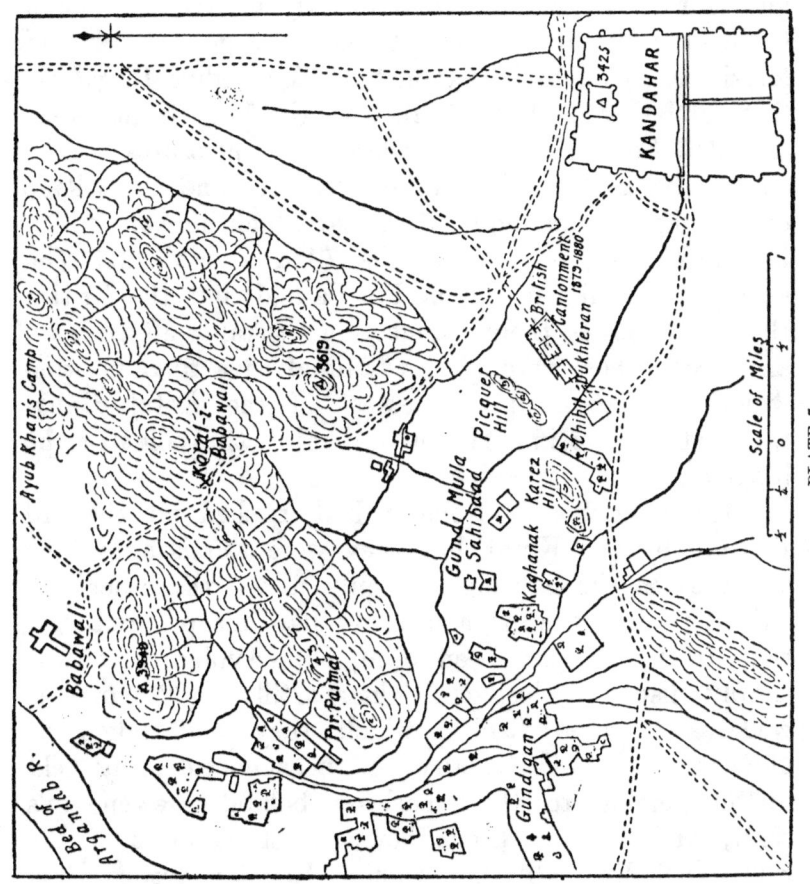

PLATE 7.

BATTLE OF KANDAHAR, SEPTEMBER 1, 1880.

great numbers. These villages had therefore to be taken before the turning movement could begin or the Cavalry get started. Brigadier-General Macpherson (1st Brigade) attacked Gundi Mulla Sahibdad with the 2nd Gurkhas and Gordon Highlanders and quickly cleared it, though the enemy put up a stout defence and a good number of ghazis remained to be bayoneted. Meanwhile Brigadier-General Baker (2nd Brigade), with the 72nd Highlanders and 2nd Sikhs, gradually cleared the enclosures to the left of the 1st Brigade's line of advance and the village of Gundigan, but only after hard fighting, in which Lieut.-Colonel Brownlow of the 72nd was killed. The enemy now fell back upon Pir Paimal, but the British Brigades followed them up, meeting resistance all the way, and drove them through Pir Paimal to a final position which they took up south-west of the Kotal-i-Babawali, which was immediately taken at the point of the bayonet.

Meanwhile Sir F. Roberts had pushed on the 3rd Brigade by the Kotal, but they were too late to take any part in the fighting and only joined the other two Brigades after the Afghan army had disappeared and their deserted camp been occupied. Ayub's force had simply dispersed, losing all their artillery (30 guns) as well as 2 guns R.H.A. which they had taken at Maiwand. Gough's Cavalry had been considerably held up in getting to their position behind the enemy's right, and by the time they got there most of the rout, including all the Afghan Regular troops, had passed, going west and north-west. They accounted for about 350 tribesmen in the pursuit. At 2 p.m. Roberts had ordered Nuttall's Brigade (3rd Sind Horse and 3rd Bombay Cavalry) in pursuit, over the Kotal-i-Babawali. They followed some fifteen miles to Mansurabad, killing about 100 of the enemy, thus getting a bit of their own back over Maiwand.

The total casualties in the Kabul—Kandahar force on September 1 were 35 killed, 213 wounded. Six hundred of the enemy were buried between Kandahar and Pir Paimal alone, so their total killed probably amounted to quite double that number.

This ended the Afghan War, and, though Kandahar continued to be occupied for the time being, the relief of the Kabul troops at once began. Our 2nd Battalion, however, were not to get back to India yet awhile, and were detailed to take part in an expedition through the Mari country under Sir Charles MacGregor, where, although they had no fighting, those who went through it say that they had a harder time than they had had either marching from Kandahar to Kabul under Stewart or back again under Roberts.

On September 8, 1880, the Battalion left Kandahar for Quetta, arriving there on the 19th. On the 28th it marched again, reaching Sibi on October 7. On the 8th Lieut.-Colonel J. J. Collins died of dysentery and was buried at Sibi next day, Major W. G. Byron taking temporary command. On October 11 the Battalion left Sibi for the Mari country, as part of the Mari Field Force under Brigadier-General Charles MacGregor, sent to punish the Maris for raids on the new line of railway then being laid down between Sibi and Quetta. On November 6 Kahan, the capital of the country, was reached, and the Chief of the Maris accepted the terms laid down by the Government. On the 8th the Battalion began its return march to India. In a farewell order on the break-up of his force General MacGregor says : " The 2nd Battalion 60th Rifles have proved by their splendid soldierly qualities that they cannot be surpassed by any Battalion in the

Army." MacGregor was not a man who was given to paying compliments, and, as Roberts's Chief of the Staff, he must have had an intimate knowledge of all the battalions that had taken part in the hard fighting in Northern Afghanistan.

On November 24, 1880, the Battalion reached Meerut after an absence of over two years.

CHAPTER III

THIRD BATTALION

WE left the 3rd Battalion just arrived in Malta in April 1882. On July 7 of that year a telegram was received from the War Office ordering the Battalion on active service in Egypt. They embarked on the 8th on H.M.S. *Agincourt*.

There left Malta with the Battalion :—

Majors C. P. Cramer, E. L. Fraser, H. A. H. Ward.
Captain W. S. Anderson.
Lieutenants E. S. St. Aubyn, H. G. L. Howard-Vyse, F. M. Beaumont, P. Marling, E. T. Scudamore-Stanhope, W. H. Kennedy, R. L. Bower.
Lieutenant and Adjutant C. R. R. McGrigor, Quartermaster J. Wilkins.
700 Other Ranks.

There joined them at Cyprus :—

Lieut.-Colonel C. Ashburnham, Lieut.-Colonel W. L. K. Ogilvy.
Surgeon-Major T. C. Tolmie.
Paymaster J. E. Orange.

H.M.S. *Agincourt* left Malta on July 8 for Cyprus, arriving at Limasol on July 14.

On the 15th the *Agincourt*, in company with the *Northumberland* with the 1st South Staffordshire Regiment on board, sailed for Port Said, arriving there at 11 a.m. on the 16th. They left the same evening for Alexandria, reaching that port in the early morning of the 17th.

Egyptian Campaign of 1882

By the middle of May 1882, Arabi, a native Egyptian Colonel in the Egyptian Army, had, by a bloodless military revolt, made himself master of Egypt, the Khedive, Tewfik, retaining little more than his title. This revolt affected the European Powers in three ways, as internal disturbances would imperil, firstly, the life, property, and business of the European inhabitants—then mostly French and British subjects and amounting to some 90,000; secondly, the free passage of the world's commerce through the Suez Canal; and, thirdly, the payment of interest on the Egyptian foreign debt.

On May 20 the allied British and French Fleets entered Alexandria Harbour to offer an earnest of support to the threatened interests. The immediate consequence of this move was that on June 11 rioting broke out in Alexandria between Moslems and Christians, with the result that many Christians were massacred; most of the remainder fled the country, the whole course of business was disorganised, and in a few weeks many even of the Mahometan population were starving.

As the Sultan of Turkey, the Suzerain of Egypt, would take no active steps to restore order, and in fact encouraged Arabi, it became evident that France or Great Britain, or both, would have to do so by force of arms.

Plans for sending an expeditionary force were at once begun at the War Office, and it is interesting to note that Sir Garnet Wolseley, the Commander-in-Chief designate of the expedition, in a memorandum dated July 3, 1882, in stating his requirements for an advance on Cairo from Ismailia, says:

'It may be expected that the Egyptian Army would

make its stand somewhere in the neighbourhood of Tel-el-Kebir,' and ' if the Egyptian Army is well defeated in the field any further resistance would be insignificant.'

While the political situation was developing and pending the decision as to whether Egypt should be occupied or not, and if so by whom, every preparation was being made for an advance by Ismailia. The first step was to prepare a small force which should rendezvous at Cyprus and be ready to seize Port Said at short notice. Major-General Sir Archibald Alison, K.C.B., who was sent out to command this force, reached Cyprus on July 14, the 1st South Staffordshire Regiment, 3rd K.R.R.C., and a Company of R.E. arriving from Malta about the same time.

The line of advance on Cairo by Ismailia was obviously better than that from Alexandria. The route by Ismailia had the Sweet-Water Canal alongside of it all the way; it led as far as the limit of cultivation at Zagazig—except for the first few miles—over hard desert, that is a firm surface of pebbles which have the appearance of having been rolled in, and, except for an occasional patch of soft sand, was, for wheeled traffic, as good as a metalled road. The distance from Ismailia to Cairo is under 100 miles. The route from Alexandria to Cairo led either through the Delta, which at time of High Nile—August to November—is all under water and can only be crossed by the narrow bunds bordering the irrigation canals, or else along the edge of the Western Desert, mostly through soft sand; the distance from Alexandria to Cairo is 120 miles. The former route also had the advantage of directly covering the Suez Canal. However, between Sir Archibald Alison's departure from England and his arrival at Cyprus, events had taken place which entailed his small force being switched off to Alexandria instead of carrying out its designed duty of seizing Ismailia.

The presence of the allied Fleet in Alexandria Harbour had not been able to prevent the massacre of many of the Christian population on June 11, though it had saved many lives by taking off refugees ; but even its own safety was becoming endangered by the activity of the Egyptians in mounting guns and strengthening the works which commanded the harbour. The British Admiral, Sir Beauchamp Seymour, called on them to stop this work, which they agreed to do, but went on with it under cover of night. It became evident that the British Fleet could not remain longer—the French Fleet had already sailed away—unless some of the forts were handed over to our care. On July 10 Sir Beauchamp Seymour, after taking off the last of the refugees, sent an ultimatum announcing that he would commence a bombardment of the forts in twenty-four hours if certain of them were not given up within twelve hours. The bombardment began at 7 a.m., July 11, and continued all day, and by night-time all the forts were silenced. Landing parties, sent ashore on the 13th, found the forts evacuated, but the city had been set on fire, the greater part of the European quarter destroyed, and the whole place was being looted by the mob.

To restore order in Alexandria thus became the first duty of the British forces, naval and military, and, although the landing parties from the Fleet were enough to police Alexandria, they in turn had to be protected from a possible attack by Arabi's Army, which lay at Kafr-ed-Dauar, only 14 miles away.

Sir Archibald Alison, on his arrival at Cyprus, hearing of the bombardment, decided that, as hostilities had begun, now was the time for his force to carry out its allotted task and seize the Canal. Arrived at Port Said, he heard more fully what was going on and saw that his force was urgently required at Alexandria ; so, sailing again at once, he arrived there on July 17. The same day the South Staffordshire and the R.E. Company were landed; also a Battalion of Marines. The 3rd K.R.R.C. disembarked next day, and bivouacked at the Moharrem Bey railway-station. On the evening of the first day of landing a body of Mounted Infantry—two Officers and thirty men—was formed, under Captain E. T. H. Hutton, K.R.R.C., from men of the South Stafford and K.R.R.C. who had previously served in the Mounted Infantry in South Africa. They were mounted from the Khedive's own stables.

On the 18th a party of the Mounted Infantry patrolled ten miles towards the enemy, and from this time onward daily rendered most valuable service.

Sir Archibald Alison's first object was to secure Alexandria from attack. As he now had 3,755 men landed (including seamen and marines) with 9 guns, and could be reinforced by the Navy by another 1,200 men; and as his left flank could be protected if required by the guns of the Fleet; this was not difficult, so long as Lake Mariut did not dry up—quite a possible contingency if the Egyptians succeeded in diverting the waters of the Mahmudiyeh Canal. This Arabi proceeded to do, but the results were too gradual to have any effect before the situation had changed and all chances of an attack on Alexandria removed.

Ou July 24 Sir Archibald Alison sent a force under Colonel W. Thackwell, 1st South Staffordshire Regiment, consisting of 1st South Staffords, 3rd K.R.R.C., Mounted Infantry, and 4 naval guns to occupy the Er Ramleh position, which they did without opposition and started entrenching. The Mounted Infantry, backed by an armoured train and 300 3rd K.R.R.C., the whole under

Colonel C. Ashburnham, 3rd K.R.R.C., had already occupied Mallaha Junction and cut the line beyond it, on July 22.

'An unfortunate incident occurred on the night of August 1–2 which got into the papers with the same unpleasant results as followed the scare in the Zulu War after the relief of Etshowe. In the early morning four men of our 3rd Battalion ran in from a piquet, reporting that their Company had been cut to pieces; the truth being that some Egyptian Cavalry had made a half-hearted attack on the piquet and after some firing on both sides retired, having inflicted no casualties on our men and leaving one wounded horse behind.'

Sir Archibald Alison's second object was to keep up the idea generally prevalent that the British Expeditionary Force was destined to advance by the Delta, based on Alexandria. To maintain this rôle and also to ascertain the truth of native reports that Arabi was preparing to retire from Kafr-ed-Dauar, he decided to make a reconnaissance which would test the enemy's dispositions on August 5. As he had no intention either of becoming seriously engaged—his force was greatly inferior in numbers to the enemy—or of making too evident his deliberate intention to retire when he had done what he wanted, he did not move till 4.30 p.m.

The force employed was disposed in two columns :—

Left Column (Lieut.-Colonel Thackwell, 1st South Staffordshire Regiment) :—

1st South Staffordshire Regiment, ½ Battalion.
2nd D.C.L.I., ½ Battalion.
3rd K.R.R.C., 6 Companies.
Mounted Infantry.
2 9-pounder Naval Guns (hand drawn).
About 1,000 men.

Right Column (under personal command of Sir Archibald Alison) :—
A weak Battalion, Royal Marine Artillery.
A weak Battalion, R.M.L.I.
Armoured train (with 40-pounder gun).
2 9-pounder Naval Guns (hand drawn).
About 1,000 men.

The Left Column followed the course of the Mahmudiyeh Canal, the Right that of the railway. The 3rd K.R.R.C. led the advance of the Left Column with their left on the Canal and drove back the Egyptian outposts, which showed fight and were immediately reinforced. The Battalion pushed on under a heavy but ill-aimed fire—most of the bullets going over their heads—and drove the enemy out of a village on the banks of the Canal. They were then halted and, darkness coming on soon afterwards, the force retired on Ramleh. As Arabi reported to Cairo that the Left Column consisted of 3 Battalions of Infantry, 3 Squadrons of Cavalry and 4 guns, the Right of 3 Battalions of Infantry and one battery of Artillery with a regiment of Cavalry in the centre, the British Force seems to have put up a very successful bluff. Hutton's Mounted Infantry must have been ubiquitous.

The only casualty in the Battalion this day was one Rifleman slightly wounded. The Mounted Infantry of the Battalion lost Lieutenant H. G. L. Howard-Vyse and one Rifleman killed and one Rifleman wounded. Howard-Vyse was a particularly promising Officer who had already seen service in the Boer War of 1881.

In the *London Gazette* of August 8, Lieut.-Colonel C. Ashburnham, C.B., was appointed A.D.C. to the Queen with consequent promotion to full Colonel in the Army.

Meanwhile the Expeditionary Force from England was

on its way out, the first to arrive being the composite Regiment of Household Cavalry on August 14. Wolseley himself reached Alexandria on the 15th, having been delayed by illness, from which happily he had by this time completely recovered. All the troops, as they arrived, were landed at Alexandria, so as to keep up the impression that the intended line of advance was to be from that port. This was all the more necessary because Admiral Hewett had, on August 2, occupied Suez with a force of Marines, preparatory to the arrival of the Indian Contingent (a mixed Brigade), which sailed from Bombay on August 9, and Arabi was showing signs of countering this movement by moving troops to the eastern front. It will be seen that the idea, which has been very prevalent among uninstructed writers on this campaign, that Wolseley's change of base to Ismailia was something quite new, the result of a great strategic brain-wave after his arrival at Alexandria, is entirely erroneous. His intention from the first was to advance from Ismailia, and all his operations and landing of troops at Alexandria, beyond what were required for the immediate protection of the place, were planned deliberately to deceive the enemy, in which he was entirely successful, as he not only deceived Arabi, but all the Press and military critics throughout Europe.

The operation of occupying Ismailia, establishing a base there, seizing an advanced position within striking distance of the Egyptian positions at Tel-el-Kebir, concentrating a force of more than two Divisions at that point, passing all this force up 50 miles of narrow canal where one ship going aground might make incalculable delay, at the same time erecting landing facilities at Ismailia, which at the time of our first arrival were almost non-existent, necessitated that perfect co-operation between Navy and Army which has so often, though not invariably, been a feature of the Wars of our Empire. The plans for the first great move of this combined operation were settled at a conference between Admiral Sir Beauchamp Seymour and Sir Garnet Wolseley on August 16. On the morning of August 20 landing parties from H.M. ships occupied Ismailia and all other points of importance along the line of the Suez Canal up to that place. These points were only held by small guards of Egyptian troops, and there was practically no resistance. In the afternoon it was reported that the enemy had 2,000 men at Nefisha—the point just outside Ismailia where the Suez branch of the Fresh-Water Canal separates from the Ismailia branch—and intended to try to retake Ismailia. Their camp was immediately shelled by H.M.S. *Orion* and *Carysfort*, a train was wrecked, and the enemy abandoned the place. At the same time the force at Suez occupied the Canal south of the Bitter Lakes, and on the 21st occupied Serapeum and connected up with the Expeditionary Force at Ismailia.

Meanwhile Sir G. Wolseley had embarked the 1st Division at Alexandria and, in order further to distract attention from the Suez Canal, the whole fleet of 6 ships-of-war and 17 transports anchored in Abukir Bay about 4 p.m. on the 19th, as if to carry out a long-talked-of attack on the forts there. At the same time orders had been issued for an attack on the Egyptian lines at Kefr-ed-Dauar by the 2nd Division. The fact that the preparations for this attack were all camouflage was kept so secret that even Sir Edward Hamley, the General Officer Commanding the Division, did not know when giving his own orders that it was not real business. At nightfall the Fleet steamed off for Port Said, arriving there soon after sunrise on the 20th. Some delay was caused by having to let three ships out of the Canal which were passing north—the Canal was much narrower then than now, and passing a much more delicate operation—and half a battalion of the Royal West Kent Regiment was rushed through in light craft to reinforce Ismailia.

Our 3rd Battalion had embarked on the troopship H.M.S. *Euphrates* on the 18th, together with the 2nd D.C.L.I., and tied up at Kantarah for the night of the 20th–21st. Wolseley reached Ismailia at 9 a.m. on the 21st, and sent out the Royal West Kents and a naval Gatling gun to occupy Nefisha, reinforcing them with a battalion of Marines as soon as they were landed. Our 3rd Battalion disembarked at Ismailia at noon and at once occupied the railway-station. The embarkation then went on as fast as the very inadequate facilities would permit, and it was not till the afternoon of the 23rd that the Household Cavalry landed, being the first Cavalry to disembark, nor till the evening of that day that the first of the Artillery landed—two guns R.H.A. By this time 9,000 men were on shore, but very little had been done in the way of landing stores or the all-necessary R.E. material, which alone could improve the landing-places and join them up with the railway.

At this time the water in the Fresh-Water Canal was rapidly falling, by which not only was the water-supply of Ismailia and Suez endangered, but, if the fall continued, the British force would be deprived of a very valuable means of transport in their advance. It was known that the part of the Canal where the most serious damage could be done by cutting it was at El Magfar, 7 miles from Ismailia, where the Canal flows through a bit of country below its own level, where therefore the water can be let off by cutting the bank. Above that point the Canal, after leaving the cultivated country where the fellaheen would object to being deprived of its water, flows generally between high banks where the flow can only be obstructed by damming—a much more difficult operation than cutting the bank. It was known that the Egyptians had made a dam across the Fresh-Water Canal near Magfar.

The following orders were issued on August 23 :—

Two guns R.H.A., three squadrons Household Cavalry, a detachment 19th Hussars, and the M.I. to march at 4 a.m. on the 24th and to report at Nefisha to Major-General Graham, who was in command there with the Royal West Kent Regiment, the 2nd York and Lancaster Regiment, and a Battalion of Royal Marine Artillery. The 2nd D.C.L.I. to Nefisha, to occupy that place.

East of El Magfar the Cavalry found the enemy's outposts and easily drove them in. From the reports of prisoners it was found that the enemy had constructed a second dam at Tel-el-Mahuta and that a considerable Infantry force was entrenched there. The Cavalry were held up by hostile Infantry half-way between El Magfar and Tel-el-Mahuta.

Sir Garnet decided on taking the opportunity, by defeating this force, to make his projected seizure of Kassassin, within striking distance of Tel-el-Kebir, at one bound.

At 7.30 a.m. he ordered the Infantry to continue their march and the two guns R.H.A. to press on as rapidly as possible.

At 8.30 a.m. orders were sent to Ismailia for the Brigade of Guards, and all Cavalry and Artillery that might be ready, to push on to the front, and for the D.C.L.I., left at Nefisha, to come on.

By 9 a.m. Graham had the left of the York and Lancaster Regiment on the Canal at the first dam and the remainder of the Battalion echeloned back to the right, the guns 600 yards to the right of the railway; the Royal Marine Artillery on their right, then the Cavalry, and on the extreme right the Mounted Infantry.

Sir Garnet then ordered General Willis (commanding the 1st Division), who accompanied him, to take command.

The enemy were in position on higher ground some 3,500 yards away. Our Cavalry moved out to threaten the enemy's left and prevent any extension by them to that side.

Our position and the ground to the immediate front of it was soft, hillocky sand, which gave good cover and smothered the enemy's shells. The enemy's position was on hard gravel, where shells had great effect.

Soon after 9 a.m. the enemy advanced with all three arms to within 2,000 yards of our guns, but his right was held up by the York and Lancaster Regiment.

Retiring on his right, he tried to advance on his left, but was held up by the fire of the Mounted Infantry.

By 9.40 a.m. he had four guns in action and dropped a shell very nearly into the Headquarters Staff. When these had taken cover, the guns turned their attention to the Cavalry and Mounted Infantry.

Soon after 10 a.m. two more guns opened and obliged the mounted troops to fall back. The enemy's shrapnel, however, was bursting very high and their percussion shell failed to explode.

As reinforcements arrived by train, the enemy prolonged their line to their left, pressed our mounted troops back, and enfiladed our line with six fresh guns.

The position would now have been none too pleasant if the Egyptians had made a determined attack.

At 3 p.m. some of the R.M.A. came to the assistance

of the R.H.A. in working their guns, the men being worn out.

The Guards Brigade arrived at 6.20 p.m., after a trying march, with the four remaining guns of the R.H.A. Battery.

At 5.20 p.m. Sir Baker Russell had come up with 350 sabres of the 4th and 7th Dragoon Guards. Five minutes earlier the enemy's guns and Cavalry had come well down the forward slopes towards our right flank, but did not advance within small-arm range.

At nightfall Sir Garnet Wolseley left General Willis with orders to attack at dawn, and returned to Ismailia.

After midnight A-1 Battery R.A. arrived and relieved the R.H.A.

To return to our 3rd Battalion: the Battalion paraded at 9 p.m. on the 24th and started to march across the desert to take part in the fight that had been going on all day. When the moon set, they halted till daylight. They then resumed their march.

At 5.30 a.m., when Sir Garnet reached the front from Ismailia, where he had spent the night, he found the Division advancing. Graham's Brigade were next the Canal, the Guards Brigade on their right, the Cavalry, M.I., and R.A. battery on the extreme right front, with the 3rd K.R.R.C. and R.M.L.I. Battalion in second line.

(Till September 12 our 3rd Battalion were Divisional Troops, 2nd Division; the 2nd D.C.L.I. Divisional Troops, 1st Division. The battalions of R.M.A. and R.M.L.I. were not a part of the Expeditionary Force, but were borrowed from the Fleet.)

Four guns, A-1, R.A., moved between the Infantry Brigades; two guns on the right of the Guards.

It soon became evident that the enemy had abandoned his works. Sir Garnet sent orders to the Cavalry to push round the enemy's left and cut off his retreat; but the horses, just off shipboard, were not equal to any extended operation. The M.I., mounted on Arabs, in hard condition, were not thus handicapped.

Sir Drury Lowe pressed on as best he could and soon found himself confronted by a strong force of Infantry, with Artillery and Cavalry, in position about Mahsama. They were soon turned out by the fire of his Artillery, which had been reinforced by the two field guns on the right of the Guards, and by that of the M.I.

The enemy gradually fell back, leaving their camp at Mahsama in Sir Drury's possession, together with seven Krupp guns, a large number of rifles, stores of all kinds, and 75 railway wagons, the one thing Sir Garnet most wanted.

If it had not been for this capture of supplies it would have been necessary for the troops to fall back till the two dams at El Magfar and Tel-el-Mahuta should be cut and obstacles on the railway line removed.

The advance was continued as the condition of the troops would allow, and Graham's Brigade reached the Cavalry bivouac at Mahsama at dawn on the 26th.

At the same time the Cavalry had occupied the position around the canal lock at Kassassin, where later in the day they were relieved by Graham's Brigade. The whole of the Canal and railway as far as Kassassin was thus in Sir Garnet Wolseley's hands.

Our 3rd Battalion, as already related, had arrived in time to join in the advance of the 25th, though they did not come under fire. After the action they moved down to the Canal at Tel-el-Mahuta, arriving there about noon. They had had a very hard march, mostly through heavy sand, and the last few hours in great heat, with no water except what the men carried in their water-bottles. One man died of heat apoplexy.

On the 26th and 27th the Battalion was employed digging down the dam across the Canal at Tel-el-Mahuta and the obstruction the enemy had piled up across the railway.

The following table of distances from Cairo on the railway will be useful in studying the account of these and subsequent operations :—

Tel-el-Kebir (railway-station).	68	miles.
Tel-el-Kebir (enemy's position)	70	,,
Kassassin	77	,,
Mahsama	82	,,
Tel-el-Mahuta	87	,,
El Magfar	90	,,
Nafisha	95	,,
Ismailia	$97\frac{1}{2}$	,,

There now followed a period occupied in opening the communications between Ismailia and the front by Canal and railway.

On the 27th the first of the railway engines brought from Alexandria, which had to go on to Suez to be landed, came up by rail to Ismailia. On the 28th, the Indian Cavalry Brigade having reached Ismailia from Suez, the whole of the Cavalry was formed into a Division under Sir Drury Lowe; the British Brigade under Sir Baker Russell, the Indian Brigade under Brigadier-General H. C. Wilkinson. On the same day Sir Edward Hamley got orders to begin the move of his Division to Ismailia, leaving Sir Evelyn Wood with his Brigade to defend Alexandria.

All this time the force at Kassassin Lock would not have been in a very comfortable position if the enemy had been more aggressive fighters. It was necessary to hold the lock itself, as it was one of the points where the

Canal flowed above the surrounding country and a cut in the bank would drain it dry. The force under Graham (3 battalions, 2 guns R.H.A., and small detachments of Cavalry and M.I.) was not large enough to extend its position to the high ground which commanded the lock. On August 25 the enemy began to advance as if they meant to attack in earnest. After taking all day to make up their minds to it, the enemy did, shortly before sunset, begin a movement as if to turn Graham's right flank, which was out in the desert. General Drury Lowe was called up from Mahsama with two regiments of Cavalry and 4 guns R.H.A. The Egyptian advance was brought to an end by a brilliant moonlight charge of the Household Cavalry, who wiped out the Infantry on the extreme left, the bad light alone letting the guns escape, the Egyptian Cavalry taking care not to get within charging distance.

All the part the 3rd Battalion took in this incident was that they marched at about 6 p.m. on the 28th, bivouacked at Mahsama, and arrived at Kassassin at 6 a.m. on the 29th. Captain Pigott, K.R.R.C., Commanding M.I., was severely wounded on the 28th.

For the next twelve days the work of landing troops and getting up stores went on uneventfully. General Sir Edward Hamley with Sir Archibald Alison's Brigade reached Ismailia on September 1, and the Indian Cavalry Brigade was sent up to join the rest of the Cavalry at the front. On the 7th the railway was ready to carry enough stores for the whole army and provide a surplus. Orders were therefore given for the move forward of Sir Archibald Alison's Brigade, the Indian Contingent, and the remainder of the Artillery. The last of the troops were timed to reach Kassassin on September 12.

On September 5 a draft of Reservists under Major

W. Forster joined the Battalion from the Depôt; strength: 5 Officers, 252 O.R.

On September 9 Arabi, misled by the reports of his Bedouin allies into the belief that Kassassin was only lightly held, whereas it was by this time occupied by about 8,000 troops of all arms, not including the Guards Brigade 10 miles away at Tel-el-Mahuta, thought to capture it by a combined attack from Tel-el-Kebir—7 miles away to the west—and Es Salahiyeh—twice that distance to the north.

Patrols of Indian Cavalry, sent out at 4 a.m., soon came in contact with the advancing enemy, and reports of their general advance reached General Willis, commanding all the troops at the front, soon after 6.15 a.m. He first ordered the troops to take up a position which had been already prepared in case of attack, in which the 3rd Battalion had their left resting on the Canal. The first shots of the action were fired about 7.15 a.m. by the armoured train which was alongside of our Battalion as the Battalion was getting into position. These immediately drew the fire of the Egyptian Artillery, the consequence being that shells began to fall among the Battalion and caused a few casualties.

Orders were at the same time sent to the Guards Brigade to come up and attack the left of the Salahiyeh Column, while the Cavalry Division was sent out between the two columns of the enemy with orders to keep them apart. This was done by the Indian Brigade acting against the left of the Tel-el-Kebir Column, while Sir Baker Russell did the same against the right of the Salahiyeh force. The M.I., who were with the Indian Brigade, were particularly active in checking the advance of the enemy's artillery by their fire until they were relieved by Infantry, when they were sent over to Sir Baker.

At 7.45 a.m. General Willis ordered an advance of his whole force, the 3rd Battalion and Royal Marine Light Infantry being in front line. The enemy at once fell back, keeping up a heavy but ill-aimed fire of artillery and musketry. The advance continued till 10.30 a.m., by which time our troops were within 5,000 yards of the Tel-el-Kebir lines. During the advance our 3rd Battalion captured one gun, the Royal Marine Light Infantry two, and the Cavalry one, with teams and limber complete. It is probable that if this success had been immediately followed up, the Tel-el-Kebir position would have been taken the same day, at considerable loss to our troops; but the victory would have been incomplete: preparations were not sufficiently far advanced for following up a victory with the whole force, and the Cavalry could not have gone straight on to Cairo, which was an important part of the plan; as an immedate occupation, following a victory, was necessary to save that city from the fate of Alexandria.

General Willis, knowing the Commander-in-Chief's views, halted the troops, and Sir Garnet, who was that day changing his General Headquarters from Ismailia to Kassassin and had arrived on the field during the course of the action, after a thorough personal reconnaissance, ordered them back to camp. The Salahiyeh force had been hunted back, by the 1st Cavalry Brigade, too rapidly for the Guards Brigade to get a blow in at them. It was a long and hot day for the troops, who had no water but what they carried in their water-bottles. The losses of the 3rd Battalion in the action were 2 men killed and 28 wounded.

On the afternoon of September 12 a fourth Brigade was formed of the two Battalions of Divisional troops (the 2nd D.C.L.I. and 3rd K.R.R.C.), under command of Colonel C. Ashburnham, C.B., A.D.C.

Wolseley was now ready to strike his blow, which was to finish the war. All his force, with which he was to make it, was assembled at Kassassin; the last battalion to arrive being the Royal Irish Fusiliers, who marched in on the afternoon of the 12th.

The conditions for a night march, followed by an attack at dawn, were ideal. It was known that the enemy were slack in the matter of outposts and that they sent no patrols out till daylight. Although information from spies, deserters, or prisoners as regards the enemy's dispositions were almost *nil*, the enemy's entrenchments had been well reconnoitred, especially on the 9th, when Colonel Redvers Buller,[1] the head of the Intelligence Branch, had reached a hill, to the left rear of Arabi's line, which practically overlooked the whole of his entrenchments.

The country to be crossed was absolutely open; undulating desert with a hard and smooth surface. There were neither inhabitants nor animals that might be disturbed and give the alarm.

Everything was done to prevent any sign in the camp of intended movement. At dusk the camp was struck, and soon after dark the force moved out to its place of assembly in the desert, north of the railway line, where it formed up in the formation in which it was to advance.

This was as follows: On the right the 1st Division (Willis); Second Brigade (Graham) in front line, Guards Brigade (H.R.H. the Duke of Connaught) in second line; on the left the 2nd Division (Hamley); the Highland Brigade (Alison) in front line; 4th Brigade (Ashburnham) in second line. All the Artillery was massed between the two second-line Brigades. The Cavalry Division was to

[1] General Rt. Hon. Sir Redvers Buller, V.C., G.C.B., G.C.M.G., Colonel Commandant 1st Battalion 1895—1908.

move some time later than the Infantry, but to time its advance so as to be ready to turn the enemy's left and get round behind him as soon as the attack should be launched.

The Indian Contingent under Sir Herbert Macpherson, which was to advance along the south side of the Canal, with the Naval Brigade on its right, between Canal and railway, was timed to start one hour later than the main force, as it was to advance through an inhabited area and could not hope to do so without creating an alarm.

The main force began its advance at 1.30 a.m.

The Highland Brigade moved in the formation in which it was going to attack, half-battalion columns of double companies (it must be remembered that till just before the Great War there were eight companies in a battalion), in the following order from right to left : 1st Black Watch, 1st Gordon Highlanders, 1st Cameron Highlanders, 2nd Highland Light Infantry. It started with intervals between the half-battalion columns, but these gradually disappeared during the march. The 4th Brigade followed the Highlanders at a distance of 1,000 yards; the 3rd King's Royal Rifle Corps having one company strung out in connecting files to keep touch.

The right Company of the Camerons was the company of direction, and was led by Sir Garnet's Naval A.D.C., Lieutenant Rawson, R.N., who steered by the stars. About 3.15 a.m. the leading Brigade, 2nd Division, halted for about twenty minutes. As the order to halt had to be passed along from the centre, the two wings, before they halted, had swung inwards without knowing it, forming a crescent, and when they resumed the march they almost met. The Brigade had to be halted again to get straightened out, and this took another twenty-five minutes.

At 4.55 a.m., when it was known that the enemy's entrenchments must be very near and when as yet only the faintest light was showing in the eastern sky, some enemy's piquets were dimly seen about 150 yards off and a few shots were fired by their sentries.

At this time, though it had been expected that the 1st Division would be the first to strike the enemy's entrenchments, which had their left a good deal thrown forward (see Plate 8), the force had assumed the form of an irregular echelon from left to right. The 1st Division had not started in the formation in which they were going to attack and had changed formation more than once on the march; consequently they did not strike the enemy's trenches till ten minutes or a quarter of an hour after the Highlanders had attacked. When the shots just mentioned were fired, the word was passed to the Highland Brigade to fix bayonets without halting. As they did so, the Egyptian bugles sounded the alarm, and when the attackers were within 150 yards of the entrenchments the whole line of them was lit up by the flashes of rifles.

Though there was no wire in those days and its predecessor, abattis, was impossible in this treeless desert, the entrenchments meant first a ditch, anything up to 6 feet deep with very steep sides; then a parapet of 4 or 5 feet with a slope of $1:2$. This represents what the Highlanders had to surmount to get at the enemy, so, what with the difficulty of scrambling up the parapet and the stout resistance at first encountered, they did not have a walk-over, and it took a good twenty minutes' fighting before they had cleared the front line of parapet of the enemy. The Black Watch and Highland Light Infantry on the right and left came up against two strongpoints in the enemy's works and had a much harder task than the Gordons and Camerons; the Highland Light Infantry were at one time actually driven back by the counter-attack of a Black Battalion. While part of the 3rd King's Royal Rifle Corps were sent to reinforce the Black Watch, the remainder of the Battalion went to the assistance of the Highland Light Infantry, and it was not till about 5.40 a.m. that the left-hand work was carried. Captain Archer, with his own Company and some men of the D.C.L.I., attacked and captured a small work, taking 4 guns and 40 prisoners.

By this time, while Graham's Brigade had carried the works in their front, which were much less of an obstacle than those stormed by the Highlanders, and the remainder of the Highland Brigade was pushing on into the second line of works, the Cavalry Division had got right behind the enemy's left rear and some of our guns had been got across the ditch and parapet, after a little spade work had made the slope easier, and had opened fire on the enemy's second line. The enemy had so far put up a stout resistance, especially against the Highland Brigade, and they had fallen back fighting all the way; but now, their rear threatened by the Cavalry and their left flank rolled up by the advance of the 1st Division, their retirement became a stampede. The Highland Brigade pushed on through the deserted Egyptian camp to the railway-station, from which two train-loads of Arabi's reserve, which had not been engaged, managed to get away before the station came under the fire of our guns.

The Indian Contingent, which had come under fire soon after the main action began, had overcome all resistance and driven the enemy from their entrenchments south of the Canal about 6 a.m.

The Cavalry Division went on to occupy Cairo. They arrived at Abbasiyeh, outside Cairo, on the afternoon of

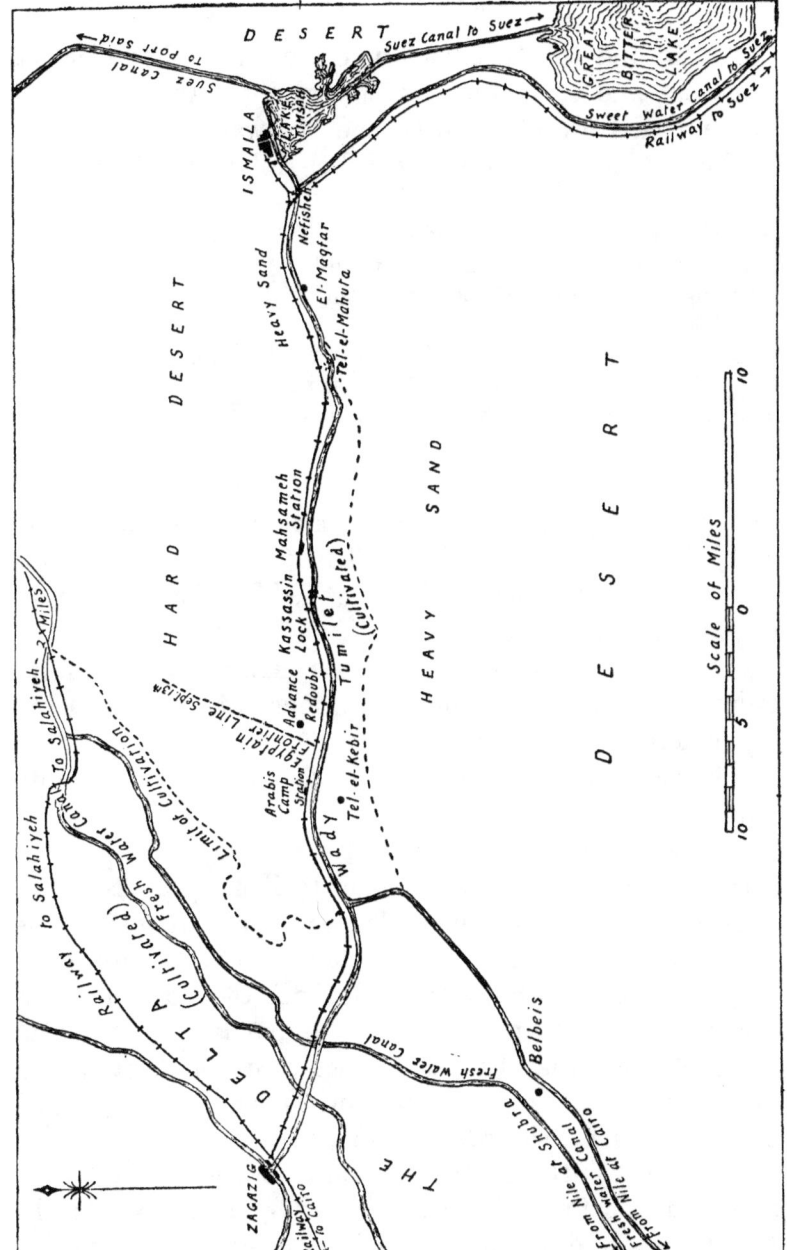

PLATE 8.

MAP TO SHOW WOLSELEY'S ADVANCE FROM ISMAILIA ON CAIRO.

the 14th, and the Governor of Cairo, and other officials, came out and surrendered that evening. Arabi followed suit immediately afterwards, and the war was over.

The numbers engaged at Tel-el-Kebir were :—

British rather over 17,000 of all ranks, 61 guns.
Arabi's force was about 20,000, with 75 guns.
58 guns were captured, of which the Indian Contingent took 15.
The total losses of the British force at Tel-el-Kebir were : 47 killed, 382 wounded, 30 missing.
The loss of our 3rd Battalion was 20 wounded.

At 7.40 a.m. General Macpherson started with the Indian Contingent for Zagazig, which he reached himself with a squadron of Cavalry at 4.10 p.m. The rest of his force got in that night, having marched 30 miles and fought an action in $16\frac{1}{2}$ hours.

During the following days the Army pushed on to Cairo, and Arabi's garrisons, in various parts of the Delta, surrendered one by one.

On the 26th the Khedive made his state entry into Cairo.

To return to our 3rd Battalion : On the morning of the 14th they got orders to move on to Zagazig as escort to some batteries of Artillery. They marched at noon ; the heat was very great, and many men fell out. After going about 4 miles, the Battalion halted till the sun got lower. The march was resumed at 4 p.m., and at 10 p.m., the road being blocked, they halted 5 miles short of Zagazig and bivouacked. They moved on next morning and bivouacked near the railway-station.

On the 16th the Battalion trained to Benha, and on the 26th left for Cairo by train at 12.30 p.m. While the Battalion was detraining at Cairo station some Egyptian artillery ammunition blew up in a train that was being shunted in the station. Surgeon-Major Tolmie and one Rifleman were wounded by flying pieces of shell. The Battalion only just got clear of the station in time to avoid a series of explosions which killed and wounded a good many natives, set the station on fire, and destroyed most of the station and a large quantity of stores. The Battalion then marched to Ghezireh and bivouacked. On the 30th all the troops in Cairo marched past the Khedive in Abdin Square, the Battalion forming part of the Brigade commanded by Major-General Sir Evelyn Wood, V.C., K.C.B.

On October 2 Sir Evelyn Wood presented to Quartermaster J. Wilkins the D.C.M. granted him for his services at Ingogo, and which had been refused at the time on the ground that, as he had got a commission since the action, he was no longer qualified to receive the decoration.

On October 29 the Battalion moved from Ghezireh to Abdin Barracks.

CHAPTER IV

Third Battalion: The Sudan

On the breaking up of the Expeditionary Force our 3rd Battalion became a part of the Army of Occupation in Egypt.

On February 3, 1883, Field-Marshal Lord Napier of Magdala, G.C.B., G.C.S.I., presented the V.C. to No. 3804, Private Frederick Corbett, 3rd K.R.R.C., which had been awarded him for conspicuous bravery during the reconnaissance upon Kafr-ed-Dowr on August 5, 1882, and also the D.C.M. to Q.M.S. Gaffney for distinguished conduct in the late campaign. The ceremony took place on parade on the Abdin Square, Cairo.

On April 17 four companies were detached to Kasr-el-Nil Barracks. On the 21st cholera broke out in Cairo, and three companies from Kasr-el-Nil were sent to Suez, under Major J. G. Crosbie. On July 23 the remainder of the Battalion, with Headquarters—less A Company (Captain Archer)—followed them there. The Battalion lost 20 N.C.O.s and Riflemen in five weeks from cholera, of whom half died at Suez or near it.

On September 11 Headquarters and seven Companies returned to Cairo, and the Battalion was again stationed with Headquarters and four Companies at Abdin Barracks, the other four, under Major Crosbie, at Kasr-el-Nil.

The Sudan, 1884

The British Government, in accepting the task of restoring order in Egypt, had unwittingly made itself responsible for finding a solution of the problem of Egypt's vast dependency, the Sudan. This province had been misgoverned by Egyptian—that is, Turkish—officials, ever since its conquest under Mehemet Ali, some sixty years before, except during the Governorship of Gordon Pasha,[1] who warned the Khedive on his retirement that by introducing good government into the Sudan he had made it impossible for any Turk to govern there again. It should be remembered that in those days the governing class of Egypt were Turks by descent, and all officials who were not foreigners were of Turkish race. The official of Egyptian race is a product of our occupation.

In 1881 one Mohammed Ahmed, a native of Dongola, had taken up his abode on an island on the White Nile and given out that he was the Mahdi, foretold by Mahomet, and had a divine mission to reform Islam and the world generally. In July 1881 the Governor-General of the Sudan, hearing that this man's influence was spreading among the surrounding tribes, sent a deputation with a small military escort requesting Mohammed Ahmed to come to Khartum and discuss matters with him. Mohammed Ahmed declined this invitation to walk into the Pasha's parlour.

To this rebuff the Pasha replied by sending, in August, 200 Regular soldiers, with orders to arrest the offender. The Mahdi turned out with a force of 4,000 followers and fell on the Egyptians, of whom only 80 escaped alive to their steamer.

The Governor of the Sudan—or it should be said one Governor after another—did what he could with the forces at his disposal, with almost continuous failure as a result. By the end of 1882 the greater part of the Sudan, with the exception of places held by Egyptian garrisons, may

[1] Major-General C. G. Gordon, C.B. (Chinese Gordon).

be said to have been 'up' in favour of the Mahdi. The British Government 'cared for none of these things.' They had taken the responsibility for restoring good government in Egypt, including the reorganisation of the Egyptian Army, but considered that the rebellion in the Sudan was a matter with which Egypt must be left to deal herself. The Egyptian Government did what it could by conscribing some 10,000 of Arabi's old army and sending them up to Khartum. Service in the Sudan, never popular with the Egyptian soldiers, was less so than ever now, and the conscripts had to be brought in chained together. The result of making war with this unpromising material was that in November 1883 the only Egyptian field Army, under Hicks Pasha, a retired officer of the Indian Army, was wiped out by the Mahdi's forces in an attempt to reconquer Kordofan.

The immediate outcome of this disaster was that H.M. Government postponed the impending reduction of the Army of Occupation. At the same time the Egyptian Government was informed that H.M. Government would not employ either British or Indian troops in the Sudan, and that the Egyptian Army, then being raised under Sir E. Wood, was intended for the defence of Egypt only. Finally, on the Egyptian Government approaching the Sultan with a request for the loan of Turkish troops to reconquer the Sudan, they were informed that so long as the British occupation lasted they must take their orders from the British Government and that, in this case, the orders were that the Sudan should be evacuated. After a resignation and change of ministry these conditions were accepted, and the question arose of how the various Egyptian garrisons in the Sudan should be withdrawn. During 1883 the tribes of the Eastern Sudan had been raised for the Mahdi by Osman

Digna, the grandson of a Turkish merchant and slave-dealer, who himself had been a partner in a good trading business in the Sudan and ports of the Red Sea till his fortunes had been considerably impaired by the capture of one or two cargoes of slaves by British cruisers. The disgruntled Osman took up the cause of the Mahdi and became his Emir for the Eastern Sudan, the home of the Fuzzy-Wuzzy. He laid siege to Sinkat, some 50 miles from Suakim, and to Tokar, 16 miles from Trinkitat, on the coast of the Red Sea to the south of Suakim. In November 1883 a force of 550 men from Suakim went by sea to Trinkitat and marched to the relief of Tokar. They were attacked by not more than 200 tribesmen and stampeded, leaving 11 officers and 148 men on the ground. Among the killed was Captain Moncrieff, R.N., British Consul at Suakim.

In December an attempt was made to relieve Sinkat with 700 black troops, recently raised for the purpose near Massowah. They were attacked by 2,000 to 3,000 Arabs and wiped out. They put up a gallant fight, and only 35 escaped.

The next effort to relieve the beleaguered garrisons was made by sending a force from Egypt under General Valentine Baker, then commanding the Egyptian gendarmerie. Baker's force amounted to about 4,000 men, and consisted partly of Egyptian police, partly of untrained fellaheen, and the rest made up from the sweepings of the streets of Cairo and Alexandria. This attempt was more disastrous than the previous ones. Half-way between Trinkitat and Tokar, on February 4, 1884, the force was attacked and almost annihilated. Out of 3,746 men engaged, 2,373 were killed, including 11 European officers. On the return of the remnant to Suakim, though the garrison consisted of 3,000 Egyptian troops, these could not be relied on, and Admiral Hewitt took over the defence from Baker Pasha, landing a force of seamen and marines for this purpose. On the 12th came the news of the fall of Sinkat. Tewfik Bey, a member of the reigning family, after an heroic defence and when starved out, made a final sortie in which he was killed and his force wiped out, only five men escaping the general massacre.

After these happenings public opinion became too strong for the British Government to keep any longer to its policy of non-intervention in the Sudan, and a relief force was sent to Suakim, composed partly of troops from Egypt and partly of units on their way home from India. This force, consisting of two Cavalry Regiments, five Infantry Battalions and a Battalion of Marines, 100 Mounted Infantry, and a proportion of Artillery and Engineers, was under the command of Major-General Sir Gerald Graham, V.C., with Major-General John Davis and Brigadier-General Sir Redvers Buller, V.C., commanding the Infantry Brigades.

On February 8 our 3rd Battalion got their orders, and embarked at Suez on the 16th in the s.s. *Bokhara* and *Osiris*. The following Officers sailed with the Battalion:—

Colonel Sir Cromer Ashburnham, K.C.B.
Lieut.-Colonel W. L. K. Ogilvy
Major J. G. Crosbie
Major E. L. Fraser
Captain W. S. Anderson
Captain E. W. Herbert
Lieutenant Hon. C. S. G. Canning
Lieutenant G. C. Baker
Lieutenant H. E. B. Riddell
Lieutenant F. M. Beaumont
Lieutenant Hon. E. T. Stanhope
Lieutenant W. H. Kennedy,
Lieutenant G. L. B. Killick
Lieutenant R. L. Bower
Lieutenant G. N. Prendergast
Lieutenant W. H. Salmon
Lieutenant C. E. Ross
Lieutenant and Adjutant C. R. R. McGrigor
Lieutenant and Quartermaster J. Wilkins

Lieutenant P. Marling with 27 O.R., embarked in H.M. troopship *Orontes* with the Mounted Infantry.

Elliott & Fry, Ltd.
FIELD-MARSHAL THE RT HON. FRANCIS LORD GRENFELL, G.C.B., G.C.M.G.

On February 24, while the relief force was disembarking at Trinkitat, news was received that Tokar had fallen. The defence had not been an heroic affair. Most of the soldiers and the townspeople had been in favour of surrender, and the Governor had fallen in with their views and given up the place without being seriously attacked and while still in possession of an abundance of ammunition and supplies.

Though the object of the expedition seemed to have vanished with the fall of both the places to be relieved, the Government decided that the force should advance to Tokar notwithstanding. Whether this was done so as not to disappoint the troops, to show the Arabs what we might have done if we had not been too late, or to safeguard Suakim by giving Osman Digna a thrashing, was never explained.

Our 3rd Battalion disembarked at Suakim on February 19, re-embarked on the 21st, and landed at Trinkitat on February 23, where Lieut.-Colonel Ogilvy was appointed Base Commandant and Disembarking Officer.

The force was divided into two Brigades, as under :—

First Brigade (*Buller*)	*Second Brigade* (*Davis*)
3rd K.R.R.C.	1st Black Watch
1st Gordons	1st York and Lancaster Regt.
2nd Royal Irish Fusiliers	Royal Marine L.I.

Mounted Troops (Brigadier-General Herbert Stewart), 10th and 19th Hussars, and Mounted Infantry. Also 2 Batteries R.A., 9- and 7-pounders. Naval Brigade, Gatlings and Gardners.

On the 26th, after a reconnaissance by the mounted troops, Fort Baker, two miles inland across marshy ground, was occupied by the Gordon Highlanders and Royal Irish Fusiliers.

The next two days were spent in transporting three days' supplies for the force, including water, to Fort Baker, where by the evening of the 28th the whole force was concentrated. The enemy had for the last few days been assembled, about 2,000 strong, a couple of miles away, and had kept up a continuous fire on our outposts.

At 8 a.m. on the 29th the force advanced in a square formation: front face, 1st Gordon Highlanders; right, 2nd R.I.F. and 3rd K.R.R.C.; rear, 1st Black Watch; left, R.M.L.I. and 1st Y. and L. The Naval Gatlings and Gardners were at the two front corners, the R.A. 7-pounders at the two rear corners of the square. The Cavalry, except for those covering the front and flanks of the march, followed in rear.

The first two miles were heavy and marshy and the guns were being dragged by hand, so progress was slow.

After a mile had been covered, the enemy opened with rifle fire, but retired slowly before the British force, keeping within about 1,200 yards.

About 10 a.m. reports came in from the Mounted Infantry, who had been sent out to get in touch, that the enemy were in position to the left front.

By 11.20 a.m. the square was directly in front of the enemy's position, which was about 800 yards away and consisted of a line of rough earthworks facing west by north, having on its right a battery of two Krupp guns and two brass howitzers and on its left two Krupp guns and one brass howitzer.

The guns were manned by Egyptian gunners, from the garrison of Tokar. Graham marched the square on, across the enemy's front, under a heavy but ill-aimed fire which mostly passed overhead, till he reached a point about 900 yards due west of the enemy's left battery. Here the square halted, turning to its left, which brought

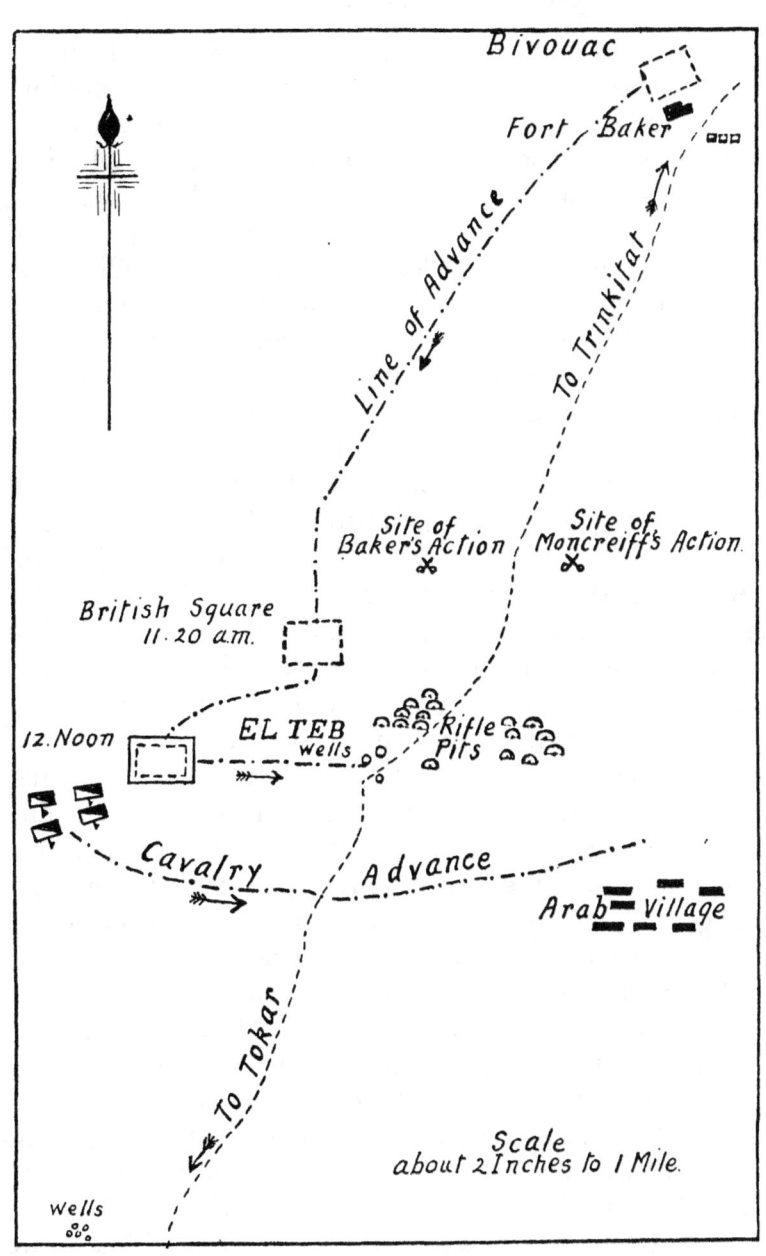

PLATE 9.
BATTLE OF EL TEB, FEBRUARY 29, 1884.

the York and Lancaster Regiment and Marines in front, and while the men lay down the British guns came into action and speedily knocked out the enemy's battery. The order was then given to advance. As the leading Battalions reached the entrenchments, the Arabs began to come out of cover and charge, not *en masse*, but in isolated groups of from 20 or 30 down to single men. When the battery on the left had been accounted for, the sides of the square wheeled up and the force moved on in an irregular line, sweeping the whole length of the enemy's position, but meeting with the stoutest resistance all the way. Most of the charging Arabs were shot down before they could get to close quarters, but not all of them, and there was a good deal of hand-to-hand fighting. Though the advance had begun about noon, it was not till after 2 p.m. that the battery on the right was taken. By this time all resistance had ceased and the enemy was in full flight. While their front line were fighting with such determination, a large body of the enemy, which must have been in reserve in rear of the position, was seen moving away. Colonel Stewart took the Cavalry round the British right and charged this mass of men, riding through them several times, but incurring pretty severe loss in doing so, the Arabs fighting to the last and hamstringing the horses with their swords as they passed.

Our 3rd Battalion sustained a great loss in the death of Quartermaster J. Wilkins, who was shot dead early in the action. As has been already told, he showed great gallantry at the Ingogo as R.S.M. and had only recently received the D.C.M. which he earned on that occasion.

The total losses of the force were 4 Officers, 26 O.R. killed (of whom 3 Officers and 13 O.R. fell in the Cavalry charge), 17 Officers and 142 O.R. wounded.

The numbers engaged and losses of the Arabs are

variously estimated, but the most reliable estimate seems to have been that about 3,000 men held the position and the reserves charged by the Cavalry were another two or three thousand.

There were 825 bodies actually counted on the ground.

Besides the Quartermaster, our 3rd Battalion's losses at El Teb were : died of wounds, 2 N.C.O.s and Riflemen ; wounded, 4 N.C.O.s and Riflemen.

The force bivouacked at the wells near the battlefield and marched next morning to Tokar. A few shots were fired at the mounted troops as they neared the town, but any enemy there was had left by the time the main force arrived, leaving the Egyptian garrison behind them, some still in possession of their arms.

The next day the Cavalry visited the enemy's abandoned camp at Dubba, three miles off, where was found much of the loot taken at Baker's defeat, including 1,500 Remington rifles and a 7-pounder gun. The troops then marched back to Trinkitat, where they began re-embarking for Suakim. Our 3rd Battalion embarked in s.s. *Utopia* and H.M.S. *Dryad* on March 8 and 10, and landed at Suakim the same day. On the 9th the change of base from Trinkitat to Suakim was complete, and the Black Watch, on that day, marched out and occupied a zariba, constructed by Baker some weeks before, eight miles on the road to Sinkat, this being the first step in the next move of the campaign, which was to beat up Osma Digna's camp at Tamaai, a few miles farther on the road to Sinkat.

The 9th and 10th were spent in forwarding stores and water to Baker's zariba, and on the 11th the whole force, except the Cavalry and Mounted Infantry, was assembled at that spot. The march was made in the evening on account of the heat, and the troops were not all in till midnight. The mounted troops arrived at daybreak and pushed on to reconnoitre. At 10 a.m. it was reported that the enemy were in great strength about six miles farther on. Dinners were ordered and at 1 p.m. the force marched, not in one square as at El Teb, but in echelon of Brigades, the 2nd Brigade leading, the 1st Brigade following from 600 to 900 yards to its right rear. The heat was great, the march was much obstructed by mimosa scrub, and progress was slow; the country also was gradually getting hilly. About 5 p.m. the scouts reported that the enemy, about 4,000 strong, were advancing to the attack. The force was immediately formed up where a clear field of fire of about 100 yards could be obtained, and work was begun in forming a zariba out of the mimosa scrub. The enemy appearing on a ridge about 1,200 yards away, they were shelled by two 9-pounder guns and disappeared again. The men bivouacked where they stood, and the enemy kept up a dropping fire most of the night. At sunrise a body of the enemy was again dispersed by artillery fire. The mounted troops arrived soon afterwards from Baker's zariba, where they had spent the night, and the Mounted Infantry went out to reconnoitre. At 8 a.m. the whole force continued the advance, in the same formation as on the previous day. The order of General Davis's Brigade, which General Graham accompanied, was: front face, half battalion Y. and L. Regiment, half battalion Black Watch; right face, half battalion Y. and L. Regiment; left face, half battalion Black Watch; rear face, R.M.L.I.

The march led across a plateau, intersected by dry watercourses, leading down to a deep and wide ravine about 60 feet deep and 100 yards wide, and it was soon reported by the Cavalry that this ravine was full of Arabs.

When the square got to within 200 yards of the ravine the Arabs began a series of broken and irregular rushes against the front and right of the square, which was stopped by rifle fire. At this moment General Graham—so it is said, and I can't find that it has ever been contradicted—personally gave the Black Watch the order to charge, which they did up to the edge of the ravine. As the Y. and L. Regiment, who were so far receiving most of the enemy's attention, were halted and firing, the advance of the 42nd made a break in the square, into which the Fuzzy-Wuzzies poured. The result was very nearly a complete disaster. To add to the confusion and to the great advantage of the attackers, there was not a breath of wind, which in those days of black powder was a necessity if a firing line was to see a yard in front of it after the first few rounds. It is unnecessary, if it were possible, to describe in detail what happened in the next few minutes; all that seems certain is that officers and men kept their heads and there was not a sign of panic, although in the soldiers' battle that followed, the whole square, which had ceased to be a regular formation, but a mass of hastily formed groups intermingled with Arabs, was borne back by sheer weight of numbers for about 500 yards; until, partly by its own efforts and partly by the support of Buller's Brigade and the Cavalry, the attack was driven off and the Brigade sorted itself out into line with the Marines on the right, Y. and L. Regiment in the centre, and 42nd on the left.

Meanwhile Buller's Brigade, formed with Gordons right and front, R.I.F. front and left, 3rd K.R.R.C. in rear, had been attacked at the same time as the 2nd Brigade, but as it was then some 500 or 600 yards from the ravine it had a clear field of fire and no Arab got within eighty yards of it.

After beating off his own assailants, Buller moved his square to its left and brought a heavy cross-fire to bear on those of the other Brigade. At the same time the Cavalry had been taken by Stewart round to the enemy's right and, dismounting, brought their fire to bear from that flank. This was too much for the Arabs, and they were soon streaming back into and across the ravine. The 2nd Brigade, after re-forming and replenishing ammunition, again advanced, and by 11 a.m. were back at the edge of the ravine, having recovered the guns, which had for a time been in the enemy's hands. The 1st Brigade moved on across the ravine and, on reaching a ridge half a mile off, which the retreating enemy occupied for a time but did not defend, found themselves looking down on the tents and huts of Osman Digna's camp, which was occupied before midday.

Our losses were: 5 Officers, 105 O.R. killed; 7 Officers, 103 O.R. wounded. Of the Officers killed, three were in the Naval Brigade, which had shown the greatest gallantry in the defence of its Gatling guns. It was no thanks to General Graham that the whole 2nd Brigade was not cut up, as his order to the 42nd to charge was indefensible. As usual, the numbers and losses of the enemy are uncertain, but the number engaged was probably not far short of 10,000, and some 1,000 of them lay dead on the spot. After destroying the enemy's camp and with it half a million small-arm ammunition and a large quantity of artillery ammunition, captured from Baker's force at El Teb, the force returned to Suakim on March 15.

The losses of our 3rd Battalion at Tamaai were: died of wounds, 1 Rifleman; wounded, 1 Sergeant, 5 Riflemen, of whom one was wounded the day before the action and two the day after.

On March 25 Graham again advanced with his two

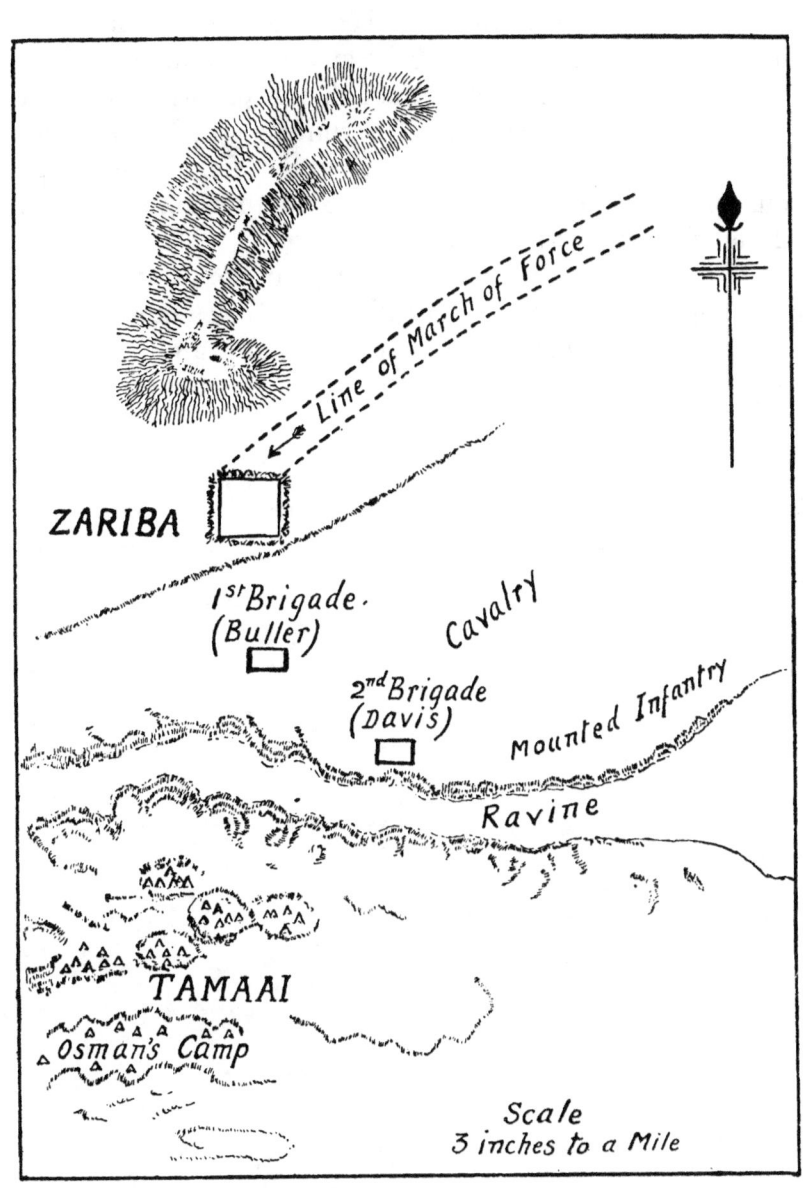

PLATE 10.
BATTLE OF TAMAAI, MARCH 13, 1884.

Brigades to a zariba eleven miles from Suakim. The troops suffered very much from the heat and fell out in great numbers. Next day he again advanced and destroyed the village of Tamanieb. Though the enemy were seen in the distance in considerable numbers and had been reported to be anxious to renew the fight, they kept out of range, and the force returned to Suakim on the 28th without further fighting.

The force was then broken up, our 3rd Battalion remaining at Suakim till May 10, when they embarked on H.M.S. *Orontes* for Egypt, landing at Alexandria on the 18th.

CHAPTER V

First Battalion

The end of 1877 found the 1st Battalion at Portsmouth, with detachments at Tipnor and Marchwood.

On December 19 Colonel C. A. B. Gordon retired from the Service and was succeeded in Command by Lieut.-Colonel J. D. Dundas.

On January 1, 1878, the helmet, the most hideous headdress ever conceived by man and the one least suited to our uniform, took the place of the busby.

About this time the collapse of Turkey in the Russo-Turkish War brought us to the brink of war with Russia, and in April the Army Reserve was called out for the first time since its formation.

On April 1 the establishment of the Battalion was raised to 1,000 rank and file, and soon afterwards a party of Reservists and fifty privates from the 2nd Middlesex Rifle Militia—afterwards our 7th Battalion—joined the Battalion. At the same time I and K Companies went to Winchester to be amalgamated with the Rifle Depôt.

In July, peace having been assured, the Reservists were retransferred to the Reserve. On August 27 H.Q. and five Companies moved from Portsmouth to Winchester, leaving a Company at Portsmouth which rejoined H.Q. on October 9.

The detachments from Tipnor and Marchwood rejoined on February 15, 1880. On June 29 the Battalion moved temporarily to Aldershot, where it was encamped on Rushmoor Bottom for the summer drills.

On July 13 it marched from Aldershot to Ascot, taking part on the 14th in a Review before the Queen in Windsor Great Park, returning to Ascot the same evening and to Aldershot next day.

On July 26 the Battalion railed to Winchester, but returned to Aldershot on August 7, where it was quartered in the North Camp.

On December 22 the Battalion moved to Athlone.

During the latter years of the nineteenth century and the beginning of the twentieth the 'eighties' were always referred to in Ireland as 'the Bad Times,' though they were tame compared with what was to follow. However, the 'No Rent Campaign' was then at its height, and troops throughout Ireland were scattered in small detachments and were frequently called out in aid of the Civil Power.

Though the troops were seldom, if ever, compelled to take action—the law breakers, though they looked upon the R.I.C. as fair game, always looked upon the arrival of the troops as the time to stop—this entailed a good many long marches and exposure to all kinds of weather.

While the Headquarters remained at Athlone, about half the Battalion was scattered in detachments throughout Mayo and Roscommon.

On July 2, 1881, by the capsizing of a sailing-boat on Lough Ree, Sergeant-Major Mitchell (the father of several good Riflemen), Colour-Sergeant James Thompson, Sergeant Isaac Steward, and Sergeant John Crowley (Master Tailor) were drowned. The only one of the party to be saved was a Frenchman, the Officers' mess-cook.

On September 20 H.Q. and four Companies moved from Athlone to Curragh Camp, there to be stationed.

On January 7, 1882, Colonel Dundas retired and was succeeded by Lieut.-Colonel G. Hatchell.

On August 9 three Companies moved to the Royal Barracks, Dublin. On the 10th they were joined by H.Q. and the remaining company from the Curragh, the four Companies from detachment in the West of Ireland rejoining the same day.

On February 2, 1883, Sergeant Danvers, of the Battalion, was granted an annuity of £10 with a silver medal ' for meritorious and distinguished conduct in assisting the Civil Power on the occasion of the assassination of a Police Constable in Dublin on November 27, 1882.'

The Battalion, after two years in Dublin, moved to Limerick on August 8, 1884 ; H.Q. and six Companies being quartered in New Barracks, two Companies in Castle Barracks.

On November 5, 1885, H.Q. and four Companies moved to Kinsale, the other four Companies going on detachment to Cork Harbour—two Companies at Fort Carlisle and two at Haulbowline.

On January 7, 1886, Lieut.-Colonel George Hatchell went on half-pay, and was succeeded in command by Lieut.-Colonel Astley Terry.

On August 20 the Battalion left Kinsale, sailing the same day from Queenstown for Portsmouth, arriving at Parkhurst, Isle of Wight, on the 23rd, and sending detachments to East Cowes and Marchwood.

The Battalion was inspected by Her Majesty the Queen at Osborne on February 7, 1887.

On July 6 the Battalion moved to Aldershot to take part in Queen Victoria's Jubilee Review. There they formed part of a Brigade of Rifles, of which the other Battalions were : our own 2nd Battalion, the 2nd Battalion Rifle Brigade, and the 1st Battalion Royal Irish Rifles.

The Review took place in the Long Valley on July 9.

It had been a hot and dry summer and the dust was such as can never have been seen in the British Isles before or since. It was a dead still day, and the dust raised by marching troops went up in a pillar of cloud. Except on the saluting base, where the ground was watered, the troops were enveloped all day in a fog of dust. The soldier of to-day, who does not possess a tunic, or, if he does, seldom wears it out-of-doors, has much to be thankful for. The Battalion returned to Parkhurst on the 11th.

On July 15 Colonel C. P. Cramer assumed command of the Battalion in place of Colonel Astley Terry, who had been allowed to stay on over the Jubilee Review, though his time had been up on June 30.

On May 1, 1888, the Battalion moved to Aldershot, being stationed in the Centre Infantry (Salamanca) Barracks.

Aldershot was then a peaceful place compared to what it has been since the South African War; still, there was some attempt made there to train troops for the Field, especially after the arrival of Sir Evelyn Wood. There was ground to train on, there were numerous field-days, and what were known as Flying Columns were sent out for a week or so at a time to carry out a sort of Brigade training. There was plenty of ground and plenty of time for company training, but as such things as tactical exercises without troops were unknown outside the Staff College, there were very few company officers who had any idea how even to begin to train their companies, and company training consisted in most cases of a series of cut-and-dried performances taken word for word from the exceedingly formal Drill-book of the day.

In January 1890 the new magazine (Lee-Metford ·303) rifle was issued to the Battalion.

In October the Lee-Metford rifles were returned, and the Martini-Henry, which was still in use in India, was re-issued to the Battalion previous to its move to that country.

The Battalion embarked at Portsmouth on November 25, 1890, for India, in H.M.S. *Crocodile*: strength, 21 Officers; 825 Other Ranks.

The voyage, as was usual with the old troopships, was not without incident. In the middle of the Indian Ocean the main crank broke. The ship drifted about, fortunately in a flat calm, for twenty-four hours, when she was picked up by H.M.S. *Serapis*, a homeward-bound troopship, and towed into Bombay Harbour on December 26.

The Battalion disembarked on the 27th and, after the usual stay of a few days at Deolali, arrived at Rawal Pindi on January 8. On its way up-country the Battalion was inspected at Umballa by H.E. General Sir Frederick Roberts, Commander-in-Chief in India.

The movement of troops by rail in India in those days was a leisurely performance. They travelled by night and spent the day in rest-camps. The Battalion halted at Khandwah, Hoshangabad, Jhansi, Tundla (near Agra), and Umballa—not a bad way of seeing a little of the country for new arrivals who were about to spend some years in the Punjab.

At Rawal Pindi the Battalion was quartered at West Ridge; the Officers in tents, the men in huts.

Within three months of their arrival they were fortunate enough to see active service on the Frontier.

NORTH-WEST FRONTIER, 1891–2–5
HAZARA AND MIRANZAI, 1891

In the cold weather of 1890–1 occurred one of the periodical outbreaks of unrest on the North-west Frontier of India. An expedition was sent to the Black Mountain, on the Hazara Border, under Major-General W. K. Elles, C.B., Commanding the Rawal Pindi District. The expeditionary force consisted of two mixed Brigades with Divisional Troops; a Reserve Brigade was also formed at Rawal Pindi, consisting of one squadron 11th Bengal Lancers, 1st K.R.R.C., 19th Bengal Infantry, and 27th Punjab Infantry.

Brigadier-General Sir William Lockhart, commanding the Punjab Frontier Force, was designated for command of this Brigade, should it be called up.

Towards the end of March the Bunerwals, a large trans-Indus tribe, an expedition against whom had resulted in some hard fighting in 1861 and who had given no trouble since, began to show signs of joining in. The Reserve Brigade was consequently called up, and a fourth Brigade was formed at Hoti Mardan, the H.Q. of the Guides.

Our 1st Battalion marched from Rawal Pindi on Good Friday, March 27, to Jani-Ka-Sang, a short march of 11 miles. The next day's march was 15 miles, and on the third day on reaching Haripur, 13 miles, at 1 p.m., they got orders to do another march of 8 miles that afternoon, and, starting at 5 p.m., did not reach their bivouac till after dark. They forded a river and bivouacked the other side of it, so as to save time in the morning. Next morning an early start was made so as to get over the best part of the last march into Durband, the base of the expedition, in the cool of the morning, as the weather was beginning to 'stoke up.' It was then found that they were on an island, and had only crossed a branch of the river the previous evening and had another to cross in the dark. What with the delay caused by fording the river in the dark and the time taken to load the pack transport, at which neither Officers nor men had had any experience, the sun was up before the Battalion got well under way. By the time they reached the first place where there was water and they could halt for breakfast—some 15 miles—a great number of men had fallen out (some with heat apoplexy), the transport was all over the place, and the rearguard miles behind. A halt was made for some hours, and a fresh start was made at 3 p.m. to march the remaining nine miles into Durband, but it was still very hot in the stifling Indus Valley and the men immediately began to fall out again. Another halt was made till the cool of the evening, when the Battalion pulled itself together and got into Durband in rather better shape.

The truth is that, although the Battalion had been detailed for the Reserve Brigade for the best part of a month, nothing whatever had been done either to get them fit or to teach officers or men their work. There are two essentials for active service on the North-west Frontier, physical fitness and a thorough knowledge of pack transport. The 1st Battalion at this time had very few Officers who had seen any active service, and only one who had served on the Indian Frontier. The few, including the C.O., who had been on service before had done it in South Africa, where they had not encountered the camel. Another fact which had not been realised was that the British soldier cannot march in heat on an empty stomach. The writer has on three occasions seen a Battalion of the Regiment completely laid out, and on each occasion it has been owing to a combination of heat and something having gone wrong with the breakfast arrangements.

The Bunerwal threat passed away and the Reserve Brigade twiddled their thumbs at Durband for a few days, when, a fresh outbreak having taken place on the Miranzai Border, Sir William Lockhart was given command of the new expedition and the Reserve Brigade went off to join him.

To punish the Orakzais, an important tribe of Pathans living to the north of the Miranzai Border, who had been raiding into British territory, an expedition had been sent under Sir William Lockhart in January of this same year. The enemy offered no resistance, his country was thoroughly penetrated by the various columns, towers were blown up and fines imposed. The clans made full submission and agreed to the terms dictated, which included the occupation of the Samana Ridge, along the crest line of which ran the border, by posts of Border Police with mule roads connecting them. Though there was no fighting, the troops had suffered severely from the severity of the climate, thirty-three severe cases of frost-bite having been treated in hospital.

The Field Force was finally broken up on March 1, leaving the 29th Punjab Infantry to protect the working parties on the Samana. Very soon after the dispersal of the force reports came in that the young men of the clans which had been visited were being taunted with cowardice by their *mullahs* and womenfolk for not having shown fight, and that further trouble might be expected.

At the beginning of April the 29th Punjab Infantry was stationed along the foot of the southern slope of the Samana with one post only actually on the Ridge. On the morning of April 4 the guards for the working parties went out as usual. During the morning all the guards were simultaneously attacked. The 29th Punjab Infantry made an attempt to clear the range of the attackers, but found themselves completely outnumbered, and it was with difficulty that the next day the post at Tsalai was relieved and withdrawn. The losses in the attack and subsequent fighting were 14 killed and 7 wounded.

This temporary success encouraged the enemy. Nearly the whole of the Orakzais came out and were joined by a certain number of adventurous spirits among the Afridis, the most important tribe on the frontier and the next-door neighbours to the Orakzais to the north.

Orders were sent for Sir William Lockhart to march his Brigade to Kohat at once.

Our 1st Battalion left Durband on the afternoon of April 7 and marched 8 miles. Next day they marched 23 miles to Haripur. On the 9th they marched 8 miles to a camping ground, where they left the left half Battalion, the right half and H.Q. going on to Hassan Abdal, another 13 miles. They entrained there next morning and detrained at Kushalghar in the afternoon, crossing the Indus and camping on the other side of it, the left half Battalion joining them there. Two more marches of about 16 miles each brought them to Kohat on the 12th. Here the Battalion halted till the 15th and stored all kit beyond the lightest active-service scale. The march from Durband had shown that the men were now quite fit, as hardly a man had fallen out, in spite of the daily increasing heat. The opportunity was taken during the two days' halt to have all ranks thoroughly instructed in loading pack animals, and from Kohat on the transport gave no further trouble.

On the 15th the Battalion marched to Chilibagh and on the 16th to Hangu, two short marches. At Hangu they joined the rest of their Brigade, which now included the 1/5th Gurkhas, and the two Regiments made great friends. Another Battalion of the Brigade was the 1st Punjab Infantry (Coke's Rifles), who had fought alongside of the Battalion on the Ridge at Delhi.

On April 16 Lockhart's force was ready for action, disposed as follows :—

First Column at Hangu
(Colonel J. M. Sym, C.B.).
No. 3 Mountain Battery, R.A.

1st K.R.R.C.

Half No. 5 Co. Bengal Sappers and Miners.
1st Punjab Infantry
27th Bengal Infantry
1/5th Gurkha Rifles.
Divisional Troops :
  5th Punjab Cavalry (2 Squadrons).
  19th Bengal Lancers
  Punjab Garrison Battery (3 guns).

Second Column at Durband
(Lieut.-Colonel A. H. Turner).
No. 3 (Peshawar) Mountain Battery.
Half No. 5 Co. Bengal Sappers and Miners.
3rd Sikh Infantry.

2nd Punjab Infantry
15th Bengal Infantry

Third Column at Durband
(Lieut.-Colonel C. C. Brownlow).
No. 2 Mountain Battery R.A. (3 guns).
6th Punjab Infantry
19th Bengal Infantry
29th Bengal Infantry

The force totalled about 7,400 men, and was augmented later on by half a Battalion of the Manchester Regiment and the 1/4th Gurkhas.

On the 17th No. 1 Column left Hangu at dawn, the G.O.C. accompanying it, and reached Lakka, a stiff climb of 1,300 feet, without opposition. The G.O.C. then ordered the second Column to meet him at Durband Kotal and the 3rd to advance by Pat Durband on Sangar. The first Column then moved west along the crest, the 1st K.R.R.C. leading.

The second Column got orders to cross the ridge when

the first had passed, to move down to Shifaldara and up the Khanki River to Gwada. As the leading Company of the 1st Battalion came in sight of Tsalai, a solitary stone tower, they came under rifle fire, the first sign they had seen of the enemy. The two leading Companies were deployed and advanced under a smart but ill-aimed fire, supported by the fire of the Mountain Battery. They reached the tower to find it evacuated. During the advance the C.O. (Colonel C. P. Cramer) and 3 N.C.O.s and men were wounded, as were Major C. C. Egerton (Lockhart's A.A.G.) and his orderly. Gogra (another tower) and Sangar, a fortified village, were then occupied without further loss.

The third Column, having driven some of the enemy out of Dhar, joined the first at Sangar, and the two Columns bivouacked on the terrace surrounding the village. The second Column, reinforced by the 27th B.I., had meanwhile occupied Gwada, with a loss of 1 killed and 4 wounded.

It had been a severe day for troops, on account of the hard climbing, the distance covered, the fierce sun, and the shortage of water. Men had only what they carried in their water-bottles and got very little more that night. On the 18th the 1st and 3rd Columns cleared the Mastan plateau of the enemy with a loss of of 1 Officer and 6 Other Ranks wounded, the first Column then returning to Sangar.

On the 19th the second Column was withdrawn from the Khanki Valley to Sangar for convenience of supply, and was followed up by the enemy all the way. Meanwhile the enemy, strongly reinforced, had begun an attack on the third Column, closing in on three sides of them and sniping their piquets. On the 20th, as the O.C. third Column did not feel himself strong enough to drive off the enemy the 1st K.R.R.C., 2nd P.I., 1/5th Gurkhas and Peshawar Mountain Battery were sent up as reinforcements. The

5th Gurkhas attacked Saragarhi under cover of the fire of the Peshawar Battery with the 1st K.R.R.C. in second line. The enemy made no stand, but did not give themselves enough start in the ensuing race down the Khud, and the Gurkhas took a pretty heavy toll of them, their losses being subsequently ascertained to have been about 300 killed and wounded. Our men only got in some long-range shooting at the disappearing enemy, to whom they probably did little damage. After destroying the towers and villages of Saragarhi and Ghuztang, the troops returned to their bivouacs.

The casualties for the day were 1 man K.R.R.C. killed (sniped on the line of march); 1 Officer and 6 men, from other Corps, wounded.

On the 21st the second Column advanced to Gulistan without opposition.

For the next few days Sir William Lockhart with the second Column, strengthened by two Infantry Battalions, cleared the country along the Samana as far as the Chagru Kotal, meeting with some opposition and inflicting considerable loss on the enemy, with very little on our side. By April 24 the enemy had had enough of it, and on that and the following days *jirgas* (deputations) came in and submitted to terms.

The fighting was over, but various parts of the country had still to be visited. On April 27 Lockhart with the first Column (less half a Battalion K.R.R.C.) marched to Hangu. On the 29th he started to march round the north-east end of the Samana Range by Mir Asghar—Dran—Kharai—Starkili—Gwada, reaching Sangar on May 3.

On the 9th the half Battalion K.R.R.C. which had been left behind joined the second Column at Gulistan as also did a half Battalion of the Manchester Regiment.

On the 10th the Column started for a march up the

Khanki Valley as far as Mamuzai Bazar, returning to Gulistan on the 15th.

This concluded the operations, the tribes having accepted all the conditions dictated to them. The British losses from the outbreak on April 4 to the end of the Expedition had been 28 killed and 73 wounded.

The 1st Battalion, after a false start which took them as far as Baliamin, being recalled to Mastan on the 18th, finally left that place to return to India on the 22nd. Marching as far as Kushalgarh, they trained to Rawal Pindi on the 28th, going on by half Battalions to Gharial, in the Murree Hills, the next day and the day after, arriving there on May 31 and June 1. Though they had not had much fighting, they had had a lot of hard marching, had a good training in frontier service conditions, and came back a very different Battalion from the one that set out.

On June 30, 1891, Colonel C. P. Cramer retired on retired pay, and Major the Hon. Keith Turnour took over command pending the arrival of Lieut.-Colonel H. B. MacCall, who was on sick-leave in England.

In November the Battalion marched down again from Gharial to West Ridge.

Lieut.-Colonel MacCall joined and assumed command on January 27, 1892.

In April H.Q. and four Companies marched up to Ghora Dhaka, Murree Hills, for the hot weather, the remaining half Battalion (less half a Company on detachment at Campbellpore) moving into Church Lines, Rawal Pindi, the first place at which the Officers had slept under a roof since their arrival in the country.

On September 7 the Battalion was warned that it was to form part of the Isazai Field Force, under Major-General Sir William Lockhart.

Isazai Expedition, 1892

In the summer of 1892 Hashim Ali, ex-chief of the Isazai Clan, whose banishment had been one of the terms of peace at the end of the Black Mountain Expedition of the previous year, returned and began to make trouble.

An expedition was therefore prepared in September to turn him out and punish the tribes who had broken faith by permitting his return.

A force of two Brigades was concentrated at Durband, under Sir William Lockhart, on October 2.

On September 23 the Headquarter Companies started to march from Ghora Dhaka, via Abbotabad and Oghi, and on the 26th the half Battalion from Rawal Pindi railed to Hassan Abdal and marched by Haripur, the two halves meeting at Durband on October 1, where the Battalion joined the 2nd Infantry Brigade, under Brigadier-General A. G. Hammond, V.C.

The expedition came to nothing, as the enemy not only put up no fight but cleared right out of the country.

The 2nd Brigade crossed the Indus, marched up to Baio—a village on a hill, 4,000 feet above the river, overlooking the Indus Valley on one side and the whole country of Buner on the other—burnt a few villages, destroyed and ate up a considerable area of crops, and returned to Durband on October 8, where orders were received for the breaking-up of the force.

From the professional point of view it was particularly unfortunate that there should have been no enemy to experiment on, as one Company of the Battalion had had the Lee-Metford served out to them—the first that had been issued in India—and there was a detachment of the K.O.Y.L.I. with a Maxim gun in the force, the first to be sent on active service in India.

On October 10 the Battalion started on its return march to Rawal Pindi. Malarial fever, which was almost entirely confined to men of the half Battalion which had spent the hot weather in Rawal Pindi, began to show itself at this time. On reaching Jani-Ka-Sang, one march from Rawal Pindi, two cases of cholera broke out, and the Battalion went into quarantine camp close by at Margala, not being allowed to return to Rawal Pindi till October 28. During the time it remained in camp, though there was no more cholera, the malaria got worse and worse, and by the time the Battalion left nearly half its strength had preceded it to hospital in Rawal Pindi.

On arrival at Rawal Pindi the Battalion was stationed in Church Lines. Here a draft of 317 N.C.O.s and men joined it from the 4th Battalion, who were leaving Burmah for home.

In November the Lee-Metford Rifle was, for the second time, issued to the whole Battalion.

Starting on April 15, 1893, the Battalion marched to Gharial for the hot weather.

In November 1893 the Battalion marched down to West Ridge, Rawal Pindi. After taking part in cold-weather manœuvres, the Battalion marched to Peshawar in January 1894, reaching that station on the 24th.

B and G Companies went to Cherat for the hot weather, starting on May 10 and returning on October 28.

On March 10, 1895, the Battalion sustained a great loss in the death of their Adjutant, Lieutenant L. C. Maclachlan, who was killed at polo. He had a strong and attractive personality, and had been a great success during the few months that he had held the Adjutancy. He would, if he had lived, undoubtedly have gone far. He was a fine horseman and had a peculiar aptitude for games. He was one of five brothers, of whom two were killed in the

Great War—Brigadier-General R. C. Maclachlan in the Rifle Brigade and Lieut.-Colonel A. C. Maclachlan in our own Regiment. Another brother, N. C. Maclachlan, in the Seaforth Highlanders, was accidentally killed when on active service on the North-western Frontier.

On March 16 the Battalion was warned for service with the Chitral Relief Force.

The Chitral Relief Expedition, 1895

Chitral is a small Muhammadan native State, lying between northern Kashmir and Kafiristan, with the Hindu-Kush to the north of it and the jumble of petty Pathan States known as Kohistan to the south. Its people are unconnected racially with their neighbours, and are probably of Aryan race with a considerable dash of Mongol blood. Up till the eighties of last century their history, which had been the usual combination of civil war and assassination, had not brought them into touch with the Indian Government. In the early eighties the reigning Mehtar (Prince), to protect himself from annexation by Afghanistan, made, with the approval of the Indian Government, a treaty with the Maharajah of Kashmir, by which he acknowledged that ruler as his suzerain, on receipt of the promise of an annual subsidy. The policy of the Government of India was to control the foreign relations of Chitral in accordance with our interests.

Chitral was visited by British missions in 1885–6 and 1888–9, from the second of which the Mehtar obtained a subsidy of Rs. 6,000 per annum and a consignment of rifles.

It is not necessary to relate in detail the assassination of successive Mehtars and consequent political reactions— including the not uninvited intervention of the Indian

Government—since the death of Aman-ul-Mulk in 1892. Suffice it to say that the outcome had been that, by the first week in March 1895, Surgeon-Major Robertson, the British Agent, was besieged in Chitral Fort by Sher Afzal, one of the claimants to the Mehtarship, backed by Umra Khan, a Pathan chieftain who had made himself master of a great part of Kohistan and had for some time been inclined to interfere in Chitral affairs. The garrison of Chitral consisted of about 100 of the 14th Sikhs, 300 4th Kashmir Rifles (Imperial Service Troops), 52 Chitralis, and 85 followers, a total of 543 persons. Supplies, on half-rations, were estimated to be enough to hold out for two and a half months. Ammunition was very short— about 300 rounds per rifle. After the wounding of Captain Campbell (Central Indian Horse) on March 3, the garrison was commanded by Captain Townshend[1] of the same Regiment.

There were two ways of relieving Chitral: one from Gilgit over the Shandur Pass, most of it roadless, through a mountainous country, at that time of year considered impassable. The other led from Naoshera, on the Kabul River, by the Malakhand Pass, into the Swat Valley; thence across the Panjkora River through Jandol (Umra Khan's Headquarters), by Dir and the Lowari Pass, into the valley of the river which flows past Chitral and has various names in different parts of its course. The latter route is much the easier physically, but a force following it would have to fight the whole way against warlike and fanatical tribes.

The story of the march from Gilgit to Chitral by Lieut.-Colonel Kelly, with his 400 Sikh Pioneers and one section of a Mountain Battery, and the relief of Chitral by them

[1] Major-General Sir C. V. Townshend, K.C.B., D.S.O. (the defender of Kut).

on April 20, does not come into our regimental history, but every soldier should read it.

On March 14, though they had not yet heard that our forces in Chitral had been actually attacked, the Government of India—anticipating trouble if Umra Khan did not comply with their demand that he should withdraw from the part of the Chitral Valley which he had recently occupied—ordered the mobilisation of a Division. A week later, on receiving definite news of the attack, orders were issued for the immediate dispatch of the relieving force, under Lieut.-General Sir Robert Low, K.C.B.

The strength of the force was three Infantry Brigades and Divisional Troops, and the 1st Brigade, made up of 1st Bedfordshire Regiment, 1st K.R.R.C., 15th Sikhs, and 37th Dogras, was commanded by Brigadier-General A. A. Kinloch, C.B., who had recently commanded our 2nd and 4th Battalions.

The first object of the expedition, as stated by the Government, was "to relieve Chitral territory from invasion by Umra Khan."

To reach Umra Khan's country of Bajaur it was necessary to pass through the territory of other tribes, notably the Swatis. A proclamation was sent "to all the people of Swat, and the people of Bajaur who do not side with Umra Khan," setting out the purposes of the expedition and promising that the Government of India had no intention of "permanently occupying their territory or interfering with their independence." Very much the same as the communication addressed by Germany to Belgium in 1914 explaining the necessity for taking a short cut through their country to get at France; the only difference in the situation—apart from our not being the aggressors—was that we had not guaranteed the neutrality of Swat in case of war with its neighbours.

Meanwhile the Division had been concentrating at Naoshera, and on March 30 Divisional Headquarters, with the 2nd and 3rd Brigades, moved to Hoti Mardan and were followed by the 1st Brigade on the 31st.

Our 1st Battalion had left Peshawar on March 29 (strength, 18 Officers, 801 Other Ranks), and marched to Hoti Mardan, which it reached with the rest of the 1st Infantry Brigade on the 31st.

There are three passes leading from Mardan into Swat, the Morah, Shakot, and Malakhand. It was Sir Robert Lowe's intention to use the two latter, as the former is next door to the powerful Bunerwal tribe, to whom it was inadvisable to give an excuse for joining our enemies. The strongest tribes and most important chiefs had so far declared their intention to keep out of a quarrel which did not concern them, but it is difficult for the fanatically Muhammadan Pathan to neglect a chance of a fight with the Kafir, and large numbers of tribesmen had already assembled in the three passes, determined to oppose our passage.

On April 1 Sir Robert Lowe, with the 2nd and 3rd Brigades, marched to Jalala, i.e. towards the Malakhand Pass, while the 1st Brigade marched to Landkhwar, towards the Shakot Pass. On the same day Lowe got information that the Morah and Shakot were defended by 13,000 and 6,000 men respectively; while only some 300 were believed to be holding the Malakhand. He therefore decided to make a feint against the Shakot with his Cavalry and to advance with the rest by the Malakhand.

His intention was to make a night march and attack on the 2nd, but heavy rain prevented this; consequently, all three Brigades were concentrated south of the Malakhand on the morning of the 2nd. The feint deceived no one, and the tribesmen had time to transfer most of their strength to the Malakhand to meet the attack.

The enemy held their position as shown in Plate 11, and to attack it entailed a very steep climb of 1,500 feet on its left, where ran the track over the Pass, and 2,000 feet on its right. The General's plan was to turn the enemy's right with the Guides and 4th Sikhs and make a frontal attack with the other two Battalions of the 2nd Brigade (2nd K.O.S.B. and 1st Gordon Highlanders); then, when the pass had been taken, to push on the 1st Brigade, which was equipped entirely with mule transport, as far as the Swat River.

At 8 a.m. on April 3 the 2nd Brigade left Dargai and moved up the valley, each Battalion turning to climb the hillside at the point shown in the sketch. Three Mountain Batteries opened fire from point A, but, finding the range too great, shortly moved on to B, whence they shelled the *sangars* opposed to the Guides and 4th Sikhs, as well as those which were arranged in tiers below the pass itself. When the Borderers and Gordons began their ascent, the guns moved on to point C, to give the attack even closer support. When the attack of the 2nd Brigade was well under way, the General brought up the 1st Brigade, which had left Shakot, four miles south of Dargai, at 7 a.m. Our 1st Battalion were sent up the hill between the K.O.S.B. and the Guides, while the Bedfords and 37th Dogras, passing in rear of the Gordons, attacked the enemy's extreme left, overlapping it considerably. The troops fought their way up the hillside, which was often almost perpendicular, turning the enemy out of *sangar* after *sangar*. Just before the summit was reached a short halt was made to re-form, and then, with bayonets fixed, the Gordons, Borderers, and Riflemen carried the crest with a simultaneous rush. The Sikhs

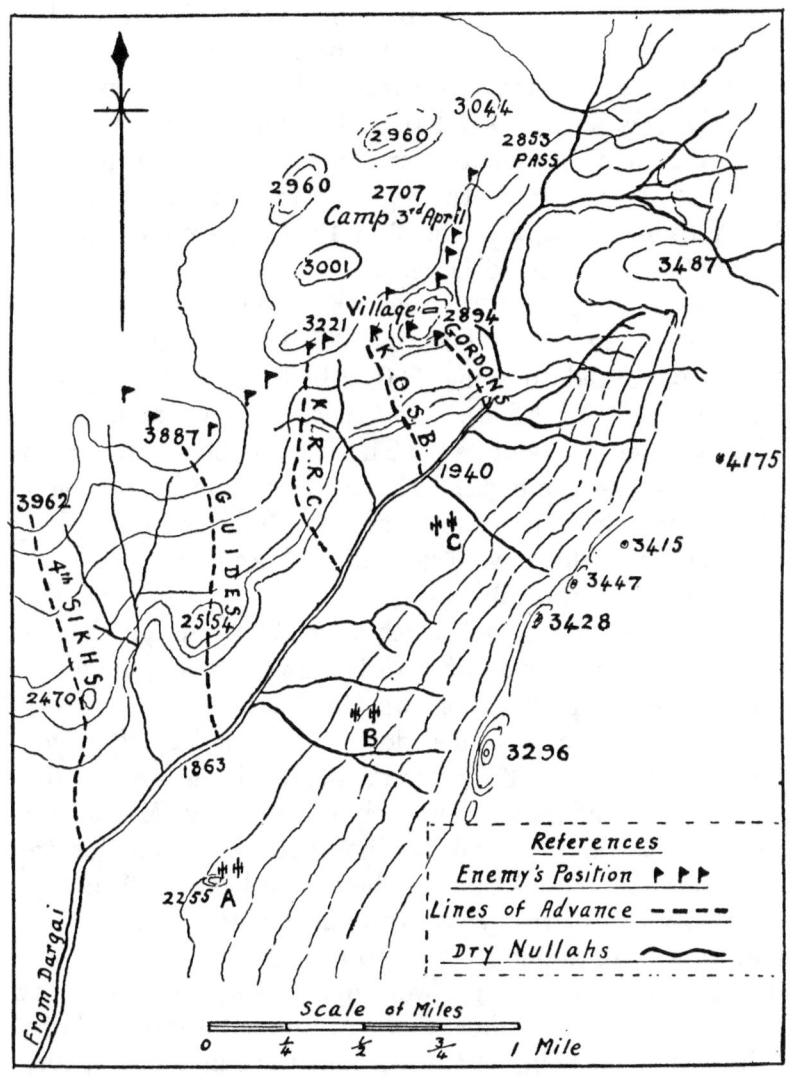

PLATE 11.
MAP TO ILLUSTRATE ACTION AT THE MALAKHAND PASS, APRIL 3, 1895.

and Guides carried the right of the position at the same time. Our 1st Battalion had done a wonderful performance in getting up in time to charge level with their neighbours on the right and left, as the 2nd Brigade were half-way up before the Riflemen were started. The action had now lasted five hours, the enemy had had enough for that day, and were pursued by the Bedfordshires and 37th Dogras as far as Khar in the Swat Valley. These two Regiments rejoined their Brigade next morning, the K.R.R.C. having spent the night on the captured position. For reasons of supply, the 2nd Brigade, except the 4th Sikhs, had returned to Dargai.

The enemy's strength was estimated at about 12,000 men, of whom from 3,000 to 4,000 had firearms. Their losses amounted to some 500 killed (the Swatis alone admitting a loss of 300). The British losses amounted to 11 killed and 51 wounded. The loss of the 1st Battalion was 4 killed, 4 wounded. The 1st Battalion in the course of the attack came across an old Buddhist road, long disused, but which was well aligned and had originally been very substantially built. Two days' work on this road opened it for camel transport. At 1 p.m. on the 4th the 1st Brigade moved on into the Swat Valley, while the 2nd Brigade relieved them on the Pass.

The 1st Brigade pushed down to Khar, having a hard fight on the way. They were attacked by a force of five or six thousand men, new arrivals from the Morah and Shakot Passes, who had not got across in time for the defence of the Malakhand. They were beaten off, chiefly by the 37th Dogras, who bore the brunt of the attack, and a party of about 1,200, who had the temerity to come down into open country, were charged and scattered by two troops of the Guides Cavalry under Captain Adams, thirty of them being cut down and the remainder driven into the hills. The casualties in the Brigade were 2 killed, 18 wounded. The 1st Battalion took no part in the fight.

On the morning of the 5th nothing was seen of the enemy till two squadrons of the Guides Cavalry reported a force near Thana, the chief village of Swat, 8 or 10 miles from Khar.

This was the end of the fighting as far as the 1st Battalion was concerned, as the 1st Brigade was left to guard the communications through the Swat Valley. The Official History says that Sir R. Lowe selected his senior brigadier for this duty owing to its importance, but the real truth was that Kinloch was a " difficult " subordinate and the 1st Brigade was left behind owing to differences between its commander and his Commander-in-Chief. That the 1st Brigade was originally intended to be the one to push on ahead is shown by the fact of its being the only one to be equipped throughout with mule transport.

The consequence was that the 2nd Brigade was pushed on, and, after further fighting at the crossing of the Panjkorah River, which finally disposed of Umra Khan, the 3rd Brigade took the lead.

On the 21st, when Gatacre (G.O.C. 3rd Brigade) was approaching Dir, news was received that Kelly had relieved Chitral and that Sher Afzul and his followers had fled. The 3rd Brigade, or a portion of it, went on over the Lowari Pass, but there was no more fighting. Sher Afzul was captured by the troops of the Khan of Dir, one of the tribal leaders who had been driven out of his dominions by Umra Khan and who had joined forces with us for the purpose of recovering his kingdom.

The troops occupied the line between Chitral and India throughout the hot weather without incident, except for a few attacks on individuals by fanatics, one of which (that on Captain W. R. Robertson,[1] Lowe's Intelligence Officer) might, if successful, have seriously affected the interests of the British Empire in the Great War. The troops were withdrawn in the autumn, leaving small garrisons in Chitral, the Malakhand, and Chakdara, and ever since—except during the big outbreak all along the North-western Frontier in 1897—the reliefs for the garrison of Chitral have used the road through Swat and Dir without molestation.

On May 15 the Battalion moved to the Laram Range and was employed for the next fortnight in making a road over the Laram Kotal.

On June 1 it settled down for the hot weather at Dostai, near the Laram Kotal, and remained there till September 25, when it started on its return march to India. Naoshera was reached on October 2, and there the Battalion entrained for Jullundur, where it arrived on October 5.

[1] Field-Marshal Sir William Robertson, G.C.B., G.C.M.G., K.C.V.O., D.S.O., Chief of the Imperial General Staff 1915–18.

CHAPTER VI

Fourth Battalion

The Third Volume of the Annals ended with the close of Hawley's period of command of the 4th Battalion. He was succeeded by Lieut.-Colonel C. Williamson on October 13, 1873.

After a brief stay at Portland, the Battalion moved to Devonport in July 1874.

The Martini-Henry rifle was issued to the Battalion in October of that year.

On June 5, 1875, Colonel Williamson was succeeded by Lieut.-Colonel R. W. Hinxman.

In July 1875 the Battalion moved to Dublin, being quartered in Ship Street Barracks with a detachment at Linen Hall.

The Battalion seems to have kept up the good reputation for shooting which it had held under Hawley, as, for the musketry year of 1875-6, it was third on the list of regiments stationed in the United Kingdom, while B Company was the best shooting company in the Army for that year.

In May 1876 the Battalion moved to Fermoy, with detachments in Cork Harbour.

On November 2, 1876, the Battalion embarked on H.M.S. *Serapis* at Queenstown for India. Strength: Officers, 23; Other Ranks, 656.

The names of the Officers who embarked with the Battalion are given in Vol. III, Appendix A, and need not be repeated, but the name of Lieutenant M. C. B. Forestier-Walker should be added.

The *Serapis* reached Bombay on December 6, and the Battalion arrived at Agra on the 14th and 16th.

In March a detachment of 6 Officers and 155 O.R. moved to the hills for the hot weather.

The standard of musketry, in those days, must have been a good deal higher in India than it was at home, as we find in an otherwise excellent report by the inspecting General, for their first year in India, comment is made on the indifference of their musketry practice. No such comment occurs again, and for the year 1886-7 we find them third in order of merit, and second in the following year, of the troops in India.

The only other remarks which approach unfavourable criticism in the Inspection Reports of this Battalion over a long period of years are that in those of 1874 and 1896 H.R.H. the Colonel-in-Chief notices that the expenses of the Officers' Mess are very high and should be reduced.

One gathers that this order must have been complied with more in the letter than in the spirit, by reducing the Officers' Mess bills without correspondingly reducing the expenditure, for we find in his remarks on the Inspection Report of 1878 H.R.H. notices that " there is a large mess debt which should be reduced."

Among the Inspection Reports of all four Battalions during the period covered by this volume we never find one that is not a good one, but those of the 4th Battalion during the eighties of last century are the most consistently laudatory.

Inspection Reports may not be very reliable guides, but the marked efficiency of this Battalion during a period when its Commanding Officers were certainly not all " flyers " inclines one to think that, though the mantle of Hawley may not have been worn by all his successors, his system automatically enabled the Battalion to retain its pre-eminence in the Regiment until the other Battalions had become leavened by Hawley's men.

In 1878 about 100 men went to the hills for the hot weather.

In 1879 4 Officers and 317 Other Ranks went up to Chakrata and were moved to Meerut in November.

Headquarters and five Companies marched from Agra on February 14, 1880, for Dagshai, which they reached on March 15. The Detachment from Meerut joined them in April.

The Battalion left Dagshai on October 15, 1881, and marched to Ferozepore, which they reached on November 3. Their strength was then only 17 Officers, 568 Other Ranks, which was very weak for an Indian Battalion, but they received a draft of 1 Officer, 213 Other Ranks from home, soon after reaching Ferozepore.

Lieut.-Colonel K. G. Henderson had succeeded Colonel Hinxman on June 5, 1880, but exchanged with Lieut.-Colonel J. S. H. Algar in November 1882, and went to the 2nd Battalion.

The Battalion left Ferozepore on December 12, 1884, and marched to Peshawar, where they arrived on January 21, 1885.

These long marches on change of station were one of the pleasantest features of soldiering in India and were enjoyed by all ranks. They were given up for financial reasons long ago, and anyhow would have since been abolished as taking up too much of the short period of the year that can be devoted to serious training.

The Battalion spent three years at Peshawar, sending half a Battalion to the local hill-station, Cherat, every hot weather.

In those days, whatever it may be now, Peshawar was a hotbed of malaria of a most malignant type. A

Battalion that had spent the hot weather there looked as if they had been boiled and bleached, and it took the greater part of the magnificent cold weather for them to recover their physical fitness.

The ill-health of the Battalion is reflected in its Inspection Reports, which during these years, however complimentary they are as to their efficiency, contain some caustic remarks as to their behaviour.

Colonel Algar was succeeded by Lieut.-Colonel Astley Terry, on October 9, 1885, who never took over command but exchanged with Lieut.-Colonel A. Morris on January 7, 1886.

The Battalion left Peshawar on December 27, 1887, and marched to Chakrata, which they reached on April 2, 1888.

Shortly after their arrival at Chakrata, H.R.H. Philippe, Duc d'Orléans, was attached for duty with the Battalion. He remained with it for about a year, and was then for some months attached to the 1st Battalion at Aldershot. He never held a commission in the Regiment, but used to wear our uniform.

The Battalion came down to Meerut for the cold weather of 1888-9, returning to Chakrata in March.

On November 11 the Battalion started to march to Pur, which they reached on the 20th, to take part in siege operation.

These Siege Camps were looked upon as a 'bow-and-arrow' business and as a *fatigue* for the training of the Royal Engineers. Little did those who took part in them think that the next European war the Regiment was to be engaged in would consist of little else.

After the Pur Camp the Battalion moved on to Meerut to a big concentration of troops in the Meerut Command.

They left Meerut on January 15, 1890, and marched to Allahabad, which they reached on February 21.

On March 22, 1890, Captain G. G. H. Allgood, Adjutant of the Battalion, was killed at polo.

Colonel Morris was succeeded, on January 7, 1890, by Colonel A. A. A. Kinloch, who exchanged from the 2nd Battalion.

Colonel Kinloch was the best-known big-game shikari of his day. In his young days there was no musketry done in India in the hot weather either in the plains or in the hills. The Musketry Staff generally went on leave. Kinloch followed a long spell as Regimental Musketry Instructor by a still longer one as a Musketry Staff Officer. He had six months' leave out of every year for some fifteen years in succession. He had shot nearly every kind of animal in India and Kashmir. After he was married, his wife used to accompany him, and it used to be said that most of his numerous family had been born at over ten thousand feet above sea-level. In those days camping in Kashmir was very much cheaper than living in cantonments. What times we missed by not being born sooner!

Colonel Kinloch got a brigade command before he had finished his time, and was succeeded on October 15, 1890, by Lieut.-Colonel R. Chalmer.

The Battalion left Allahabad in October *en route* for Burma.

Headquarters and four Companies reached Thayetmyo on January 14, 1891. The other half Battalion reached Myengyan on the 1st. A party from the Battalion at the same time left for Upper Burma to join the Mounted Infantry.

On April 4, 1891, Headquarters and four Companies, with a Mounted Infantry Detachment, embarked on

H.M.I.M.S. *Sladen* with orders to join the Tammu Column, Manipur Expedition, under Brigadier-General T. Graham, C.B. Strength : 8 Officers, 363 Other Ranks, 33 Mounted Infantry.

The Officers who embarked were :

Lieut.-Colonel R. Chalmer, Major G. G. Grimwood, Captain W. D. Stuart, Lieutenants C. A. G. Clarke, H. H. A. Walsh, 2nd Lieutenant C. L. E. Eustace, Lieutenant and Adjutant R. S. Oxley,[1] Captain and Quartermaster E. J. Crane.

Lieutenant E. J. Dewar, 2nd Lieutenant R. J. Vernon, and 48 Mounted Infantry joined at Pokoko from Myengyan.

Captain C. J. Markham, Lieutenant A. Blewitt, Lieutenant R. P. Cobbold, and 2nd Lieutenant G. H. Prevost joined at Manipur. 2nd Lieutenant C. J. Sackville-West [2] acted as A.D.C. to Brigadier-General Graham.

Manipur Expedition, 1891

Manipur is a small protected State in the borderland between Assam and Burma. Its chief claim to fame is that polo was introduced into India in the sixties of last century from that State, where it had been played from time immemorial, the only other polo played in the world at that time being in the small hill States to the north of Kashmir. The Manipuris had been taken under British protection at their own request, to save them from the Burmese, when that nation was independent. In 1890 a revolution had taken place, in which the chief mover was a younger brother of the Raja, who held the office of Commander of the Forces, or Senapati.

The Raja having voluntarily abdicated, the Govern-

---

[1] Brigadier-General R. S. Oxley, C.B., C.M.G.
[2] Major-General Lord Sackville, K.B.E., C.B., C.M.G.

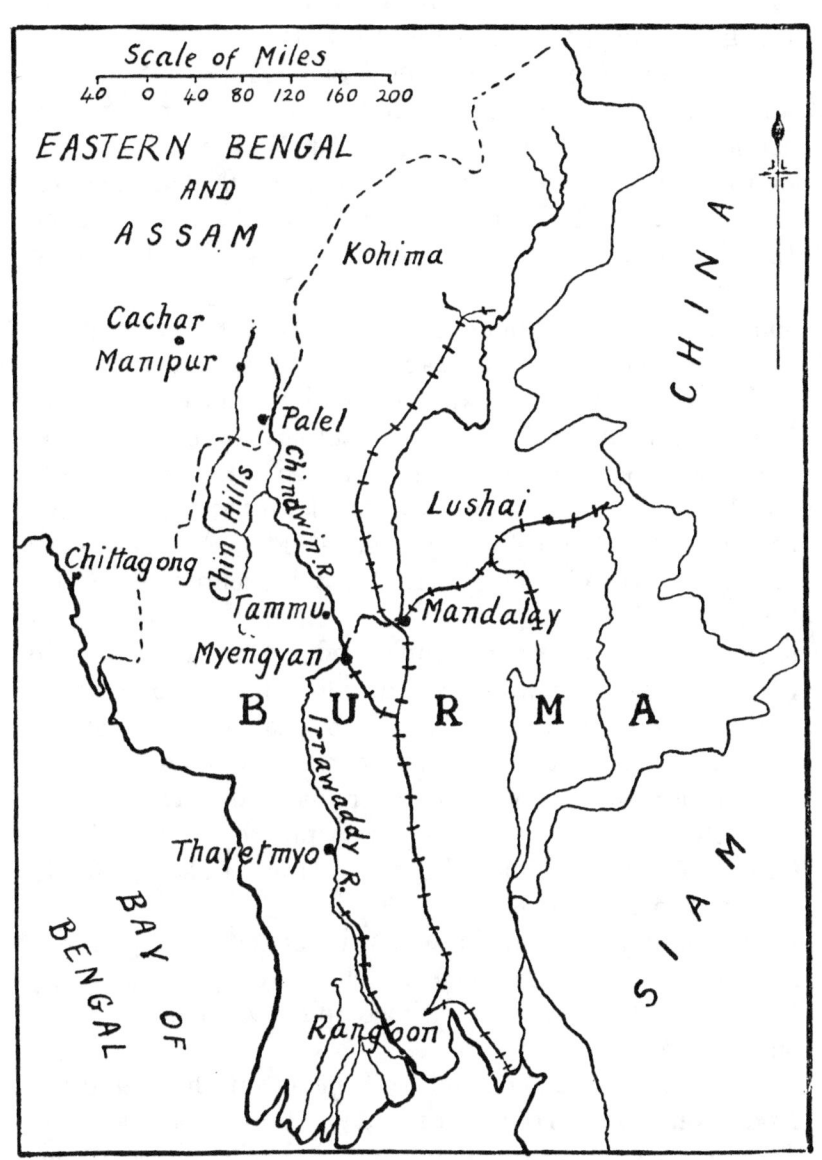

PLATE 12.
BURMA.

ment of India recognised his second brother as Regent, and, as the Senapati was likely to be a source of future trouble, decided to deport that official.

The Chief Commissioner of Assam, Mr. Quinton, with an escort of 400 Gurkhas, under Lieut.-Colonel Skene, set out for this purpose, and arrived at Manipur, the capital of the State, where there were already 100 Gurkhas, on March 22, 1891. After several attempts to persuade the Senapati to surrender peaceably had failed, British troops, early on the 24th, surrounded his house. After some fighting, in which one British Officer was mortally wounded, the house was taken, but the Senapati was not in it. Firing went on all day, and in the evening the Chief Commissioner invited the Manipuris to discuss terms. He was asked to meet the Senapati outside the fort, which was in the occupation of the Manipuris. He went, attended by Lieut.-Colonel Skene, Mr. F. Grimwood, I.C.S., Mr. H. W. Cossins, I.C.S., and Lieutenant W. H. Simpson. They were invited to enter the fort, which they did, and were there murdered. On receipt of the news, the senior Officer left decided, for reasons which have never transpired, to retire to Cachar. The retreat was harassed by the enemy and was not made in very good order—in fact was not a credit to our arms. Fortunately, the retreating party was met on the 26th by Captain Cowley, who had been sent from Cachar with 200 Gurkhas to their relief.

A punitive expedition was immediately organised, consisting of three Columns, which, starting from Cachar, Kohima, and Tammu, were timed to converge on Manipur on April 27.

Our 4th Battalion reached Kendat on the Chindwin River on the 17th. Next day they marched for Tammu, where they arrived on the 21st. On the

25th they reached Palel, and joined the remainder of their Column, made up of 2 guns No. 3 Mountain Battery, the 2/4th Gurkhas, and 200 men 12th (Burma) Madras Infantry.

At Palel news was received that the enemy were holding an entrenched position 5 miles north, at Bapam. The position was attacked by Captain F. M. Rundall, 2/4th Gurkhas, with 250 of his Regiment, 50 of the 12th Burma Regiment, 43 Mounted Infantry and 4 guns. The Manipuris put up a stubborn resistance and stood till they were turned out at the point of the bayonet, when they fled, pursued by the Mounted Infantry, and the expedition met with no further opposition. The British loss in this engagement was 2 killed and 13 wounded.

On April 27 the force entered Manipur and found the place deserted and the palace burnt.

The Kohima (Assam) and Cachar Columns arrived the same day, under Brigadier-General Collett, C.B., who assumed command of the combined forces.

This was the end of the campaign and the troops soon returned to their stations. The Regent and his brother were fugitives and the work of establishing order was left to the Military Police.

On May 1 two Companies under Captain Stuart started on the return journey, the remainder following next day.

Cholera broke out on the way down, and both parties were detained for some time in cholera camp.

Headquarters reached Thayetmyo on May 25 and Captain Stuart's Detachment on the 30th. Twenty-nine men died of cholera and four from other causes during the expedition.

Half of the Battalion was detailed to take part in the

cold-weather operations of 1891–2 in the Chin Hills. It was distributed as follows :—

HAKA SECTION
Brungshe Column

F Company, 100 strong; Officers, Lieutenant J. K. Watson, 2nd Lieutenant C. J. Sackville-West.

They left Myengyan on December 25, 1891, and reached Haka on January 30, 1892.

The Column visited and obtained the submission of several villages, but had no fighting. Major R. H. Gunning commanded the Column.

Tlang Tlang Column

G Company, 100 strong; Officers, Captain C. J. Markham, 2nd Lieutenants A. J. Sainson and W. H. L. Allgood.

The Column left Haka February 5, 1892, and returned on March 4. Several villages were visited and some destroyed. Lieutenant J. K. Watson commanded the Coolie Corps on this Column.

Tashon Column (Major R. H. Gunning)

F Company, 100 strong; Officers, Lieutenant C. J. Sackville-West, 2nd Lieutenant W. H. L. Allgood.

This Column left Haka on March 10 and was broken up at Falam on April 3. There was no fighting. Lieutenant Watson commanded the Coolie Corps.

FORT WHITE SECTION
Kanhow Column

B Company, 50 strong, under 2nd Lieutenant R. Beaumont, left Fort White in January and returned in the middle of April. They visited Manipur and several villages.

Nivengal Column

A Company, 137 strong; Officers, Captain Stuart, Lieutenant Eustace, 2nd Lieutenant W. J. Long.

They left Fort White on March 10 and visited Falam, meeting the Tashon Column there, and other villages. Major M. C. B. Forestier-Walker accompanied the Column as Intelligence Officer.

The Column was afterwards converted into the Burma-Lushai Column for the relief of Captain Shakespear, Superintendent of the Southern Lushai Hills, who was besieged by rebels.

They marched through Lushai Land—relieving Captain Shakespear—to the coast of Chittagong, thence by steamer to Rangoon, arriving there at the end of May after very severe marching, but no fighting.

Thirty-two men under 2nd Lieutenant Beaumont were sent from Fort White to Botong, starting on May 2. They had a slight engagement on the Manipur River, and returned to Fort White on the 14th.

The men from Haka returned to Myengyan in April; those from Fort White at the end of May.

From a report to Headquarters Madras Army, by Major-General R. C. Stewart, C.B., A.D.C., Commanding Burma District, dated Rangoon, June 6, 1892, the following is an extract:—

> 'I wish to place on record the appreciation I have for the Officers and men of the 4th K.R.R.C. who have served in the several expeditions in the Chin Hills during the past season. They have done most excellent work and displayed a keenness which was pleasant to see.'

The following farewell order was published by the

G.O.C., Burma District, on the departure of the Battalion from Burma:—

'The 4th K.R.R.C. being about to leave the Burma Command, the Major-General desires to place on record his high appreciation of the services done by this Battalion with the Manipur Field Force and the various Columns on the frontier during the past two years and more, especially with the Nivengal Column, which he has already had the pleasure of bringing to the notice of the Commander-in-Chief. The Major-General desires to convey his cordial thanks to Lieut.-Colonel R. Chalmer, his Officers, N.C.O.s, and men for their excellent service in the field and for their equally good conduct in quarters.'

The half Battalion from Myengyan, consisting of A, B, C, and F Companies, under the command of Major Walker, arrived at Thayetmyo on board H.M.I.M.S. *Irrawaddy* on October 24, 1892.

Headquarters and the remainder of the Battalion embarked next day. The *Irrawaddy* reached Rangoon on the 29th, where the Battalion transhipped to H.M.I.M.S. *Canning*, in which they arrived at Bombay on November 9. They transhipped next day to H.M.S. *Malabar*, and sailed at once for home.—Strength: 21 Officers, 432 Other Ranks—a large draft having gone to join the 1st Battalion.

The following Officers, W.O.s, N.C.O.s, and Riflemen, who had sailed for India with the Battalion in 1876, returned with it in 1892: Major Forestier-Walker, Captain and Quartermaster Crane, Sergeant-Major O'Shea, Quartermaster-Sergeant Bright, Colour-Sergeant Wheatley, Colour-Sergeant Nolan, Colour-Sergeant Turner, Quartermaster-Sergeant Holmes, and Sergeant Healy. Of these, Major Walker alone had served in other Battalions during the tour of the 4th Battalion in the East.

The Battalion reached England on December 5 and was stationed at New Barracks, Gosport, with companies on detachment at Fort Blockhouse.

In August 1893 Headquarters and half the Battalion attended manœuvres near Swindon under Lieut.-General Sir Evelyn Wood, V.C., etc.

On October 4 the 3rd Battalion came over from Parkhurst, Isle of Wight, and the two Battalions were inspected together by H.R.H. the Duke of Cambridge, the Colonel-in-Chief. Lieut.-General Hawley, Colonel Commandant, was present, and there was a great gathering of past Officers.

The Battalion moved to Dover on May 30, 1894.

On October 15, 1894, Lieut.-Colonel H. R. Mends succeeded to the command.

In May 1896 the Battalion moved to Tournay Barracks, Aldershot.

In August they won the Duke of Connaught's Shield (obstacle race); fourteen teams of 2 Officers, 8 Sergeants, and 96 rank and file competed. They won this event again in 1897 and 1898.

On June 22, 1897, the Battalion lined the streets in Piccadilly and St. James's Street for Queen Victoria's Diamond Jubilee.

On July 1 they took part in a Review before Her Majesty on Laffan's Plain.

In August 1898 the Battalion went to Salisbury Plain for manœuvres, moving to Cork, on change of station, after the manœuvres were over.

On October 15 Lieut.-Colonel E. W. Herbert succeeded to the command.

On June 6, 1899, the Battalion marched to Kilworth Camp, $27\frac{1}{2}$ miles. Five men were taken to hospital at Fermoy and ten others fell out. The day was exceptionally hot, and thirteen of the fifteen casualties were attributed to the want of protection from the sun by the field-service cap of the period, which gave no shade to the eyes.

On October 23 the Battalion paraded for a Memorial Service in honour of their comrades of the 1st Battalion killed at Talana Hill.

The following letter of sympathy from the O.C. 17th Lancers was published in Battalion Orders :—

'BALLINCOLLIG,
'*October* 23, 1899.

'DEAR COLONEL,
'I have only just returned or I would have written before, as I do now, on behalf of all ranks of the 17th Lancers, to express our deepest sympathy with your Regiment for the great loss they sustained during the most gallant action last Friday of your 1st Battalion. We have known you so well that we feel your loss almost as if it were our own, and I am anxious to express to you our feelings of the utmost regret for your losses and of admiration for the gallant feat in the accomplishment of which they were sufferers.
'Yours very sincerely,
'[*Signed*] H. FORTESCUE, Major,
'Commanding 17th Lancers.'

On November 4 a party of all ranks went to Queenstown to see the 3rd Battalion off to the South African War.

Though it was not to be for another two years that the Battalion went out as a Battalion to South Africa, many Officers and other ranks were going out all the time to the Staff, the Mounted Infantry, and drafts to the Battalions out there.

On July 30, 1900, the following telegram was sent to Lord Roberts, then Commander-in-Chief in South Africa :—

'Lord Roberts, Pretoria. Have won your cup at the Curragh—1,300 strong—anxious for work.'

(The cup referred to was given by Lord Roberts when Commander-in-Chief in Ireland to be shot for by teams of young soldiers in the Irish Command.)

The reply of congratulation which Lord Roberts sent having gone astray, the following letter was received some time later by the C.O. from the Hon. Aileen Roberts :—

'DEAR COLONEL HERBERT,
'Father is very vexed that a telegram of congratulation he sent you on hearing that the Battalion had won his prize at the Curragh had been returned from that place. He is sending it again, but he wants me to explain the delay in its reaching you and to tell you how delighted he was that a Battalion of the 60th should hold his cup.'

In October the Battalion and the whole Regiment sustained a severe loss in the death, from enteric fever at Pretoria, of Brevet-Major H.H. Prince Christian Victor of Schleswig-Holstein, G.C.B., G.C.V.O., who had been serving on the Staff in South Africa since early in the war.

Prince Christian Victor joined the 1st Battalion at Aldershot in 1888. He went with them to India two years later, and served in the Hazara Expedition in 1891 as Orderly Officer to Major-General Sir William Ellis till his Battalion came up to the front, when he rejoined them and accompanied them to the Samana. He served with the 1st Battalion in the Isazai Expedition of 1892. Not long afterwards he was transferred to the 4th Battalion, and got his company in March 1896, being gazetted next day to a Brevet-Majority which he had earned in the Ashanti Expedition of 1895-6. He served in the Nile Expedition of 1898, and went out on Special Service to South Africa in October 1899. He afterwards became A.D.C. to F.M. Lord Roberts, Commander-in-Chief, and held that post when he died.

He was devoted to his profession, and was one of the best and keenest of regimental Officers. He was a very good rifle shot and did a great deal for the musketry of the 1st Battalion during the few years he served with it. He was a very fine cricketer, only just missing his Blue during his short spell at Oxford, and, as he came on a great deal at the game after joining the Regiment, there is little doubt that he would have made a name in first-class cricket if he could have devoted the time to it. He was universally popular with all ranks in the Regiment.

On January 31, 1901, a party of two Officers and 100 Other Ranks went to London to attend the funeral of H.M. Queen Victoria.

At last the Battalion got their long-awaited orders for South Africa, and embarked on the hired transport *Roslin Castle* on December 11, 1901. Strength, 25 Officers, 814 Other Ranks.

The Officers who embarked with the Battalion were :—

Lieut.-Colonel E. W. Herbert; Captains F. Douglas-Pennant, Hon. J. R. Brownlow, G. C. Shakerley, C. C. Herbert-Stepney, H. C. R. Green, M. L. Porter; Lieutenants S. A. G. Finch, K. S. Smith, F. W. L. Edwards, C. V. L. Poe; 2nd Lieutenants C. A. Blacklock, G. Wynne-Finch, C. J. T. R. Wingfield, A. A. Soames, E. A. Pratt-Barlow, F. O. Grenfell, A. J. Hunter, E. G. St. Aubyn, G. A. S. Mure, H. C. M. Porter, L. Aylmer, A. P. Evans; Captain and Adjutant W. H. L. Allgood; Lieutenant and Quartermaster T. O'Shea.

They reached Capetown on the 31st and Durban on January 3, 1902, entraining for Harrismith next day.

CHAPTER VII

SECOND BATTALION

FIRST BOER WAR, 1881

WE left the 2nd Battalion at Meerut in November 1880, after their return from Afghanistan. On December 30, 1880, the Battalion was warned for active service in Natal on account of the outbreak in the Transvaal.

Lieutenant-Colonel J. Algar, having been promoted in place of the late Colonel Collins, assumed command on January 2, 1881.

On the 3rd the Battalion left Meerut for Bombay, where it arrived on the 10th, embarking on H.M.S. *Euphrates*.

The following embarked with the Battalion :—

Lieut.-Colonel J. Algar ; Major W. G. Byron ; Captains G. L. McL. Farmer, R. Chalmer, W. Tilden, H. S. Marsham, J. N. Blackwood-Price, G. Astell ; Lieutenants H. R. Mends, R. C. Wilson, H. R. Lovett, H. D. Banks, A. Davidson, R. E. Golightly, E. J. M. Stuart-Wortley, R. G. H. Couper ; 2nd Lieutenants Lord Tewkesbury ; Adjutant Lord F. Fitzgerald ; Acting Paymaster Captain T. P. Lloyd ; 709 of all ranks.

The following Order shows the reputation which the 2nd Battalion left behind it :—

Extract from General Orders by H.E. the Commander-in-Chief in India.

'HEADQUARTERS, FORT WILLIAM.
'*January* 1, 1881.

'The 2nd Battalion 60th Rifles, being about to leave India for service in Natal, H.E. the Commander-in-Chief cannot allow them to quit the country without referring to the eminent services they have rendered during the recent operations in Afghanistan.

'The 2nd Battalion 60th Rifles has, throughout the war, maintained its high reputation for efficiency. In the march from Candahar to Cabul; at Ahmad Khel; in the memorable march from Cabul to Candahar under Sir Frederick Roberts; in the action at Candahar; and in the subsequent expedition to the Marri country, the 60th Rifles were remarkable for their discipline and marching powers. In the operations above described the Regiment marched 1,000 miles in 100 days, no light feat anywhere, but in such a country as Afghanistan it is one well worthy of record in the annals of the British Army. In bidding farewell to this distinguished Regiment, Sir Frederick Haines had hoped to wish it a speedy and happy return to England; but England claims its services in another quarter of the globe, a call most heartily and cheerfully responded to. This may delay their return home for a while, but H.E. knows full well that the opportunity thus afforded to it of adding to the lustre of the British Arms and to its own renown will be utilised to the utmost.

'By Order

'[*Signed*] G. R. GREAVES, Major-General,
'A.G. in India.'

On January 25, 1881, H.M.S. *Euphrates* reached Durban, and the Battalion disembarked that afternoon.

On the 27th the Battalion left Durban by train and camped about 10 miles from Pietermaritzburg.

On the 28th the news came of Colley's reverse at Laing's Nek, and the Battalion was ordered to the front. Newcastle was reached on February 17.

On the 21st the Indian Column (15th Hussars, 2/60th and 92nd (Gordon) Highlanders) were inspected by Sir George Colley.

The Battalion remained in camp at Bennett's Drift, Newcastle, Majuba having brought the war to an untimely end, where it was inspected on May 19 by Major-General Sir Evelyn Wood, V.C.

Numbers present: 26 Officers, 744 Other Ranks.

On November 9 the Battalion, under orders for England, left Newcastle by march route, passing Ladysmith on the 13th, Estcourt on the 15th, reaching Richmond Road near Pietermaritzburg on the 21st. Distance from Bennett's Drift, 183 miles.

The Battalion remained at Richmond Road till December 7, when it entrained for Durban, sailing for England on the *Dublin Castle* on the 13th and arriving at Portsmouth on January 11, 1882.

The Battalion trained the same day to Winchester, where it was presented on arrival with an address by the citizens of Winchester.

The N.C.O.s and Riflemen were entertained at dinner at the Guildhall, Winchester, next day.

Detachments of one Company each went to Tipnor and Marchwood on the 16th.

On March 11 the Battalion formed part of the Indian Brigade inspected on Southsea Common by H.R.H. the Duke of Cambridge, who expressed himself highly satisfied with the appearance of the Battalion.

On July 3 the Battalion was inspected by H.S.H. Prince Edward of Saxe-Weimar, the Commander-in-Chief's remarks on this inspection being as follows:—

'HORSE GUARDS,
'*March* 3, 1883.

'This is a most favourable report in every respect, and H.R.H. has been pleased to express entire satisfaction with the admirable condition of the Battalion. . . .

'[*Signed*] R. B. HAWLEY, D.A.G.'

On November 23, 1883, Lieut.-Colonel Algar exchanged to the 4th Battalion with Lieut.-Colonel K. G. Henderson.

During the late summer and autumn of 1882 a strong

detachment from the Battalion was stationed in Kensington Barracks for the purpose of finding the Guards and duties in London in the absence of a Brigade of Guards in Egypt.

The Battalion was inspected by H.S.H. Prince Edward of Saxe-Weimar on August 21, 1882.

The Commander-in-Chief's remarks on this inspection were :—

'From this report, and from what the Duke of Cambridge saw himself of the Kensington Detachment, H.R.H. considers the Battalion in excellent order.'

The strength of the Battalion had fallen considerably since its return from abroad, as an Army Circular of May 21, 1884, raises its establishment from 480 to 610 privates.

Lieut.-Colonel K. G. Henderson was promoted Colonel on June 5, 1884.

The Battalion was inspected by H.S.H. Prince Edward of Saxe-Weimar on July 23, 1884.

The Battalion furnished a draft of 1 Sergeant, 32 rank and file for service with the Mounted Infantry in Egypt on August 22, 1884.

Colonel K. G. Henderson gave up command on September 9, 1884, having received an appointment in Egypt, and was succeeded by Lieut.-Colonel W. G. Byron.

The Battalion moved from Winchester to Devonport on October 3, 1884.

Lieut.-Colonel W. G. Byron was promoted Colonel on March 2, 1885. He died in London on June 5, 1895, and was succeeded by Lieut.-Colonel Charley, who exchanged with Lieut.-Colonel W. L. K. Ogilvy without taking over command. Colonel Ogilvy was posted to command the Battalion on September 2, 1885.

On July 8 the Battalion was inspected by Major-

General Lyons, C.B., Commanding Western District; 23 Officers, 824 Other Ranks.

The Battalion was inspected by H.R.H. the Field-Marshal Commanding-in-Chief on October 2, 1885, with the rest of the garrison.

Remarks by the Commander-in-Chief on annual inspection for 1885 :—

'This is a fine Battalion, and its creditable condition confirms the opinion formed of it by H.R.H. in the autumn.'

The establishment of privates was raised to 710 on April 1, 1886.

On June 17, 1886, the Battalion embarked on H.M.S. *Jumna*, disembarked at Portsmouth on the 19th, and railed to Shorncliffe, there to be stationed.

On July 23, 1886, the Battalion was inspected by Colonel Sir Baker Russell, K.C.B., Commanding the troops at Shorncliffe. Strength: Officers, 24; Other Ranks, 704.

Remarks by Commander-in-Chief on this inspection :—

'It has given H.R.H. much satisfaction to find the Battalion in all respects in a very creditable and efficient condition.
'[*Signed*] E. BULWER, D.A.G.'

The Battalion was inspected on April 13, 1887, by H.R.H. the Commander-in-Chief, who complimented the Battalion on its general efficiency.

The Battalion moved to Aldershot on July 7, 1887, for Queen Victoria's Jubilee Review. It formed a part of a Brigade of Rifles camped on Rushmoor Green under Colonel C. G. Slade, R.B. The other Battalions of the Brigade were 1st King's Royal Rifle Corps, 1st Royal Irish Rifles, 2nd Rifle Brigade.

The Brigade formed the 6th Brigade, 3rd Division, 1st Army Corps, and marched past the Queen on July 9th at her Jubilee Review.

The Battalion returned to Shorncliffe on the 11th.

Colonel Ogilvy retired on July 15, 1887, and was succeeded by Colonel A. A. A. Kinloch, dated July 1, 1887. (Colonel Ogilvy's time was up on July 1, but he was allowed with other Commanding Officers to remain on for the Jubilee Review.)

The Battalion was inspected by Colonel Sir Baker Russell on July 19, 1887. Strength: Officers, 23; Other Ranks, 500.

The Battalion left Shorncliffe on January 14, 1888, sailed from Dover in H.M.S. *Assistance* for Kingstown, and reached its new station, Enniskillen, on January 18, 1888.

One Company went on detachment to Londonderry, another to Belturbet.

On January 25 Colonel Kinloch, 5 Officers, and 100 rank and file were sent to Dunfanaghy, Donegal, to aid the Civil Power during some political trials.

This party, in marching order, did the $22\frac{1}{2}$ miles from Letterkenny to Dunfanaghy on a very hilly road in seven hours, including a halt of one hour.

One hundred more men were subsequently sent up from Londonderry.

Colonel Kinloch, 4 Officers, and 100 rank and file returned to Enniskillen on February 20, leaving A Company (3 Officers and 100 rank and file) to be stationed at Dunfanaghy.

The Detachment at Dunfanaghy had some very hard work and rough living during their stay in North Donegal. They were constantly being called out at all hours and in any weather, in aid of the Civil Power, to support the

Royal Irish Constabulary at evictions, arrests of offenders, and trials. It was very noticeable that although the police frequently met with resistance of the most violent type, whenever the troops were asked to take action the resistance immediately ceased. On several occasions the Officer in command of the Detachment was given an order by the magistrate present to fire. On each occasion the threat to do so was sufficient and resistance ceased. The explanation of this is said to have been that the people knew that the police never would shoot under any circumstances, firstly, because they knew that if they did so they would probably be let down by the authorities afterwards ; and, secondly, that they had to go on living in the country and would be marked men. On the other hand, the people believed that when an Officer in command of troops said he was going to shoot, he meant what he said.

The Battalion was inspected by Major-General S. M. Wiseman-Clarke, C.B., Commanding Belfast District, on July 19, 1888. Strength: Officers, 23; Other Ranks, 778.

The following is an extract from a letter received from the Chief Secretary's Office, Dublin Castle, on September 24, 1888 :—

'H.E. desires to take this opportunity of acknowledging the valuable services rendered by Colonel Kinloch, and placing on record his appreciation of the excellent bearing of the men of the King's Royal Rifles since they first went to Dunfanaghy.'

The Battalion was inspected by Major-General Wiseman-Clarke, C.B., Commanding Belfast District, on July 15 and 16, 1889. Strength: Officers, 23; Other Ranks, 671.

Headquarters moved from Enniskillen to Dublin on

January 10, 1890. The Detachments from Londonderry and Dunfanaghy arrived in Dublin on January 13. Headquarters and five Companies were stationed at Richmond Barracks, three Companies at Portobello.

A letter, bearing the signatures of nine magistrates of different political parties and religious persuasions, testifying to the good conduct of the men of the Regiment during their two years' stay at Dunfanaghy, having been received at Dublin Castle, was forwarded to the Commanding Officer in a very complimentary letter from the Chief Secretary, expressing the appreciation of the Lord Lieutenant of the Battalion's services in Donegal, during the last two years, ' under very trying circumstances.'

On January 7, 1890, Major G. L. McL. Farmer, on promotion to Lieutenant-Colonel, exchanged with Colonel Kinloch, who went to the 4th Battalion.

Major-General Keith Fraser, C.M.G., Commanding Dublin District, inspected the Battalion on July 4 and 5. Strength: Officers, 22; Other Ranks, 675.

The Slade-Wallace equipment, 1888 pattern, was issued to the Battalion in May.

The sealskin busby was taken into wear in December, in place of the helmet.

The Annual Inspection for 1891 took place on July 29 and 30. Strength: Officers, 24; Other Ranks, 838.

The Battalion sailed from Kingstown for Gibraltar on December 1, 1891, in H.M.S. *Himalaya*, to relieve the 3rd Battalion.

The following Officers embarked with the Battalion:—

Lieut.-Colonel G. L. McL. Farmer; Major G. S. Baynes and Brevet-Major E. J. M. Stuart-Wortley, C.M.G.; Captains Lord Tewkesbury, H. Buchanan-Riddell (Adjutant), T. E. M. S. Pilkington, and E. W. Thistlethwayte; Lieutenants F. A. Browning, C. S.

Chaplin, H. W. Christian, J. H. G. Feilden, C. Gosling, J. A. Hope, and W. G. A. Orde-Powlett; 2nd Lieutenants N. Lord, H. R. Blore, L. P. Irby, C. A. K. Pechell, and G. C. Shakerley; Quartermaster A. Wynn. Strength: Officers, 20; Other Ranks, 748.

One hundred N.C.O.s and Riflemen were taken on the strength at Gibraltar from the 3rd Battalion.

The Battalion arrived at Gibraltar on December 7.

The Battalion was inspected by Major-General H. R. L. Newdigate, Commanding Infantry Brigade, Gibraltar, on December 5, 7, and 8, 1892. Strength: Officers, 26; Other Ranks, 988.

Commander-in-Chief's comments: 'H.R.H. considers the report is satisfactory. The percentage of third-class shots is high.'

The Annual Inspection for 1893 took place on December 11. Strength: Officers, 28; Other Ranks, 985.

Commander-in-Chief's comments: 'H.R.H. considers this Battalion to be in excellent order in all respects.'

On January 7, 1894, Lieut.-Colonel Farmer completed his period of command and was succeeded by Lieut.-Colonel the Hon. Keith Turnour.

The Battalion was inspected by Major-General E. Hopton, C.B., on November 28 and 29, 1894. Strength: Officers, 28; Other Ranks, 884.

Commander-in-Chief's remarks: 'H.R.H. is gratified to find that this Battalion continues to be in all respects in a thoroughly efficient condition.'

On January 13, 1895, Headquarters and six Companies embarked in the hired transport *Victoria* for Malta, arriving there on the 17th. The other two Companies followed in the course of the next month.

The Officers who left Gibraltar for Malta were:—

Lieut.-Colonel the Hon. Keith Turnour; Major M. C.

B. F. Forestier-Walker ; Captains H. B. Addington, C. F. Sewell, T. L. N. Morland, and J. Curteis ; Lieutenants H. W. Christian, C. A. K. Pechell, J. A. Hope, L. P. Irby ; 2nd Lieutenants U. O. Thynne, M. L. Porter, E. F. Ward, C. E. Balfour, G. F. B. Hankey, A. I. Paine, J. Spottiswoode, C. E. de V. Beauclerk, H. C. R. Green, and S. F. Mott ; Lieutenant and Adjutant J. H. G. Feilden ; Lieutenant and Quartermaster A. Wynn.

Field-Marshal H.R.H. the Duke of Cambridge, Commander-in-Chief, landed in Malta on March 3. He dined with the Officers of the Battalion on the 7th.

Lieut.-Colonel the Hon. Keith Turnour retired on September 18, 1895, and was succeeded by Lieut.-Colonel G. G. Grimwood.

The Battalion was inspected on December 18 and 19, 1895, by Major-General the Hon. H. Parnell, C.B., Commanding Infantry Brigade, Malta. Strength : Officers, 28 ; Other Ranks, 1,042.

The Battalion embarked on the hired transport *Victoria* on July 16, 1896, for the Cape of Good Hope. Strength : Officers, 27 ; Other Ranks, 961.

The Officers who embarked were :—

Lieut.-Colonel G. G. Grimwood ; Majors E. W. Herbert and F. A. Fortescue ; Captains H. R. Addington, A. Blewitt, Hon. J. R. Brownlow, G. A. J. Soltau-Symons, E. Northey, and H. B. Nicholson ; Lieutenants J. A. Hope, L. P. Irby, H. R. Green, M. L. Porter, E. F. Ward, C. E. Balfour, R. Chester-Master, and S. F. Mott ; 2nd Lieutenants G. F. Hankey, A. I. Paine, J. Spottiswoode, C. E. de V. Beauclerk, H. F. Foljambe, W. B. Du Pré, L. W. de Saumarez, and A. T. Rickman ; Adjutant-Lieutenant G. C. Shakerley ; Quartermaster-Captain A. Wynn.

The Battalion arrived at Cape Town on August 4 and was quartered in the Main Barracks.

In 1897 a Mounted Infantry Company was formed in the Battalion and detached for duty at Wynberg. Strength as follows:—Captain Northey,[1] Lieutenants Chester-Master and Mott, 2nd Lieutenant Paine, 123 Other Ranks.

The Battalion was inspected on November 22 and 23, 1898, by Colonel Morgan Crofton, D.S.O., Commanding Troops, Cape District. Strength: Officers, 28; Other Ranks, 984.

The Battalion embarked on the hired transport *Avoca* for Calcutta on March 15, 1899. Strength: Officers, 19; Other Ranks, 712.

The Battalion arrived at Calcutta on April 5, 1899, and was quartered at Fort William.

At midnight on September 7–8, 1899, the Battalion was ordered by telegram to hold itself in readiness for active service in South Africa.

Lieut.-Colonel G. G. Grimwood was granted an extension of command for six months from September 18 with Brevet of Colonel from September 10.

Headquarters and seven Companies embarked on s.s. *Purnea* on September 18. Strength: Officers, 15; Other Ranks, 711.

The following Officers embarked with the Battalion:—

Brevet-Colonel G. G. Grimwood; Major H. Gore-Browne; Captains C. Gosling, C. L. E. Eustace, and A. J. Lainson; Lieutenants E. F. Ward, F. S. Mott, and L. W. de Saumarez; 2nd Lieutenants C. H. N. Seymour, L. A. E. Price-Davies, G. Makins, and the Hon. A. F. W. Harris; Lieutenant and Acting Adjutant H. R. Green; Captain and Quartermaster J. Dwane.

[1] Major-General Sir Edward Northey, G.C.M.G., C.B.

The following Officers, attached for duty, accompanied the Battalion :—

Captain Fox-Strangways and Lieutenant Eckford, R.I.R.; Lieutenants Green and Rutter, E. Lancs; Lieutenant R. C. Maclachlan, R.B.; Lieutenant Birch, D.C.L.I.; Lieutenant Tod, Scottish Rifles; 2nd Lieutenant Wingate, K.O.S.B.; and Major E. W. Gray, R.A.M.C.

G Company and Transport under Major Bowen embarked on s.s. *Nurani* on September 20. Officers, Major R. S. Bowen and Lieutenant M. L. Porter. Strength: Officers, 2; Other Ranks, 122.

CHAPTER VIII

THIRD BATTALION

(Period between Sudan Campaign and South African War)

ON their return to Egypt in May 1884 the 3rd Battalion were quartered at Ramleh Barracks, near Alexandria.

In August 1884 Headquarters and the right half Battalion moved to Cyprus, where they remained till June 1886. On May 30 of that year the left half Battalion left Alexandria on H.M.S. *Himalaya*, picked up the right half on June 2, and disembarked at Gibraltar on the 11th. They remained there till they were relieved by the 2nd Battalion in December 1891.

Lieut.-Colonel W. L. K. Ogilvy succeeded Sir Cromer Ashburnham in command of the Battalion on November 1, 1884, but on June 6, 1885, he exchanged with Colonel J. Charley and went to the 2nd Battalion. Colonel Charley retired on July 1, 1887, and was succeeded by Lieut.-Colonel G. T. Whitaker.

Lieutenant H.R.H. Prince Albert Victor of Wales, 10th Hussars, was attached to the Battalion at Gibraltar for a few months in 1887.

Lieut.-Colonel G. T. Whitaker died on April 15, 1890, and was succeeded by Lieut.-Colonel H. D. Browne.

On the night of March 17–18, 1891, the Italian emigrant ship *Utopia* was wrecked in Gibraltar Bay with great loss of life. The gale which was blowing made the task of the steamboats from the British warships in the Bay, which went to the rescue, both difficult and dangerous. A boat from H.M.S. *Immortalité* got on the rocks owing to its steering gear breaking down. Assistance was given by both Officers and Riflemen of the 3rd Battalion, and Sergeant McQue of the Battalion particularly distinguished himself and was awarded both the Albert Medal and an Italian medal.

The following letter was forwarded to the Commanding Officer by the G.O.C. Gibraltar Infantry Brigade :—

'COLONIAL SECRETARY'S OFFICE, GIBRALTAR,
'*July* 15, 1891.

'SIR,

'I am directed by the Governor to inform you that the Secretary of State for the Colonies has conveyed to His Excellency the thanks of the Board of Trade for the services rendered by all the Officers and men of the 3rd Battalion of the K.R.R.C., who, on the night of the 17th of March last, on the occasion of the wreck of a launch from H.M.S. *Immortalité*, rendered assistance in saving life.

'I am to express the Governor's high sense of satisfaction at this recognition by H.M. Government of the valuable services rendered by those Officers and men, and I have the honour to request that you will be good enough to cause these expressions to be conveyed to them through the O.C. the Battalion and duly placed on record in its archives.

'I have, etc.,
'CAVENDISH BOYLE,
'*Colonial Secretary.*'

The Battalion left Gibraltar in H.M.S. *Himalaya* on December 8, 1891, landing at Portsmouth on the 14th. They were stationed at Parkhurst, Isle of Wight.

The ·303 magazine Lee-Metford Rifle was issued to the Battalion in April 1892, and the Slade Wallace equipment in June of the same year.

On October 4, 1893, the Battalion crossed to Gosport,

where, with the 4th Battalion, it was inspected by the Colonel-in-Chief of the Regiment, H.R.H. the Duke of Cambridge, Commander-in-Chief.

Lieut.-Colonel H. D. Browne was placed on half-pay on April 16, 1894, and was succeeded by Lieut.-Colonel and Brevet-Colonel R. S. Fetherstonhaugh.

On January 24, 1895, the Battalion marched to Osborne to be inspected by Her Majesty Queen Victoria.

The Battalion moved to Shorncliffe on February 9.

On November 27 Captain W. S. Kays with 25 Other Ranks left for Aldershot to form part of a Composite Battalion there being formed for service in the Ashanti Expedition of 1895–6.

They had a strenuous time in a pestilential climate, though there was no fighting, but they all returned on February 22, 1896, with a very complimentary report from their C.O., Lieut.-Colonel F. Stopford, Grenadier Guards.

A Detachment of 29 N.C.O.s and men left for Aldershot on April 27, 1896, for service with the Mounted Infantry in Rhodesia. They embarked on May 6.

The Battalion took part in the manœuvres of the South-eastern District in September 1896. There they attracted the favourable notice of the Commander-in-Chief, Lord Wolseley, who was not as a rule lavish with compliments.

Extract from Battalion Orders

'*October* 1, 1896.

'The O.C. has been desired by the Commander-in-Chief to convey to the Officers, N.C.O.s, and men of this Battalion how much he was struck by their smartness and that he has seldom seen a better battalion.'

166 THE KING'S ROYAL RIFLE CORPS [CHAP. VIII.

The Battalion moved to Aldershot, Salamanca Barracks, on January 27, 1897. On April 16, 1898, Colonel Fetherstonhaugh retired, and was succeeded by Lieut.-Colonel R. Gunning, who, however, exchanged with Lieut.-Colonel R. G. Buchanan Riddell, who had been appointed to the 1st Battalion on February 17, 1899.

The Battalion moved from Aldershot to Kilkenny on September 10, 1898. On October 9, 1899, they were mobilised for service in South Africa. Strength : Officers, 28 ; Other Ranks, 1,073.

They embarked from Queenstown in s.s. *Servia* on November 4 and disembarked at Durban on the 28th.

THE FIRST BATTALION

THE WRECK OF THE 'WARREN HASTINGS'

On July 1, 1895, Lieut.-Colonel McCall completed his period of command, and was succeeded by Lieut.-Colonel M. C. B. Forestier-Walker, who took over command on the 30th.

After a quiet year at Jullundur, the Battalion, on November 20, 1896, was placed under orders for Mauritius and the Cape. They left Jullundur on November 30, reaching Deolali on December 5. Leaving all time-expired men at that Depot, they sailed for the Cape on the R.I.M.S. *Warren Hastings* (Commander G. E. Holland, D.S.O., R.I.M.) on December 10. On December 28 the ship arrived at Cape Town and disembarked B, D, E, and F Companies, under Major R. H. Gunning, for Wynberg. On January 6, 1897, the *Warren Hastings* sailed for Mauritius, having on board Headquarters, A, C, G, and H Companies, half a Battalion of the 2nd York and Lancaster Regiment, under Major W. J. Kirkpatrick, and 25 men of the Middlesex Regiment. The following Officers of the 1st Battalion were on board :

Lieut.-Colonel M. C. B. Forestier-Walker,
Major H. Gore-Browne,
Captain G. N. Prendergast,
Captain M. H. K. Pechell,
Lieutenant C. Gosling,
Lieutenant L. B. Cumberland,
2nd Lieutenant J. Taylor,
2nd Lieutenant B. J. Majendie,
Captain and Adjutant Hon. A. R. M.-Stuart-Wortley,[1]
Hon. Lieutenant and Quartermaster J. W. Dwane.

The only passengers in addition to the troops were Lady Muriel Gore-Browne, three Officers' wives of other Corps, thirteen wives of Other Ranks, and ten children.

The story of the dramatic ending of the voyage cannot be better told than it is in Colonel Walker's report, which is given in full. Commander Holland's report is equally good, but more technical.

'MAURITIUS,
'*January* 28, 1897.

'SIR,

'1. I have the honour to forward, for the information of the Major-General Commanding, the following report of the circumstances connected with the loss of the R.I.M.S. *Warren Hastings*, of the troops on board of which I was in command.

'2. The ship left Cape Town on 6th instant with the Headquarters and four Companies of 1st Battalion King's Royal Rifles, four Companies 2nd Battalion York and Lancaster Regiment, and one Warrant Officer and 24 men Middlesex Regiment, *en route* to this island, where she was due at midday on 14th instant. The total number of troops on board was 22 Officers, 4 Warrant Officers, 940 Non-commissioned Officers and men, 4 ladies, 13 women, and 10 children.

'3. At 2.20 a.m. on the night of the 13th and 14th instant, I

[1] Lieut.-General Hon. Sir A. R. Montagu-Stuart-Wortley, K.C.B., K.C.M.G., D.S.O., Colonel Commandant 1st Battalion, 1925.

was awakened by a shock, and realising from the grating sound what had occurred, I dressed hurriedly and went up to the bridge to report myself for orders to the Captain of the ship, Commander G. E. Holland, D.S.O., R.I.M. All this time drenching rain was falling in torrents, and making a great noise, pouring on the awnings and decks, and the night was so intensely dark that it was impossible to distinguish anything more than a few feet away, and impossible to make out where the vessel was, or to see anything at all of the land, or the nature of the rocks on which she was lying, though it was believed that the vessel had struck on the coast of the Island of Réunion. The sea at the time was calm, though there was a moderate swell. The engines were then working at full speed ahead, and were kept so until stopped by the water.

' 4. I received orders from Commander Holland to have all the troops fallen in down below, the guard alone being on the upper deck, and these were ordered down almost immediately after, leaving only such sentries as were necessary.

' 5. On receiving a report that the rock against which the ship's bows were resting appeared to afford landing-space, Commander Holland, at 3.25 a.m., sent Lieutenants Dobbin and Windham, R.I.M., down over the bows, with blue lights, to investigate and report, and informed me that, if practicable, he would commence landing the men, in a similar way, as soon as possible. In order to facilitate this, I gave directions that the men should be formed up by regiments, the King's Royal Rifles on the port side and the York and Lancaster and details on the starboard side of the ship, so that the two forward companions could be used simultaneously.

' 6. Up to this time, though the vessel was bumping heavily, she was lying on a fairly even keel, and Commander Holland therefore considered that the disembarkation of the ladies, women, and children could with safety be deferred till daylight, as it could then be carried out with so much more safety and convenience to them ; and orders were therefore issued, on his learning from the Officers sent that landing was feasible, for the disembarkation of the men to commence. I had previously given instructions that such of the men as were able should fetch their rifles and boots, and at 4 a.m. disembarkation commenced by rope ladders on either side of the bow.

' 7. At the same time, by Commander Holland's direction, I detailed two Officers, 1st Battalion King's Royal Rifles, the one, Major Gore-Browne, to land with the men and take command on shore, the other, Captain Prendergast, whose excellent knowledge of French was likely to be of good service, to proceed to the nearest village and try and make any arrangement possible for the reception of the ladies, women, and children, and men. Very soon after 4 a.m. the vessel gave a heavy bump, and a lurch to starboard, and as she appeared heeling over everyone was ordered on the upper deck. The men came up by various companies, and the regularity of the disembarkation was not interfered with. At 4.20 a.m., owing to the list increasing, Commander Holland deemed it necessary that the ladies, women, and children, and such sick as required assistance, should be landed at once, and for this purpose suspended the disembarkation of the men till it was satisfactorily completed.

' 8. The sea was by this time beginning to wash over the upper deck on the starboard side, and I received instructions to get all the men as far as possible over to the port side of the ship, and as Commander Holland considered that she was now in imminent danger of heeling right over and probably sinking in deep water, it became necessary to expedite the disembarkation, and orders were therefore given to discard both rifles and boots; this order was the more necessary as it was impossible to move along the deck without using both hands to support oneself. At about this time, 4.35 a.m., the electric light, which most fortunately had lasted so long, gave out, but happily it was almost daylight.

' 9. The list to starboard still continuing to increase, Commander Holland, about 4.55 a.m., gave permission to men who were good swimmers to drop off and swim ashore on the port side, a distance of some 30 yards, and the first man who did so, Private McNamara, 1st Battalion King's Royal Rifles, was successful in carrying a line to the land, by aid of which some three or four ropes were carried and made fast, and were the means of assisting a considerable number of men to the shore. Though the swell at the time was only moderate, the waves were breaking on the rocks with considerable force, and the backwash was sufficient to prevent anyone landing without assistance, and groups of men were all along the shore helping others as they came near. By this time, too, in addition to the ladders already mentioned, one or two ropes had been hung over the bows, by which men clambered down on to the rocks.

'10. The disembarkation of the troops was completed by 5.30 a.m., and I then, by Commander Holland's directions, left the bridge and went ashore. Here I learned that we were on the Island of Réunion, and within about half a mile of the village of Saint-Philippe, and that Captain Prendergast was there making all the arrangements he could. A little later, as it seemed that the vessel had settled down and showed no immediate signs of any further heeling over, Commander Holland authorised attempts being made to save the light baggage and anything else possible, and for this purpose I ordered two parties of 50 men each to be detailed from the King's Royal Rifles and York and Lancaster Regiment to assist, and to form a chain over the rocks from the wreck to the mainland of the island, where the baggage could be collected, a distance of about 100 yards. The party of the former Regiment was subsequently increased by about 25 or 30 more men, and the remainder of the troops I directed to be marched to the village. It was then found that, providentially, no lives among the troops had been lost.

'11. About 9 a.m. the parties mentioned above were relieved by some 80 or 100 men of the York and Lancaster Regiment, and these continued to work until 10 a.m., when the First Lieutenant of the ship, Lieutenant St. John, who was in charge at the time, considering the wreck to be unsafe, directed everyone to leave, and the whole of the troops, with the exception of a small guard placed over the baggage saved, with sentries close to the ship to prevent any looting, were then collected in the village of Saint-Philippe. The baggage was subsequently brought up the village, and the sentries, being relieved by the local French police, were withdrawn. Commander Holland had previously proceeded to the village and placed himself in telegraphic communication with the British Consul at Saint-Denis, and had also made every possible arrangement for the supply of rations to the troops, a considerable portion of which had to be brought from Saint-Joseph, about $10\frac{1}{2}$ miles distant, a sufficient quantity not being procurable at Saint-Philippe. This involved a certain amount of delay, but, fortunately, some preserved beef and biscuits had been saved from the wreck and were available for immediate issue.

'12. During the day a reply was received from the Consul stating that the B.I. s.s. *Lalpoora* was at Pointe des Galèts, and available to take on the troops, and I was informed she would probably be chartered for this purpose. Saint-Pierre, the nearest place with a harbour where there would be any chance of embarking the men, is distant from Saint-Philippe about 21 miles, and it was absolutely necessary that everyone should be got on there as soon as possible, as the smaller towns and villages would be unable to find the requisite provisions for so large a force. Carriage for the ladies, women, and children, and sick, was essential, and, in addition, there were some 350 men without boots, who could not possibly march the distance; Commander Holland had, therefore, asked the aid of the local authorities at Saint-Pierre and Saint-Joseph to secure as many carriages and carts as could be got, and, having arranged that the men capable of walking should march the following day, the 15th instant, to Saint-Joseph, and that the ladies, women, children, and sick, and as many men as the carts procurable could carry, should also start the following morning and go right through to Saint-Pierre, he left for the latter place at 8 p.m., 14th instant, taking me with him, with a view to making all further arrangements necessary.

' 13. The command of the troops remaining at Saint-Philippe devolved on Major Kirkpatrick, York and Lancaster Regiment.

' 14. The people of the village had been most kind in providing the best accommodation at their disposal, the sick being put up in the Mairie and the women and children in the convent. The men were quartered in two empty enclosures, the best sleeping-accommodation which was available being given them, and they were made as comfortable as could be expected under the circumstances. Commander Holland and I reached Saint-Pierre about 2.15 a.m. on the 15th instant.

' 15. It had been his intention to have the B.I. s.s. *Lalpoora* brought round there, but she could not have entered the harbour, and the sea, on the morning of the 15th instant, was too high to admit of any boats passing in or out, so she was ordered to remain at Pointe des Galèts, and as the railway begins at Saint-Pierre, arrangements were made for a special train to convey everyone to the former place to embark. The old barracks at Saint-Pierre were placed at our disposal and afforded sufficient and excellent accommodation, especially as it was not intended that anyone should stop there more than a few hours.

'16. I had directed Major Kirkpatrick to proceed in command of the party, about 600 strong, marching from Saint-Philippe to Saint-Joseph, and left it to him to decide whether, after a rest and a meal there, the men were fit to complete the march to Saint-Pierre the same day. About 12 o'clock I redeived a telegram from him saying he intended to halt at Saint-Joseph for the night. The ladies, women, children, and sick arrived during the course of the day in carts and carriages, and at 8 p.m. a special train was got off, in which Commander Holland left, with the whole of them, nearly all the crew of the R.I.M.S. *Warren Hastings*, and as many of the men without boots as had arrived up to then, together with two Officers, in all about 400.

'With the kind assistance of the Mayor of Saint-Pierre more carts had been placed at our disposal for the purpose of bringing up the remaining men from Saint-Philippe, and instructions were sent by Commander Holland to Lieutenant St. John, who with Captain Prendergast, 1st Battalion King's Royal Rifles, had remained in charge, telling him to bring everyone along, and to arrange to arrive at Saint-Pierre by 3 p.m. on the 16th instant.

'I also sent orders to Major Kirkpatrick to march so as to arrive not later than 11 a.m. that day, so as to enable the men to get the meal provided for them, and to be ready to entrain at 12.30 p.m. Going down to the barracks at 8 a.m. on the 16th, I found that Major Kirkpatrick's party, about 600 strong, had arrived all right, and as Commander Holland, after inspecting the *Lalpoora* at Pointe des Galèts, returned to Saint-Pierre by the forenoon train, I left myself with about 400 men by the 12.50 p.m. special train, and embarked with them on the *Lalpoora*, where I found the ladies, women, and children, and the whole of the men who had gone on the preceding night, already settled down. I had left Major Gore-Browne, 1st Battalion King's Royal Rifles, in command of the men remaining at Saint-Pierre, and this party, being joined by those with Lieutenant St. John and Captain Prendergast from Saint-Philippe, left that night with Commander Holland, and reached Pointe des Galèts about 4 a.m. on the 17th instant, when the whole of those from the R.I.M.S. *Warren Hastings* (with the exception of Lieutenants St. John and Windham, R.I.M., and 10 Lascars remaining behind for salvage purposes) were embarked on the *Lalpoora*, which sailed at 3 p.m. that afternoon and reached Port Louis, Mauritius, at 6 a.m., 18th instant.

'17. It is impossible sufficiently to thank Mr. Bennett, the British Consul, for all he did for us. Not being able to leave himself at that particular time, he immediately on receipt of the news of the disaster sent his Secretary, Mr. Piat, down to meet us, and he joined Commander Holland and myself, between Saint-Joseph and Saint-Pierre, on the night of the 14th instant, and was untiring in his efforts to assist us in every possible way from that time until we sailed.

'18. I have already mentioned the kindness and hospitality of the inhabitants of Saint-Philippe when we landed there. All, from the Mayor downwards, showed the greatest anxiety to be of service to us, and the many isolated acts of kindness in the giving of coffee, food, and clothing to individual men are much too numerous to mention. I would, however, draw special attention to what was done for us by Monsieur Coulon, who placed his house and everything he possessed at the disposal of the ladies, and had food available all the day for any of them, or of the Officers who required it, and finally, when practically eaten out of house and home, was with the greatest difficulty prevailed upon to accept any recompense.

'Monsieur Alfred Chaton, Sous-Officier of Gendarmerie, was also most obliging and unsparing in his efforts to save the men fatigue by taking on himself and his gendarmes nearly all the guard duty necessary at Saint-Philippe, which, after what everyone had gone through, was an inestimable boon.

'Major Kirkpatrick reported to me that he had received very material assistance from the Mayor of Saint-Joseph, and I can speak myself to the services cheerfully rendered to us by the Mayor of Saint-Pierre in the collection of extra carts, without which it would have been impossible to get the men up from Saint-Philippe as soon as we did. I might mention numerous other instances, but I trust these will be enough to show the really kindly spirit in which these ship-wrecked British troops were received by the officials and inhabitants of the Island of Réunion, and I would further respectfully express a hope that when this is represented to the Government, some steps may be taken to convey to the Governor and officials of this island our grateful thanks for all they did for us.

'19. I enclose a report received from Major Kirkpatrick,

York and Lancaster Regiment, giving his account of what took place, and I have to express my entire concurrence in his remarks.

'20. During the time everyone was being got ashore from the wreck, I was an eye-witness from the bridge of numerous acts of devotion and gallantry in saving life, and several other cases were afterwards brought to my notice, which I did not see myself, but which I consider are thoroughly well authenticated, and I have therefore the honour to submit the following list with the hope that the conduct of those named may be brought to the notice of the proper authorities. In this list I have, to avoid repetition, omitted any mention of names already brought forward by Major Kirkpatrick, in the report already alluded to, except in one case, where the details came more under my own personal observation :—

'(1) No. 7679, Private N. McNamara, 1st Battalion King's Royal Rifles, was the first man to attempt to swim to the shore on the port side, as has already been mentioned, carrying a light line, by means of which ropes were carried over and made fast, thus enabling many men to escape.

'(2) No. 6168, Private E. Carr, 1st Battalion King's Royal Rifles, swam out some distance to the assistance of Mr. Gadsden, R.I.M., Chief Engineer of the ship, and brought him ashore.

'(3) No. 4421, Private G. Howes, 1st Battalion King's Royal Rifles, at the time a patient in hospital, dived in and attempted to save a native cook, who was drowned. He had afterwards to be himself helped out of the water.

'(4) No. 7291, Lance-Corporal R. Newby, 1st Battalion King's Royal Rifles, dived from the ship and assisted a man of the York and Lancaster Regiment (name unknown) to a rope, by which he was got ashore.

'(5) No. 5680, Private W. J. Grisley, 1st Battalion King's Royal Rifles, swam out with a buoy to the assistance of Private J. Brown, 1st Battalion King's Royal Rifles, by which he was saved.

'(6) No. 6131, Private M. Arrowsmith, 1st Battalion King's Royal Rifles, was on the rocks near the bow of the ship ; when a child of one of the York and Lancaster Regiment, which was being brought down the ladder, slipped and fell into the sea, Private Arrowsmith, although unable to swim, jumped in with a rope and was pulled out again with the child in his arms.

'(7) No. 6547, Private L. A. Wootton, 1st Battalion King's

Royal Rifles, swam out to the assistance of Private G. Taylor, 1st Battalion King's Royal Rifles, and, after bringing him ashore, went in again with a buoy to Private Danner, 1st Battalion King's Royal Rifles, who was getting exhausted. Private Danner missed the buoy, and Private Wootton then supported him to the rocks.

'(8) Lieutenant Windham and Sub-Lieutenant Huddleston, R.I.M., were instrumental in saving several lives, but I have been unable to get particulars, except in the case of Lance-Corporal Robinson, 1st Battalion King's Royal Rifle Corps, who could not possibly have got ashore but for assistance, and who was saved by them both; and Private Diamond, 1st Battalion King's Royal Rifles, whom Sub-Lieutenant Huddleston saved, being afterwards himself dashed insensible against the rocks, and picked out of the surf by Serjeant J. Allen and No. 7030, Private C. Croft, both 1st Battalion King's Royal Rifles, at great risk to themselves.

'(9) Mr. Tyler, Bandmaster, 1st Battalion King's Royal Rifles, was in the water, on the starboard side, and unable to make any headway against the backwash of the waves, or to get near the shore; Lieutenant Gosling, 1st Battalion King's Royal Rifles, endeavoured to reach him, but after going some 20 yards was washed back, thrown on the rock and injured. Second Lieutenant Forman, Royal Artillery, at once went in with a rope and a life-buoy, and swimming out to Mr. Tyler, gave him the buoy. When, however, the men on the shore began to haul on the rope, it parted. Second Lieutenant Forman stayed with Mr. Tyler, and Lieutenant Gosling then made a second attempt to reach him, but failed and was brought ashore. Second Lieutenant Bayley, York and Lancaster Regiment, then swam out with a rope, and the whole three were then brought close in to shore, when Second Lieutenants Forman and Bayley were hauled up on the rock, over which the sea was then washing. In endeavouring to pull Mr. Tyler in the buoy slipped, and the backwash carried him out at once. Just at the time one of the boats belonging to the ship, which had washed loose, was drifted sufficiently near the rocks to be got hold of, but was all the time being dashed against them, and actually being broken up. It was caught and manned by Colour-Serjeant Jones, who was at the time a hospital patient, Serjeants H. Howarth and R. Downe, Corporals R. Hodgson and C. Young, and Privates Nos. 6206

W. Parkinson, 6040 G. Kaley, 6064 T. Jones, 5756 J. Connell, 7441 T. Steele, 8094 P. Pickersgill, all King's Royal Rifles, and attempted to be rowed out to where Mr. Tyler, who was much exhausted, was.

'Not being able to get the boat out, Serjeant Downe dived from the stern and swam to him, supporting him till he could be got on board; but the sea afterwards swept him out of the boat and he was pulled in again by Corporal C. Young and No. 6231, Private C. B. Jones, and was eventually landed in safety, though insensible, together with the crew of the boat.

'21. In conclusion, I would wish to bring to the notice of the Major-General Commanding the admirable behaviour of all the troops on board from the time the vessel struck.

'The most perfect discipline was maintained; everyone fell in quietly when the order was given, and remained awaiting further orders, without noise or any sign whatever that anything more than usual was expected of them. When it is remembered that the great majority of the men were below decks at the time, and could not see, though they could not but be conscious of the danger in which they stood, of the extent of which, however, they had no chance of forming an opinion, the order maintained appears the more praiseworthy.

'From my position on the bridge, where I could see distinctly, I was particularly struck by the way in which, when the disembarkation of the men was stopped to allow the ladies, women, and children to get ashore, the former quietly stood on one side to permit them to pass, and then resumed their own disembarkation in perfect order, when, all the time, it appeared to be a question of moments when the vessel would heel over.

'I have, etc.,

'M. F. WALKER, *Lieut.-Colonel, K.R.R.,*
'*Late Commanding Troops, R.I.M.S. " Warren Hastings."* '

The names of the men of the York and Lancaster Regiment who particularly distinguished themselves do not appear in Colonel Walker's Report; but no account of the wreck can be complete without the story of Private Roe of that Regiment, who was on sentry on one of the lower decks and was found, after all the troops were supposed to be on shore, by an Officer sent below to make sure that no one had been left behind, standing up to his knees in water with every intention of remaining on his post till he should be relieved. The Officer had seen no one and was returning on deck, when he heard a voice say, 'Please, sir, am I to stay here?' Surely this British soldier makes a fitting companion to the Roman sentry whose skeleton was found at Pompeii, still at his post though buried in a shower of volcanic ash, as an instance of fortitude and discipline.

The cause of the wreck seems to have been a change in the usual current. Though observations had been taken the previous day, the ship when she struck was eight miles out of her position as it should have been by dead reckoning. The torrents of rain that were falling drowned any sound of breakers. The darkness was so intense that, to quote Commander Holland's report, 'although the vessel was actually on rocks, close to very large boulders, and having, within a distance of only about 60 yards from the bow of the ship, the cliffs and high land of the island, we could see from the vessel's bridge absolutely nothing.' It may also be mentioned that a volcano in full eruption only a few miles away was totally invisible.

The report of Mr. C. W. Bennett, H.M. Consul at Réunion, tells us how what was no more than a perilous adventure might easily have been a tragedy. He says :—

'On the whole rugged coast there was only one spot where there was any chance of saving life on a wrecked vessel, and a merciful Providence guided the *Warren Hastings* there. Had the wreck taken place 10 yards one side or other of this spot for a distance of over 20 miles on either side, the vessel would have sunk in deep water, and the passengers and crew who escaped death from sharks would have met a hardly less cruel one by being dashed, bruised and bleeding, upon sharp, pitiless, inaccessible lava-cliffs.'

About a fortnight elapsed before the news of the wreck reached England. The unexpected delay had caused the Colonel to remark that the people in England did not seem to care whether they were drowned or saved, but when the whole story had been realised ample amends were made. On March 6 Her Majesty Queen Victoria sent to the Colonel the following cablegram :—

'I wish to express my great satisfaction with the admirable discipline shown by the troops under your command on the occasion of the wreck of the *Warren Hastings*, particulars of which have only just been received by me. I much regret the loss of private property sustained by all ranks.

V. R. I.'

Many congratulatory telegrams followed, including a letter from H.R.H. the Duke of Cambridge, our Colonel-in-Chief, as follows :—

'You may easily imagine how much I have been distressed at the sad calamity which has befallen the wing of the Battalion of the King's Royal Rifles (60th) in being shipwrecked on board the *Warren Hastings*, together with a wing of the York and Lancaster Regiment, on their voyage to Mauritius; but, whilst deeply deploring this catastrophe, I am full of admiration at the admirable discipline of both Corps, which has resulted in the saving of life of every soul on board, including sick, women, and children. It is a noble example, set to the Army and to the world at large, as to what discipline can effect under the most trying circumstances, and I hope you will express to the Officers, N.C.O.s, and Rank and File of your Battalion my admiration of their conduct. But for their calm and perfect behaviour it is more than probable that great losses of life would have resulted.

'As Colonel-in-Chief of the gallant Corps I feel more than ever proud of being associated with so splendid a Regiment.'

The guardians of the public purse were not so sympathetic, and it was only after the matter had been taken up in Parliament that something approaching to an adequate compensation was given to the troops for the losses they had incurred.

Captain Holland was made an honorary member for life of the Officers' Mess. Such a recognition was the least that could be given by the Battalion for his splendid coolness and courage.

The following is an extract from a special Army Order, issued on March 13, 1897, by Field-Marshal Viscount Wolseley, Commander-in-Chief :—

'The Commander-in-Chief feels great gratification in making known to the Army the substance of the report from the G.O.C. at Mauritius regarding the remarkable courage and exemplary discipline displayed under most trying circumstances by the troops on board the R.I.M. troopship *Warren Hastings* when that ship, steaming full speed, struck the rocks during a pitch-dark night and was wrecked near the village of Saint-Philippe in the Island of Réunion at 2.20 a.m. on the 14th of January last.

'The troops on board consisted of the H.Q. and four Companies 1st Battalion King's Royal Rifle Corps, and four Companies 2nd Battalion York and Lancaster Regiment, and a Detachment of the Middlesex Regiment. They at once fell in on the main deck in perfect order. [The Army Order goes on to describe in detail the incidents already related.] . . . With the exception of two natives, all on board, to the number of 993 besides the crew, reached the shore, saved in many cases by the individual gallantry of comrades. The following N.C.O.s and men are named by Lieut.-Colonel Forestier-Walker, 1st Battalion K.R.R.C., who was in command and was the last soldier to leave the ship, as having particularly distinguished themselves upon the occasion :—

'1*st Battalion, K.R.R.C.*

Colour-Sergeant Jones.
Sergeant J. Allen.
    ,,   R. Downe.
    ,,   H. Howarth.

Corporal R. Hodgson.
,, C. Young.
Lance-Corporal R. Newby.
Private M. Arrowsmith.
,, E. Carr.
,, J. Connell.
,, C. Croft.
,, W. J. Grisley.
,, G. Howes.
,, C. B. Jones.
,, T. Jones.
,, G. Kaley.
,, N. McNamara.
,, W. Parkinson.
,, R. Pickersgill.
,, T. Steele.
,, L. A. Wootten.

'Commander Holland speaks in the highest terms of Lieut.-Colonel Forestier-Walker, who is entitled to great praise for his conduct.

'Lieut.-Colonel Forestier-Walker reports that the conduct of the Officers generally was admirable, and gives exceptional credit to the following :—

'*1st Battalion, K.R.R.C.*

Major H. Gore-Browne.
Captain G. N. Prendergast.
Lieutenant C. Gosling.

'Commander Holland reports the behaviour of the troops throughout as beyond all praise. Discipline was twice very seriously tested ; first, when, after the vessel struck, the men were ordered to fall in below on the main and troop decks ; secondly, when their disembarkation was suspended to enable the women and children to be landed. Had there been any attempt to crush or struggle forward, there would have been great loss of life, as, owing to the position of the vessel, it was impossible to walk on the deck without holding on to the rails or ropes, and any struggle or pushing would inevitably have resulted in many being drowned. From first to last perfect discipline was maintained and all orders issued were instantly obeyed, without noise, confusion, or hesitation.

'The Commander-in-Chief is proud of the behaviour of the troops during this trying time ; he regards it as a good example of the advantages of subordination and strict discipline, for it was by that alone in God's providence that heavy loss of life was prevented.

'The Commander-in-Chief again closes the Order with expressing his admiration of the coolness, courage, and resource shown by Commander Holland and sympathises with him and his brave Officers.

'[*Signed*] WOLSELEY.'

Our 1st Battalion passed two uneventful years in Mauritius. On December 29, 1898, Colonel Forestier-Walker was appointed A.A.G. in Egypt and was succeeded in command by Lieut.-Colonel R. H. Gunning, who had for a few months been commanding the 3rd Battalion and who exchanged with Lieut.-Colonel R. G. Buchanan-Riddell, promoted to fill Colonel Walker's vacancy.

The Headquarters Wing embarked at Port Louis, Mauritius, in the R.I.M.S. *Clive* for Natal on March 5, 1899, and reached Durban on the 21st : strength, 9 Officers, 424 Other Ranks. Their station was Pietermaritzburg, where they were joined by the other half Battalion from the Cape on May 11 : strength, 7 Officers, 499 Other Ranks.

The same month a Mounted Infantry Company was formed from the Battalion at Maritzburg, and a detachment of 3 Officers, 150 Other Ranks, and a Mounted Infantry section went to Etshowe, Zululand.

On September 25, in expectation of the outbreak of war, the Battalion started to march to Ladysmith : strength, 17 Officers, 767 Other Ranks.

The following officers were with the Battalion :

    Lieut.-Colonel R. Gunning.
    Major W. P. Campbell.[1]
       ,,   C. A. T. Boultbee.
       ,,   F. M. Beaumont.
    Captain O. S. W. Nugent, D.S.O.[2]
       ,,   E. Northey.
    Lieutenant F. M. Crum.
          ,,   B. J. Majendie.
          ,,   R. C. Barnett.
          ,,   J. Taylor.
          ,,   J. H. Davidson.[3]
    2nd Lieutenant G. H. Martin.
             ,,   A. D. Legard.
             ,,   C. F. Hawley.
             ,,   R. G. Stirling.
             ,,   W. J. Hambro.
    Captain and Adjutant H. R. Blore.

The Battalion was encamped there till October 5, when it went to join Penn Symons's Brigade at Glencoe, where it arrived on October 7.

On October 12 it was officially intimated that the South African Republics had declared war against Great Britain.

On the 14th Captain M. H. K. Pechell, Lieutenant H. S. Marsden, and 2nd Lieutenant R. E. Reade joined the Battalion, as did, on the 18th, Captain the Hon. A. R. M.-Stuart-Wortley, Lieutenant R. G. Jelf,[4] and Lieutenant R. Johnstone.

---

[1] Lieut.-General Sir William Pitcairn Campbell, K.C.B., Colonel Commandant 4th Battalion 1918–23, 2nd Battalion 1923.
[2] Major-General Sir Oliver Nugent, K.C.B., D.S.O.
[3] Major-General Sir John Davidson, K.C.M.G., C.B., D.S.O.
[4] Brigadier-General R. G. Jelf, C.M.G., D.S.O.

CHAPTER IX

THE SOUTH AFRICAN WAR, 1899—1902

IT is unnecessary to go into the very controversial question of the causes of the South African War further than to say that, from the history of the country, it was inevitable that, some day, it would be settled by force of arms whether South Africa, as a whole, should come inside or go outside the British Empire, unless one side or other were prepared completely to surrender its claims.

In August 1899, when it appeared more and more certain every day that war would break out at an early date, when it was known that the Boer Republics could put at least 50,000 men into the field, the British forces in South Africa amounted to something under 10,000 men. A driblet of some 2,000 men was ordered out early in August. On September 8 orders were given for a further reinforcement of just over 10,000 men, rather more than half of which came from India, the remainder from England and different colonial stations. Nearly all these additional troops had landed in South Africa before the outbreak of war. The main expeditionary force did not begin to leave England till after the invasion of Natal.

The difficulty of the British political situation, all along, had been that any attempt on the part of the Government to dispatch reinforcements, which would bring their force in South Africa to anything approaching an equality with that of the Boer Republics, was certain to bring on war and at the same time to give to the rest of the world the impression that the British were the aggressors; so that, whether they acted or did not act, they were bound to find themselves on the outbreak of war in great numerical inferiority on the scene of action. This is just what happened. The dispatch of reinforcements in September was answered by Kruger's ultimatum on October 9, followed immediately by the invasion of Natal. It had all along been anticipated that the first act of the drama would be an invasion of Natal, and in the measures to be taken to prepare for this move political and strategical considerations clashed.

The salient formed by Northern Natal, with the Transvaal on one side of it and the Orange Free State on the other, made any attempt to hold the frontier line or—in view of the probability of the Orange Free State joining the Transvaal in the event of war—even to try, with the small force available, to occupy any part of the triangle against an invading force, very bad strategy. From the political point of view it was most undesirable that Northern Natal, with its mixed population of Kaffirs, loyal British settlers, and Dutch—who, though they had long remained uncomplainingly under British government, might be expected to sympathise more or less actively with their kinsmen over the border—should be invaded. This was urgently pointed out by the Natal Government in a dispatch to the Colonial Office dated September 6, 1899.

The result was a compromise which, in the event, turned out as ineffectually as a compromise generally does in war, by which the main force occupied Ladysmith, the junction of the railway lines from the Transvaal and Orange Free State respectively, while a detachment was sent forward some 50 miles to Glencoe, to cover the Dundee coal-fields. Sir George White,[1] who had been sent out

[1] Field-Marshal Sir George W. ite, V.C., G.C.B., G.C.S.I., G.C.I.E., G.C.V.O.

from England to take command in Natal, on his arrival on October 7, disliking this dispersion of force, wished at once to withdraw the Glencoe detachment; but the proposal was met with such a protest by the Governor of Natal, who drew so alarming a picture of the moral effect of a withdrawal—which would be looked upon as a defeat—on the Dutch of Cape Colony and the 750,000 natives in Natal and Zululand, that Sir George gave in. It is easy to be wise after the event, but, in our worst troubles a month or two later, when, to those who could not appreciate the reserve strength of the British Empire, it must have seemed that the whole British Army could make no impression on the Boers and were on the way to be themselves driven into the sea, there was never a hint of trouble with the natives; and, anyhow, a worse moral effect was likely to be produced by the total destruction of the Glencoe detachment—which would have been inevitable if the Boer leaders had not failed to co-operate—than by its withdrawal before the outbreak of war. By this time there was no doubt that the original view, that the Boers' first move would be the invasion of Natal, was the correct one; nor that—following on President Kruger's ultimatum of October 9—this invasion might be expected at any hour.

The disposition of the Boer forces for this purpose was as follows:—

The main force of about 11,300 men with 16 field guns and 3 6-inch Creusots, under General P. Joubert, the Boer Commander-in-Chief, was concentrated opposite the apex of the Northern Natal salient. On the eastern border of Natal facing the Dundee detachment was General Lukas Meyer, with 2,870 men. A Free State contingent of some 9,500 burghers occupied the passes over the Drakensberg.

The distribution of the British forces in Natal on October 11, 1899, was as follows :—

Dundee [1] :—
    18th Hussars.
    1 Squadron Natal Carbineers.
    3 Companies Mounted Infantry.
    Detachment Natal Police.
    3 Batteries Royal Field Artillery.
    1st Leicestershire Regiment.
    1st King's Royal Rifle Corps.
    2nd Royal Dublin Fusiliers.

Ladysmith :—
    Two Regular Cavalry Regiments.
    3 Batteries Royal Field Artillery.
    1 Mountain Battery.
    1 Company Royal Engineers (less one Section).
    4 Regular Infantry Battalions.
    3 Regiments of Colonial Mounted Troops,
    with other odds and ends.

At different points in the Line of Communications :
    2 Regular Infantry Battalions (including 2nd K.R.R.C.).
    3 more Regiments of Colonial Mounted Troops.

    A small Infantry Detachment 1st K.R.R.C. with one Section M.I. in Zululand.

According to the terms of Kruger's ultimatum of October 9, a state of war ensued at 5 p.m. on the 11th.

Major-General Sir W. Penn Symons, who had all along been in favour of holding Dundee, arrived there and took command on the 12th. He had not long to wait for news of the enemy. On the 13th he heard that a strong commando was concentrating east of De Jager's Drift, only a

---

[1] The 1st Royal Irish Fusiliers and one Section 23rd Company Royal Engineers arrived on October 15 and 16.

short march away. Next day a Boer patrol was encountered on the British side of the Buffalo River. Joubert got on the move on the 12th, but only reached Newcastle on the 18th. He had, however, already made his dispositions for dealing with Symons. Erasmus with 5,000 men was to march straight on Dundee while Lukas Meyer made a simultaneous attack from the east; Kock, who had entered Natal by Botha's Pass, was to occupy the Biggarsberg, cutting the railway between Dundee and Ladysmith. All these movements were known to Symons, and on the 19th he received detailed warning that he would be attacked that night by Erasmus from the north, Meyer from the east, and Viljoen (detached from Kock) from the west.

On the evening of October 19 Lukas Meyer, with 3,500 men and 7 guns (4·75 mm. and 3 pompoms[1]), started on his march to make the agreed attack—in concert with Erasmus—on Penn Symons's force. He crossed the Buffalo River at De Jager's Drift about 9 p.m. At 2.30 a.m. a Mounted Infantry piquet of the Dublin Fusiliers was encountered at the road junction east of Smith's Nek. The piquet retired after a few shots had been exchanged. An hour before dawn the Boer advanced guard was on the summit of Talana Hill. Meyer occupied Talana Hill with 1,800 men, with the rest holding Lennox Hill to the south of the Nek. He placed two of his 75s near the rear edge of the top of Talana with one pompom on the forward crest, and sent the other two 75s and two pompoms to Lennox Hill.

Talana is a flat-topped hill about a mile to the east of Dundee, the intervening country being intersected by wire fences with the sunken bed of the Sand Spruit crossing it

---

[1] "Pompom" was the name given to the 1-inch to 1½-inch quick-firer, much used in the South African War, but which has since gone out of fashion.

from north to south. From the western crest of the hill a very steep and rocky face drops 160 feet to a nearly flat terrace 50 to 80 yards wide, which is commanded throughout from the top. This terrace was bounded along its outer edge by a low stone wall, below which the ground again falls steeply, leaving 10 to 15 yards of ground dead to the top of the hill but open to fire from Lennox Hill and from a spur running out from the northern end of Talana. From the wall above mentioned other walls run down the hill giving some protection from flanking fire. These walls formed the enclosures of Smith's Farm, which stood among trees near the foot of the hill and about 400 feet from the summit. Below the farm stood a group of copses of eucalyptus trees covering a space about 500 yards square. From the edge of this wood an open glacis sloped away for about 800 yards to the Sand Spruit.

At 3 a.m. the report from the Mounted Infantry piquet that the Boers were advancing reached General Symons. He sent two companies of the Dublin Fusiliers to support the piquet, which they joined in the Sand Spruit to which it had fallen back, but otherwise he seems to have carried on as if there was not an enemy within a hundred miles.

At 5 a.m. of a wet and misty morning the British troops stood to arms as usual in their camp west of Dundee. As they stood on parade, musketry fire was heard to the east. It was the piquet of Dublin Fusiliers in the Sand Spruit exchanging shots with the Boers. The parade having been dismissed, a message from Headquarters at 5.20 a.m. assured C.O.s that all was clear. Various companies moved off for training round the camp and the horses of two batteries and all the transport animals went off to water a mile and a half away.

At 5.30 a.m. the mist lifted and revealed the summit of Talana—5,000 yards away—alive with men. Ten minutes later a shell dropped into the western edge of the town, followed by a rapid succession of them into the middle of the camp. Fortunately they failed to explode in the sodden ground. The Cavalry and Mounted Infantry, who had not left camp, quickly got out of sight behind a neighbouring kopje. The Infantry fell in again and were doubled off to the shelter of a ravine to the south of the camp.

Symons at once decided to attack. While one battery replied to the Boer fire from their own gun-park, another, ready horsed, galloped forward through the town and, turning to the right, came into action immediately west of the colliery extension of the railway. Within twenty minutes of the first shell falling into the camp they had opened fire on the crest of Talana at a range of 3,750 yards. They were quickly joined by a second battery, and in a few minutes the Boer guns were temporarily silenced. Meanwhile, the Infantry had moved so quickly that they were already east of the town. The Leicestershire Regiment, one company from each of the other Regiments, and the third battery were left to defend the camp from the expected attack by Erasmus from the north. The Cavalry, with the Mounted Infantry attached to them, were left awaiting orders under cover near the camp.

By 7 a.m. the three attacking Battalions were under cover in the Sand Spruit, where the Dublin Fusiliers picked up their two companies which had gone out in the small hours.

Here Penn Symons gave his orders for the attack: Dublin Fusiliers, first line; K.R.R.C., second line: Royal Irish Fusiliers, reserve. Brigadier-General Yule to command the attack.

At 7.20 a.m. the right-hand company of the Dublin

Fusiliers emerged from the bed of the Sand Spruit and advanced in extended order towards the woods of Smith's Farm about 800 yards away, the other companies following in echelon from the right. As soon as they got into the open they came under a heavy fire from Talana itself and from Lennox Hill to their right front. Men began to fall, and they broke into a double. On reaching the wood, they pushed through it and lined the wall on the far side, where they were within five or six hundred yards of the crest of Talana. Here our 1st Battalion, who had left the Spruit just behind the Dublin Fusiliers, came up and prolonged the line to the right. The Dublin Fusiliers had during their advance been all the time inclining to the left.

A donga which entered the wood at its north-eastern corner had the appearance of forming a covered way, at least as far as the level terrace below the crest. The three leading companies of the Dublin Fusiliers at once tried to push on up this donga, but it proved to be a fatal trap. It soon changed from its oblique direction to a vertical one, straight up and down the hillside, and then faded to nothing. On reaching the point where it was swept with rifle fire from the top, they suffered heavy casualties, could make no further progress, and had to hang on under what cover they could find. Meanwhile the 1st K.R.R.C., with four companies under Colonel Gunning lining the wall at the front edge of the wood, and three under Major W. P. Campbell holding the enclosures round Smith's Farm, kept up a telling fire on the crest of Talana and on the numerous Boer snipers who were annoying them from the crest and slopes of Lennox Hill. The R.I.F., with two companies, lined the northern edge of the wood and kept the right of the enemy's position on Talana under fire. The remainder of the Battalion were in reserve inside the wood. The Maxim guns of all three Battalions occupied the south-eastern corner of the wood and, directing their fire on Smith's Nek and Lennox Hill, did a good deal to keep down the fire from those places. Such was the situation at 8 a.m., at which hour the two batteries from near the station advanced to a new position between Dundee and Sand Spruit, one battery opening fire on Talana Hill at 2,300 yards, the other on Lennox Hill at 2,500. Unfortunately, owing to limitation of ammunition supply, the fire was not as rapid as could have been wished.

The momentum of the attack had now died away and the battle for a while developed into a shooting match. The reason for this is not apparent, as Yule had a battalion in hand with which to give it a fresh start.

After an hour of this Penn Symons seems to have lost patience. Instead of getting hold of the commander of the attack and giving him his orders or—supposing that he was determined to take direct command of the attack into his own hands—giving orders to Commanding Officers as to the next move, he himself rode into the wood, dismounted, and went up into the front line at the north-eastern corner of the wood, which was occupied by some of the R.I.F., and began to pass down the line calling on the men to press on. First Major Hammersley, of his Staff, was hit and immediately afterwards the General himself was shot in the stomach. Though he must have been suffering agony he turned, after telling General Yule to carry on, walked back to his horse, mounted, and rode back to the first-aid post without letting a sign of pain escape him. He was carried back to the dressing-station, where the Medical Officer at once pronounced his wound to be fatal.

The only direct effect of General Symons's action was

that one company of the R.I.F., which he had himself ordered forward, followed the donga already mentioned, by which the Dublin Fusiliers had tried to advance, and were held up at the same place. Another company followed them with the same result.

Meanwhile, the K.R.R.C. had resumed the advance. Four and a half companies, leaving two in Battalion Reserve—one company had been left in camp and a half company was escorting the Artillery—broke cover on the right, beginning from the enclosures round Smith's Farm. They came under a heavy fire, chiefly from Lennox Hill, but so rapid was their advance that they suffered few casualties. As they reached the wall bounding the upper terrace, mentioned in the description of the position, they found it unoccupied by the enemy. That this breastwork, within 400 yards of the wood and commanding every inch of the intervening space, some of which was dead from the top of the hill, should not be held was not the intention of the Boer commander. He had given direction for it to be held, but the prospective garrison, not liking the look of it as being isolated and exposed, had failed to obey his orders.

On seeing the Rifles reach the wall, the R.I.F. came streaming out of the wood straight up the hill, prolonging the line to the left. A company and a half of them, working round to the left and avoiding the dongas, got to within 500 yards of the enemy's extreme right. Another half company, which had been with the K.R.R.C. in Smith's Farm, advanced with that Regiment. With the Rifles and R.I.F. were mixed many of the Dublin Fusiliers, there having been considerable intermingling of units when the front of the wood was first occupied. Many of those also who had got held up by following the donga succeeded in getting up into the front line by retracing their steps to the wood. In fact, the advance of the Rifles produced a general rush up the hill all along the line, followed by a gradual reinforcement of the front line.

The advance was once more brought to a standstill. The Boer fire was intense and all our men could do was to lie down and shoot back. This went on for the best part of two hours; the line behind the wall, in spite of casualties, gradually gaining strength as more and more joined it from the rear.

At 11 a.m. the O.C. Royal Artillery got an order to cease fire to allow the Infantry to assault. This he did, but the assault not taking place immediately and the Boer fire on our guns increasing, he reopened again. At 11.30 the order was repeated. The Artillery again ceased fire, and this time galloped forward and opened again from a spot between the Sand Spruit and the foot of Talana, whence their fire could reach the top, past the left-hand edge of the wood, at a range of 1,400 yards. Under their rapid bombardment the enemy's fire slackened and then ceased, and again the order was signalled to cease fire. Colonel Gunning, who had by this time got up his two reserve companies from Smith's Farm, passed the word "Get ready to go over." Then, on the word "Advance," the whole line began scrambling over the wall, dashing across the flat terrace to the final climb up the precipitous escarpment that led to the crest. As they appeared over the wall they were met by a blaze of fire from the crest. Many fell, but the others continued to make the best of their way up on hands and knees. As they neared the top many of the Boers began to leave the position, while others ran forward and shot point-blank at their assailants who were clawing their way up to them.

What with the casualties from fire and the physical

difficulties of the ground, the attack was losing impetus, and the Artillery, owing to the indifferent light, not seeing how far some of our men had got and thinking that the attack had failed, again opened a rapid fire on the crest, the losses from which were by no means confined to the enemy. For a moment both sides drew back, which seems on our side to have had the effect of closing up the line and on the other of starting a general retirement; then, as the Boer fire ceased and that of our Artillery as well, the whole British line advanced again and stormed over the crest as the Boers disappeared in full flight down the other side.

Colonel Gunning was killed—shot through the heart—just below the crest of the hill.

The occupants of Lennox Hill evacuated it as soon as they saw that Talana was lost, and the whole of Lukas Meyer's force was in full retreat for the Drifts of the Buffalo. The two batteries of Artillery galloped forward to Smith's Nek, where a target presented itself to them such as gunners dream of and seldom see, but the C.R.A., either from some mistaken idea of chivalry or other cause, did not open fire. The Cavalry, with an equally ideal opportunity, were nowhere to be seen, and the Boer force got back to the laager they had left the night before without the material losses and even greater moral damage which they would have suffered if their defeat had been converted, as it should, into a rout.

It is unnecessary to go into the tragedy of the Cavalry further than to say that the O.C. 18th Hussars, at the end of an ineffective day, ran into some of Erasmus's column, was surrounded, and surrendered with a portion of his own Regiment, the Mounted Infantry Company of the R.D.F., and one section Mounted Infantry of the K.R.R.C.

What exactly was Penn Symons's appreciation of the rôle of his detachment will never be known. He does not seem to have considered it his duty to occupy the town of Dundee or defend the coal-fields from the Boers—which was the ostensible, political, unstrategic, and wholly inexcusable reason for his being there—as he had made no defensive preparation of any kind. He seems to have looked on his force as a striking force, with a roving commission to hit one or other of the separate Boer forces and beat them in detail as they invaded Natal. Whether this was what he had in his mind, or how he would have carried it out if the co-operation of Erasmus and Lukas Meyer had not missed fire, none can say; but, in the event, he gained a brilliant success in turning a force of about equal strength to his own—in everything except Artillery—out of a very strong position, without undue loss to his own force, and probably a good deal less than his opponents would have suffered if only the Cavalry had been well handled.

In his report of the engagement, Major W. P. Campbell, who had succeeded to the command of the Battalion on the death of Colonel Gunning, favourably mentioned the following for their conduct in the action:—

Lieut.-Colonel R. H. Gunning.
Major C. A. T. Boultbee.
Captain O. S. W. Nugent, D.S.O.
Captain M. H. K. Pechell.
Captain the Hon. A. R. M.-Stuart-Wortley.
Captain and Adjutant H. R. Blore.
Lieutenant J. H. Davidson.
Lieutenant R. Johnstone.
Lieutenant R. C. Barnett.
2nd Lieutenant G. H. Martin.
Major O. R. A. Julian (R.A.M.C.)

Bandmaster F. Tyler, Colour-Sergeants Rush, Edwards, and Taylor, and sixteen other N.C.O.s and Riflemen.

The casualties in the Battalion were :—

Killed

Lieut.-Colonel R. H. Gunning.
Captain M. H. K. Pechell.
Lieutenant J. Taylor.
Lieutenant R. C. Barnett.
2nd Lieutenant N. J. Hambro, and thirteen N.C.O.s and Riflemen.

Wounded

Major W. P. Campbell.
Major C. A. T. Boultbee.
Captain O. S. W. Nugent, D.S.O.
Captain the Hon. A. R. M.-Stuart-Wortley.
Lieutenant F. M. Crum.
Lieutenant R. Johnstone.
Lieutenant G. H. Martin.
83 N.C.O.s and Riflemen, of whom 10 died of wounds.

Missing

One Rifleman.

Most of the wounded, including Major Boultbee, Captain Nugent, Lieutenants Crum and Johnstone, had to be left at Dundee and became prisoners of war. Of these Major Boultbee, Lieutenant Johnstone, and 31 N.C.O.s and Riflemen were sent into Ladysmith by the Boers on November 2, on parole. The remainder were prisoners till Lord Roberts entered Pretoria.

The Retreat from Dundee

Brigadier-General Yule having thus disposed, for the time, of one of the Boer forces, against whose intention of making a combined attack on him Symons had been warned the day before, might still expect the arrival at any moment of Erasmus from the north and Viljoen from the west. On the afternoon of the 18th Erasmus's advanced guard had come into collision with a squadron of the 18th Hussars, north of Hatting Spruit, not much more than 10 miles as the crow flies from Dundee; but

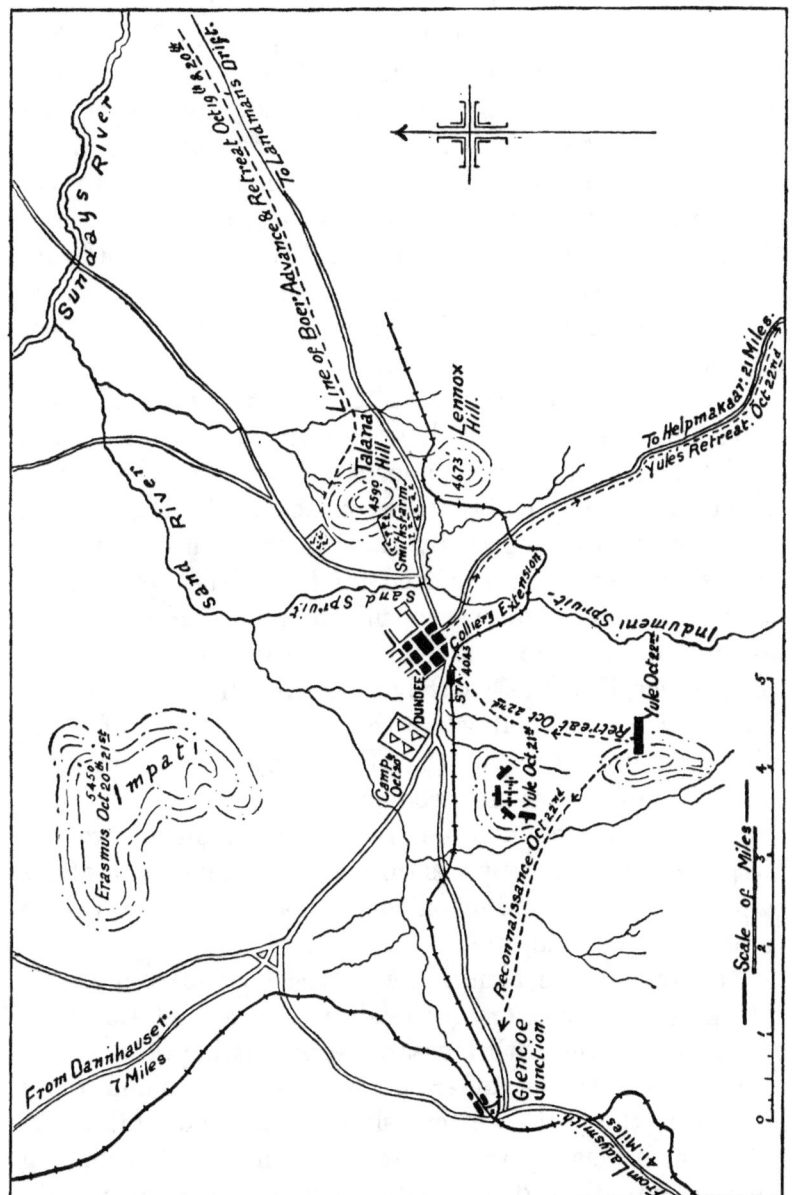

PLATE 13.

TALANA, OCTOBER 20, 1899.

it does not appear that any effort had been made to keep in touch with them at the time, or to get warning of their whereabouts while the battle of Talana Hill was being fought. After collecting the wounded, Yule withdrew his Infantry into camp, which the last of them reached in a deluge of rain about 6 p.m. Nothing had been seen of the Mounted Troops since the morning, but at 7 p.m. Major Knox of the 18th Hussars returned with two squadrons. He had been sent off on a wild-goose chase, and it was only by his able handling of his command that he escaped the fate of the rest of his Regiment.

By daylight on the 21st the Boers, expected from north and west, had still shown no signs of activity. The British mounted patrols reported no signs of the enemy to the east, but quickly found contact on the Dannhauser Road, which runs north by the western flank of Impati. Boer forces were also reported farther to the west. Yule had never shared Symons's optimism, and could not expect his diminished force to deal with the greatly superior force under Erasmus as they had with Meyer. Still, he did not like to retreat while there was a chance of being reinforced from Ladysmith. He reorganised the Staff—that of Symons having been practically wiped out—and selected a position where he proposed to stand his ground. He pointed out the new position, about a mile south of the camp, to his commanding officers at noon and ordered them to occupy it by 2.30 p.m.

Meanwhile, the camp, except the hospital tents, was struck and the baggage got ready to move. At 1.35 p.m. a squadron of the 18th Hussars, reconnoitring on the west side of Impati, came under the fire of four guns and many rifles from the north-western slopes of the mountain. At 3.30 p.m. it was reported that the enemy were mounting guns on Impati, and soon afterwards shells began to fall, first into the deserted camp and then into the British entrenchments. A few casualties resulted, and the range was a long way outside our field guns' power to reply. On taking up his new position, Yule had wired to Ladysmith asking for reinforcements. The first answer came in the form of congratulations from the Commander-in-Chief on his promotion to Major-General. The next was that the Commander-in-Chief was at that moment engaged in fighting the enemy at Elandslaagte. As night fell, the Boer fire died away, and by 5 a.m. on the 22nd Yule had taken up a fresh position, two miles farther south and out of range of Impati.

At 8 a.m. on the 22nd news came, not from Sir George White, but from the Prime Minister of Natal, that the British force from Ladysmith had, the day before, completely defeated a Boer force of over 1,000 strong at Elandslaagte, and that the Cavalry were pursuing them. Yule immediately decided to march to Glencoe Junction to get across the Boer line of retreat.

At 10 a.m. the march on Glencoe was started across the spur of Indumeni with the mounted troops and a battery of Field Artillery as advanced guard. So far from cutting off the Boers, the mounted troops found them strongly posted on the high ground north and west of the station, while the baggage, seeking an easier route farther to the north, came under the fire of a heavy gun from Impati, the fire of which was impartially distributed between the baggage, a battery which tried ineffectually to reply to it, and the hospital tents in the old camp. It seems that there is no reason to blame the enemy for making the hospital their target, as the Red Cross was so placed and so small as to be invisible to them. A partial engagement took place about Glencoe Junction between the mounted troops and the enemy, during which a troop of the 18th

Hussars were cut off and could not rejoin. They, however, made straight for Ladysmith, which they reached next day. Seeing that nothing was to be done in the Glencoe direction, Yule withdrew his force to their previous night's bivouac, which was reached at 1 p.m. He then decided to retire on Ladysmith. At 6.30 p.m. a telegram arrived from Sir George White saying that no reinforcements could be sent and ordering him to fall back on Ladysmith.

The shorter and easier way by Glencoe Junction being thus closed, the retreat had to be made via Beith and Van Tonder's Pass, which entailed going back almost into Dundee before turning east and then south. At 9.30 p.m. the march was begun, the Column being guided by Colonel J. G. Dartnell, a veteran of the Indian Mutiny and Zulu War, who had lived many years in Natal. On this first night's march the 1st K.R.R.C. were advanced guard. They were through the pass of Blesboklaagte by 4.30 a.m. on the 23rd, fourteen miles from the starting-point, and at Diwaas, when the force was well clear of the pass, they halted for a few hours' rest. At 10 a.m. the march was resumed, with the R.I.F. relieving the K.R.R.C. as advanced guard. The heat was great, progress was slow, and at 2 p.m. the Column closed up and bivouacked a mile to the west of the junction of the Ladysmith and Helpmakaar roads and waited for night. At 11 p.m. the Column set off again to make its way through Van Tonder's Pass, which meant a steep and bad road for six miles which would lead them clear of the Biggarsberg Range. The Column went well; in spite of the difficulties, the vanguard had reached and crossed the Waschbank River by 6 a.m. on the 24th, the tail of the Column not getting in till 10 a.m.

About 8 a.m. heavy artillery fire was heard to the westward, and Yule, urged thereto by his senior Officers,

LIEUTENANT-GENERAL SIR EDWARD T. H. HUTTON, K.C.B., K.C.M.G

resolved to take his mounted troops to co-operate. This firing was Sir George White's fight at Rietfontein, at which our 2nd Battalion was present and which will be referred to again. Yule, though by this time almost prostrate with illness and fatigue, himself went in command of this detachment, which consisted of two batteries of Field Artillery, two squadrons 18th Hussars, and two companies Mounted Infantry. The remainder of his force were left under Lieut.-Colonel Carleton, R.I.F., who recrossed the Waschbank River and took up a defensive position on the left bank, the far side from their destination—always a risky thing to do in South Africa in the rainy season. Yule marched nine miles to the sound of the guns without seeing anything, and when, at 2 p.m., the firing died down, he gave the order to return. His detachment reached their bivouac at 4 p.m. and the Infantry started to re-cross the river. The greater part of them had only just done so when a deluge of rain came down, which, within an hour, converted the Waschbank from a mere trickle to an impassable torrent. A piquet of the R.D.F. and a patrol of the 18th Hussars were cut off for a considerable time.

At 4 a.m. on the 25th the Column set out again by the southernmost of the two roads to Ladysmith. At 8.30 a.m. the advanced guard reached Sunday's River—seven miles—and by noon the rearguard was across. The troops were rested here till 1 p.m., when the march was resumed. At 3.45 p.m., after covering another four and a half miles, the Column again halted and prepared to bivouac for the night.

At 5 p.m. a patrol of the 5th Lancers arrived from Ladysmith with orders to Yule to come straight on in, as the enemy were reported to be closing in on him on all sides; at the same time informing him that a column, under Lieut.-Colonel J. A. Coxhead, R.A., was on its way to come to his help, if attacked. This detachment, consisting of the 5th Lancers, two half battalions of Infantry, and a battery R.F.A., came to a spot a mile east of the Nek between Bulwana and Lombard's Kop and remained there till all the Dundee force had passed.

At 6 p.m. Yule's force began their last night march into Ladysmith, and a terrible one it was. No sooner were they started than another deluge came down which converted the track into a bog. It was as much as the Infantry and more than the Transport could do to keep moving. At 9 p.m. the whole Transport stuck for two hours. From then on throughout the night it was one long struggle for the rearguard to get the wagons along. The mules were already exhausted by overwork and short rations and were incapable of effort. In the pitchy darkness it was impossible to tell which wagons had been definitely abandoned and which it was still hoped might be extracted from the slough. In spite of this, only some half-dozen wagons were abandoned and they were recovered next day.

At 3.30 a.m. on the 26th the foremost of Yule's mounted troops reached Coxhead's bivouac. An hour later the Leicestershire Regiment and 1st K.R.R.C. arrived, much exhausted but in good order. After a short halt they continued their march and entered the town at 6 a.m. The other two Regiments, with the Transport, came in a few hours later. The victors of Talana had rejoined Sir George White, who, at one time, can hardly have hoped to see them again.

The Dundee detachment had indeed covered itself with glory. Sent out, no one knows why, to do no one knows what, they had inflicted a smart defeat on one portion of greatly superior forces seeking to overwhelm them, shown that they could turn a Boer force of equal numbers out of a strong position, and had then, after challenging those same superior forces for two days to attack them, slipped clean away and rejoined their Commander-in-Chief without losing a man or a wagon. The march from Dundee to Ladysmith does not, on the map, appear anything wonderful, judging by time and distance only. Judging by the marching conditions, it was as fine a feat as the taking of Talana. The weather was as unfavourable as could well be; the heat was extreme when the sun shone; when it did not it was generally deluging with rain, converting the unmetalled tracks into a regular Slough of Despond. It has not been previously mentioned that the Transport Column was increased by thirty-three wagons loaded with stores which were snatched from under the noses of the enemy on the first night of the retreat. After dark Major Wickham, of the Indian Commissariat, took the wagons, with two companies of the Leicestershire Regiment to load them, to the deserted camp, loaded them up and joined the Column as it passed the outskirts of Dundee. The brilliance of this performance can hardly have been appreciated by the rearguard on that last night-march into Ladysmith, but it was not to be long before every full wagon-load of stores brought in by the Dundee Column was to be a subject of sincere thanksgiving.

On October 25 Major H. Gore-Browne was posted to the 1st Battalion and assumed command from that date.

On the same day the following officers joined the Battalion: Major W. J. Myers (7th K.R.R.C.), Lieutenant H. C. Johnson and Lieutenant and Quartermaster T. C. McNally. Myers had not long left the Regiment and was, at the outbreak of war, Adjutant of the Eton College Rifle Volunteers. Unable to get leave to rejoin the Regiment and being of an independent temperament, he came without it, and was killed in action two days after rejoining.

LADYSMITH, BEFORE THE CLOSING OF THE DOOR

On October 13 Sir George White arrived in Ladysmith, where he had under him two regiments of Regular Cavalry, three batteries R.F.A., one Mountain Battery, one company R.E., four battalions of Regular Infantry, three regiments of Colonial Mounted Rifles, and a few oddments of Colonial troops. Our 2nd Battalion was at Pietermaritzburg, with the newly raised Imperial Light Horse and one squadron 5th Dragoon Guards which had just landed at Durban. Having acquiesced, against his better judgment, in the separation of his force for political reasons which were in themselves unsound, Sir George found himself faced with the task of repelling an invasion by considerably superior numbers with a divided force. The one bright spot in the situation was that the Boer forces were also divided, and his hope was to strike one or other of them a blow before they could concentrate.

At the outbreak of war the Free Staters, his nearest enemy, showed no sign of offering Sir George the opportunity he desired. They merely sat in the passes of the Drakensberg waiting till the Transvaalers were so far advanced that they could, with them, strike a simultaneous blow. White, seeing that there was every prospect of being besieged in Ladysmith, had spent his time organising its defences. He was reinforced during this period by the 2nd K.R.R.C. and the Imperial Light Horse. On the morning of the 18th the Free State Columns were on the move down every pass from Olivier's Hoek to Müller's.

By 8 a.m. Acton Homes, twenty-five miles west of Ladysmith, was occupied by 3,000 Boers, and the same day a piquet of Natal Carbineers was driven out of Bester's Station, ten miles to the north-west. On the 19th Kock, who, with a commando of foreigners, had been sent on by

Joubert to get touch with the Free Staters, occupied the Biggarsberg and, marching all night, reached Elandslaagte at daybreak on the 20th, where his advanced guard had captured a supply train, on its way to Glencoe, the previous day.

Sir George White decided to strike a blow at Kock. On the 20th he held his hand, as the activity of the Free Staters gave him the impression that he was about to be attacked himself; but on the 21st a mixed Brigade under Major-General J. D. P. French attacked and completely broke up the Boer force (at Elandslaagte), which lost 200 killed and wounded (including their commander mortally wounded), nearly 200 prisoners, and 2 guns. The British loss was 263 of all ranks, killed and wounded. It was no part of Sir George White's strategy to hold on to Elandslaagte and French's force returned to Ladysmith next day.

On October 23, anxious for the safety of the Dundee force, Sir George heard that a Free State force of about 6,000 men had taken up a position covering six miles from west to east with its centre on Intintanyoni Mountain, two miles north of Modder Spruit Station. Determined that, if he could not hope for another Elandslaagte, he would at any rate divert the attention of this force from General Yule's Column, he left Ladysmith at 5 a.m. on the 24th with two regiments of Regular Cavalry, two of colonial Mounted Troops, two batteries R.F.A., a mountain battery, and four Infantry Battalions, including the 2nd K.R.R.C. Sir George White took up a position on a ridge facing the Boer centre, with his mounted troops keeping the right and left of the enemy in check. The two forces, about a mile apart, spent the day practising long-range rifle fire at each other, neither side feeling strong enough to attack. At 3 p.m. Sir George, having accomplished his object of keeping the Boer force busy, withdrew unmolested to Ladysmith, covered by his Cavalry. The British loss was 114, that of the Boers 44. Our 2nd Battalion were not engaged. This engagement was known as Rietfontein.

The Boer forces continued to close in on Ladysmith. On the day on which the Dundee force marched in, Erasmus had got touch with the Free Staters under A. P. Cronje— their commander in the affair at Rietfontein—on his right ; on the 27th with Lukas Meyer on his left. Strong Cavalry reconnaissances on the 27th and 29th gave Sir George White such information of the enemy's situation as induced him to try a very ambitious scheme of attack. Large encampments of Boers were reported to the east and south-east of Lombard's Kop. Long Hill and Pepworth Hill were both strongly occupied, with guns on both. White's scheme was to take his whole force, except for fractions of units left to guard his camp, and then, with a mounted force, under French, to guard his right and a detached force of two Infantry battalions and a mountain battery to keep off the Free Staters, with all the rest of his force to attack the Transvaalers about Long Hill and Pepworth Hill.

The forces allotted for these various tasks were as follows : the 8th Infantry Brigade, under the temporary command of Colonel G. G. Grimwood, 2nd King's Royal Rifle Corps (in the absence of Colonel F. Howard), consisting of 1st and 2nd King's Royal Rifle Corps, 1st Leicestershire Regiment, 1st King's (Liverpool Regiment), and 2nd Royal Dublin Fusiliers, were to attack Long Hill from the south-east, supported by the fire of two brigades Royal Field Artillery and the Natal Field Battery. That position taken, they were to hold it, while the 7th Infantry Brigade, under Colonel Ian Hamilton,[1] consisting of the 2nd Gordon Highlanders, 1st Manchester Regiment, 1st Devon Regiment, and 2nd Rifle Brigade—the latter being due to arrive

[1] General Sir Ian Hamilton, G.C.B., G.C.M.G., D.S.O.

from Maritzburg during the night—and to which was attached the 5th Dragoon Guards, 18th Hussars, Imperial Light Horse, and two companies Mounted Infantry, were then to attack Pepworth Hill, being in their turn supported by the whole of the Artillery. Major-General French,[1] with the 5th Lancers, 19th Hussars, and Colonel Royston's Colonial Mounted Troops, was to cover Grimwood's right and rear. The 1st Royal Irish Fusiliers, 1st Gloucestershire Regiment, and No. 10 Mountain Battery, under Lieut.-Colonel Carleton, R.I.F., were to take up a position about Nicholson's Nek, five or six miles due north of Ladysmith, and prevent either a move of the Free Staters from west to east to the relief of the Transvaalers, or the retreat of the Transvaalers by that route should they be compelled to attempt it.

Never was a more complete fiasco. Grimwood's Brigade reached their place of assembly before dawn on the 30th, but, soon after daylight, found themselves, instead of attacking towards the north-west, resisting an attack from the south-east and east. French's Cavalry had been held up at an early hour, and, so far from clearing the ground of the enemy to the south and east of Grimwood, they were in the end reduced to prolonging Grimwood's line to his new right and so preventing him from being cut off from Ladysmith.

Carleton's detachment met with disaster even before they met with the enemy, as their mules stampeded during the night march and left them without artillery or any reserve of rifle ammunition. They were surrounded in the morning, and by 1.30 p.m. all that was left of them were prisoners of war.

Hamilton's Brigade was broken up during the day, units being sent here and there to cover the Artillery,

[1] Rt. Hon. the Earl of Ypres, K.P., G.C.B., O.M., G.C.V.O., K.C.M.G.

reinforce the line held by the 8th Brigade and the Cavalry, and finally to cover the retirement.

At 11 a.m. Sir George White, realising that his scheme had failed, decided to withdraw. The 8th Brigade began their retirement at 11.30 a.m., commencing on the left. At the first sign of movement the Boer rifle fire, which had died down, reopened in full fury, and it was only the action of the 13th Battery Royal Field Artillery, which by galloping forward and opening again at shorter range kept the fire down and attracted the greater part of it to themselves, that enabled the Infantry to get across the open ground without being decimated.

The Times History of the War in South Africa gives an uncomplimentary account of the command of this Brigade in the action which has not, so far as we know, been contradicted and which those who care to may read. In consequence of this want of higher control, the retirement was rather of the nature of a go-as-you-please, and it speaks well for the discipline of the troops that it became nothing worse. The account referred to makes special mention of the admirable way in which a company of our 2nd Battalion, under Captain E. P. Pearce-Serocold,[1] covered the retreat on the extreme left. The 8th Brigade made its way back into Ladysmith, covered and followed by the 7th Brigade, the Artillery and Cavalry; and by 2.30 p.m. all the troops were back in camp.

Fortunately the Boers had no Louis Botha in supreme command that day, or the fate of Ladysmith might have been settled then and there. As it was, they made no effort seriously to follow up the British retirement.

The heroes of the day had been the Royal Field Artillery. They had begun the action at daylight by taking on the Boer Artillery in preparation for the expected

---

[1] Brigadier-General E. P. Serocold, C.M.G.

attack of the 8th Brigade. Finding themselves outranged by the Boer guns, they had advanced to within their own range of them and fairly silenced them. They then had to spend the day in support of Grimwood's defensive position, at the same time being under fire from the Boer guns they had silenced at the start. After being in action for hours on three fronts, they showed the greatest self-sacrifice in covering the withdrawal.

If the field gunners played the most heroic part, the most dramatic event of the day was the arrival on the field of the naval guns. The British retirement had not long begun and every yard of ground to be covered was under fire of the enemy's long-range guns on Pepworth Hill, which our Field Artillery were at that time unable to reach. Captain the Hon. Hedworth Lambton, R.N.,[1] with two 4·7-inch guns, three 12-pounder 12-cwt. quick-firing guns, and some smaller pieces, detrained in Ladysmith at 10 a.m. when the enemy's 6-inch shells were bursting over the station. The 12-pounders detrained ready for immediate use and, drawn by teams of bullocks, were soon on their way to the field of battle. They joined Hamilton's Brigade just as the retirement was beginning and were ordered to withdraw, and in doing so had one gun, which was afterwards recovered upset by the enemy's shell fire. Coming into action nearer the town, they soon silenced the Boer guns on Pepworth Hill. This welcome reinforcement not only greatly relieved the Infantry in their retirement and made possible the withdrawal in its turn of the much-exposed Field Artillery, but was an incalculable asset, moral and material, to the defence throughout the succeeding siege, which, without the naval pieces, had only two 6·3-inch howitzers capable of reaching the Boer long-range guns.

[1] Admiral of the Fleet the Hon. Sir Hedworth Meux, G.C.B., K.C.V.O.

The following were mentioned for distinguished conduct by the O.C. 1st Battalion in his report of this engagement :—

> Major W. J. Myers (7th K.R.R.C.)
> Major O. R. A. Julian (R.A.M.C.)
> Lieutenant H. C. Johnson.
> Bandmaster F. Tyler.
> No. 1016, Rifleman A. Thompson.

The casualties in the two Battalions were :—

1st Battalion
Killed
Major W. J. Myers.
Lieutenant H. S. Marsden.
Lieutenant J. L. Foster (attached from 2nd Battalion).
1 Rifleman.

Wounded
Lieutenant H. C. Johnson and 32 N.C.O.s and Riflemen.

2nd Battalion
Killed
Major E. W. Gray, R.A.M.C., and 7 Riflemen.

Wounded
Major H. E. Buchanan-Biddell and 27 N.C.O.s and Riflemen.

Missing
15 N.C.O.s and Riflemen.

CHAPTER X

COLENSO

WHEN Sir Redvers Buller left England for South Africa, his plan was to invade the Free State from the south with the Expeditionary Force, leaving Sir George White to contain the Boers in Natal. On arrival at Cape Town on October 31 he was faced with the situation which followed White's defeat outside Ladysmith on the previous day. If he could have begun his invasion of the Free State at once, he could thus have relieved the pressure on White by drawing off the Free Staters to defend their own country; but the first units of the Expeditionary Force were not due for another ten days and the disembarkation of the whole force would not be completed till early in December. It would thus be another month before he could make any pressure felt by direct advance on the Free State, and meanwhile, even if White's force could look after itself, Natal was in danger. There were as usual two aspects to be considered: the purely strategic, and the political, which affected the strategic. The chief considerations in the former aspect were that the initiative was now with the Boers and that events would not give Buller time to carry out his original plan; that Sir George White must be relieved, as a disaster to him would not only mean the loss of the actual strength of his force, but would free his opponents for operations elsewhere—Natal or Cape Colony, as they might choose. The political consideration was that any great success by the Boers would mean the immediate addition to their force of all the disloyal Dutch in Cape

Colony, who were only waiting to see how things were going before coming down definitely on the Boer side of the fence. All this meant that Natal must be strongly reinforced, but at the same time an invasion of Cape Colony must be prevented and Kimberley must be relieved. The invaders of Cape Colony would speedily have all the disloyal Dutch on their side, while the fall of Kimberley, which was of no importance strategically, would have had a tremendous moral effect.

By November 4 Buller had worked out his plan. General Clery and Headquarters 2nd Division were to go straight on to Natal from Cape Town, and were to be followed by three brigades made up from the first battalions to arrive. Lord Methuen, with one Division, was to relieve Kimberley. General French, just escaped from Ladysmith and destined to command the Cavalry Division, was to form a flying column at Naaupoort, as troops were available, and check any invasion of Cape Colony; while Gatacre, commanding the 3rd Division, did the same farther east. All this meant a complete break-up of the organisation of the Expeditionary Force as an Army Corps. Of the Infantry of the 2nd Division only the 4th Brigade (Brigadier-General the Hon. N. Lyttelton)[1] went to Natal, the other brigade—there were only two per Division in the original organisation of the Army Corps—going to Lord Methuen. Of the 3rd Division Infantry only one battalion went to Gatacre, all the rest going on to Natal. General Lyttelton's Brigade was made up of the 2nd Scottish Rifles, 3rd K.R.R.C., 1st Durham Light Infantry, 1st Rifle Brigade. Our 3rd Battalion sailed in the hired transport *Servia* on November 4 and disembarked at Durban on the 28th.

Leaving, from the necessities of the case, his Headquarters' Staff at Cape Town, Sir Redvers left that place on

[1] General the Rt. Hon. Sir Neville Lyttelton, G.C.B., G.C.V.O.

November 22, accompanied only by his Personal Staff, and reached Durban on the 25th. On his arrival the situation seemed to be improving. Methuen had twice driven the Boers out of a defensive position, though without inflicting much loss on them; French and Gatacre were both holding their own. In Natal the enemy had attempted a raid to the south and, though they had caused Clery at Estcourt some anxiety for his communications, they had started too late to do any great harm before the British reinforcements began to arrive, and they were now falling back. By December 6 Buller was at Frere, and had at his disposal a Mounted Brigade (Colonel Lord Dundonald) consisting of the Royal Dragoons, 13th Hussars, Thorneycroft's and Bethune's Mounted Infantry, the South African Light Horse (the last three all being newly raised Colonial Corps), and detachments of Imperial Light Horse, Natal Carbineers, and Natal Police : a Naval Brigade (Captain E. P. Jones, R.N.) of two 4·7-inch and fourteen 12-pounder guns; two brigades R.F.A.—they were called Brigade Divisions in those days—the second being a battery short; four Infantry Brigades, each of four battalions; a Field Company R.E. and a Pontoon Troop. In addition, two battalions of Regular Infantry, three of Colonial Infantry, and four naval 12-pounders held the line of communication.

The problem now confronting Buller was the crossing of the Tugela. The river was only fordable at a few places and only bridged at Colenso. For thirty miles up or down stream from Colenso the country to the north of the river was a tangled mass of hills commanding the southern bank nearly everywhere. Buller seems to have considered two plans : one, an attack on Colenso immediately in front of him, which, after crossing, offered a difficult route to Ladysmith, but had the advantage of keeping his line of communication covered; the other, by Potgieter's Drift (of which more later), which offered an easier route beyond the river but meant a flank march away from the railway. He first inclined to the latter plan, and so informed Sir George White, giving him instructions as to co-operation. On December 13 he changed his mind and signalled to White that he was coming by Colenso and that the probable date of the attack would be the 17th. The reason for this change appears, from his own dispatches, to have been that the news of the reverses at Magersfontein and Stormberg had shaken his confidence, and that he chose the plan which would entail the least danger of disaster in case of failure.

The Boer force in Natal at this time was roughly about 20,000 men, of whom some 5,000 to 6,000, under Louis Botha, were holding the line of the Tugela, most of the remainder being round Ladysmith, within easy reach. Most of Botha's force were disposed to guard the Colenso crossing and had skilfully entrenched that part of the line; but should Buller have chosen some other point for crossing, the Boers' superior mobility and power of observation given them by the high ground on their side of the river would always have enabled them to forestall him, if not before he had seized a crossing-place, at any rate before he had penetrated very far. The only Boer force on the right bank was one of some 800 men occupying Hlangwhane, which certainly appears from the map to be a point the occupation of which was equally essential to the Boers if they wanted to defend the Colenso crossings as to the British if they hoped to force them.

Buller's plan was to gain a footing on the left bank of the Tugela by seizing a group of heights known as the Colenso Kopjes, of which the southernmost, Fort Wylie, is on the east side of the railway, the others being on the west side, to the north of the Colenso railway bridge.

The main attack was to be carried out by the 2nd

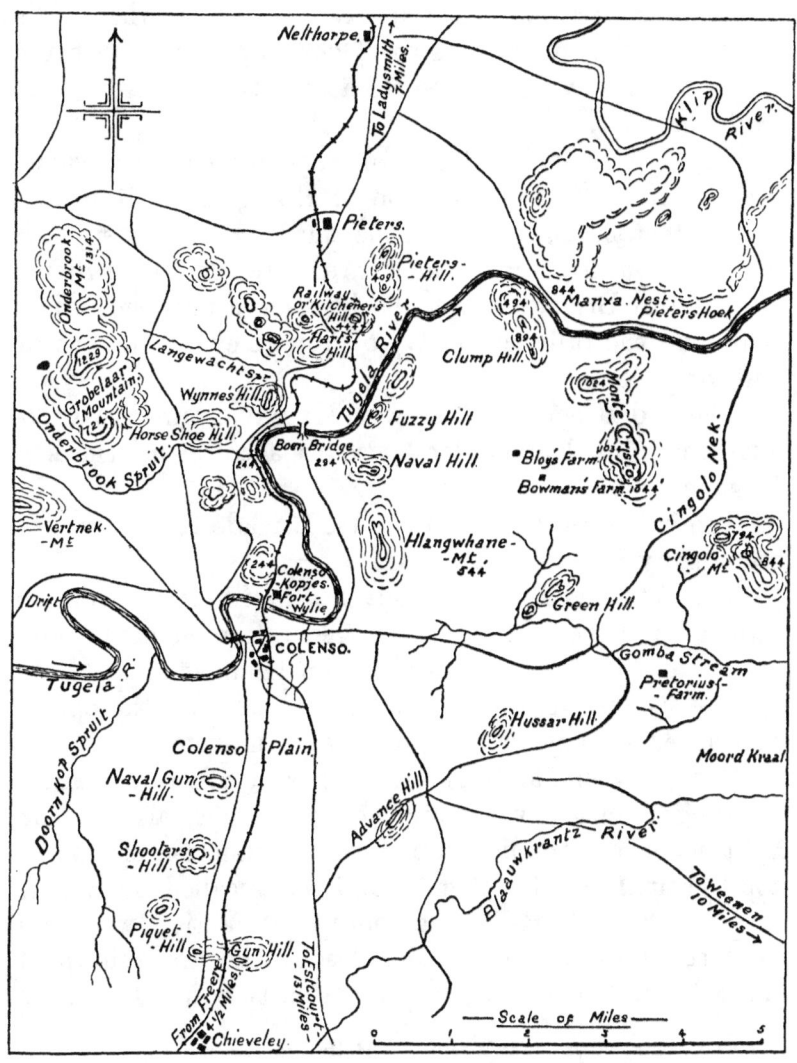

PLATE 14.

COLENSO, DECEMBER 15, 1899. RELIEF OF LADYSMITH, FEBRUARY 14-28, 1900.

Brigade (Hildyard's), who were to cross by the railway bridge,[1] the crossing to be covered by the fire of No. 1 Brigade R.F.A. less one battery, reinforced by six naval 12-pounders.

The 5th Brigade (Hart's) was to cross at the Bridle Drift near the junction of the Doornkop Spruit with the Tugela, and, having crossed, to attack the Colenso kopjes from the west.

The 6th Brigade (Barton's) was ordered, in a vague way, to move in the direction of Hlangwhane Mountain and protect the right flank of the 2nd Brigade, and support it or the mounted troops who were directed on Hlangwhane.

The 4th Brigade was to be in reserve between Bridle Drift and the railway, ready to support either the 5th or 2nd Brigade.

The 2nd Brigade R.F.A. with six naval guns (two 4·7-inch and four 12-pounders) was to accompany the 4th Brigade.

The battery taken from the 1st Brigade R.F.A. was to accompany the Mounted Brigade.

The Mounted Brigade received a half-hearted order to 'cover the right flank of the general movement' and 'endeavour to take up a position on Hlangwhane.'

Everything went wrong from the start and the operation never got beyond the preliminary movements.

Owing to mistakes in the map and other misunderstandings, Hart never found the drift, got his brigade right down into the big loop above the junction of Doornkop Spruit, lost a lot of men, and was recalled by Buller.

No. 1 Brigade R.F.A., in coming into action, went too far to the front and came under close and accurate shrapnel and rifle fire. After an hour in action they had lost most

---

[1] The Orders say, 'the iron bridge.' Both bridges were of iron, but it is evident that the railway bridge was intended.

of their men, fired off most of their ammunition, and were too exposed to get reinforcements of either one or the other. What was left of them were obliged to abandon their guns and take cover in a donga close behind them.

About 8 a.m. Buller decided that without No. 1 Brigade R.F.A.—and doubtless also influenced by the failure of Hart's Brigade to find a crossing—he was not strong enough in artillery to carry out the attack. By this time two of Lyttelton's battalions had gone off to cover Hart's retirement; two of Hildyard's battalions and one of Barton's were being employed in preparing with their fire to cover the withdrawal of the guns.

Lord Dundonald, commanding the Cavalry Brigade, had embarked on an attack on Hlangwhane, but, having actually fewer men to employ in the attack than the number of its Boer garrison, he asked for the assistance of Infantry. Having already decided to abandon the main attack, Buller saw no reason for persevering with the attack on Hlangwhane.

There was nothing for him now to do but to get his force, with as little further loss as possible, back to where they started from in the morning. He himself rode forward to where the naval guns were in action a few hundred yards in rear of the abandoned guns. Here he sanctioned a series of gallant attempts to save the guns, for which several Victoria Crosses were given, one who earned it, but was only awarded it after his death, being Lieutenant the Hon. F. H. S. Roberts, K.R.R.C., who was acting as A.D.C. to General Clery until he could join Sir George White's Staff.

Despairing of saving the guns without great loss of life, Buller decided to abandon them and to withdraw the Infantry, which, at the time, was so placed as to be able to prevent their removal by the enemy. General Lyttelton, on taking two battalions of his brigade to cover Hart's retirement, had left the remaining two (Scottish Rifles and K.R.R.C.) under Lieut.-Colonel Buchanan Riddell, commanding 3rd K.R.R.C. Our 3rd Battalion, with Major R. C. A. Bewicke-Copley in temporary command, had been moved forward and extended some 500 yards in rear of the guns which were now about to be abandoned. When the general retirement began, Major Bewicke-Copley was ordered to remain out, covering it, and to furnish the outposts. He therefore took up a piquet line with his left resting on the railway.

At 2 p.m. he was ordered to fall farther back. He twice submitted a request to be allowed to remain out so as to save the guns after dark, but permission was refused, and he fell back to a position immediately covering the camp.

The British casualties amounted to 1,139 of all ranks, which would not have been serious if anything had been gained or the battle had ever really begun. As things were, with the force back where it started in the morning, having left half its field artillery behind it and with the Boers practically untouched—their losses were 29 all told—the moral effect of such a failure was crushing, most of all to the Commander-in-Chief.

On the evening of December 15 Buller sent a despondent telegram to the Secretary of State for War, in which he proposed to abandon Ladysmith and take a defensive position to cover Southern Natal. Next day he sent the notorious message to Sir George White which will be referred to in the account of the Defence of Ladysmith.

The Government, replying on the 16th, would not hear of the abandonment of Ladysmith, informed Buller that the 5th Division, now in process of disembarkation, was at his disposal—through a misunderstanding of his instructions he had thought that the Government had definitely detailed this Division for the relief of Kimberley—and promised further reinforcements, of which the 6th Division had already begun to embark. On the same day they decided that Buller had enough to do in commanding the Ladysmith Relief Force, and appointed Field-Marshal Lord Roberts as Commander-in-Chief in South Africa, with Major-General Lord Kitchener as his Chief of the Staff.

CHAPTER XI

THE TWIN PEAKS

BULLER now sat down to await reinforcements and to plan his next effort for the relief of Ladysmith. The intervening period was uneventful so far as active operations are concerned. The Boers made no attempt to follow up their successes by an aggressive policy, being content to carry on with the reduction of Ladysmith by starvation, their one great and unsuccessful attack on January 6 being their only attempt to take it by storm.

Owing to scarcity of water at Chieveley, nearly half the force was withdrawn to Frere, which Buller made his Headquarters, leaving Clery in command at Chieveley.

January 6, the day of the attack on Wagon Hill, was the eve of Buller's start for a fresh attempt. On receipt of Sir George White's report of a serious attack, Buller ordered Clery to make a demonstration against Colenso with a view to retaining the garrison there and preventing them going off to reinforce the attack on White, or to forcing a crossing if they had already done so. Clery moved out at 2 p.m., bombarding the whole line of trenches and advancing his Infantry to within 3,000 yards of the river. There was little or no reply to the fire, but scouts reported that the enemy's trenches were fully manned, so Clery returned to camp after dark.

Having been reinforced by the 5th Division (Lieut.-General Sir Charles Warren), Buller now felt strong enough for a second effort to relieve Ladysmith. His intention was, this time, to try his original scheme of crossing at Potgieter's Drift. There were both advantages and disadvantages in this scheme, as there are in most schemes in war. There was no question of turning the enemy's position. The high ground north of the Tugela followed the river's course to the west as far as Venter's Spruit, where it turned north and then north-east right round to the other side of Ladysmith; to the east it followed the river to the borders of Zululand. Buller might march to either side, he would find no flank. The Boers by their superior mobility could always forestall him. Wherever he attacked, there he would find them waiting for him, and his attack would be a frontal one. The advantages of the Potgieter's scheme were that in that neighbourhood there was high ground on the right bank which commanded a good deal, though not all, of the other bank. The country between the river and Ladysmith was not quite so difficult as by the Colenso route. There was only one high range, after crossing which the country was more or less open. The drawbacks to the scheme were: transport difficulties owing to distance from the railway; the danger of a flank march within striking distance of a very mobile enemy—the obstacle offered by the river and the want of enterprise so far shown by the Boers made this consideration not a very serious one; and thirdly, that the necessity for leaving a force to cover railhead seriously diminished his striking force—Warren had only brought him two Infantry Brigades, so that, leaving one at Chieveley, he was only one brigade stronger, in Infantry, than at Colenso.

Before starting on this operation there was a considerable re-shuffling of the force. The 2nd Division (Clery) now consisted of the 2nd Brigade (Hildyard), the 5th Brigade (Hart), a squadron 13th Hussars, and one brigade R.F.A. The 5th Division (Warren) consisted of the 4th Brigade

(Lyttelton), the 11th Brigade (Woodgate), one squadron 13th Hussars, and one brigade R.F.A.

Corps Troops included the 10th Brigade (Coke), Headquarters and 1 squadron 13th Hussars, 61st Howitzer Battery R.F.A., 78th Battery R.F.A., two naval 4·7-inch guns, and eight naval 12-pounder guns.

Major-General Barton was left at Chieveley with his own Brigade (6th), some mounted troops, and four naval 12-pounder guns. A further small mixed force garrisoned Frere.

It would be tedious to follow in detail all the operations which culminated in the fight for Spion Kop, but, briefly, they were as follows. Buller's first move was to concentrate at Springfield. The move began at dawn on January 10. There had been a tropical downpour for the previous three days, the country was a bog, the spruits in flood, and the steamy heat very trying to man and beast. By nightfall Dundonald with 700 men and 4 guns had reached Potgieter's Drift and occupied the hills overlooking it (Mount Alice and Spearman's Hill) without opposition. Next morning some men of the South African Light Horse swam over, captured the ferry-boat and brought it back to their own side under a shower of bullets.

Spruits had to be bridged, wagon convoys had to go backwards and forwards, and it was not till the 15th that the force was concentrated at Springfield with sixteen days' provisions and forage.

The Boers, to whom every move was visible, spent the time entrenching a line from Spion Kop to Vaal Krantz.

On examining, from Mount Alice, the position which guarded Potgieter's Drift, Buller at once decided that the only way to take it was to begin by crossing higher up and attacking the western end of the crescent and clearing first Bastion Hill and then Spion Kop. His plan was to put

Sir Charles Warren in command of the force which was to carry out this operation, which was to consist of the whole of the 2nd Division, one extra Infantry Brigade, the Divisional Artillery from Warren's own Division, and nearly all the mounted troops. Buller himself, with the remainder of the force, would remain opposite Potgieter's Drift, attracting the attention of the enemy by crossings at Potgieter's and Skiet's Drifts, and ready to join in the attack on the main position when the time was ripe.

Warren marched to Trickhardt's Drift on the night of the 16th–17th and began crossing next morning. The remainder of the force marched down to Potgieter's Drift on the afternoon of the 16th, and during the night the kopjes just across the drift were occupied by two battalions of Lyttelton's Brigade and a howitzer battery. A detachment was also sent to take up a position which denied the use of Skiet's Drift to the enemy.

It is not proposed here to thrash out the question of whom to blame for all the sins of omission and commission of the British leaders during this disastrous campaign, but it may be taken as a generally accepted fact that Warren's action was dilatory and unenterprising.

The 17th was spent in getting troops and transport across the Tugela, and no forward movement of troops was made beyond taking up a position on some heights, not two miles from the drift, to cover the crossing.

On the 18th Dundonald was sent on, presumably to find the Boer right and reconnoitre generally the line by which Warren proposed to advance, though the orders given him were not very decided. His advanced guard surprised a party of some 300 Boers on the march and inflicted losses of about 50 in killed, wounded, and prisoners, with only 3 casualties on the British side—the first success any of Buller's force had had since they landed in Natal. Dundonald received no encouragement from Warren in his desire to ride right round the Boer flank, and the 19th was wasted. Warren, on this day, had come to the conclusion that his only way to carry out Buller's plan was to fight his way through by the Fairview—Rosalie Road which runs between Green Hill and Three Tree Hill. This he started to do on the 20th, and by the evening of that day he had taken Piquet Hill, Three Tree Hill, and Bastion Hill. On the 21st and 22nd he could get no farther, and on the evening of the 21st he asked the Commander-in-Chief to reinforce him by the 10th Brigade (Talbot Coke) and a battery of howitzers, the latter being especially required as, from the formation of the ground, his Field Artillery could not get at the Boer guns and trenches.

The howitzers and the 10th Brigade arrived during the course of the 22nd. By this time it was clear that the Boer right extended well beyond the British left and that a further advance on the present front would be met by an enfilade fire from both flanks. Though Dundonald's scouts continued to report no large bodies of Boers in the direction of Acton Homes, Warren seems to have remained prejudiced against going farther to that flank or even letting his mounted troops do so. These had been practically idle since the 18th, except that on the 20th Dundonald had, on his own initiative, captured Bastion Hill with the South African Light Horse and Thorneycroft's Mounted Infantry, who were relieved next day by Infantry. Warren therefore decided to take Spion Kop before going any farther. The attack was to be made by night, and as it was late on the 22nd before the decision was reached, the attack was deferred till the night of the 23rd–24th.

Major-General Woodgate (11th Brigade) was ordered to carry out this attack with the battalions of his brigade and part of Thorneycroft's Mounted Infantry. The long and precipitous climb of over 1,000 feet in the dark was successfully accomplished and, the Boer piquet on the top being rushed, the hill was occupied by 4 a.m. In darkness and thick fog the British started to entrench a position, but the nature of the surface—bare rock, in places covered with a veneer of soil, and big boulders—made digging impossible and their shallow trench and low parapet combined could not produce more than 18 inches of cover. As day dawned they saw that the hill, instead of being flat-topped like most South African kopjes, had a distinct crest from which a gentle slope for a short distance ended in a very steep one. Thus their trench, which followed the crest, had dead ground within 200 yards of it. They started afresh to get cover along the rim of the steep slope from which they might include the whole hillside in their field of fire. As the mist lifted, they soon knew what they were in for. Every inch of the hill-top forward of the main crest was under a cross-fire through an arc of some 140°, of which they formed the centre. Immediately on receipt of the news of the capture of the hill, the Boers started to make another Majuba of it. It had soon been found that the front edge of the hill-top was untenable, and by 8 a.m. the Boers had reached the top of the steep slope, and on the north-east, where they had covering fire from a knoll only 300 yards away, they got within 50 yards of the British trenches. At 8.30 a.m. General Woodgate was killed by a shrapnel bullet in the head. All day the fight for the top went on, the many casualties being replaced by reinforcements, but nothing was done by Sir Charles Warren to enlarge the front of his attack or, by advancing against Green Hill—Leng Kopje—Rangeworthy Heights, give the Boers something else to think of than the ejectment of the garrison from Spion Kop. His attention seems to have been so absorbed by the struggle on Spion Kop that he did not take the obvious step to relieve the situation there by carrying on with the main operation, to which the capture of Spion Kop was to be only a preliminary.

He did send one message to Lyttelton, asking him to give assistance on his side, and it was Lyttelton's action, on receipt of this message, followed by another (anonymous) direct from Spion Kop, which very nearly converted failure into complete success.

Lyttelton from the first had done all he could to relieve the pressure on Spion Kop. Before dawn he had sent out the Durham Light Infantry and Rifle Brigade, who, under cover of the 64th Battery R.F.A. and naval guns, began a vigorous demonstration against Brakfontein, but at 8 a.m. Buller, fearing that they would get too much involved, recalled them.

On receipt of Warren's message about 10 a.m., he sent the Scottish Rifles over to the right bank and ordered them, with two squadrons of Bethune's Mounted Infantry, to recross the river at Kaffir Drift and, climbing Spion Kop, to come in on the right of the British position there. They were stopped by Major-General Talbot Coke (commanding 5th Division) before they reached the top, but were sent on again by him half an hour later with orders to reinforce on right and left. This they did, arriving at the top when things were very critical and probably saving the situation; but they would have helped more if some part of the Battalion had been directed farther to the right so as to include Aloe Knoll in their line of attack, a spot from which a most galling enfilade fire had been poured all day into the British right at a range of 300 yards.

No sooner had the Scottish Rifles started than Lyttelton got the appeal direct from Spion Kop already mentioned. The only British General who grasped the fact that the way to relieve the situation there was to widen the front of attack rather than pour more troops on to a shell-trap, he ordered our 3rd Battalion to follow the Scottish Rifles over the Kaffir Drift and then to attack the Twin Peaks.

These peaks are a part of the ridge of which Spion Kop is the highest point. They are about half a mile apart, and the western one is 2,000 yards from Spion Kop and 200 feet lower. The eastern peak, the Sugar Loaf, is another 150 feet lower.

They were held by 200 Boers of the Carolina Commando, under Schalk Burgher.

The Battalion moved off about 11.30 a.m. and began to ford the river by the Kaffir Drift. The water was deep and rapid, so the crossing had to be done in single file and took some time. As soon as each company got across, rolled great-coats were removed and piled on the riverbank. The Battalion then formed up in two half battalions. On the right, A and B Companies in first line, C and D in second; on the left, E and F in first line, G and H in second. The right half battalion, under Colonel Buchanan Riddell, was directed against the right peak, known as Sugar Loaf Hill; the left half battalion, under Major Bewicke-Copley,[1] against the left peak.

At 2 p.m. the advance began. Each company deployed in two lines, a half company in each, at eight or ten paces' interval, with 150 yards between lines.

A mile and a half of flat, open ground intervenes between Kaffir's Drift and the foot of the Twin Peaks, and the right of the Regiment followed the river in its curve to the north. The enemy brought no guns to bear on the attack, neither was any support afforded by our own Artillery if we except two 4·7-inch naval guns on Mount Alice, which fired only four shells all the afternoon, the

[1] Brigadier-General Sir R. C. A. Bewicke-Copley, K.B.E., C.B.

last of which was more dangerous to the leading men of B Company than to the Boers.

The Boer rifle fire began at about 1,500 yards' range, and as soon as it became fairly warm, the leading half companies doubled forward to the shelter of a deep donga which crossed the plain about 300 yards from the foot of the slope. This donga was about 900 yards from the top of the hill and became the object of much attention from the Boer riflemen, while the attackers opened a heavy fire in return. But the advance was not delayed. The open space in front was soon covered by rushes of twenty or a dozen men at a time, and, in the dead ground at the foot of the hill, the men collected preparatory to the climb. Very slight losses were incurred in this early stage of the attack; Major Thistlethwayte of G Company and Captain Briscoe of E Company were, however, among those wounded.

The position, like Majuba and Spion Kop, was not so strong as it looked, most of the slope being dead to frontal fire from the top. Here and there it was exposed to a cross-fire from one side or other, but the defenders on the top could only fire down the slope by coming forward to a point where they were exposed to the covering fire of the attackers.

The slope, though steep, almost precipitous, had open ledges at three or four points which were exposed to a cross-fire, and it was in crossing these that most of the casualties occurred. It was at a ledge, about half-way up, that Lieutenants R. J. Grant, of G Company, and H. G. French-Brewster, of E Company, were killed at the head of their companies. About this time, also, Captain R. Beaumont, of A Company, and Colour-Sergeant McLoughlin of E Company, were wounded. Lieutenant Blundell had five bullets through his clothing without a wound.

The right half battalion were annoyed during their advance by the enemy from the direction of Brakfontein firing on their right rear, but beyond detailing some men of A Company to return the fire, they took no notice of it. Shortly afterwards this Company was effectually checked by fire from a concealed Boer trench about two-thirds of the way up the hill. B Company, however, were led forward by Major Kays [1] (who was shortly afterwards severely wounded in the hand) and cleared the trench, enabling A Company to advance again.

Crawling, climbing, running, firing from every rock and at every opportunity, the Riflemen worked their way up the hill. When our men got to within 150 yards of the trenches on the summit the Boers gave up the struggle and fled, two only waiting gallantly to the last and escaping unhurt.

The Sugar Loaf was taken at 5.15 p.m. and the left peak a few minutes later. Two guns, which had been firing from near the Sugar Loaf at Spion Kop, were withdrawn about an hour earlier.

Though the majority of the Carolina Commando never stopped till they had left the Twin Peaks eight miles behind them, a few bolder spirits still clung on behind bits of cover on the farther slope, and every head appearing over the crest was a target for their rifles. In this way the Colonel was killed, shot through the head. Beloved and respected by everyone in the Regiment, he had on that day but added to the admiration and devotion of those he led.

With two hours of daylight left, the Battalion set to work to make themselves secure in the position they had captured so brilliantly. Mules with entrenching tools and ammunition were got up close to the top of the left

[1] Brigadier-General W. S. Kays, C.M.G.

peak. Night came down, and the occupants of the Twin Peaks were full of confidence that their success, properly exploited, was the precursor of a complete victory, and so it should have been. To quote from the 'Official History of the War' describing the situation at nightfall from the Boer point of view :—

'By the capture of the Twin Peaks, the troops on Spion Kop had been largely relieved of the gun and rifle fire which had raked their right flank. Still more important were the effects on the enemy. The long day's battle had worn out the spirit of the Boers. Their utmost efforts . . . had failed to recapture Spion Kop. Before sunset they had abandoned all hopes of doing so, and it only needed such a blow as the sight of the Carolina men fleeing from the Twin Peaks to shatter their crumbling opposition. By nightfall every laager and most of the guns were on the move to the rear, the stormers of Spion Kop, utterly exhausted, slipped away one by one, four of the commandos from the actual front were riding for the passes, and there arose signs of a panic throughout the whole Federal forces. But General Louis Botha . . . urged the impossibility of retreat. . . . One objection he was unable to answer, and it chilled even those who agreed to stand by him. The Twin Peaks were in the hands of the British on the flank. . . .'

Yes! But the fatal order had already gone out for their evacuation. Buller had disapproved from the first of Lyttelton's independent action, and our 3rd Battalion had no sooner started their attack than he ordered their recall. It is not known how far the Battalion had got when the message reached them, but, anyhow, Colonel Buchanan Riddell exercised a wise discretion by putting it in his pocket, where it was found after his death.

The order to retire was repeated after dark, and this time there was nothing for it but to obey.

Sadly, but 'in perfect order,' the retirement was

carried out, and by 2 a.m. next morning all had re-crossed the river—this time by a pontoon bridge, thrown by the Engineers during the day—except for a few of the wounded who could not be found in the darkness.

Though the prospective gains of their attack had been thrown away, the Battalion could feel that it had not been wasted altogether, as it had shown what well-trained Infantry could do and that Majuba was a game that two could play.

This was fully realised by both their Brigadier and their Commander-in-Chief.

General Lyttelton, addressing them next day, said :—

' I have been a Rifleman for over thirty years, and never, in the course of my experience, have I seen a finer bit of skirmishing and fighting. The men of the 60th, led as I knew they would be led, behaved as Riflemen should.'

A few days later their Commander-in-Chief and Colonel Commandant addressed them on church parade. These were his words :—

' I have lost in two of your Officers one of my oldest friends and the son of one of my oldest friends. But had God seen fit to give me a son, I would have been proud if he had lost his life the other day with the 3rd Battalion 60th Rifles.'

The losses in the action were :—

Killed : Lieut.-Colonel R. H. Buchanan Riddell, Lieutenant R. J. Grant, 2nd Lieutenant H. G. French-Brewster, and 19 N.C.O.s and Riflemen.

Wounded : 4 Officers, 73 N.C.O.s and Riflemen.

The situation when darkness fell was that of about 4,500 men of the British force that had ascended Spion Kop, of whom over 1,000 had not yet been engaged, over 1,000 were killed, wounded, or missing.

Warren's only plan for next day was to hold on to Spion Kop and get guns up on to it during the night. Not a suggestion of any further action elsewhere ; not an order to the Mounted Troops, who had now been inactive since they captured Bastion Hill on the 20th. Thorneycroft, the soul of the defence all day on Spion Kop, who had been placed in command there by Buller after Woodgate's death, over the heads of several seniors, knowing nothing of the capture of the Twin Peaks—anyhow, their evacuation had already been ordered by Buller—saw before him for next day's programme only a repetition of the one just passed, and so on till his men's limit of endurance was reached. He, therefore, after vain attempts to get a reply to messages to Warren asking for orders, decided to withdraw his force during the night and issued his orders for that operation about 10 p.m.

If only Thorneycroft had known the general situation : that the capture of the Twin Peaks had had such a moral effect on the Boers that it was only the personal magnetism of Louis Botha that prevented a general and disorganised retreat ; if he had had any reason to suppose that the next day would not be a repetition of the past one, there can be no doubt that he would have held on ; and if only Warren could have roused himself to find some better rôle for Hildyard's Brigade and the Cavalry than that of spectators, the battle might still have been won—though Buller had taken the first step to making this unlikely by ordering the withdrawal of our 3rd Battalion from the Twin Peaks.

Warren's first intimation of the evacuation was from Thorneycroft himself, who arrived at his Headquarters about 2 a.m. on the 25th. Warren accepted the situation in that he did not give immediate orders for the reoccupation of the hill ; though he sent out patrols to find out whether the Boers had come back. They had. In the small hours their scouts found Spion Kop and Twin Peaks abandoned, and both hills were promptly reoccupied.

The Boer General sent in a request for an armistice to bury the dead, which showed that at least he had no intention of counter-attacking. This was agreed to by Buller, who had already made up his mind to accept defeat for the time, retire behind the Tugela, and try again elsewhere. The withdrawal across Trickhardt's Drift began the same evening and most of the transport was across by morning. The Boers on Rangeworthy Heights kept up a brisk fire all day, but made no other move, and the retirement was continued after dark. At 1 a.m. on the 27th the troops on Three Tree Hill, the last to go, were withdrawn and were over the bridge by dawn. By the afternoon the Army was in camp round Hatting's Farm, south of Mount Alice, and the campaign of Spion Kop was over.

CHAPTER XII

Vaal Krantz

No sooner was his force back on the right bank of the Tugela than Buller had ready a new scheme for the relief of Ladysmith. He seems to have been very sanguine of success, and on January 28 addressed some of his troops on church parade and told them that he had now really got the key to Ladysmith and they would be there within a week. His troops, whose confidence he never lost even after further failure, were as confident as himself and in the best of spirits. During the next few days reinforcements arrived, consisting of two 5-inch guns Royal Garrison Artillery, a battery Royal Horse Artillery, two squadrons Regular Cavalry, and drafts for the Infantry. The Cavalry was reorganised; Colonel Burn-Murdoch, 1st Royal Dragoons, being put in command of the 1st Cavalry Brigade (three regiments Regular Cavalry) and Lord Dundonald commanding the 2nd Mounted Brigade, made up of all the other mounted troops, mostly colonial.

The Boers meanwhile were taking things easy, many of the men and some of their commanders had gone off to visit their homes, no one in particular being left in command on the Tugela; in fact, if Buller's next move had been swift and decided they would have been taken at a considerable disadvantage. Unfortunately it was neither swift nor decided. From the first order in his Operation Orders for the next effort it is evident that Buller had made up his mind that Vaal Krantz was the extreme left of the enemy's position and that he need fear no interference with his plan from anyone to the east of that point.[1] His plan was to make a show of attacking the Brakfontein Heights from the direction of the kopjes near Potgieter's Drift, and then to cross the river below Munger's Drift, attack and capture Vaal Krantz, and then put the Cavalry Brigade through between Vaal Krantz and Green Hill. Presumably he intended then to roll up the Boer position on Brakfontein Heights. The plan would have been a most effective one if only all ground east of the Skiet's Drift—Ladysmith road could have been put 'out of bounds.' As things turned out, Vaal Krantz was simply a repetition of Spion Kop—an isolated position taken in the enemy's line, made a cockshy by the Boers for a certain time, and then a withdrawal.

At 6 a.m. on February 5 Colonel A. S. Wynne, who had succeeded Woodgate in command of the 11th Brigade, advanced from behind the kopjes and deployed as if to attack Brakfontein. Six field batteries came into action behind them and a howitzer battery just west of the kopjes. For a long time no fire was drawn from the Boer position, their riflemen having orders not to open fire till the attack got within 400 yards. At last, at 11.45 a.m., when the Infantry had got within 1,000 yards of the enemy's trenches, the Boer Artillery, three guns and a pom-pom, opened on our guns, and for the next hour and a half kept up a fire which did little damage, Wynne's Infantry making no further advance.

Meanwhile our Engineers, covered by the 4th Brigade and the fire of our heavy guns on Zwart Kop, which had opened fire on Vaal Krantz at 9.15 a.m., were throwing a pontoon bridge across the Tugela 1,500 yards south of

[1] General Lyttelton, in his 'Eighty Years,' says that Buller told him that Hart's Brigade was to clear Doornkop, but there is no mention of it in his orders.

Munger's Drift. Starting at 10.25 a.m., they had finished the bridge by 11.15 a.m.

The intention was that immediately the bridge was ready, the six field batteries in action north of the kopjes should withdraw in succession, at ten minutes' interval, cross the Tugela by a pontoon just north of Zwart Kop, and come into action a little farther east to cover the crossing of the river and attack on Vaal Krantz by the 4th Brigade. There was an unfortunate delay in the withdrawal of the guns owing to the message reporting the completion of the bridge miscarrying, and the preliminary bombardment of Vaal Krantz seems to have been unnecessarily prolonged. It was not till 2 p.m. that Lyttelton at last got the order to move. The two leading battalions, Durham Light Infantry and Rifle Brigade, dashed over the bridge a company at a time with very little loss, though exposed to a fairly severe rifle and pom-pom fire from various points which the covering Artillery had not been able to locate. They formed up under the far bank and moved upstream under its cover. After going half a mile the bank ceased to cover them, and they climbed out and extended across some mealie-fields which reached to the foot of the slopes of Vaal Krantz. With the Rifle Brigade on the right and the Durham Light Infantry on the left they advanced rapidly to the attack, and soon swept off those of the garrison that had survived the bombardment.

A line was immediately taken up facing north-east, with the left thrown back facing north-west. The Rifle Brigade were on the right, the Durham Light Infantry on the left. The remaining two battalions of the brigade, K.R.R.C. and Scottish Rifles, which had followed the attacking battalions—with some loss too, as the fire had all been from the east and south-east—came into local reserve, the K.R.R.C. behind the Durham Light Infantry and the Scottish Rifles behind the Rifle Brigade. The Devonshire Regiment from Hildyard's Brigade had crossed the bridge behind them with orders to attack Green Hill to the east of Vaal Krantz. They were, however, followed by an order telling them to conform to the movements of the 4th Brigade. The fact was that Buller had already abandoned the attack as hopeless. The successful assault of Vaal Krantz did not reinspire him sufficiently to cause him to carry on with his plan, which so far was working well, though it may have taken longer than he originally intended. It did, however, leave him in a state of indecision as to what to do next, so that, instead of immediately ordering the withdrawal of Lyttelton's Brigade during the night, he left them there with every prospect of another Spion Kop next day.

Lyttelton's position was not an enviable one. Wynne's false attack had come to a standstill before noon, and if it ever did draw any Boer forces to its front it certainly ceased to do so after 1.30 p.m., at which hour Wynne started to withdraw his force to the kopjes. From that hour the Boer Artillery could turn its sole attention to the defence of its left. Consequently, after taking Vaal Krantz, Lyttelton was exposed, not only to musketry fire at close range from the north and medium range from the north-east and east, and artillery fire at close range from Green Hill, but he was within reach of long-range guns on Brakfontein, and by next morning the Boers had mounted a 94-pounder (Creusot) gun on Doornkop to the south-east. The sole advantage the defenders of Vaal Krantz had over those of Spion Kop seems to have been that on this occasion the British Artillery were better placed for counter-battery work and could do something to keep down the enemy's fire. The 4th Brigade spent the night digging in—or rather piling up sangars—and replying to the enemy's fire, which was persistent and ever nearer, doing both to such good purpose that their losses were much fewer than might have been expected.

During the night Buller, who does not seem to have realised the weakness of the Vaal Krantz position, reverted to his original intention, as shown by his orders, of using it as an artillery position which would clear the way for his proposed advance. He therefore sent a message to Lyttelton before daylight, proposing an attack on Height 360. Lyttelton, to whom it was obvious that, so long as nothing was done to right and left, even if he took 360 he would be worse situated than he was already, answered that it could not be done.

The day of the 6th was spent on Vaal Krantz very much as that of January 24 on Spion Kop, a constant bombardment varied by an attempt to recapture the hill by an Infantry attack. Botha, the victor of Colenso and Spion Kop, had returned from Pretoria during the night, and immediately, as he invariably did, put new life into the Boer operations. About 3 o'clock in the afternoon the enemy began a heavy bombardment of the left of Lyttelton's line, whilst, under cover of the smoke from burning grass which had been set alight by our shell fire, their riflemen advanced to within 300–400 yards and opened a terrific fire on the extreme left of the front line, which gave way, and the Boers rushed forward to occupy the vacated position, whence they would have enfiladed Lyttelton's line at close range. They were met by a very prompt counter-attack by the half of our 3rd Battalion in local reserve, who charged with fixed swords. The advancing Boers, seeing them coming, thought better of it and were very soon back at the place from which they started. The whole affair was over in ten minutes.

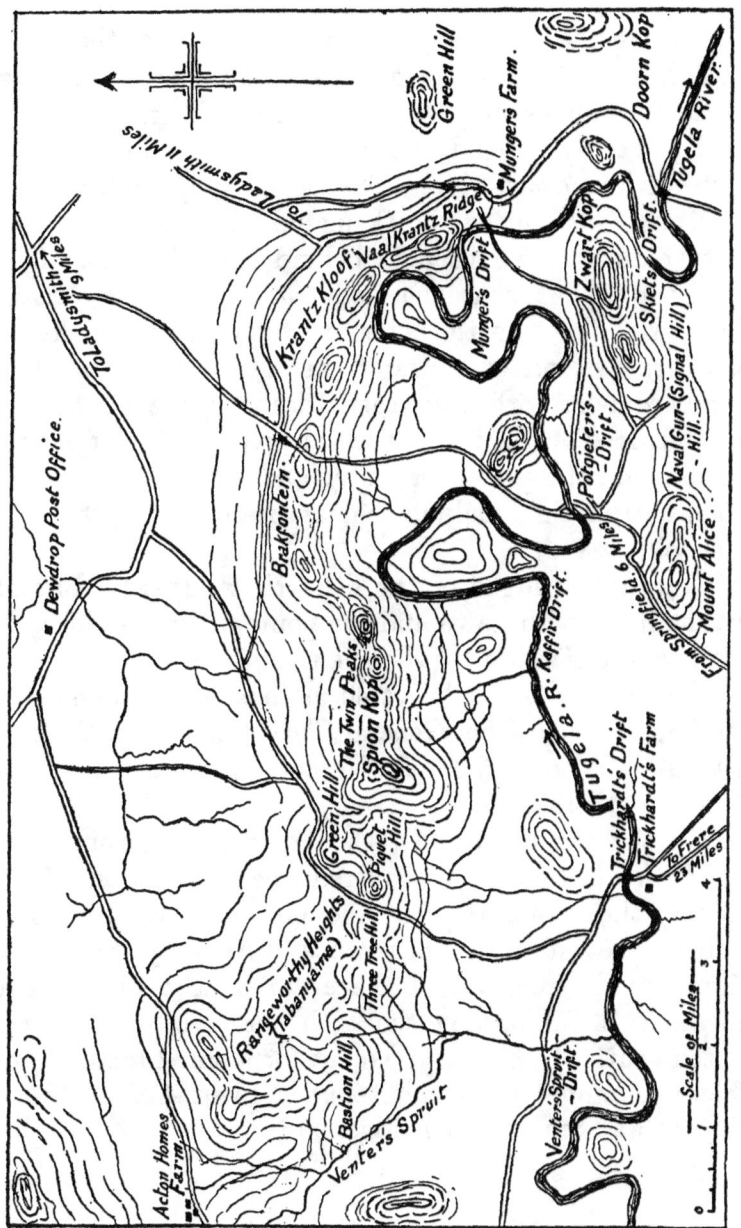

PLATE 15.

SPION KOP AND TWIN PEAKS.

During the day the pontoon bridge east of the kopjes was dismantled and thrown across just below Vaal Krantz. By it, towards evening, Hildyard's Brigade crossed and relieved the 4th Brigade on Vaal Krantz, who retired to just north of Zwart Kop. The Devon Regiment, replaced at Munger's Farm by the Connaught Rangers, came into reserve to its own brigade behind Vaal Krantz. Hildyard's Brigade spent the night improving the existing defences, doing so with such effect that they spent the day of February 7 on Vaal Krantz, under a heavier and closer bombardment, with fewer casualties than the 4th Brigade had incurred on the 6th. Towards evening Buller decided to abandon the present attempt and have another try at Colenso, this time making the capture of Hlangwhane his first objective.

During the night of the 6th–7th Hildyard's Brigade was skilfully withdrawn and the pontoon bridge picked up without interference by the enemy.

On the 7th General Lyttelton took over command of the 2nd Division from General Clery—placed on the sick-list—and Colonel C. H. B. Norcott, Rifle Brigade, took over the 4th Brigade.

On the 8th the 2nd Division marched to Springfield, while the 5th Division covered the evacuation of the kopjes, the dismantling of the pontoon bridge at Potgieter's, the withdrawal of the heavy Artillery from Zwart Kop, and the removal of the accumulation of stores at Spearman's Camp. By the 12th the force was concentrated south of Chieveley, except for a small mixed force, chiefly mounted troops, left under Lieut.-Colonel Burn-Murdoch at Springfield Bridge.

CHAPTER XIII

THE RELIEF OF LADYSMITH

FAR from being discouraged by his three failures, Buller seems to have looked forward to his new task with undue optimism. On the afternoon of the 7th, before Vaal Krantz had been evacuated, he sent a message to White telling him that he intended to ' slip back to Chieveley, take Hlangwhane, . . . and the next night try to take Bulwana from the south. I hope to be at Hlangwhane on Saturday ' [February 10].

There was never any remote prospect of adhering to this time-table. From the wording of his message to White, Buller seems to have thought that he could leave the bulk of the Boer force in position opposite Potgieter's Drift, snap up Hlangwhane by a surprise attack, and thus clear the right bank of the Tugela by a *coup de main.* Even if he had acted up to this idea—that is, if he had rapidly reinforced the detachment at Chieveley and attacked Hlangwhane before bringing the bulk of his force away from before Potgieter's, so proclaiming his intentions to the Boers—he would have been disappointed. There was to be no snapping up of Hlangwhane or clearing the right bank by a surprise attack. Barton, who had been left behind during the recent operations with orders to keep the Boers constantly on the alert in the Colenso area, had done his work far too well for that. His activities, even while the Spion Kop operations were at their height, had alarmed the Boers for the safety of their left flank, and by the time Buller had resolved to try this line of advance again they were holding a much more extended position on the right bank of the Tugela than they did at the battle of Colenso, and turning them out was going to be a big operation. In fact, there was no question of surprising the Boers. They had the double advantage of interior lines and superior mobility. This, combined with their defensive powers, would always enable them to bring the bulk of their force to the threatened point in good time, whatever plan of attack Buller might spring on them. Ladysmith could only be relieved by 'hard pounding' and heavy losses which Buller, so far, had not been able to make up his mind to incur.

Whatever his expectations had been when he told White on the 7th that he hoped to have Hlangwhane on the 10th (changed next day to the 12th), he must soon have realised the impossibility of their fulfilment, as his operations for the clearing of the right bank were deliberate in the extreme.

The Boers had by this time occupied and entrenched the line Hlangwhane—Green Hill—Cingolo—Monte Cristo, and Buller would have to clear this line before he could settle upon a definite plan for crossing the river.

Except for the detachment already mentioned under Burn-Murdoch, another smaller one under Lieut.-Colonel Bethune, far to the right at Greytown, and one battalion—much reduced by losses at Spion Kop—sent to the lines of communication, Buller now had his whole force concentrated about Chieveley. The 11th Brigade, from which two battalions had been detached, was now reinforced by the Rifle Reserve Battalion (Major the Hon. E. J. Montagu-Stuart-Wortley, K.R.R.C.),[1] made up of drafts

[1] Major-General the Hon. E. J. Montagu-Stuart-Wortley, C.B., C.M.G. M.V.O., D.S.O.

for the 1st and 2nd K.R.R.C. and 2nd Rifle Brigade, then in Ladysmith.

On the evening of February 11 Buller ordered Dundonald to seize Hussar Hill, which was lightly held by the enemy. This was done next morning, and Buller spent the day on it reconnoitring the enemy's position. For some reason that is not apparent, he ordered its evacuation in the evening. The rearguard was followed up and suffered some loss, and the place had to be retaken two days later.

Orders for the next move were issued on the 13th, and were confined to the occupation of Hussar Hill by the 5th Division and its use as an artillery position. Early next morning these orders were expanded to include the advance of the 2nd Division to the reverse slopes of Hussar Hill, after its capture, pending orders for a further attack towards Cingolo. Hussar Hill was occupied by the 5th Division at 9 a.m. almost without loss. Except for some desultory artillery fire, the only opposition shown was against the 4th Brigade, towards Moord Kraal, which was occupied by the 3rd Battalion, who were recalled by Buller's order. Artillery was brought up into position and the enemy's line shelled on Green Hill and thence to Hlangwhane. Nothing more was done on the 14th, and the two Divisions bivouacked on the line they had occupied.

On the 15th Lyttelton came up on Warren's right and occupied Moord Kraal Hill. From there he reported to Buller that the Boer position appeared more extensive than had been expected and that he would require more troops if it was to be dealt with, that is, if its left flank was to be turned. Buller, from his reply to this message, seems to have been already seized with another fit of pessimism. After warning Lyttelton to be careful, he adds : 'We are holding a large number of Boers off Ladysmith, which is, after all, all we can expect to do.' His mood of the 7th had not lasted long.

On the 16th, early in the morning, Lyttelton sent forward two battalions to try to locate the Boer position on Cingolo. They got to within a mile and a half of the foot of the hill without getting any information, or even drawing fire, except from snipers when they were retiring. A Cavalry patrol did, however, reach the south-eastern crest of Cingolo, whence, though sniped at, they saw no signs of entrenchments.

By night of the 16th Buller's force was bivouacked in one line; the right facing Cingolo, the left at Gun Hill, north of Chieveley. The Composite Regiment of Mounted Infantry was on the extreme right, Thorneycroft's on the left, and the South African Light Horse in reserve in rear of the centre.

Buller has been severely criticised for the deliberation of his movements during these four days, and one is certainly tempted to wonder why he could not have reached the position he occupied on the 16th by the evening of the 13th. His reply to Lyttelton, quoted above, certainly makes strong evidence for the prosecution, but he was undoubtedly severely hampered by the question of water-supply, a difficulty the like of which arm-chair critics are apt to ignore.

Whatever the reasons for delay, all prospect of catching the Boers napping had long departed; the general locality of the attack had been made clear and they had had three days in which to bring every available man to the threatened point.

On the evening of the 16th a preparatory order was given for the attack on Cingolo Ridge and Green Hill next day. At daybreak on the 17th final orders were given to Lyttelton to clear Cingolo and then swing round and attack Green Hill from the north-east. One of Warren's Brigades was to move on the left of the 2nd Division with another in reserve. His third brigade was to hold Hussar Hill, and Hart's Brigade, which during these operations had been directly under the Commander-in-Chief, was still on the extreme left.

At daybreak on the 17th the British Artillery, from Moord Kraal Hill on the right to Gun Hill on the left, opened a bombardment of the enemy's lines. At 6.30 a.m. the 2nd Division began its advance, Hildyard's Brigade leading. Progress was slow, as the country was rough and the bush very thick. The leading battalion (2nd West Yorks) came under fire at 9 a.m. from the northern slopes of Cingolo. Hildyard then sent another battalion (2nd Queen's) out to his right to work up the south-eastern spur of Cingolo. While this flank attack was developing, the rest of the Division halted. At 1 p.m. the Queen's reached the crest of Cingolo and found the mounted troops already in possession. Dundonald had worked right round the hill and attacked it from the north-east, driving the garrison off, some time before the arrival of the Queen's.

Owing to difficulties of communication it was some time before Lyttelton became aware of the success of the turning movement, and it was not till 4.10 p.m. that he was in a position to report to Buller that he was in possession of the whole of Cingolo and that he was about to attack Monte Cristo, suggesting at the same time that Warren should attack Green Hill. It would seem that Warren would have been usefully employed attacking Green Hill while Lyttelton was engaged at Cingolo, but Buller seems to have had a prejudice against using more than a small portion of his force at one time. He now, considering that it was late in the day to embark on a fresh attack, ordered a halt.

During the night four field guns were with difficulty dragged up on to Cingolo for the purpose of covering an attack on Monte Cristo next day. The orders for the two Divisions for the 18th are interesting for the reason that, while Lyttelton's orders point to a further advance against Cingolo Nek and Monte Cristo, Warren's orders detail Barton to support the 2nd Division, after sending a Staff Officer to Lyttelton to find out what he wanted him (Barton) to do; the other brigade of the 5th Division to be in reserve, but no mention is made of an attack on Green Hill.

At 6.40 a.m. on the 18th the 2nd Brigade began their advance on Monte Cristo. Half an hour later the 4th Brigade also advanced, keeping to the left rear of the 2nd Brigade, through the thick scrub between Green Hill and Cingolo. Covered by the fire of the naval guns and 5-inch guns, Royal Garrison Artillery, from Hussar Hill and the four guns, Royal Field Artillery, which had been dragged up on to Cingolo during the night, and by long-range rifle fire by the supporting battalions of their own Brigade, the two leading battalions of the 2nd Brigade—though under artillery fire from guns placed to the north of Green Hill and Hlangwhane and from Pieter's Hill, as also under musketry fire from the works on the ridge joining Green Hill to Monte Cristo—crossed the Nek without heavy loss and began to work up the steep slopes of Monte Cristo. Here they were in dead ground, and by the time they reached the southern crest the Boers had fallen back to the farther ridges of the hill. By 10.30 they had reached this crest, where they were reinforced by the rest of the Brigade, less half a battalion left in reserve on the Nek. At the same time Dundonald's men were continuing their turning movement by pressing forward along the eastern slopes of Monte Cristo.

While this was going on the 4th Brigade had wheeled round half left, facing the ridge between Green Hill and Monte Cristo, with Barton's Brigade on its left, facing Green Hill. When the 2nd Brigade began to appear on the top of Monte Cristo, the 4th Brigade was sent forward to the attack, supported by a battery which had crossed the Gomba early in the morning. At 12.30 p.m. Lyttelton stopped the 4th Brigade to let Barton get level with them. Meanwhile, the 2nd Brigade had been pushing on. Checked by the heavy fire along the top of Monte Cristo, they worked round under the eastern crest and then cleared the whole of the higher part of the hill from east to west. As they reached the western edge of the hill they found themselves firing down on a Boer laager and trenches defending it near Bloy's Farm, at a range of about 700 yards. As soon as the 2nd Brigade appeared again on the western edge of Monte Cristo, the 4th Brigade and Barton's, which had now drawn level with it, were sent forward and were very soon on to and over Green Hill and the ridge joining it to Monte Cristo. But the Boers in front of them had too good a start and were by this time retiring in the distance in good order, having begun their retreat as soon as Monte Cristo was seen to have fallen. It certainly would appear that much greater results would have been obtained if the attacks on Green Hill, Monte Cristo, and the ridge joining them had been made simultaneously. Whatever the reason, it was not shortage of artillery which prevented the two attacks being simultaneous. There was plenty of artillery which could have been used against Green Hill which was not used against Monte Cristo.

Thus, early in the afternoon, the whole line Monte

Cristo—Green Hill was in British possession (the extreme northern end of Monte Cristo had not been occupied by Hildyard's Brigade, but the Boers had evacuated it), two abandoned laagers, in rear of the captured positions, had been taken, and there was something like a general move on the part of the Boers from the right bank of the Tugela to the left. The 4th and 6th Brigades had not had a hard day; the 10th and 11th had done nothing. The success of the day had been great, but one is tempted to ask if they might not have been made greater without taking any undue risks. Might not an attack on Hlangwhane, following immediately on the capture of Green Hill, have converted the Boer retreat into a rout?

However that may be, Buller thought otherwise and was content with the line he had gained for making a fresh start next day.

On the 19th good progress was made with very little fighting. Dundonald's men worked down to the river and dispersed, by rifle fire, a body of Boers on the left bank. The East Surrey Regiment (2nd Brigade) occupied a line from Clump Hill to the north-eastern spurs of Monte Cristo. Two battalions of the 2nd Brigade were employed making a road on to Monte Cristo, while the fourth battalion joined the 4th Brigade, which pushed on slowly to the north-west through thick bush.

Barton's Brigade occupied Hlangwhane, which they found had been vacated during the night, except for some knolls on its northern spurs to which a few Boers clung all day. During the morning four 5-inch guns, Royal Garrison Artillery, arrived near Bloy's Farm from Hussar Hill. In the afternoon two naval 12-pounders were established on Clump Hill and, later on, two naval 4·7-inch guns also arrived at Bloy's Farm after a two days' trek from Gun Hill. These, during the following night, were got into a concealed position on the north-western spur of Clump Hill.

From Buller's instructions, issued at 4.15 a.m. on the 20th to his divisional commanders, it is clear that he still had in his mind the plan, with which he had started these operations, of crossing the Tugela somewhere to his north-east and so side-stepping all the rough country behind the Colenso bend. His instructions to Warren dealt solely with defence, evidently to guard against the Boers re-crossing the Tugela; those to Lyttelton dealt chiefly with improvement of communications. At daylight on the 20th a small Boer rearguard was still on the northern spurs of Hlangwhane, but by 7 a.m. they had crossed the river, having tried, and failed, to destroy the bridge. Not a Boer was now left on the right bank, and during the day all the crests from Clump Hill to Hlangwhane were occupied by British troops.

Buller spent the morning reconnoitring from Monte Cristo. He soon decided that the turning movement by the north-east was impracticable. The road through Cingolo Nek to the river below Pieter's Hoek was so bad that to make it passable by wagons would take more time than he had to spare, if Ladysmith was to be relieved before it was starved out. Below the junction with the Tugela of the Onderbroek Spruit, though the right bank commanded the left, the fact of there being flat ground on the left bank meant that bridges thrown there would be fully exposed to artillery fire from all the high ground farther west. He was therefore compelled to make his crossing higher up and the rest of the day was spent in movements preliminary to crossing to the west of Hlangwhane.

By the evening of the 20th the force was disposed as follows :—

2nd Division

2*nd Brigade.*—On the eastern slopes of Hlangwhane (less East Surrey Regiment, which remained on Monte Cristo and Clump Hill).
4*th Brigade.*—Rifle Brigade and Durham L.I. north of Hlangwhane, Scottish Rifles, and 3rd K.R.R.C. at Bloy's Farm.
5*th Brigade.*—Still detached at Chieveley.

5th Division

11*th Brigade.*—From Hussar Hill to Hlangwhane.
10*th Brigade.*—One battalion on Hlangwhane, remainder on Green Hill.
6*th Brigade.*—On the northern spurs of Hlangwhane.

The Mounted Brigade (less Thorneycroft's Mounted Infantry at Colenso) were east of Hlangwhane with piquets watching the Tugela from Monte Cristo downwards. Burn-Murdoch's detachment was ordered in from Springfield to Chieveley.

At this time Buller was under the impression that the Boers were in full retreat and that he had only a rearguard before him. Such indeed had been the position for the two previous days. On the 19th even Botha was disheartened and telegraphed to Joubert recommending a retirement of the whole force to the Biggarsberg; but Joubert would have none of it, and the Boers were given time to recover. By the morning of the 21st they were well dug in from Vertnek Mountain on the right to Pieter's Hill on the left.

Buller's idea was for Warren to cross the pontoon bridge as soon as it was ready, taking his own Divisional Artillery with him; and then push north, covered by the remainder of the Artillery, firing from the right bank. The bridge was ready by 2.45 p.m., but by this time Buller had information that the slopes of Grobelaar Mountain were still held. Coke's Brigade, then on the point of crossing, was ordered to push due west and clear the high ground running north from the Colenso loop of the river, above the railway and the flat ground beyond.

The advance of the 10th Brigade soon showed that they had more than a rearguard to deal with. As soon as they got beyond the Colenso kopjes they came under a heavy fire from the lower slopes of Grobelaar, Horse-shoe Hill, and Wynne's Hill. The right companies of the battalions in first and second line crossed the Onderbroek Spruit south of Horse-shoe Hill and there came under such a heavy fire that they were pinned down, unable to advance or retire. About 3 p.m. the 11th Brigade crossed the pontoon bridge and occupied the high ground in rear of the 10th Brigade. As soon as it was dark the 10th Brigade was withdrawn to the Colenso kopjes, on the left of the 11th Brigade. The leading battalion (Somerset Light Infantry) had had a loss of 91 killed and wounded. Sir George White reported during the day that a considerable number of the enemy had arrived by rail, from the north, at Modder Spruit Station. The Boers, so far from being on the run, were being reinforced.

By the evening of the 21st Buller had across the river the 10th and 11th Brigades, a battalion of Hart's Brigade, which had been ferried across at Colenso, three field batteries, and two naval 12-pounders. The 2nd Division and the 6th Brigade were concentrated about Hlangwhane, while the remainder of Hart's Brigade was distributed between Colenso and Chieveley. During the morning of the 22nd the 2nd Brigade, two battalions of the 4th Brigade (2nd Scottish Rifles and 3rd King's Royal Rifle Corps), and two battalions of the 5th Brigade crossed the river; thus nearly the whole force was crowded into a triangle of about two miles by two by one and a half. The 1st Cavalry Brigade had joined the force on the right bank—an unfortunate decision, as they had been doing good work at Springfield in constantly threatening the Boers with a crossing higher up, and had led them to detach considerable forces to guard against such a move. With the British force crowded on to such a small front it was more than ever necessary to keep the Boers at full stretch.

On the morning of the 22nd Warren, who had had no orders as to any further movement, sent the Commander-in-Chief a sketch of his proposals for action. They were for the 11th Brigade to take Wynne's Hill (supported by one battalion 10th Brigade), passing by Horse-shoe Hill, and gave details of the artillery support he required. General Wynne protested against making this attack with all the high ground on his left held by the enemy, but meanwhile General Lyttelton had been ordered to support the attack of the 11th Brigade. He thereupon issued orders that the 4th Brigade should support the attack by sending forward one battalion echeloned in rear of the left flank of the 11th Brigade followed by another, while the 2nd Brigade followed in reserve. The order stated that the General Officer Commanding would accompany the supporting battalion of the 4th Brigade. This shows what importance he placed on the action of this battalion, and that he intended to see for himself how to employ it. If only this order could have been carried out simultaneously with the advance of the 11th Brigade, all might have gone well, but the only two battalions of the 4th Brigade available—the other two were a long way off on the other side of the river—the 2nd Scottish Rifles and 3rd King's Royal Rifle Corps, were at the moment holding an important part of the line, and it was not till nightfall that our 3rd Battalion, the first of the two to be returned, was sent off on its new errand.

Consequently at 2 p.m. the 11th Brigade went off unsupported. As they advanced, artillery fire and the rifle and machine-gun fire of some of the 6th Brigade from the right bank kept the Boer fire down; the garrison of Horse-shoe Hill being kept back to the rear edge, the route of the 11th Brigade past their hill was dead ground to them. The Brigade thus reached the lower slopes of Wynne Hill with little loss. Major-General Wynne was wounded early in the action and was succeeded temporarily by Colonel Crofton, Royal Lancaster Regiment, but Colonel F. W. Kitchener, West Yorkshire Regiment, was selected for the command next day. As they mounted the hill, the Royal Lancaster Regiment on the right, the South Lancashire in the centre, and Rifle Reserve Regiment on the left, they began to come under fire from three sides, which when they reached the top and pushed on towards the Boer position along the further crest got very much heavier, especially from Horse-shoe Hill. Part of the Rifle Reserve Regiment was then directed against Horse-shoe Hill and succeeded in reaching the forward crest, thereby easing the situation, but not enough for the Brigade to be able to continue its advance.

At 3 p.m. Warren asked Lyttelton to reinforce Wynne's Brigade by sending one battalion to Wynne's Hill and another to Horse-shoe Hill. Lyttelton ordered up the 2nd Brigade from the Colenso kopjes. This would take time, and there was no time to spare. As soon as dusk should bring a cessation of our artillery covering fire, a determined counter-attack by the Boers on Wynne's Hill was likely to deprive the 11th Brigade of their precarious hold on it. Fortunately about sunset our 3rd Battalion had been relieved from the front line and been sent up to assist the 11th Brigade. Major R. C. A. B. Bewicke-Copley, who was in command, directed the Battalion on Horse-shoe Hill and the west end of Wynne's Hill.

As darkness fell and the British gun-fire ceased, the Boers counter-attacked so vigorously against the west end of Wynne's Hill that two companies of the Royal Lancaster Regiment were driven back across the plateau to the southern crest. At this moment half of our 3rd Battalion were just coming up for the purpose of relieving the front line. The Officer Commanding one of these companies, Captain the Hon. R. Cathcart, grasping the situation at once, fixed swords and charged the advancing Boers, who fell back with considerable loss to their own works. Cathcart pressed on to within 70 to 100 yards of the enemy's line, where he came under such a heavy fire that he was obliged to take cover in a stone cattle-kraal. Here Cathcart was killed whilst arranging for the defence of the place, and was succeeded in command of the company by Lieutenant D. H. Blundell-Hollinshead-Blundell. This Officer, though soon aware of his isolated position, saw at once what a help he would be to an advance by our side next morning if only he could stay where he was. He therefore decided to hang on there for the night. Meanwhile the East Surrey Regiment and the Devons, from the 2nd Brigade, had come up into the front line, part of the East Surrey occupying that part of the line in front of which our single company was isolated. Thus, although with considerable intermingling of units and overlapping of commands, the line was made secure for the night; but the situation was unsatisfactory as, unless something were done as soon as daylight came, the enfilade fire from both flanks would be as bad as ever and the reinforcement of our line would only increase the losses. Heavy firing went on all night, and several times parties of Boers got so close to our line on Wynne's Hill that they had to be driven back by a bayonet charge.

During the night Lieutenant H. Wake,[1] from the cattle-kraal, succeeded in making his way back to 11th Brigade Headquarters to report the situation of the detachment, surrounded on three sides and almost out of ammunition. Guided by Wake, two companies of the East Surrey took up a position to cover the retirement of Blundell's detachment. When this was done, Wake crept forward again with orders to Blundell to slip away. The retirement began one man at a time and for some time escaped notice. At last the Boers detected the movement and opened a heavy fire on the space to be crossed. There was then nothing to be done but to make a dash for it, and what were left of the Riflemen darted back together and re-formed in rear of the East Surrey.

Of these, one company immediately withdrew to the southern crest under cover of the fire of the Rifles; but the other, with which was the Commanding Officer of the Battalion, Lieut.-Colonel Harris, had got too far into the open, and after losing their Commanding Officer and Company Commander had to remain where they were for fourteen hours, till nightfall enabled them to rejoin their Battalion.

The only other important move of the night of the 22nd–23rd was that the Queen's seized and entrenched some kopjes on the right bank of the Onderbroek Spruit, from which the right of the Rifle Reserve Regiment was being enfiladed.

On the evening of the 22nd, Buller gave orders for an attack next day by Hart's Brigade on the hill since named after him, his Brigade being reinforced by the 1st Rifle Brigade and Durham Light Infantry from the 4th Brigade.

[1] Colonel Sir Hereward Wake, Bart., C.M.G., D.S.O.

The morning was spent in getting artillery into position to support this attack.

Leaving its bivouac at 5 a.m., the 5th Brigade was, by 7 a.m., just south of the Onderbroek Spruit.

The attack, which did not take place till 5 p.m. owing to the length and difficulty of the route, was a gallant and costly failure. The assault was not delivered till after the Artillery had been obliged to cease fire owing to the failure of daylight. A few men reached the Boer trenches, only to be shot down or made prisoners, and the remnants of the leading battalions were driven back as far as a stone wall some 200 yards below the forward crest, where they re-formed.

The fire fight about Wynne's Hill and Horse-shoe Hill had been going on all day, and in the evening the 11th Brigade had been withdrawn under cover just south of Hill 244.

The distribution of the troops on the night of the 23rd–24th was as follows :—

The 5th Brigade, with two battalions of the 4th attached, was clinging to the slopes of Hart's Hill. To their left came the 2nd Brigade holding the front edge of Wynne's Hill, two battalions of the 6th Brigade doing the same on Horse-shoe Hill and the 2nd Scottish Rifles and 3rd K.R.R.C. holding the kopjes south of Horse-shoe Hill and across the Onderbroek Spruit from it. The 11th Brigade was in reserve. The 10th Brigade held the Colenso kopjes with the Mounted Brigade on their right—less Thorneycroft's Mounted Infantry, who were on their left. The Cavalry Brigade was on the right bank of the river near the pontoon bridge, and the remaining two battalions of the 6th Brigade were escort to the Artillery on the right bank. As the Boer bridge, partially repaired, was not fit for wheeled traffic, besides being badly exposed, and the

Colenso bridges were still out of action, the pontoon bridge was practically the only link with the right bank.

At daylight on the 24th Hart's front line behind the stone wall came under a very harassing enfilade fire from both flanks, and the senior officer on the spot withdrew them to the railway line. The position was reoccupied with little loss by the Rifle Brigade and Durham Light Infantry. It began to look as if things had come to a deadlock unless Hart's Hill could be taken, which would entail the taking of the hill immediately to the north of it at the same time. Buller on the 24th at first intended to continue the operations of the previous day by renewing the attack on Hart's Hill; but before the arrangements for the fresh attack were complete, information came to him which caused him to change his mind. A track was found leading down to the river about a mile above Hart's Hill to a place suitable for throwing a bridge. The track was well covered from view and fire, and with little work could be made practicable for wheeled transport. He therefore determined to bring a great part of his force back across the river, send them over again by the proposed bridge, and then make a strong attack on the left of the Boer position which, if successful, should open the road to Ladysmith.

On the 25th a truce was agreed to for the purpose of bringing in the wounded, many of whom had lain out in the open for nearly forty-eight hours, but this did not prevent the movement of troops. By 10 a.m. on the 25th all the guns from the left bank, except one field battery, had been brought back to the right, and by nightfall they were nearly all in their new positions ready to cover the coming attack.

After dark on the 25th the Boers made attacks on various points of the line, but were easily repulsed. These were probably not intended to be driven home, but to find out if the British were really retiring. The 26th was occupied in bringing troops across from the left bank to the right, and dismantling the pontoon bridge.

During the fighting of the 22nd and 23rd, formations had been so mixed up that there was scarcely a Brigade which had not battalions detached from it and had absorbed units from other Brigades. The 4th Brigade, for instance, had lost the 3rd K.R.R.C. and half of the Scottish Rifles, but had taken on the East Surrey Regiment from the 2nd Brigade. The front was now divided into two sections divided by the Langewacht Spruit, Warren commanding all troops to the right of it and Lyttelton all to the left. The 3rd K.R.R.C. and four companies Scottish Rifles were in the front line immediately south of Horse-shoe Hill.

The plan for the 27th was that as soon as the pontoon was ready in its new place, the 6th Brigade was to cross by it, followed by the 11th. They would then move up the covered way formed by the river till opposite their objectives; the 6th Brigade would then attack Pieter's Hill, the 11th Brigade Kitchener's Hill, and the 4th Brigade, already on the left bank, Hart's Hill. The attacks were to be made in succession from the right, the 11th and 4th Brigades not starting their attacks till that of the Brigades next on their right was well under way. The task of Lyttelton's troops was to keep up such a heavy fire as to prevent the Boers in front of them leaving their trenches and going to reinforce any of the points attacked.

The attack was a complete success, and by evening the Boers were in full flight from every part of the line, but so well covered by their rearguard that Buller's Infantry were unable to pursue; not that they were in any condition to pursue after the hard work of the last fortnight. Even if they had been fit to march they could not have been supplied, as Buller's first occupation, so far as wheeled transport is concerned, was to get supplies and medical requisites to the garrison of Ladysmith.

On the evening of the 27th the mounted troops got orders for the 28th. Dundonald was to work north and north-west towards Ladysmith, Burn-Murdoch to cross the Klip and reconnoitre towards Umbelwana. Next morning the advance of the mounted troops was unfortunately delayed by an accident to the pontoon bridge, and Dundonald did not cross till nearly 8 a.m., Burn-Murdoch, who had been told to cross the bridge and await orders, an hour later.

Reports from all parts of the line were now reaching General Headquarters that the enemy had retired, which were confirmed by signals from Ladysmith saying that the Boers were in full flight.

The mounted troops were soon held up by the enemy's rearguard, sufficiently to prevent them, unless supported by artillery, doing any damage to the retreating Boers; but Dundonald, leaving the bulk of his Brigade near Nelthorpe, got into Ladysmith before dusk with a part of the Imperial Light Horse and Natal Carbineers.

The 28th was spent by the Infantry in sorting themselves out, detached units rejoining their formations.

On March 1 the relieving force, less 5th and 10th Brigades, marched towards Ladysmith and bivouacked at Nelthorpe. An effort to speed the parting enemy was made by Sir George White, who sent out a column made up from every man or animal thought fit to walk, but they were soon found to have misjudged their strength and to be incapable of any useful effort. On the same day Buller entered Ladysmith, had an interview with Sir George White, and returned to Nelthorpe. He meanwhile steadily declined to allow a Cavalry pursuit. He was convinced that Cavalry could do no good unsupported by Artillery and Infantry. He had either to use his single bridge for supplying a pursuing force or for supplying Ladysmith, and he decided in favour of Ladysmith.

A convoy of seventy-three wagons laden with food and medical stores entered Ladysmith during the day.

On March 3 the relieving force marched through Ladysmith.

CHAPTER XIV

SIEGE OF LADYSMITH

THE events of October 30 obliged Sir George White to give up all hope of an active defence and to resign himself to being besieged. As things turned out, it was the best use to which his force could be put, while awaiting the reinforcements from home, as the Boers were attracted by the bait and devoted all their efforts to besieging him instead of proceeding to the invasion of Natal, the prevention of which had been his first object.

To the Boer Commander-in-Chief the choice between taking Ladysmith or invading Natal, leaving a part of his force to contain Sir George White's force, was chiefly a moral and political one.

It appeared that the loss of Ladysmith with its garrison and vast accumulation of stores would be a greater blow to British prestige and a greater encouragement to rebellion by the Cape Dutch and intervention by European Powers than would a successful invasion of Natal. He therefore set about the siege with all the force at his disposal, with every hope of taking the place before it could be relieved.

Ladysmith, as the map shows, lies in a loop of the Klip River and is surrounded by an outer and inner ring of hills. The outer ring which completely surrounds the town, with a radius averaging from 7,500 to 8,000 yards, in places rising to some 700 feet above the town level, would have been far too extensive a perimeter for White's force to hold. He therefore had no choice but to hold the inner ring—or horse-shoe, as it is open to the south-east—

which is slightly lower and less continuous than the outer ring, having an average diameter of about four miles, giving a perimeter of about twelve and a half miles, three of which were in the flat, open country through which the Durban railway ran and the Klip River wound its way till they disappeared together through a narrow cleft in the outer ring. Now that the naval guns had arrived and made good his deficiency in long-range artillery, and considering that siege warfare was not likely to be the Boers' strong suit, with ample supplies for at least a couple of months, in spite of a certain shortage of artillery ammunition, Sir George White must have sat down in Ladysmith with every confidence of being able to hold out till the arrival of relief.

The perimeter was divided into four sections, as shown on the map, and was garrisoned as follows at the beginning of the siege :—

Section A (Colonel W. G. Knox)
1st Devon Regiment.
1st (King's) Liverpool Regiment.
2 Companies 1st Gloucestershire Regiment.
½ Company 2nd Royal Dublin Fusiliers.

Section B (Major-General F. Howard)
6 Companies 1st Leicestershire Regiment.
2nd K.R.R.C.
2nd Rifle Brigade.
1st K.R.R.C.

Section C (Colonel I. S. M. Hamilton)
1st Manchester Regiment.
4 Companies 2nd Gordon Highlanders.
2 Companies 1st Royal Irish Fusiliers.

Section D (Colonel W. Royston) was garrisoned entirely by colonial troops.

The guns heavier than field artillery—viz. two naval 4·7-inch guns, four naval 12-pounders, and two 6·3-inch howitzers—were distributed among the sections. The troops not allotted to sections, which at first included all the field artillery, formed a general reserve.

During November 2 and 3 the Boers closed round Ladysmith, occupying the outer ring of hills mentioned above. The last train to leave before the investment was complete, which left on the 3rd, conveying Major-General French and his Staff, barely escaped capture.

The effective garrison on November 2 amounted to 13,496 of all ranks and 51 guns, of which only 8 were long-range weapons and 36 were R.F.A. 15-pounders. The civilian population numbered 5,400, exclusive of 2,400 Kaffirs and natives of India. The perimeter held by the troops had considerable drawbacks as a defensive position. The heights occupied, which were generally flat-topped with steep sides, too often had dead ground in front of the forward crest; the ground was rocky and did not lend itself to entrenching, thereby necessitating the use of that most unpleasant form of cover under shell fire, the sangar or stone breastwork. The shortness of the perimeter and the length of range of the Boer guns meant that practically every part of it was exposed to enfilade fire and much of it to reverse fire from some part of the Boers' line. Fortunately their long-range guns were not numerous and their expenditure of ammunition was economical.

The strength of the besieging force at the beginning of the siege, before any part of it was drawn off to oppose the relief force, amounted to about 23,000 men.

On November 2, and more so on the 3rd, the Boer Artillery had been active, a good many shells had fallen in the town, and there had been some casualties among the civil population. A party of 89 wounded, from

Dundee, had also been sent into the town by the Boers. Sir George White therefore wrote to General Joubert, the Boer Commander-in-Chief, asking that the sick and wounded with the non-combatant inhabitants of Ladysmith should be allowed to depart south by train. Joubert could hardly be expected to sanction this, but to his eternal credit and to that of his nation as chivalrous foes he sanctioned the formation of a neutral camp in no-man's-land, on the Intombi Spruit, agreeing to a cessation of hostilities till midnight November 5–6, to enable the arrangements to be carried out. The sick, wounded, and families were thus placed in safety, but still continued to be a drain on the supplies of the defence.

At the beginning of the siege neither side did much beyond consolidating its position, the Boers seeming to have resigned themselves to the prospect of letting bombardment and starvation do their work for them ; with no idea of forcing a surrender, before the arrival of the relieving force, by more active methods.

On November 4 the Boers occupied Limit Hill, hitherto held by a British Cavalry piquet. Our 13th Battery R.F.A. was consequently placed in position east of Junction Hill, the two 6·3-inch howitzers on Helpmakaar Ridge, and a section of the 69th Battery R.F.A. at Leicester Post.

On November 7 the Boers bombarded all day and a force of about 1,000 gathered below Middle Hill, one mile south of Mounted Infantry Hill, and opened long-range fire on Wagon Hill, as if about to attack, but nothing came of it. Four guns of the 42nd Battery were then put in position on Cæsar's Camp. Next day another 94-pounder opened from the flat top of Umbulwana, and the remaining guns of the 42nd Battery were brought up to Cæsar's Camp. On the 9th, after bombarding Cæsar's Camp from every side from 5 a.m. to 10.30 a.m., the enemy made an attack on it, getting to within 500 yards, but were driven off by the fire of its garrison, of the Manchester Regiment. Threats were also made against Observation Hill and Helpmakaar Ridge, but nothing came of them.

On October 31 Major-General F. Howard had taken over command of the 8th Brigade from Colonel Grimwood, the Brigade consisting of the 1st Leicestershire Regiment, 1st and 2nd K.R.R.C., and 2nd R.B.

Howard commanded B, or the Northern Section of the defences, but there seems to have been considerable interchange of troops among the sections, as from November 8 Wagon Hill was permanently garrisoned by three companies of the 1st K.R.R.C. More of the Field Artillery were now taken from the General Reserve and brought up into position; two guns, 69th Battery, going to Observation Hill and four to Leicester Post; four guns, 67th, to Ration Post. The troops went on entrenching, or rather erecting breastworks and traverses of stone, which secured them from anything but a direct hit. The civil population excavated dug-outs in their gardens and out of the steep banks of the Klip River.

As reinforcements arrived in Natal, and the prospect of the Relief Force being strong enough to move came nearer, a Mobile Column was formed in Ladysmith consisting of 4 regiments of Cavalry, four batteries R.F.A., 4 battalions of Infantry, 15 odd companies of Infantry, some colonial troops, and ammunition and supply columns carrying three days' rations. This force was kept fit by route marching at night, ready to co-operate with the Relief Force when it should get near enough.

Towards the end of November the enemy got more guns into position, including a 94-pounder on Gun Hill and another on Middle Hill. The British shortage of ammunition prevented any very active reply to the Boer long-range guns, but in spite of this they did little damage and casualties were few.

On the night of December 7–8 a raid was made for the purpose of destroying the 94-pounder gun and 4·7-inch howitzer on Gun Hill, which had been giving trouble. A force of 650 men, led by Major-General Sir A. Hunter,[1] the Chief of the Staff, consisting of 500 Natal Carbineers, 100 I.L.H., 18 of the Corps of Guides under Brevet-Major D. Henderson,[2] Sir George White's Intelligence Officer, and a detachment of R.E. under Captain G. H. Fowke,[3] crossed the two miles of rough, scrub-covered plain to Gun Hill in pitchy darkness, overran the piquet, fired gun-cotton charges in the breeches and muzzles of both pieces, and returned with Major Henderson and seven men wounded as their only casualties.

On the night of December 10–11 the 2nd Rifle Brigade, under Lieut.-Colonel C. T. E. Metcalfe, made a similar raid against a 4·7-inch howitzer on Surprise Hill, which was equally successful in its object, but, owing to failure of the charges to ignite, which delayed their return for half an hour, they had to fight their way back and had 58 casualties in killed and wounded and 6 missing.

By this time the advance of Buller's Relief Force was imminent. On the 7th Buller had signalled that he meant to advance by Potgieter's Drift, starting on the 12th, and that he would take five days. A later message postponed the move for six days. On the 13th Buller signalled that he meant to come by Colenso, probably on the 17th. On the 15th heavy firing to the south showed that the battle had begun, though White had received no further warning. A day of suspense was not cheered by the arrival

[1] General Sir Archibald Hunter, G.C.B., G.C.V.O., D.S.O.
[2] Lieut.-General Sir David Henderson, K.C.B., K.C.V.O., D.S.O.
[3] Lieut.-General Sir George Fowke, K.C.B., K.C.M.G.

of the news of Methuen's failure at Magersfontein. The firing at Colenso died down in the afternoon without further news from Buller till next day, when his report of the action of the day before was in terms of the lowest depths of despondency, telling White that he could do no more for another month, asking him if he could hold out so long and counselling him what to do, if he could not. White replied encouragingly, and on the 17th Buller signalled that the 5th Division were just then arriving at the Cape, that he had ordered it to join him, and that this addition would enable him to have another try. In spite of the tonic of the arrival of the 5th Division, White must have felt that the tone of Buller's late communications gave very little hope of early relief.

Food had not so far become a serious difficulty to White, though he had thought it necessary to reduce the men's rations as early as November 25; casualties had never been severe since the siege started, but the numbers of sick were mounting rapidly. The figures for enteric were more than doubling every week, and dysentery was not much better. Ammunition shortage also would become serious if the Boers, satisfied that Buller would remain inactive, were forcibly to set about the reduction of Ladysmith. This they showed no immediate signs of doing, and, up to the first week in January, things went on as before—a few casualties daily by the enemy's fire and an ever-mounting sick-list.

The chief weakness in the British position at Ladysmith lay in its want of depth. Nowhere in the perimeter was there a good second line of defence, and the capture and retention of any prominent point in it would lay the whole of the rest of it open to enfilade or reverse fire at long field-artillery range. To no part of the position did this apply more than to the Cæsar's Camp—Wagon Hill Ridge. Any part of this ridge for over two miles from east to west was higher than any other point in the perimeter, and from it one overlooked the whole interior of the position as from the rim of a saucer. This ridge is divided into two unequal parts by a nek. The eastern and much the larger of these, called Cæsar's Camp, is about two miles long, fairly flat-topped, and dumbbell-shaped in plan, forming two salients with a re-entrant between. At its widest parts the top is about 1,000 yards from north to south. The highest point is the north-west end of the plateau.

To the south the hillside falls steeply into Bester's Valley, the face being covered with scrub and boulders and much cut up by small salients and re-entrants. To the east and south-east the slope is as steep but more regular. At the west end of Cæsar's Camp is a nek, about 100 feet lower than the top of the ridge, and beyond the nek is Wagon Hill, also nearly flat-topped, but only 900 yards from east to west and 300 from north to south. The centre and extreme west of Wagon Hill form two knolls with a depression between them and a consequent re-entrant both to north and south. The easternmost of these two knolls, which had two small works on it—the easternmost of the two being a redoubt called the Crow's Nest—is the highest point in the whole ridge. The western knoll also had a small work on it and was known as Wagon Point. The southern and western faces of Wagon Hill are steep, rocky, and scrub-covered, but instead of the broad and deep valley of Bester's Spruit it has only a shallower valley to the front of it, and about one mile away to the south-west the ground rises again into Mounted Infantry Hill, of equal height to Wagon Hill.

The garrison of Cæsar's Camp on the night of January 5–6, 1900, consisted of the 1st Manchester Regiment, the 42nd Battery Royal Field Artillery, a detachment Royal

Navy with a 12-pounder gun, and a detachment Natal Naval Volunteers with a Hotchkiss. On Wagon Hill, the Crow's Nest was the Headquarters of three companies of the 1st King's Royal Rifle Corps. In the work next to the west was a squadron of Imperial Light Horse (38 men), and on Wagon Point itself another squadron Imperial Light Horse (41 men). The piquet line followed the forward edge of the plateau, but the line of resistance was along the rear edge.

On January 5 at a conference in the Boer G.H.Q. camp it was decided to attack the Cæsar's Camp—Wagon Hill position early next morning. Two thousand burghers from each Republic were to take part, the Transvaalers attacking Cæsar's Camp and the Free Staters, Wagon Hill. A reinforcement of 600 from the commandos on the Tugela was called in to make up the necessary 4,000. General Schalk Burger was to command. The same evening a party of Sappers, under Lieutenant R. J. T. Digby Jones, arrived at Wagon Hill. Their work for the night was, firstly, to finish an emplacement for a 12-pounder naval gun near the centre of the summit of Wagon Point; secondly, to erect a platform for a similar emplacement just below the extreme western point; thirdly, to mount a 4·7-inch gun, then on its way from Junction Hill, in a work which had been already prepared for it, halfway between the two 12-pounder emplacements. With the help of a fatigue party of 50 men of the Manchester Regiment the work began. Soon afterwards the 4·7-inch arrived, escorted by 2 Officers and 13 bluejackets Royal Naval Brigade, and 170 men of the Gordon Highlanders. The gun was left at the foot of the hill, in the wagon in which it travelled, until the emplacement should be ready for it. At 2.30 a.m. the fatigue party of the Manchester Regiment left for their own bivouacs. All seemed quiet and a patrol of the Imperial Light Horse which had been out to near Middle Hill had returned at 2 a.m. and reported no movement.

At 2.40 a.m. a sentry of the Imperial Light Horse piquet on the nek between the western work and Wagon Point heard someone moving in the donga below him, challenged and fired. He was answered by a blaze of rifle shots at close range. The supports of the Imperial Light Horse immediately ran forward to reinforce the piquet, which was covering the Sappers at work on the emplacement and therefore could not fall back to the line of resistance. Four men fell in this rush, and their Officer ran right into the enemy as they swarmed up the hill and was shot at close range. A moment later the Sappers came under a heavy fire from their left front at 150 yards' range. Digby Jones doused the lights, extended his men (25 of them), and returned the fire, joined by a few men of the Gordon Highlanders who had come up from where they had left the 4·7-inch gun. Jones then fixed bayonets and advanced 40 yards to the forward crest of the hill, the Imperial Light Horse on his right and left joining in with him. Here they found the enemy already above them on their left on the glacis of the small work on the crest, and in a few moments they lost over two-thirds of their numbers. Our 1st Battalion had two half companies on piquet on the left of the Imperial Light Horse. These, quickly reinforced by two more half companies, lined the crest, leaving one company in the Crow's Nest.

Soon afterwards Colonel Gore-Browne, commanding the 1st Battalion, received an urgent appeal for help from the Imperial Light Horse. He sent Brevet-Major D. Mackworth (the Queen's: attached to the 1st Battalion), with a part of the Reserve Company to try to clear the

Boers off from their point of vantage in front of the Imperial Light Horse work. With 20 riflemen Mackworth led a charge against this party, but was met by a terrific fire and fell dead with most of his followers killed or wounded round him.

Meanwhile, the Manchester Regiment on Cæsar's Camp had had fifteen minutes' warning from the outburst of fire on Wagon Hill in which to reinforce their piquets. Suddenly, their left-hand piquet was swept by a burst of fire from their left rear. A party of Transvaalers had got up to the eastern crest of the hill and occupied a point whence, when daylight came, they would sweep the whole plateau with their fire. For the time they were content to retain this position without pushing any farther, and when daylight did come they were quickly dislodged by shrapnel fire, followed by a bayonet charge by a company of Gordon Highlanders.

Against Wagon Hill the attack was prosecuted much more vigorously. The Free Staters continued to press up the hill in ever-increasing numbers, and the Imperial Light Horse in the nek, outflanked from both salients, were forced back. At the same time a party of Boers, working round the west end of the hill, attacked the 4·7-inch gun, but were beaten back by the escort, who dismantled the wheels of the wagon in which it had been brought up, so that, if captured, it could not be removed.

Reinforcements soon began to arrive. A wing of the Gordon Highlanders was encamped near Maiden Castle. Colonel Ian Hamilton, commanding the section of defence, had his Headquarters there, and assembling three companies of the Gordons, he sent one to reinforce Cæsar's Camp while he made for Wagon Hill with the other two.

At 4.30 a.m. under orders from General Headquarters the Imperial Light Horse were on their way to Wagon Hill, the other half battalion of the Gordon Highlanders to Cæsar's Camp. A little later four companies each of the 1st and 2nd Battalions King's Royal Rifle Corps, the whole under Major W. P. Campbell, were on the march from their bivouac near Observation Hill to Wagon Hill.

Soon after daybreak two batteries of Field Artillery came up from the reserve and did much to prevent the situation getting worse—one by sweeping all the ground to the immediate west of Wagon Hill, the other doing the same to the east of Cæsar's Camp, thus preventing either flank from being turned.

The first reinforcements to arrive were the Imperial Light Horse and the Gordon Highlanders from Maiden Castle. Of these the Imperial Light Horse went straight into the firing-line with their comrades on Wagon Hill, the two companies of the Gordons which Colonel Hamilton brought up being, for the time, kept in reserve in rear of the hill. The other company, which went to Cæsar's Camp, came up at the east end, where, at first, they prevented the Boers further outflanking the position and kept them busy till they were shaken by shrapnel fire, when they charged them with the bayonet, driving them out of some sangars which they had taken from the Manchester Regiment and down the hill; thus relieving Cæsar's Camp of any danger of its left flank being turned, though the Boers still held the whole of the southern crest.

At 7 a.m. the eight companies of the 1st and 2nd Battalions King's Royal Rifles reached Wagon Hill, along the top of which a terrific fire fight was going on with the opposing lines within a stone's throw of each other. The most critical situation was on Wagon Point, where the Imperial Light Horse held the southern crest, the Gordon Highlanders prolonging the line to the right. These latter had tried to advance so as to enfilade the attackers, but the Boer fire from Middle Hill and the dongas to the south-west had been too much for them and they had had to fall back. The Imperial Light Horse line was badly enfiladed by a small party of Boers, already mentioned, who had got good cover close in front of the Imperial Light Horse work, from which they could fire to either flank.

Major Campbell on arrival sent four companies up into the firing-line, between Crow's Nest and the Imperial Light Horse work, keeping four companies in reserve. He then saw that the thing which wanted doing most was that the party of Boers in front of the Imperial Light Horse work should be driven out. Major R. S. Bowen, 2nd Battalion, volunteered to do it, and, taking eight men of his company, made a gallant charge across the open. He himself was killed within ten yards of the Boer line and the whole of his little party fell with him. Shortly afterwards another attempt was made by Lieutenant N. M. Tod, Scottish Rifles, attached to our 2nd Battalion, but with the same result, Tod being killed and all his party of twelve killed or wounded. This happened about 9 a.m., and from that time the firing gradually died down on both sides and by 11 a.m. had almost ceased. Further reinforcements had arrived about 9 o'clock—the 18th Hussars at Wagon Hill and three squadrons of the 5th Lancers and two of the 19th Hussars at Cæsar's Camp. All of these were for the time retained in reserve.

On Cæsar's Camp things were much more comfortable. At 8 a.m. six companies of the Rifle Brigade had arrived and gone straight into the firing-line. Shortly afterwards came the two squadrons of the 19th Hussars, who were kept in reserve. These were quickly followed by the four Headquarters Companies of the Gordons and three squadrons of the 5th Lancers. The Lancers went into reserve and the Gordons were gradually absorbed in the firing-line.

The firing died down on Cæsar's Camp as it had on Wagon Hill, and it began to look as if the enemy had shot his bolt. They had failed to take the position by surprise in the dark. How were they to take it now after the garrison had been strongly reinforced and they had not? Though it certainly seems that the Transvaalers, opposite Cæsar's Camp, had had enough of it and their supports preferred to adhere to their task of giving long-range covering fire, the Free Staters at Wagon Hill were far from done with.

At 12.30 p.m. a party of them, led by Commandant de Villiers, formerly Chief of the Orange Free State Army, and Field Cornet de Jagers, suddenly charged over the crest-line of Wagon Point. The firing-line were caught napping and fell back. A rot might very well have set in if Lieutenant Digby Jones, R.E., had not seized a rifle and shot de Villiers dead—de Jagers falling at the same time from another bullet—and then led a bayonet charge of his Sappers, joined by a few of the Imperial Light Horse and bluejackets, which drove back de Villiers's few followers and reoccupied the front line. Major Knox, 18th Hussars, who was in reserve behind the hill, seeing some of the front line coming back, promptly led up his two squadrons into line with Digby Jones's men. Digby Jones was killed immediately afterwards, as were his subaltern, 2nd Lieutenant G. B. B. Denniss, R.E., and Major Miller-Wallnutt, Gordon Highlanders, who was with Digby Jones when the surprise attack was made and had immediately rejoined his men on the right flank.

The situation on Wagon Hill was now critical, as the Boers' fire was as hot as ever and the defenders were almost worn out. The three squadrons 5th Lancers and two of the 19th Hussars, which had been in reserve behind Cæsar's Camp, were sent to Wagon Hill, as also were two squadrons 5th Dragoon Guards, who had been acting as escort to the Field Artillery and had been relieved by the last remaining squadron of the 19th Hussars.

The Lancers and Hussars arrived about 2.30 p.m. and went straight up into the front line in front of the Crow's Nest. At the same time Major Campbell placed three companies of the King's Royal Rifle Corps in a covering position along the northern crest, where they were joined by the two squadrons of the 5th Dragoon Guards. A deluge of rain had come on which continued all the afternoon. The fire fight went on as fiercely as ever, without either side gaining any advantage.

Sir George White now resolved that Wagon Hill must be cleared of Boers before nightfall. Headquarters and three companies of the 1st Devon Regiment, under Major C. W. Park, had been brought down from Tunnel Hill, north of the town, to the iron bridge over the Klip River. These, at 4 p.m., received orders to march down to Wagon Hill. On their arrival, Colonel Hamilton ordered Park to turn out the party of Boers ensconced in front of the Imperial Light Horse work, the task in which Mackworth, Bowen, and Tod, with their small detachments, had already lost their lives.

Park formed up his men on a small terrace on the reverse slope of the hill, where space was so confined that there was only room for them in quarter column. He then fixed bayonets and gave his directions to the company officers.

On the order to charge, the Devons swept over the top, forming line as they went. At that moment the storm reached its culmination in a terrific outburst of thunder and hail. In the 130 yards they had to cross, the Devons lost an Officer and about 40 men, but the Boers did not wait for the bayonet and were soon in full flight down the hillside. The Devons occupied the position the Boers had left and came under a heavy fire from the enemy's covering troops, but the attack on Wagon Hill and Cæsar's Camp was over. The Boers were now fleeing from every part of the position. The dongas in the valley were, from the deluge, impassable except here and there, and the enemy, crowding together at the crossing-places, lost heavily.

The British casualties for January 6 totalled 424 in killed and wounded. The Boer casualties are not known, but were probably, for once, greater than those of the British. The figures do not seem high for the numbers engaged—between three and four thousand on our side—to those accustomed to the hecatombs of the Great War, but it must be remembered that the circumstances and indeed the whole manner of fighting were entirely different. When one side is much more mobile than the other and has no intention of crossing bayonets—having, in fact, no bayonets to cross—the fighting must be of a different nature from what it is when both sides are equally anxious to come to close quarters. In South Africa the losses from artillery fire were almost negligible to troops under cover, and rifle fire can never do much more to troops under cover than make them keep their heads down. The fighting on Wagon Hill was at extremely close quarters, but so long as the combatants remained under cover the losses were slight. Whenever either side made a forward movement in the open, their losses were instantaneous and heavy and were thrown away unless the attack succeeded.

The importance of the action, however, was out of all proportion to the casualties or the numbers engaged. If the Boers had taken the Cæsar's Camp—Wagon Hill position (and there were one or two very critical moments), it is more than probable that Ladysmith would have fallen. Sir George White had put in his last reserve, and it is doubtful if, once taken, the position could ever have been recaptured. Then, even if an alternative position could have been held through Maiden Castle, every yard of the rest of the perimeter and the reserves would have been commanded from the captured position.

If Ladysmith had fallen, the moral effect not only in South Africa, but throughout the world, would have been incalculable. As it was, the 6th of January was the high-water mark of the Boers' offensive. No further effort was made by them to take Ladysmith by force. The invasion of Natal, which culminated in the siege of Ladysmith, had been their only real strategic offensive, and from that day the offensive passed finally to the British.

The losses of our Battalions at Wagon Hill were :—

First Battalion

Killed : 1 Officer (Queen's Royal West Surrey Regiment : attached) ; Other Ranks, 6.

Wounded : Lieutenant R. C. Maclachlan, R.B. : attached ; Other Ranks, 23, of whom 4 died of wounds.

Second Battalion

Killed : Major R. S. Bowen ; Lieutenant N. M. Tod, Scottish Rifles : attached ; 2nd Lieutenant Raikes : attached from 1st Battalion ; Other Ranks, 7.

Wounded : Other Ranks, 23.

The following Officers and Warrant Officers were mentioned by the O.C. 1st Battalion, for distinguished conduct, in his report on the defence of Wagon Hill :

Major D. Mackworth (The Queen's).
Major O. R. A. Julian, R.A.M.C.
Captain and Adjutant H. R. Blore.
Lieutenant R. C. Maclachlan (Rifle Brigade).
Bandmaster F. Tyler.

This was the third time in this campaign that Bandmaster Tyler had been mentioned for his conduct in the field. He had already been mentioned for gallantry in the wreck of the *Warren Hastings*.

The Boers were thoroughly disheartened by their defeat on January 6, in which many of their best men had fallen, and confined themselves for the rest of the siege to shell fire and sniping. The British continued to improve their defences and casualties from hostile fire were few, but the sick-list and death-rate continued to rise and the scale of rations fell. Occasionally, as at the crisis of the Spion Kop venture, their hopes of relief were raised, even to the extent of an increase in the rations, only to end in disappointment.

By the end of January there were 1,900 sick and wounded in hospital, of whom 842 were enteric cases and 472 dysentery. The death-rate was 8 per diem. Horse meat had long taken the place of beef, and on February 9 the biscuit ration was reduced by one-half. Even the men still at duty were getting so weak that they could hardly do the short marches required for relieving posts. On February 13 the garrison were cheered by a telegram from Lord Roberts telling them that he had entered the Free State and saying that he hoped his movements would soon result in a lessening of the pressure on Ladysmith.

Soon the gun fire to the south showed that Buller had begun another attempt at relief. The enemy were constantly on the move and on the 16th even showed signs of retreat, a body of about 2,000 of them being seen heading towards Cundycleugh Pass. The rate of bombardment increased daily—often a sign of impending departure in a force that has more ammunition than it can conveniently carry away. On the 18th the British troops on Monte Cristo were actually visible from points in the Ladysmith

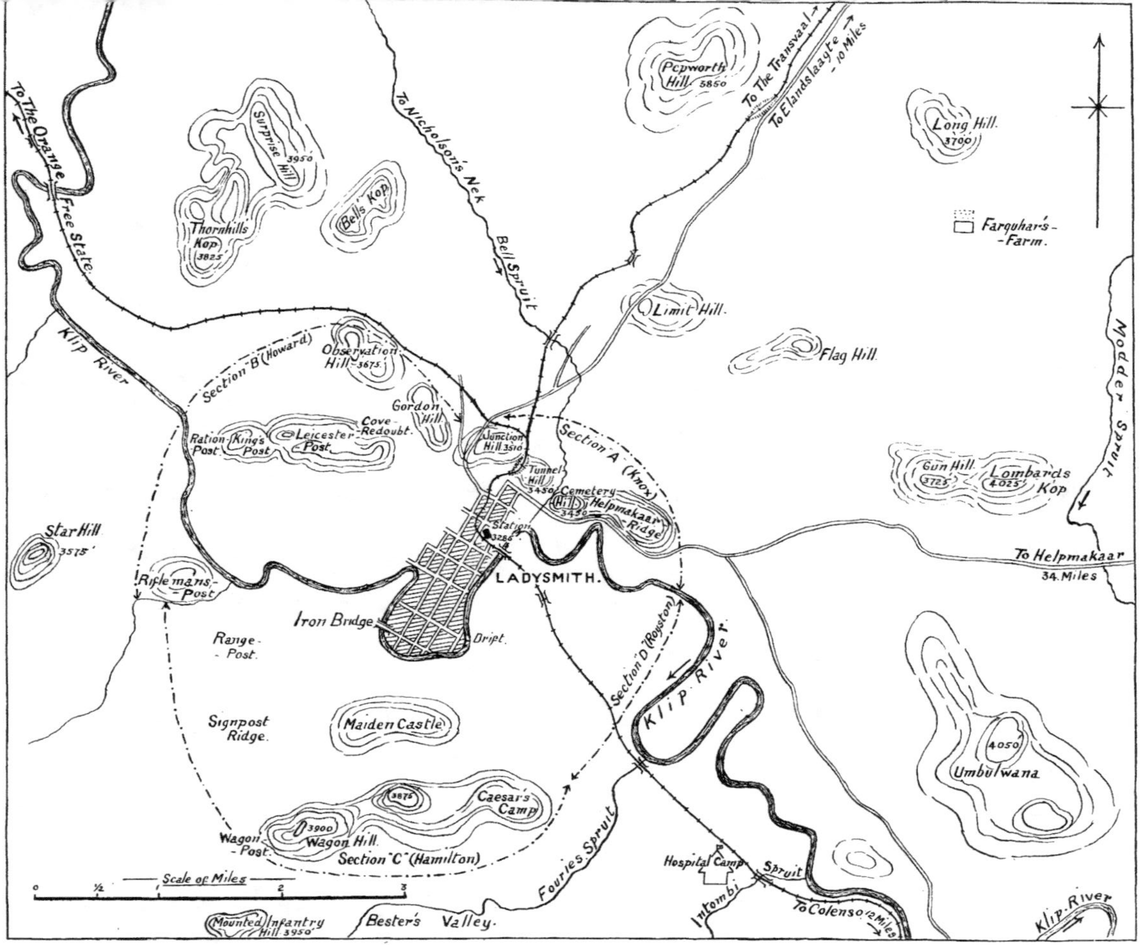

PLATE 16.

DEFENCE OF LADYSMITH.

enceinte. On the 19th Sir George White heliographed to Sir Redvers offering to co-operate when informed of the line of advance. An answer came on the 21st that Buller was coming through by Pieters, that he hoped to be in Ladysmith next day, and that Sir George could help most by marching to cut the Boers' line of retreat.

Next day came a message from Buller that he was meeting with more opposition than he expected. On the 23rd and the 24th the firing continued without further news. On the 25th it ceased altogether, and the garrison, not knowing that there was an armistice, began to ask themselves if this meant another failure. Yet another reduction of the ration scale did not look hopeful. On the 26th the firing began again, but it was cloudy and no news came through. All day on the 27th the sounds of battle were incessant and louder than ever, and at nightfall silence. Buller, not yet knowing how complete was his success, sent a message through by lamp that he was doing well, at the same time cheering the garrison with the news of Lord Roberts's success at Paardeberg. That night an alarm was started in the Boer lines by an attempt to destroy their entanglement, and at midnight a furious rifle fire broke out and ran right round their lines and lasted for half an hour. It might have been a *feu de joie* fired as a parting salute by the besiegers in honour of the defence. At dawn on the 28th clouds of dust could be seen going up from every track leading to the Free State or the Transvaal. The enemy were in full retreat and the siege was over. At 6 p.m. Dundonald with his small force of colonial mounted troops entered the town.

CHAPTER XV

NORTHERN NATAL AND EASTERN TRANSVAAL

THE Boers' retreat from before Ladysmith had been sudden and rapid but well conducted. That is, it had been anything but a stampede and, although Van Reenen's Pass was almost clear of them on March 2, and on the 5th British Cavalry reached Elandslaagte without encountering an enemy, they had got away all their guns but two, and the quantity of stores left behind was small for a besieging force which had left at such short notice.

For Buller's force, which now included the Ladysmith garrison, the relief was followed by a long period of inaction. The advantages to be gained by following up a beaten enemy are obvious; the objections to doing so in this case were so numerous and involved, as they were closely interwoven with the conduct of Lord Roberts's campaign in the Free State, that it would be beyond the scope of this work to discuss them here. Suffice it to say that Lord Roberts ordered the 5th Division (less divisional troops) and the 14th Hussars to leave for Durban *en route* for Cape Colony, and this move began on March 6 and 7. The Ladysmith garrison, man and beast, were unfit for service till they should recover their condition. This left only the 2nd Division and two mounted brigades at Buller's disposal.

While therefore the defeated Boers settled down to defend the Biggarsberg, Buller's force took up a position of observation from Job's Kop on the right—where Bethune commanded a small mounted force—through

Elandslaagte, where were the 2nd Division, right round to Tabanyama, with Dundonald's Brigade watching the passes of the Drakensberg, and proceeded to reorganise and refit.

The mounted troops now formed three brigades; two of British cavalry, under Burn-Murdoch and Brocklehurst, formed the 1st and 2nd, while Dundonald's Brigade became the 3rd.

General Clery returned and took over the 2nd Division, which was now composed of the 2nd and 4th Brigades. A 4th Division, commanded by General Lyttelton, was formed of the 7th and 8th Brigades, from the Ladysmith garrison. The 8th Brigade (Colonel and local Major-General Francis Howard) was made up of the 1st Liverpool Regiment, 1st Leicester Regiment, 1st and 2nd Battalions King's Royal Rifle Corps. The 5th Division, now commanded by Major-General Hildyard, Sir Charles Warren having taken up a command in Cape Colony, was composed of the 10th and 11th Brigades.

The 5th Division had been sent back before it embarked for Cape Colony, and a 10th Division, made up of the 5th and 6th Brigades, under Sir A. Hunter, had taken their place.

As Lord Roberts advanced into the Free State, the Boer force on the Biggarsberg was constantly being depleted to find reinforcements to oppose him. By the end of March about half of them had gone, leaving 6,000 to 7,000 men.

On April 10 the enemy brought forward some guns and shelled the 2nd Division camp at Elandslaagte and some of our piquets were fired on, presumably with the object of drawing Buller to attack the enemy in a position of their own selection. His reply was to withdraw the Division to a better defensive position. On the 16th the

2nd Division was relieved by the 5th and brought back to near Ladysmith. On April 21 the Boer forces in Natal were still further reduced, another 3,000 men for the Free State being withdrawn.

Lord Roberts was now about to begin his advance from Bloemfontein to Pretoria, and on May 2 he ordered Buller to begin operations for clearing Natal.

Buller's plan, which he had ready to put into operation as soon as he should receive the order, was to turn the south-east end of the Biggarsberg with the 2nd Division, while the 5th Division advanced along the railway. The 4th Division was to remain in reserve round Ladysmith.

The 2nd Division marched on May 7, and, moving by Modder Spruit Siding and Peter's Farm, reached the drift over the Sunday's River, on the Ladysmith—Helpmakaar road on the 10th, where it was joined by the 3rd Mounted Brigade and some extra artillery. On May 11 Buller joined and took command of the turning force which crossed and camped on the left bank of the Waschbank River, Hildyard at the same time extending his right to keep in touch.

On the 12th the force reached Vermaak's Kraal, and on the same day Bethune's mounted detachment halted four miles south of Pomeroy. On the 13th the enemy, whose numbers on this flank did not exceed 1,500 men, though with the help of some well-placed guns they put up a good rearguard action, were turned out of their position, covering Helpmakaar, by the mounted troops backed by the 2nd Brigade.

The enemy evacuated Helpmakaar during the night and Dundonald kept them well on the move next day, bivouacking at Myer's Farm while the Infantry had reached Beith. During the night a patrol entered Dundee and found it evacuated. The Boers had been clearing out of the whole Biggarsberg position all day, and by evening not a gun was left in the position. The 3rd King's Royal Rifle Corps, two squadrons of Cavalry, and one battery of Field Artillery reached Dundee at daybreak on the 15th, marching all night, and the head of the main Infantry column arrived at 1 p.m., having covered sixteen miles since 6 a.m. The force halted on the 16th, and on the 17th reached Dannhauser, some of the mounted troops reaching Newcastle the same day. On the 18th the column covered the twenty-four miles into Newcastle. On the 19th the 4th Brigade advanced in support of Dundonald, who was pressing on to reconnoitre Laing's Nek. It was soon evident that the Boers were holding this position in earnest. They were seen to be digging hard and even followed Dundonald up aggressively when he, having found out what he came to learn, was falling back on the Ingogo.

It was evident that forcing the frontier was going to be a serious operation, and Buller decided to close up his force before attempting it. Our 3rd Battalion camped this day on the ground occupied by the same Battalion in the Ingogo fight of 1881. Meanwhile the 5th Division had been following steadily up the railway-line. On the 18th they reached Hatting Spruit, where they halted till the 23rd. The 4th Division marched from Ladysmith the same day, leaving a garrison of a mixed brigade, and the two Divisions reached Newcastle on the 27th.

Towards the end of the month Buller was obliged to send two columns across the Buffalo River to deal with some Boer forces which were active there, had administered a severe check to Bethune near Vryheid, and were a threat to his communications. The appearance of those columns quickly had the desired effect, and the Boer force retired behind Utrecht.

The problem that now confronted Buller was how to turn the enemy out of the Laing's Nek position prior to invading the Transvaal : whether to attack the position direct or to turn it by the left or the right. The time Buller had spent in repairing the railway behind him had been so well employed by the Boers in strengthening their position on the Nek that our attack on it was likely to be an expensive operation. The country on the Utrecht side was very difficult, and everything pointed to a turning movement by the passes of the Drakensberg, especially as any movement to his left brought Buller nearer to Lord Roberts, who was just at that time crossing the frontier from the Free State into the Transvaal.

Before striking his blow, Buller tried to bluff C. Botha, the Boer General opposed to him, into a surrender, pointing out the inutility of further resistance now that the Transvaal was invaded. The result was a three-days' armistice, ending in a refusal by the Boer General, who had consulted higher authority, to negotiate further.[1] Buller replied on June 6 by sending the South African Light Horse to drive the Boer piquets off Van Wyk's Hill commanding the mouth of Botha's Pass, and then occupying it with the 10th Brigade and a battery of Artillery. The Boers made an attempt to recapture the hill, but were easily repulsed, and the night was spent in getting artillery into position.

On June 8 Hildyard, to whom the execution of this operation was allotted, attacked and captured Botha's Pass with his own Division, plus the 2nd Infantry, 2nd Cavalry, and 3rd Mounted Brigades.

The Boers, whose position did not actually include the Pass, but stopped about a mile to the north of it, did

[1] Our 3rd Battalion occupied themselves during the armistice in putting in order the cemetery at Mount Prospect, where was the grave of Sir George Colley with many others who fell in the short campaign of 1881.

not offer much resistance, and our casualties were only 2 killed and 13 wounded.

The Boers had not been strong enough to reinforce their right without denuding the Laing's Nek position, and Buller's superiority in numbers enabled him to divide his force with impunity. He had only to force his way north, threatening their communications, to ensure the evacuation of Laing's Nek by its garrison.

June 9 was spent in getting artillery and transport up the Pass. On the 10th the column moved on with Buller himself in command and bivouacked near the junction of the Klip River and Gansvlei Spruit. The South African Light Horse and a squadron of the 18th Hussars had a vigorous advanced-guard engagement in clearing the high ground beyond the spruit, and reported seeing a force of about 3,000 Boers halt and distribute themselves over the position of Alleman's Nek.

Next day Alleman's Nek was taken after a march of seven miles and a stout resistance by the Boers, some of whom did not evacuate their part of the position, the rest of which had been taken before nightfall, till after dark.

All through the day the Boers had been clearing out of Laing's Nek. Next morning it was found to be evacuated, and by nightfall of the 12th General Clery had occupied the abandoned position. At dawn on the 12th Buller's force pushed on towards Volksrust, but the garrison of Laing's Nek had started just in time and got clear away without the loss of a gun.

Buller bivouacked at Joubert's Farm, four miles from Volksrust, of which town he received the formal surrender next day.

Lord Roberts's wish was that Buller should, without delay, advance up the line to Standerton, and this would have been possible if C. Botha's force had kept together, whether they retired north or north-west; but the Boer leaders had already begun to realise that fighting pitched battles with the British main forces only led to defeat, and that their only hope of prolonging the war till the British were tired out or the long-expected foreign intervention occurred was a system of constant attacks on the British communications. After the evacuation of Laing's Nek they therefore proceeded to delay Buller's advance, not by directly opposing him as they had done hitherto, but by threatening his communications.

It was not long before indications of this policy began to show themselves. Pending the collection of supplies for a fresh start, the whole Army of Natal was concentrated about Volksrust and Charlestown, except the 4th Division at Ingogo. On the 13th two companies of Thorneycroft's with a Telegraph section Royal Engineers were sent back by the route of the late turning movement to pick up telephone cable. They were attacked by superior numbers and had to withdraw through Botha's Pass.

On the 15th a detachment under Major-General F. Howard, consisting of the Mounted Infantry of the 4th Division and six companies each of the 1st King's Royal Rifle Corps and 1st Liverpool Regiment, were sent to receive the submission of Wakkerstroom. They found themselves opposed by such large forces of the enemy that Buller recalled them and reinforced them by a field battery and six companies each of the 1st Leicestershire Regiment and 2nd King's Royal Rifle Corps. He then sent them out again, at the same time sending General Hildyard, who was to take command of the operation, by a more northerly route with the 3rd Mounted Brigade, the 11th Infantry Brigade, and several batteries of Artillery. This time there was no opposition and the town was surrendered at once; 193 burghers surrendered with their arms, and a large quantity of ammunition and supplies were captured. The detachment from the 4th Division returned to Ingogo on the 18th, while Hildyard moved to Zandspruit, which he reached on the 20th.

Though it was not long before Wakkerstroom was reoccupied by the enemy and C. Botha was reported to be concentrating a force at Vryheid, Buller now started his advance into the Transvaal, leaving Lyttelton's Division to protect his communications. On the 18th the first train came through the Laing's Nek tunnel, which had been partially blown in by the Boers on their retirement. On the 20th the 2nd and 5th Divisions were concentrated at Zandspruit. On the 21st the two Divisions, covered by the 3rd Mounted Brigade, reached Paarde Kop. A garrison was left at each halt, so the force gradually diminished as it advanced. Hildyard went to Volksrust on the 21st to take command of a section of the line of communication, the remains of his Division being absorbed in Clery's command.

On the 22nd Clery marched to Kromdrai and on the 23rd he entered Standerton, which had been occupied by his mounted troops the previous day without opposition. Though the railway bridge over the Vaal River had been completely destroyed, a good bag was made of 18 locomotives and 148 carriages.

Our 3rd Battalion took over the town from Gough's Mounted Infantry. On June 25 the railway line was reopened as far as the left bank of the Vaal.

Buller now proceeded to collect supplies at Standerton with a view to using it as an advanced base for a march northwards to join Lord Roberts in his advance along the line from Pretoria to Komati Poort. Meanwhile he took steps to close the gap between himself and the main army, a detachment of which occupied Heidelberg on the 27th.

On the 30th Sir F. Clery continued his advance along the railway-line with a column of all arms, made up of the 4th Infantry Brigade; Thorneycroft's Mounted Infantry; Strathcona's Horse, which had joined Buller's army at Zandspruit; a squadron 13th Hussars; a battery Royal Field Artillery; a howitzer battery and two 5-inch guns. He reached Vlaklaagte the same evening.

On July 1 he reached Val after some slight skirmishing.

Next day he reached Greylingstad. A strong body of the enemy was close in front of him, but they offered no opposition.

On July 4, leaving a garrison to look after Greylingstad, he pushed on and met General Hart, from Heidelberg, at the Zuikerbosch River. A detachment under Lieut.-Colonel Bewicke-Copley (half battalion 3rd K.R.R.C., 50 Strathcona's Horse, 60 Imperial Mounted Infantry) took over Zuikerbosch Bridge. On the 11th the Battalion returned to Greylingstad. On the 28th they marched to Heidelberg, which they garrisoned, spending the next few months in occupation of it and posts round it and taking no part in Buller's move northward.

Buller now had a line of communication of 500 miles to Durban, the greater part of which, from Ladysmith up, was constantly threatened from both sides by the scattered Boer forces, which had now adopted a settled policy of interference with the British communications. This threat was greatest from the side of the Free State and was very much lessened by Sir Archibald Hunter's successful operations, which ended on July 30 in the capitulation of General Prinsloo and the surrender of over 4,000 Boers.

On July 30 Buller got orders from Lord Roberts, whose advanced troops were near Belfast, to prepare a force of one Division and a Cavalry brigade for a march to Middelburg. The route was to be by Amersfoort, Ermelo, and

Carolina, at which place he was to get in touch with French's Cavalry by August 15. This entailed not only concentrating the required number of troops but collecting transport to carry fourteen days' supplies. By August 6 the force was concentrated at Meerzicht, very completely supplied with transport, most of which was mule drawn, the only ox-drawn wagons being those of the supply columns and supply park.

The force consisted of :—

2nd Cavalry Brigade (Major-General J. F. Brocklehurst).
5th Lancers.
18th Hussars (3 squadrons).
19th Hussars.
3rd Mounted Brigade (Major-General the Earl of Dundonald).
South African Light Horse.
Strathcona's Horse.
A. Battery Royal Horse Artillery (Chestnut Troop).
No. 2 Field Troop Royal Engineers.
The 4th Division (Lieut.-General the Hon. N. G. Lyttelton) as before, with a battalion of Mounted Infantry as Divisional Mounted Troops.
Three Field Batteries Royal Field Artillery.
61st (Howitzer Battery) Royal Field Artillery, with various units of Mountain and Garrison Artillery.

The 2nd and 5th Divisions were left guarding the line of communication.

On the morning of August 7 Buller's force advanced on Amersfoort. A considerable force of Boers had been located there on July 30, and patrols on August 6 found them still there. Buller, advancing with the 8th Brigade in the centre with Dundonald and Brocklehurst on the left and right respectively, drove the Boers—about 2,000 men with 5 guns—gradually back all day. In the evening our 1st Battalion, who had been doing most of the work—their casualties were 13 out of 19 in the whole force—

passed through Amersfoort and seized the heights beyond, the Boers disappearing in the direction of Ermelo. The transport, having been parked for a long time and not brought on close in rear of the fighting troops—a somewhat unnecessary precaution in view of our overwhelming strength—and afterwards held up at a drift, did not arrive till midday next day, and our troops spent an uncomfortable night in bitter cold. For this reason and on account of a dense fog the force remained halted on the 8th. On the 9th the force only advanced eight miles, though no opposition was offered.

On the 10th the force reached, and crossed, the Vaal River at Beginderlyn. The Boers, keeping out of reach, were marching parallel to Buller's force, and there was a slight Cavalry skirmish in the afternoon. On August 11 Dundonald occupied Ermelo, the rest of the force reaching Klipfontein. On the 12th the force closed up on Ermelo. On the 13th the column reached the source of the Vaal River at Klipstapel. On the 14th the Infantry reached Witbank and Kranspan and the Cavalry Twyfelaar, where they got in touch with French's Cavalry, which was covering Lord Roberts's advance from Pretoria to the east. Next day Buller's main body reached Twyfelaar. Here it halted pending the arrangement of plans for the next advance.

On August 21 Buller advanced to Van Wyk's Vlei to get nearer the enemy's left flank—his probable objective in the forthcoming operations—and also to give closer support to French's Cavalry, whose outposts were having rather a busy time, in constant contact with the enemy. An engagement with a party of Boers on his right flank cost Buller over 30 casualties, and next day he sent a detachment under Major-General F. W. Kitchener to clear them off, which was done with slight loss. The

11th Division (Major-General Pole-Carew) advanced to Wonderfontein on the 21st.

On the 23rd Buller reached Geluk, not without considerable fighting on his right flank, in which the 1st Liverpool Regiment lost 74 out of a total loss for the force of 105. Buller was now in close contact with the enemy's left flank, while the 11th Division were opposed to his centre about Belfast.

On the 25th Lord Roberts arrived at Belfast to take personal command of the operations.

The enemy's force under Louis Botha, which numbered about 7,000 men with 20 guns, several of which were of heavy calibre, was occupying a very strong position with their right in a very intricate hill country, while their left rested on a country so cut up by bogs and impassable spruits that, not only was it considered to be unsuitable for cavalry—it had originally been intended that French should make a turning movement round this flank—but Buller felt obliged to ask permission to move straight on Waaikraal and Dalmanutha rather than commit his force to such a country. Lord Roberts agreed to this, and decided that Buller should attack the Boer left flank, while Pole-Carew contained the enemy in front and French, supported by one Infantry Brigade, worked round his right.

On the 26th French's Cavalry Division left Geluk at 5 a.m., and passing through Belfast had by 2 p.m. cleared the enemy out of the ridges to the north which threatened the left of any advance by the 11th Division. That Division then spread out as far as Lakenvley to connect with the Cavalry. This entailed a flank march across the enemy's front. On the same day Buller pressed on to Waai Kraal, driving the enemy before him, but attacked all the time on his right and rear. The 8th Brigade and

3rd Mounted Brigade formed a right flank and rearguard and had most of the fighting.

The enemy's line now ran north and south from Swartkopjes on their right to beyond the railway. Here it turned at a right angle and ran due east towards Dalmanutha. The point of the salient was at Bergendal Farm.

Lord Roberts seems to have been content to force the Boers to quit their position by capturing the apex of the salient, probably deciding that as their flanks were unassailable any general attack in hopes of making a big capture would result in heavier losses than the prospects of obtaining it justified.

The fight on the 27th was therefore confined to an attack on Bergendal, which was carried out almost entirely by the 2nd Rifle Brigade, the 1st Inniskilling Fusiliers, and Buller's Artillery. The fight is equally famous for the gallantry of the small force of Johannesburg Police, who defended the position, and for the brilliance of the Infantry attack, especially that of the 2nd Rifle Brigade. The Police, after standing a crushing bombardment of three hours and losing half their numbers, were still equal to bringing a heavy rifle fire to bear on the attacking Infantry. They kept it up till the attackers were within charging distance, when a few of them took to their horses and got away, but out of 74 who held the position the greater part were killed, or wounded prisoners. The losses in the attack amounted to 120, of whom the Rifle Brigade lost 3 Officers and 10 Other Ranks killed, 5 Officers and 63 Other Ranks wounded. The Inniskillings, who were fortunate in having a less exposed line of advance, had 17 casualties.

Early in the day the Boers, seeing that the fall of Bergendal was inevitable, began withdrawing their right, and French, pushing on without opposition, occupied Swartkopjes, his right connecting with Pole-Carew at Lakenvley.

During the night the Boers fell back and occupied a new position about Helvetia, where they were located by Dundonald's Brigade. Buller halted at Machadodorp to prepare for a fresh attack, and French advanced to Elandsfontein with Pole-Carew in support at Middlepunt.

On the 29th the enemy, finding Lord Roberts's whole force converging on them, retired without fighting.

Bergendal was the last stand of the Boer main Army. The war was still to last for nearly another two years, but henceforth it took the form of guerilla warfare. A force of about 2,000 retired towards Lydenburg, another of the same strength towards Barberton, and a third of about 3,000 followed the railway-line, covering Nelspruit, to which Kruger and the Boer Government had retired.

On August 30 French and Pole-Carew occupied the hills above Waterval Onder, while Buller with the greater part of his force pushed on to a point overlooking Nooitgedacht, where a number of our men had been interned as prisoners of war since the occupation of Pretoria. The Boers had already released the prisoners, and 9 Officers and 1,697 men made their way into the British camp.

Lord Roberts now divided his force, sending Buller towards Lydenburg, Pole-Carew along the railway, and French to work round by Carolina on Barberton.

On September 1 Buller set out on his march into the Lydenburg district, a fearful country of precipitous mountain ranges and deep gorges. Leaving a small force of all arms behind him on the watershed between the Crocodile River and Elands Spruit, he reached Badfontein in the evening, his force being now reduced in Infantry to five and a half battalions. Continuing his march next morning, he very soon found his force held up by the enemy, who occupied a very strong position across his route, defended by three 6-inch guns and a 4·7-inch howitzer, besides lesser pieces. Deciding that the enemy's flanks were impregnable and that a frontal attack was beyond the powers of his small force, he suggested to the Commander-in-Chief that another column should be sent up the more westerly road from Belfast, to take the enemy in flank. Lord Roberts immediately complied by sending Major-General Ian Hamilton, who had joined him on August 31, up this road with Smith-Dorrien's Brigade, a few Mounted Infantry, and some guns.

As he was short of mounted troops, Buller sent him the 2nd Cavalry Brigade (Brocklehurst) with two guns Royal Horse Artillery to join him on the march.

Ian Hamilton marched on the 3rd as far as Swartkopjes. On the 4th he was opposed all day by a Boer rearguard, but, driving them in front of him, reached Palmfontein the same day, where he was in direct communication with Buller.

On the 5th Hamilton again advanced—this time without opposition—to Weinarshoek, sending on half a battalion to seize the pass of Zwagershoek, which commanded the mouth of the valley leading down to Lydenburg, being thus almost in rear of the position which Buller was facing. This move had its immediate effect on the Boers, who drew off a little to the east, covered by the fire of their heavy guns, which shelled Buller's bivouacs at a range of 10,000 yards. Next morning the enemy busied themselves in preparing a position in this direction, but were turned out of it by General Francis Howard with three battalions and a battery.

On the 6th the Boers fell right back, and Buller marched on over the abandoned position to Witklip, where he was joined by Ian Hamilton, who had sent on the 2nd Cavalry Brigade to Lydenburg, which was formally surrendered to Brocklehurst. The Boer force under the Commandant-General Louis Botha again broke up, part retiring north on Pilgrim's Rest, part withdrawing to Paardeplaats, a hill overlooking Lydenburg, blocking the road by which Buller intended to advance. Here Buller, who had reached Lydenburg on the 7th with the combined force, attacked on the 8th.

The position held by the Boers was a mountain 1,500 feet high, the front of which formed a semi-circle with its horns pointing to the front, on each of which was a 6-inch gun. The sides of the hill were steep and seamed by deep water-courses. Buller attacked with Ian Hamilton on his right and Lyttelton on his left, the outer flanks being covered by the mounted troops.

The attack was a complete success. Covered by the Artillery, the Infantry scrambled slowly up the almost precipitous mountain-sides with very little loss. It took them from 9 a.m. till 5 p.m., yet the two wings of the converging attack, which at the start covered a front of six miles, reached the summit at the same moment. The Boers then cleared off and would have lost heavily in their retirement, the route of which was confined to a narrow ridge a few yards wide with precipitous sides, if a thick mist had not come down suddenly and completely blinded the victorious British, just as they were pouring over the mountain top.

The total casualties on this day were 31 killed and wounded, of whom 1 man was killed and 21 wounded of the Volunteer Company of the Gordon Highlanders, who were caught in column of route by a 6-inch shrapnel shell at 11,000 yards' range, as they were leaving Lydenburg.

On September 9 Ian Hamilton started back with his force to rejoin the Commander-in-Chief; while Buller, leaving General Howard with two battalions of his Brigade, the 2nd Cavalry Brigade, and four guns to garrison Lydenburg, marched on against the next pass he had to cross, that over the Mauchberg.

The country was now getting rougher and rougher and the roads worse and worse. The Boers had evidently no intention, for the time, of doing more fighting than would enable them to get away their guns and transport, and the way they succeeded in doing this during the next few days was a pattern of rearguard fighting. Buller's advanced guard very soon found themselves held up by the Boer rearguard, which had taken up a position covering the pass. A deep dip separated the two forces. The 1st King's Royal Rifle Corps and 2nd Gordon Highlanders extended along the edge of this valley, and then, covered by the fire of A Battery, Royal Horse Artillery, they swept down into the valley and up the opposite slopes till they cleared the pass, with a loss of only some half-dozen wounded.

The enemy's transport train was in full view below them, and Dundonald immediately started in pursuit, but, what with the difficulties of the country and the excellence of the enemy's rearguard dispositions, he was unable to make any progress, and returned to join the rest of the force in bivouac on the pass.

On the 10th the pursuit was continued and the Boer train was frequently under long-range shell fire. The King's Royal Rifle Corps and Gordons were again in the lead, supporting Strathcona's Horse and a field battery. Though one big gun came very near capture, losing some of its detachment by rifle fire, and a number of wagons were abandoned, the rearguard were as skilful and determined as ever, and in the end the Boers got clear without the loss of a gun.

On the 11th Buller entered Spitz Kop without opposition. This was a point of great strategic importance, as it blocked the only road by which the Boer forces, being driven back on the frontier along the Delagoa Bay Railway by Pole-Carew, could break away to the north with artillery or wagons.

Buller halted at Spitz Kop till the 21st, when he moved one march to the north to the drifts on the Sabi River.

After opposing Buller's march on Lydenburg, Louis Botha had rejoined the main Army—or rather the chief portion of it—on the railway where it was occupying a position about Godwaan Station; but it soon became clear that if he continued to resist along the line of the railway, he would inevitably be surrounded. French was moving on Barberton, and Hutton, moving between French and the railway, was a more imminent danger.

On September 11 President Kruger took the train for Laurenço Marques on his way to Europe. There was nothing left to be done but a final dispersion north and south while there was yet time and as much destruction of guns, transport, railway stock, and stores as could be accomplished before departure. Leaving behind the dismounted burghers, of whom there were many, Botha went north with 2,500 men, while Smuts went south with 1,800.

The probable line of retreat for the Boers who went north from the railway ran through, or near, Pilgrim's Rest.

On September 26 Buller marched north to cut this line, taking with him the 3rd Mounted Brigade, the 1st Devonshire Regiment, 1st King's Royal Rifle Corps, 2nd Gordon Highlanders, and some Artillery.

On reaching Burger's Pass, crossing the watershed between the Sabi and Blyde Rivers, he found it occupied. The pass was cleared by the Devons, covered by artillery fire, with only five men wounded; but it had taken all day, and the enemy was a rearguard to Botha's column, which had crossed the pass the day before.

On the 27th Buller halted a few miles short of Pilgrim's Rest, which was entered by the Mounted Brigade. A very difficult pass to the west of Pilgrim's Rest gave great trouble to the transport, and it was not till October 1 that Kruger's Post was reached. This place was already occupied by Brocklehurst's Cavalry from Lydenburg. The bivouac was shelled by two heavy guns, which caused 16 casualties. A party went out in the night to attempt to destroy the guns. It was led by Major D. Henderson (Argyll and Sutherland Highlanders), Buller's Intelligence Officer, who had brought off a similar raid successfully from Ladysmith, but the birds had flown. On October 2 the force reached Lydenburg.

Here Sir Redvers received orders to hand over his command to General Lyttelton and return to England. A few days later he bade farewell to what was left of the troops he had commanded through a year of hard campaigning. Although it can hardly be denied that his own doubts as to his ability for the great position that had been thrust upon him—and which he would have shown himself well equal to if his chance had come to him ten years sooner—had been fully justified, never, through the worst of his failures, had he lost for one moment the confidence and affection of his troops. Never did the most successful of Generals receive a more touching and heartfelt ovation than did he on his departure for home.

From the date of the final break-up of the main Boer

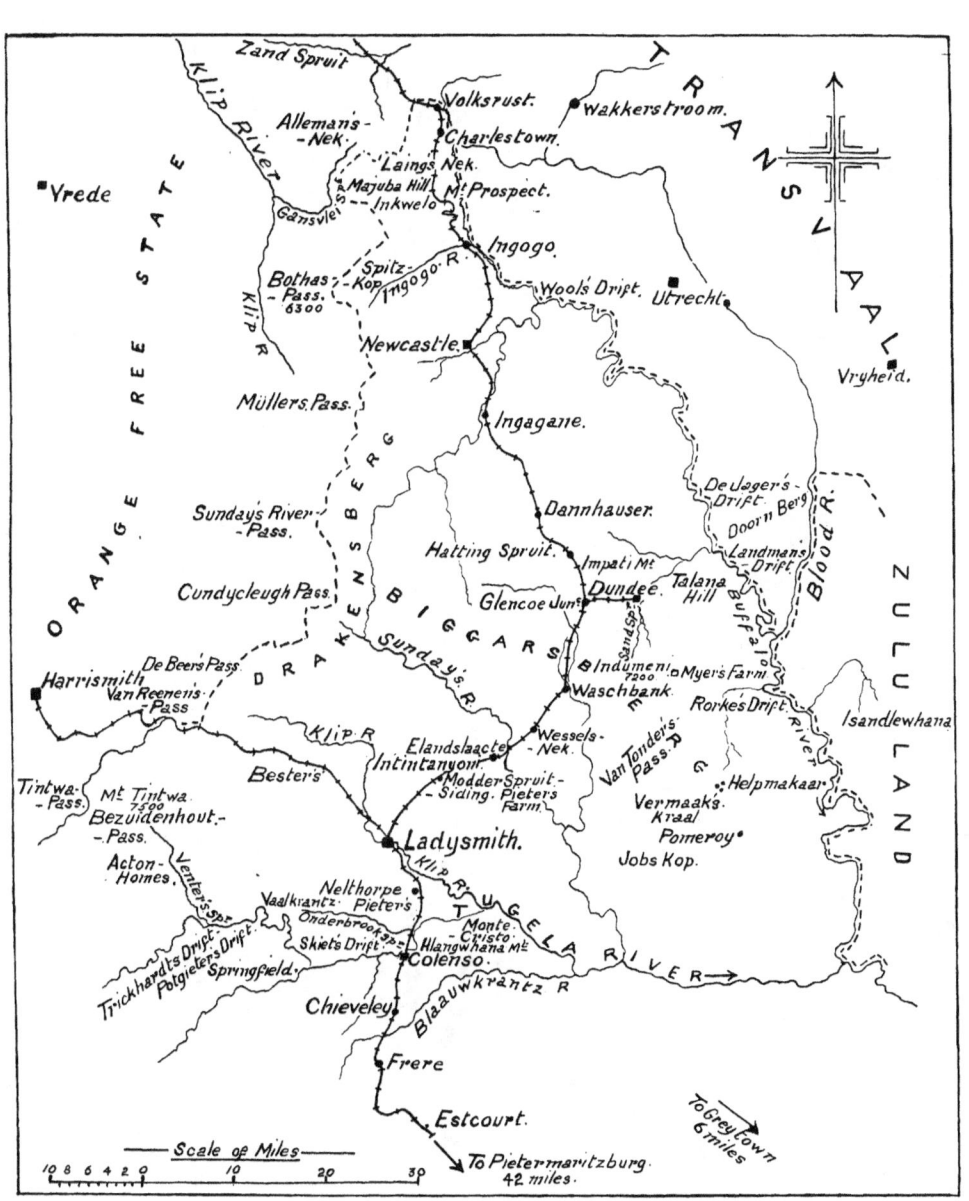

PLATE 17.
NORTHERN NATAL.

PLATE 18.

EASTERN TRANSVAAL.

force, regular operations may be said to have ceased, and the war, though it dragged on for nearly two years, consisted, for the British, of safeguarding communications and rounding up the enemy.

The Infantry were thenceforth chiefly employed in the former of these two services, the latter being mainly carried out by mounted troops.

CHAPTER XVI

THE DRIVE AND BLOCKHOUSE PERIOD

OUR 2nd Battalion left South Africa in July 1900 and took no further part in the war. Lieut.-Colonel H. Gore-Browne, who had succeeded to the command of the 1st Battalion in the place of Lieut.-Colonel Gunning, killed at Talana Hill, and had commanded it during the siege of Ladysmith, exchanged with Lieut.-Colonel Bewicke-Copley, promoted to the command of the 2nd Battalion on the retirement of Colonel Grimwood after the Relief of Ladysmith. Bewicke-Copley had never actually taken over command of the 2nd Battalion, but remained in command of the 3rd Battalion, which he had taken over on the death of Lieut.-Colonel Buchanan Riddell, until December 1901, except during such periods as he was in command of various columns. Lieut.-Colonel W. Pitcairn-Campbell succeeded to the command of the 3rd Battalion, on paper, on the death of Lieut.-Colonel Buchanan Riddell. He, however, did not actually take over command of the 3rd Battalion till after their return home at the conclusion of the war, but remained in command of the 1st Battalion, which he had taken over in Gore-Browne's place, till the end of the war. He, however, frequently left the Battalion to take command of columns during the sweeping operations, in which he made a name for himself as one of our most successful Column Commanders.

The following is an extract from Lord Roberts's

COLONEL H. DONALD BROWNE.

dispatch, published in the *London Gazette* of February 15, 1901 :—

'Lieut.-Colonel W. P. Campbell is one of the best regimental commanders that have served under my command, and I very strongly recommend him for your most favourable consideration as an officer whose advancement would be in the interests of the service.'

In the *Gazette* of April 19, 1901, Lieut.-Colonel Campbell was appointed Aide-de-Camp to the King, with the brevet rank of Colonel. In the same *Gazette*, Bandmaster F. Tyler, 1st Battalion, who had been three times mentioned by his Commanding Officer for his conduct in action, was awarded the D.C.M.

On Sir Redvers Buller's departure, his force was broken up, and the 1st Battalion rejoined their own Brigade, the 8th, from which they had been detached since September 8.

This Brigade marched on October 8, with a force under Lieut.-General the Hon. N. G. Lyttelton, by Dalstroom to Middelburg, which they reached on the 16th. The force met with opposition all the way, notably south of Dalstroom, where the Battalion fought a rearguard action.

The Battalion remained at Middelburg, taking part from time to time in the operations of various mobile columns for a few days, till May 1901.

On May 14 Headquarters and four companies under Lieut.-Colonel W. S. Kays started to join Lieut.-General Sir Bindon Blood in a big sweeping operation which he was about to undertake through the Eastern Transvaal.

On the same date four companies under Captain E. Northey[1] railed to Machadodorp, to join a column under Lieut.-Colonel W. Douglas.

[1] Major-General Sir Edward Northey, G.C.M.G., C.B.

During the course of the operations this detachment joined the column commanded by Colonel W. P. Campbell, A.D.C.

On June 23 the detached wing rejoined Headquarters.

On July 9 Lieut.-Colonel W. S. Kays took command of a column and Captain E. Northey assumed command of the Battalion.

At the close of these operations, which entailed a great deal of marching and very little fighting, Sir Bindon Blood, having swept the whole Eastern Transvaal clear of stock and inhabitants, arrived with his force at Balmoral. His column having been broken up, Lieut.-Colonel Kays resumed command of the Battalion.

On the 16th the Battalion entrained for De Aar, Cape Colony, arriving on the morning of the 19th. On the afternoon of the same day they entrained for various posts along the De Aar—Orange River Railway, and began to erect blockhouses, one to a mile, along the railway.

Lieut.-Colonel R. C. A. B. Bewicke-Copley, C.B., took over command of the Battalion on December 25.

The Battalion remained in the blockhouse line till peace was signed.

3RD BATTALION
JUNE 1900 TO END OF WAR

On June 30 the 3rd Battalion left Standerton, arriving at Greylingstad on July 2.

On the 5th a force under Lieut.-Colonel Bewicke-Copley, consisting of half of the 3rd Battalion, 50 of Strathcona's Horse, and 50 of Thorneycroft's, took over Zuikerbosch Bridge, returning to Greylingstad on the 11th.

On July 12 they started on a mobile column under General Clery, which trekked through the country north of the Natal Railway, moving every day until the 24th.

On the 28th they reached Heidelberg.

From July 29 to October 11 they were occupied in making posts on the railway from Zuikerbosch to Roodekop.

On October 12 they marched to join General Clery at Vlakfontein. Under him they toured the country till November 2, when Bewicke-Copley took over command of the Column. They were on the move all November, during which they had a few encounters with the enemy, especially on the 24th and 25th, in an endeavour to surround Stephanas Buys.

On November 28 the Battalion returned to Heidelberg. During December they were engaged in minor expeditions from Heidelberg and guarding the railway-line.

Through the first six months of 1901 the Battalion was engaged in building and occupying blockhouses along the Natal Railway.

In August they joined a mobile column commanded by Lieut.-Colonel Bewicke-Copley, which was employed in establishing a line of South African Constabulary posts on a line running north and south from the Delagoa Bay Railway to the Natal Railway. The Battalion was commanded, first by Major F. B. M. Henniker and afterwards by Major E. W. Thistlethwayte.

On December 1 the Battalion moved by rail to Machadodorp, where it occupied a line of blockhouses along the railway from Waterval Boven to Dalmanutha, and along the Lydenburg Road to Badfontein, one company being continually occupied escorting columns of supplies.

The Battalion was thus employed till peace was signed.

On December 21, 1901, Lieut.-Colonel Bewicke-Copley left to take over command of the 1st Battalion. Lieut.-Colonel W. S. Kays returned from the Mounted Infantry on July 4, 1902, and took over command of the Battalion.

The 4th Battalion spent the remaining months of the war in the blockhouse line in the neighbourhood of Harrismith. Though they were not fortunate enough to see any fighting, they had plenty of hard work, little sleep, and, in places, were continually sniped at.

There were many attempts to get through their line, but, after the wire was once up, very few were successful. The Battalion suffered no casualties and only one dead Boer was picked up.

CHAPTER XVII

First Battalion

End of South African War to Outbreak of Great War

In June 1902 the 1st Battalion vacated the blockhouse line and concentrated at De Aar, with the exception of one detachment which rejoined the following month.

In September they railed to Cape Town and embarked for Malta in the s.s. *Sardinia* on the 22nd.

By discharge and transfer to the Reserve the Battalion, which had been over 1,000 strong, was reduced to little over 600 of all ranks on embarkation.

On arrival at Malta they were welcomed by that great Rifleman Lord Grenfell, who was Governor of the island.

On March 25, 1904, Colonel R. C. A. Bewicke-Copley, C.B., completed his term in command, and was succeeded by Lieut.-Colonel C. J. Markham.

On February 27, 1905, the Battalion embarked on the hired transport *Dilwara* for the following destinations :—

Alexandria, Headquarters and D, F, G, and H Companies: 11 Officers ; 471 Other Ranks.
Crete, A, B, and C Companies (Captain H. C. Johnson, D.S.O.): 5 Officers ; 400 Other Ranks.
Cyprus, E Company (Captain M. Pratt, D.S.O.) : 3 Officers ; 100 Other Ranks.

On arrival at Alexandria, Headquarters trained to Cairo, where they occupied Abbassia Barracks.

The reason for British troops being in Crete at this time

was that in 1897 the Cretans, whose island then formed a part of the Turkish Empire, had started one of their periodical rebellions against Turkey. Though the island had been Turkish for some 250 years, the Christian inhabitants had never been really subdued and had revolted about once in a generation, which revolt was always put down in the usual Turkish manner. The revolt of 1897 brought on a war between Turkey and Greece, which ended in the rapid and complete success of the Turks. Four of the six Great Powers, Great Britain, France, Russia, and Italy—Germany and Austria standing out—calling themselves the Concert of Europe, decided that this constant succession of revolts followed by massacres must cease. They therefore occupied the island, turned the Turks out, and started a sort of self-government under a High Commissioner appointed by the Powers—the first one being Prince George of Greece—leaving garrisons of troops of all four Powers to see fair play between Muhammadans and Christians. The former, who called themselves Turks, but were for the most part of Cretan blood, formed only about one-ninth of the population and chiefly inhabited the coastal towns, the interior being almost entirely Christian.

The island was divided up into four spheres of occupation: the French held the extreme east of the island; the British next with Candia, the largest town in the island, as their station; next to them were the Russians; and the Italians were in the extreme west. The centre of Government, where also resided the diplomatic representatives of the Powers, was Canea, in the Italian sphere. Each Power had a small detachment at Canea. The arrangement worked well, though there was an extreme pro-Greek party who were not content to await events and from time to time anticipated their inevitable ultimate cession to Greece by small outbreaks which were easily suppressed, but the Powers could not be expected to keep troops in the island for ever, and, after the Turkish Revolution of 1908, the island was definitely handed over to Greece, and the allied troops left for good early in 1909.

On April 1, 1905, at the request of the British Consul-General, a party of 60 N.C.O.s and Riflemen, under Captain G. H. Martin, went from Candia to Canea, on H.M.S. *Aboukir*, to take part in a demonstration with international troops against the insurgents.

The unrest increased in May, and, although nothing very serious occurred, several minor conflicts between the gendarmerie and the insurgents were reported, also disturbances between Christians and Moslems. By desire of the Consul-General two detachments were sent into the interior of the island to assist in preserving order :—

Captain H. C. Johnson, D.S.O., with 35 N.C.O.s and Riflemen to Aios Giorgios.
2nd Lieutenant A. P. Evans with 29 N.C.O.s and Riflemen to Aios Miron.

In June Lieutenant C. D. Eyre with 64 N.C.O.s and Riflemen relieved a detachment of the Royal Sussex Regiment at Kudetse.

On July 12 parties under Captain H. C. Johnson, D.S.O., and Lieutenant C. D. Eyre were employed in surrounding the villages of Kudetse and Skylos to arrest insurgents and search for arms and ammunition. There was a certain amount of resistance and some shooting, by which 1 Rifleman was seriously wounded and 1 slightly. They were the only casualties in the Battalion during all these very minor operations.

On March 1, 1906, the detachments from Crete and Cyprus rejoined Headquarters in Egypt.

On the 29th the Battalion furnished a Guard of Honour

at the Cairo railway-station and was employed in lining the streets on the arrival of T.R.H. the Prince and Princess of Wales.

Next day H.R.H. the Prince of Wales, Colonel-in-Chief, inspected the Battalion in Review Order.

In October, the Battalion having been ordered to Khartum, F and H Companies, under Major C. L. E. Robertson-Eustace, D.S.O., moved to Ras el Tin Barracks, Alexandria. These companies were made up of all those who would become time-expired during the course of the next year or who were too young to serve in the Sudan.

The Battalion moved to Khartum in three parties, the first leaving on October 13, the last reaching Khartum on November 3.

In April 1907 the Battalion was re-armed with the new pattern short rifle.

The Battalion returned to Cairo after a year in the Sudan and occupied the Kasr el Nil Barracks.

On January 21, 1908, Major R. S. Oxley was promoted Lieut.-Colonel *vice* Brevet-Colonel C. R. R. McGrigor, C.B., to date from December 18, 1907, and posted to the 3rd Battalion, which, however, he did not join, exchanging with Lieut.-Colonel Chaplin on March 18. He took over command on April 8.

On October 5, 1908, Major C. L. E. Robertson-Eustace, D.S.O., died suddenly in the Officers' Mess. Major Eustace, who was the son of a Rifleman and born at Winchester, had seen a great deal of active service since he joined the Regiment in 1889. His campaigns were Manipur, 1891, and the Lushai Expedition, 1891-2, in the 4th Battalion Mounted Infantry; in 1896 he served with the Mounted Infantry in Mashonaland and was severely wounded; he served in the South African War from October 1899 to January 1902, and particularly distinguished himself in command of a Mounted Infantry Battalion (25th) made up entirely from our Regiment, receiving the D.S.O.

On January 29, 1909, the Battalion left Cairo for Alexandria and embarked on the hired transport *Braemar Castle* for England, disembarking at Southampton on February 12 and arriving at Gosport the same day.

A telegram of welcome was received, on arrival, from H.R.H. the Prince of Wales, Colonel-in-Chief.

The Battalion remained at Gosport, except for moves in 1909 to Wool, Dorset, and Parkhouse Camp, Salisbury Plain, for training, till September 29, 1911, when it went to Aldershot, where it was stationed till the outbreak of the Great War.

On December 18, 1911, Colonel Oxley completed his term in command, and was succeeded by Lieut.-Colonel E. Northey.

Second Battalion

July 1900 to Outbreak of Great War

On July 28, 1900, the Battalion left Ingogo Station for Durban to embark for Ceylon as escort to Boer prisoners of war.

The strength of the Battalion embarking on the hired transport *Orient* was : Officers, 14 ; Other Ranks, 810.

The names of the Officers embarking were :—

Captain J. E. Rhodes.
,, G. C. Shakerley.
,, W. Barnett.
Lieutenant E. F. Ward.
,, L. W. de Saumarez.
,, G. Makins.
,, Hon. A. F. W. Harris.
,, A. R. Leith.
,, F. G. Willan.

2nd Lieutenant G. Culme Seymour.
,, T. H. Harker.
,, G. C. Kelly.
,, H. A. Vernon.
Captain and Adjutant H. R. Green.
Captain and Quartermaster J. W. Dwane.

E Company—three Officers (Captain E. Pearce-Serocold, Lieutenant B. F. Widdrington, 2nd Lieutenant R. N. Abadie) with 100 Other Ranks—had embarked for Ceylon on the 23rd on the s.s. *Mohawk*. The Battalion reached Colombo on August 9, E Company having arrived the previous day.

The Battalion camped at Diyathlawa in charge of Boer prisoners. Lieut.-Colonel H. Gore-Browne took over command of the Battalion on September 11. During the stay of the Battalion in Ceylon the members of the Hill Club, Newara Eliya, presented them with a sum of 1,000 rupees to be funded for the purpose of giving an annual prize (to be known as the Ceylon Trophy) to the best shot in the Regiment, also a shield, as an Inter-Company Challenge Trophy.

The Battalion embarked on the s.s. *Clive* on December 31, 1900, for Bombay. Strength: Officers, 16; Other Ranks, 889.

They disembarked on January 7, 1901, and railed to Rawal Pindi.

The following is a letter received from Colonel J. Hay, late Commander 4th Gurkha Rifles, enclosing £30 from the Officers of the Gurkha Rifles for the widows and orphans of men of the King's Royal Rifle Corps and Rifle Brigade who died in South Africa :—

'*To the Officer Commanding, Rifle Depot, Gosport.*
'*March* 16, 1900.
' DEAR SIR,
I have been requested by the Officers of the Gurkha Rifles to forward to the fund for widows and orphans of the

men of the King's Royal Rifles and Rifle Brigade in South Africa a subscription they have made for that purpose. I have much pleasure in forwarding a cheque for £30 for the fund, and hope that you will not mind the trouble of sending it on to the proper quarters, as I am not aware who is receiving subscriptions.

'The subscription is sent as a token of sympathy and admiration for the gallant Rifles, with whom the Gurkhas have been so often associated, both in peace and war.

'I remain, dear Sir,

'Yours truly,

'J. HAY, *Colonel,*

'*Late Commanding* 1*st Battalion* 4*th Gurkha Rifles.*'

The following letter was received from the Headquarters of the 2nd Gurkhas, the old Delhi comrades of our 1st Battalion :—

'*To the Officer Commanding, Depot,* 60*th Rifles.*

'DEHRA DUN,
'*March* 8, 1900.

'SIR,

'All ranks of both Battalions of the 2nd P.W.O. Gurkhas have watched events in South Africa with the keenest interest, especially so the doings of their old comrades the 60th Rifles and the Gordon Highlanders.

'Their admiration of the deeds of their friends has been expressed, first by a desire to be sent out to aid them, and secondly, in a voluntary and spontaneous donation of a day's pay to the fund for the aid of families of killed, etc., in the two Regiments.

'The amount subscribed has therefore been divided into two equal shares, and it is with hearty greetings and congratulations on the added fame of their old comrades that I send the enclosed cheque for £35 2*s*. 7*d*. from all ranks of the 2nd P.W.O. Gurkhas.

'Yours very truly,

'L. HILL, *Lieut.-Colonel,*

'*Commanding* 2*nd Battalion.*'

The Battalion moved to Kuldana, Murree Hills, in April 1901. They came down again to West Ridge, Rawal Pindi, at the end of October. At the Annual Inspection on February 17, 1902, the strength of the Battalion was: Officers, 29; Other Ranks, 1,127.

On March 27 three Companies under Major H. A. Kinloch left Rawal Pindi for Kakul near Abbotabad to guard Boer prisoners. They did not arrive there till April 9, having been weather-bound for four days at Abbotabad.

On April 9 the Battalion moved from West Ridge into Church Lines for the hot weather.

The detachment from Kakul rejoined Headquarters in September.

On November 17 the Battalion trained to Umballa, where they took part in a camp of Exercise until the 29th, when they left to take part in the Delhi Manœuvres. They were brigaded with the 3rd Battalion Rifle Brigade, 1st Battalion 2nd Gurkha Rifles, and the 1st Battalion 39th Gharwal Rifles. At Delhi they took part in manœuvres till December 21. From the 22nd to the 30th they were engaged in rehearsing for the Delhi Coronation Durbar. On the 28th the Battalion assisted in lining the streets for the State entry of the Viceroy (Lord Curzon).

On January 1, 1903, the Battalion took part in the Durbar ceremonial. Thirty-three battalions were drawn up in line of quarter-columns facing the opening to the amphitheatre, and at 12 noon the leading companies of battalions fired a *feu de joie* in honour of the proclamation of King Edward VII as Emperor of India.

The Battalion left on their return journey to Rawal Pindi on January 19.

By War Office letter 61002, Inf. 812, A.G. 7, Dress, December 1, 1902, the old braided mess dress was abolished, being succeeded by the present abomination.

In the end of April 1903 the Battalion marched to Kuldana, Murree Hills, returning to Rawal Pindi (West Ridge) in October.

On October 20, 1903, Lieut.-Colonel H. Gore-Browne completed his time in command and was succeeded by Lieut.-Colonel W. S. Kays.

On leaving the Battalion Colonel Gore-Browne presented it with the ship's bell of the *Warren Hastings* on two conditions :—

(1) That it should always strike ship's time.

(2) That if no longer required, it should be returned to him.

From December 1 to the 16th the Battalion took part in the Rawal Pindi District Manœuvres.

In January 1904 the old pattern of helmet was replaced by the Wolseley, or Egyptian pattern, a much more serviceable form of head-dress. It was impossible to see to shoot, lying down, with the old helmet, without turning it back to front.

Lieut.-Colonel Kays joined and took over command on February 17, 1904.

In April the Battalion moved to Gharial, Murree Hills, for the hot weather.

During September 1904 the Battalion won the Murree Hockey Tournament from thirteen other teams.

The Battalion returned to West Ridge, Rawal Pindi, from Gharial on October 20 and 21.

On December 5 the Battalion left Rawal Pindi for Bareilly, arriving there on the 7th and going under canvas.

In February 1905 the Battalion won the Bengal-Punjab Football Tournament, sixteen teams being entered.

The same month the Battalion won the All-India Infantry Polo Tournament at Meerut, five teams being entered. The team was made up of Captain G. K. Priaulx,

Lieutenants F. O. Grenfell, E. B. Denison, and T. H. Harker.

On March 20 and 22 the Battalion left Bareilly for Rhaniket, arriving on the 25th and the 27th.

From October 18 to 25 the Battalion took part in hill manœuvres near Almorah, returning to Bareilly in November.

On November 20 the Battalion left Bareilly by train for Rawal Pindi to take part in manœuvres and a review on the occasion of the visit to India of T.R.H. the Prince and Princess of Wales.

The Battalion formed part of the 12th Infantry Brigade, 4th Division. The other Battalions of the Brigade were the 1st Royal Irish Rifles and 1st and 2nd Battalions 2nd Gurkhas.

Manœuvres took place on December 5 to 7, and on December 8 a Royal Review was held on Khanna Plain.

The Battalion left Rawal Pindi on its return journey on the 11th, reaching Bareilly on the 13th, and moved up to Rhaniket in March 1906.

The Battalion sent a party of 1 Officer, 1 Warrant Officer, and 1 Rifleman to be present at the unveiling of the statue of John Nicholson at Delhi on April 6.

This year the Battalion Signallers, who had been sixth the year before, were second in order of merit in the Army in India.

The Battalion left Rhaniket for Bareilly on November 1 and 2.

On the night of January 5, 1907, the Battalion left Bareilly by train, arriving next morning at Agra to take part in the concentration of troops held there in honour of the Amir of Afghanistan (Habibullah).

The Battalion, with the 2nd Battalion Rifle Brigade,

1st Scottish Rifles, and 1st Royal Irish Rifles, formed the 19th Infantry Brigade, 7th (Rifle) Division.

On January 8 the Battalion lined the route from Agra Fort Station on the arrival of the Viceroy (Lord Minto).

Next day they lined the route on the arrival of the Amir.

On the evening of the 10th the Band of the Battalion was detailed to play at the Amir's camp. On His Majesty expressing his dissatisfaction with the rendering of the Afghan National Anthem, the Bandmaster (Mr. W. J. Dunn) suggested to His Majesty that he might like to conduct them himself. This he accordingly did and expressed his entire satisfaction with their performance. The upshot of this encounter was that Mr. Dunn was invited by the Amir to score his National Anthem, which hitherto had been handed down by ear. This he did, with satisfactory results to the Band Fund of the Battalion.

On January 12 the Battalion took part in the grand review held in honour of the Amir.

On January 18 the Battalion left by train for Jubbulpore, where it arrived on the night of the 19th–20th. A detachment of two companies went to Saugor.

From February 8 to 24 the left half Battalion took part in the Jubbulpore Brigade manœuvres, the two companies at Saugor forming part of the opposing force.

During the hot weather a party of forty scouts from the Battalion went to Almorah for training with the 3rd Gurkhas.

The short M. L. E. Rifle, Mark 1, was taken into use during August and September. Bandolier equipment was issued at the same time. Rifle regiments were, however, permitted to retain black waist-belts, frogs and scabbards, and one pouch, for ceremonial and walking-out purposes. For Field Service Marching Order, shorts and half hose were instituted on October 1, 1907.

On October 15 Colonel W. S. Kays handed over command to Brevet-Major M. Crum, on completion of his tenure of command.

Lieut.-Colonel Sir F. B. M. Henniker was posted to the Battalion on promotion and took over command at Jubbulpore on January 16, 1908. Lieut.-Colonel Sir F. B. M. Henniker, having been invalided home, died on board the s.s. *Arabia*, off Lisbon, on August 23.

On July 31, 1908, Quartermaster and Hon. Major J. Dwane retired on retired pay.

John Dwane was one of the best known and most popular of the Riflemen of the last generation. He was born a Rifleman, being the son of a Sergeant-Major of the 1st Battalion. He was himself Sergeant-Major and then Quartermaster of that Battalion, and transferred to the 2nd in 1899. His brother, Charles Dwane, was also Sergeant-Major of the 1st Battalion, and his sister married Tim Riley, Quartermaster of the 1st Battalion and the Rifle Depot. John Dwane never married and lived in the Mess, and was always the most popular member of it. A first-rate Sergeant-Major and Quartermaster, he was always at his best in a crisis. When the Depot Barracks at Winchester were burned down in 1894, Dwane was on leave from India, staying with his brother-in-law, Riley, the Quartermaster of the Depot, who broke a tendon in his leg on the night of the fire. John Dwane took over his work and saw the Depot through a very difficult time. After seeing the Depot settled temporarily in the Portsdown Forts, Portsmouth, Dwane left to return to India. At his departure the Quarter Guard, on their own initiative, turned out and gave him a " General Salute."

Inspections were held on December 11, 1908. Headquarters and six companies took part in the annual test, December 7 to 9, by Brigadier-General A. Wallace, C.B.

Lieut.-Colonel S. W. Hare assumed command of the Battalion on December 16.

On February 2, 1909, the Battalion moved into camp at Gawari Ghat to take part in Brigade manœuvres, returning to Jubbulpore on February 6.

The Battalion embarked at Bombay on January 10, 1910, in the hired transport *Plassey*, and disembarked at Southampton on February 1, moving thence by rail to Shorncliffe, where they occupied Risborough Lines.

Here they came under the command of an old Rifleman, Brigadier-General the Hon. E. M.-Stuart-Wortley, C.B.

On May 20 the Battalion trained to London and lined the part of the route of the Funeral Procession of King Edward VII between Grosvenor Gate, Hyde Park, and the Marble Arch.

On August 2 to 4 the Battalion took part in Territorial manœuvres between Dover and Shorncliffe.

On August 22 to 24 the Battalion took part in a Brigade bivouac march in East Kent.

The Battalion left Shorncliffe on September 2 for Divisional and Army Manœuvres, detraining at Wells (Somerset) the following morning, and going into camp at Masbury. They entrained at Heytesbury (Wilts) on the 24th and returned to Shorncliffe.

The Battalion trained to London on June 21, 1911, and camped in Regent's Park.

On the 22nd they lined the western portion of Pall Mall, by which route T.M. King George V and Queen Mary returned from their Coronation. On the 23rd the Battalion lined the route of the Royal Procession through the City, the part occupied by them being in St. Paul's Churchyard. They returned to Shorncliffe the same evening.

On August 18, at 2.45 a.m., a telegram from the War

Office was received, ordering the Battalion to move to Hull on strike duty.

The Battalion—strength : Officers, 24 ; Other Ranks, 546—entrained at Shorncliffe Station at 5.15 a.m. and reached Hull at 4.5 p.m., where they were quartered in the Territorial Artillery Drill Hall. From the date of their arrival till the 24th of the month the Battalion found various posts on the railway, at the docks, and other vulnerable points, but at no place was there any disturbance.

This was the occasion of the Coal-mine and Railway Strike, when the men's leaders showed their patriotism by calling the strike off when the difficulty arose with Germany over the Agadir affair.

On the morning of the 24th all posts were withdrawn, and the Battalion left for Shorncliffe on the evening of the 25th.

At a meeting of the Justices of the Peace, held at Hull on the 25th, it was resolved to express the thanks of the inhabitants of Hull to the troops for their exemplary conduct during their stay in Hull.

In September the Battalion took part in a tactical march through East Kent with the rest of the 10th Infantry Brigade. The Brigade bivouacked at night, and by day carried out some small tactical scheme.

From September 18 to 20 the Brigade took part in manœuvres with the Dover Brigade, under the direction of the G.O.C. in C. Eastern Command.

The following is an extract from a Brigade Order published on September 21, containing the appreciation of the G.O.C. 4th Division (Major-General T. D'O. Snow) :—

'The G.O.C. requested the Brigadier-General Commanding to convey to the Brigade that in his opinion it is the finest he has ever seen.'

The other Battalions of the Brigade were the 1st Battalion D.C.L.I., 1st Battalion North Staffordshire Regiment, and the 2nd Battalion Oxfordshire and Buckinghamshire Light Infantry.

On January 10, 1912, the Battalion handed over the hutments in Risborough Line to the 2nd Battalion Seaforth Highlanders and took over the Napier Barracks, vacated by the 1st North Staffordshire Regiment.

On August 20 Lieut.-Colonel S. W. Hare completed his time in command of the Battalion and was succeeded by Lieut.-Colonel E. Pearce-Serocold.

On August 10 the Battalion moved to Ash, and was encamped there for Brigade and Divisional training till September 10. On that date they marched to Longmoor, and on the 11th and the 12th the Division was inspected by Lieut.-General Sir James Grierson, K.C.B., G.O.C. in C. Eastern Command, near Petersfield, returning to Ash on the 13th.

On the 15th the Battalion trained to Biggleswade (Beds) to take part in Army Manœuvres, returning to Shorncliffe on the 19th.

On September 30 the short L.E. Rifle, Mark III, was issued to the Battalion.

On January 10, 1913, the Battalion moved to Blackdown, to be stationed there.

From March 26 to 28 the Battalion took part in a billeting scheme in connection with the Aldershot Command Exercise. The 2nd Brigade, of which the Battalion formed part, marched to Crondall and Ewshott and were billeted there. On the 27th the march was continued to Eversley and Hartley Row. They returned to barracks on the 28th. Subsistence was found by the inhabitants. This was the first experiment in billeting on a large scale in England in peace time in recent history, and was completely successful.

On May 13 H.M. the King inspected the Battalion in Column in Drill Order. After he had inspected each Company, the Battalion marched past H.M. in fours.

On September 13 the Battalion left Blackdown for manœuvres and took part in Aldershot Command Exercise, September 15 and 16; Inter-Divisional Exercise, September 18 and 19; Army Exercise, September 22 to 26.

While in bivouac in Buckinghamshire the Battalion was visited by H.M. the King, who was accompanied by the Duke of Connaught and Prince Arthur of Connaught. The Battalion was also visited by Field-Marshal Lord Roberts and Field-Marshal Lord Grenfell. It returned to Blackdown on the night of the 27th.

From October 1 the four-company organisation was regularly adopted in the Battalion. This system had been employed for some years, off and on, for training purposes, and it had become evident that it was the only practical system by which Infantry could be handled in the field under modern conditions.

Third Battalion

South African War to Great War

After the conclusion of peace the 3rd Battalion remained in South Africa till the beginning of 1903, having reverted to the Colonial Establishment the previous November.

On February 25, 1903, they embarked at Capetown on the s.s. *Dominion* for home, disembarking at Queenstown and training to Cork on March 21.

Colonel W. P. Campbell, C.B., A.D.C., assumed command the same day.

He had succeeded to the command of the Battalion on the death of Lieut.-Colonel Buchanan Riddell in January 1900, but had been otherwise employed ever since, chiefly in command of columns in South Africa, and had never taken over command.

Most of the summer months were spent training at Kilworth Camp, except for a brief return to Cork at the beginning of August, to line the streets for the visit of H.M. King Edward VII.

Colonel W. P. Campbell completed his period of command on January 24, 1904, and was succeeded by Lieut.-Colonel C. R. R. McGrigor.

For some months the Battalion had been under orders for Bermuda, which by some practical joke on the part of the Authorities was turned into a Home Station for a time.

As the Battalion was not due to go abroad again for some years and as, ever since a Battalion of Guards had been sent there under a cloud some fifteen years previously, Bermuda had been looked upon as a penal settlement—most unjustly, as in those days it was a very pleasant station for a short time—a story very quickly got about that they had misbehaved in some way and were being sent there as a punishment. Before long the story took the definite form that the Battalion had, on receiving an unpopular form of head-dress known as the Brodrick cap—a thing like that worn by a fireman and called after the then Secretary of State—made a bonfire of them in the barrack square. The story actually appeared in the Press. This story reached Bermuda before the Battalion did, and the fact that they arrived without the Brodrick cap was looked upon as proof of its truth. The true explanation, that they had never had it issued to them, was received with derision.

The Battalion embarked at Queenstown on the s.s.

Dilwara on March 16, 1904. Strength: Officers, 23; Other Ranks, 831.

They reached Bermuda on the 27th and were split up with Headquarters and four companies on Boaz Island, two companies at St. George's, and two companies at Warwick Camp.

Bathing being the chief recreation of the men in Bermuda, by the end of their time there the Battalion had a water-polo team which was in a class by itself. In the Army Water-Polo Tournament in the garrison baths at Aldershot, to which place the Battalion went from Bermuda, the team won the final by 17 goals to nothing.

The Battalion sailed for home on the s.s. *Kensington* on October 13, 1905, and disembarked at Southampton on the 25th, arriving at Aldershot, where they occupied Salamanca Barracks, the same day.

The double-company system was introduced on December 1, 1905, experimentally, but the Battalion reverted to the eight-company system for administration on July 1, 1906, two companies continuing to work together as one on parade and in the field. It was not till shortly before the Great War that the four-company system was finally adopted.

The short Lee-Enfield rifle was issued to the Battalion on February 1, 1906.

On July 7, 1906, the Battalion was inspected by H.R.H. the Prince of Wales, the Colonel-in-Chief, who expressed his pleasure at the appearance of the Battalion, their steadiness on parade, and the march past in column.

On May 28, 1907, the Battalion water-polo team played an exhibition game before H.M. King Edward VII on the occasion of his visit to Aldershot.

The Battalion spent three training-seasons at Aldershot and made a very good name for themselves, their musketry and signalling especially receiving very favourable comments in all their inspection reports.

Colonel C. R. R. McGrigor, C.B., left on appointment to the Staff on December 18, 1907. His immediate successor, Lieut.-Colonel R. S. Oxley, did not take over, but waited to exchange with Lieut.-Colonel C. S. Chaplin, who fell to the 1st Battalion, on March 18, 1908.

The Battalion embarked for Crete and Malta in the s.s. *Sicilia* on February 13, 1908. Strength : Officers, 18 ; Other Ranks, 800. The establishment was raised on embarkation to 28 Officers and 905 Other Ranks.

The *Sicilia* reached Suda Bay on the 23rd, and there half a company disembarked for Canea, the political capital of Crete, where the High Commissioner resided together with the representatives of the occupying Powers.

Candia was reached the same day, and by next morning the remainder of the Battalion, less two companies for Malta, had disembarked. The ship then went back to Malta and landed the two companies to be quartered there.

The island had quieted down since the 1st Battalion were there and the stay of the 3rd Battalion was uneventful.

Except by the detachment at Canea, little was seen of the Allied troops.

On May 11 Colonel De la Rue, Commandant Supérieur of the Allied Forces in Crete, and a party of French Officers visited Candia and were entertained by the Officers of the Battalion. A torchlight tattoo, under the direction of Bandmaster Lovell, was given in their honour in the evening, and everything possible was done to forward the Entente Cordiale.

On June 30 a company of the 13th Regiment of Russian Infantry reached Candia, having completed the march from Rethymo, some fifty miles of very bad roads, in from eighteen to twenty hours. They were entertained by the Battalion and started their march back next day.

On May 29 and 30 an International Rifle Meeting was held at Canea, in which representatives of the British, French, Russian, and Italian Armies competed, also of the Cretan Gendarmerie and Cretan Militia.

Our men took the first four places in the competition for rank and file, and Lieutenant Atkinson won the Officers' Revolver Competition, the one practice at which the Allies expected to beat us, but we only took fourth place in the Sergeants' Competition and lost the Tile Competition to the Gendarmerie.

The prize winners were pretty evenly distributed among the different nationalities, and our representatives certainly did not sweep the board as they should.

The International Occupation was coming to an end, and in July two companies moved to Malta, followed by the rest of the Battalion in January 1909. The Battalion was stationed at Verdala Barracks.

H.M. King Edward VII visited Malta from April 21 to 25. The Main Guard at Valetta was furnished by the Battalion during the stay of His Majesty.

The Battalion took part in a Ceremonial Parade on the Marsa on the 22nd. H.R.H. the Duke of Connaught (Commander-in-Chief in the Mediterranean) personally complimented the Commanding Officer on the appearance of the Battalion in the Ceremonial Parade, and also on the way in which the Guard had performed its duties.

On May 10 the Battalion assisted in lining the streets on the occasion of the visit of the German Emperor to Malta.

In September the Battalion moved to St. George's Barracks, Pembroke.

On November 12, 1910, the Battalion embarked in the

s.s. *Rewa* for India. Strength : Officers, 21 ; Other Ranks, 878.

They arrived at Karachi on the 24th and Umballa on the 27th, when they went into camp on the racecourse, the women and children going on to Dagshai, in the Hills.

On the Battalion leaving Malta, the following Order was published by Brigadier-General G. G. Egerton, C.B., Commanding the Malta Infantry Brigade :—

'The 3rd Battalion King's Royal Rifle Corps having embarked this day for service in India, the Brigadier-General, in wishing, in the name of the Malta Infantry Brigade, farewell and every good wish to Lieutenant-Colonel C. S. Chaplin and the Officers, N.C.O.s, and men under his command, desires to place on record that this Battalion during its stay in Malta has admirably maintained the best traditions of the great Regiment to which it belongs, and in the field of sport and athletics leaves behind a record which it will be no easy matter for others to surpass.'

In April 1911 the Battalion marched to Dagshai, returning to Umballa in October.

On November 19 they moved to Delhi for the Coronation Durbar, and returned to Umballa on December 18.

On March 17, 1912, Lieut.-Colonel C. S. Chaplin completed his period of command, and was succeeded by Lieut.-Colonel C. Gosling.

The Battalion moved to Dagshai in March and returned to Umballa in November, whence they moved to Delhi, where they lined the streets for the State Entry of the Viceroy (Lord Hardinge of Penshurst) on December 23.

On March 29, 1913, they trained to Meerut, to be stationed there.

Three companies went to Chakrata for the hot weather.

On November 11 they started to march to Pur for winter training, returning to Meerut on December 18.

On April 1, 1914, the four-company system was adopted.

Two companies only went to the Hills this year, one to Chakrata, the other to Rhaniket. They rejoined Headquarters soon after the outbreak of the Great War, and on September 27 the Battalion received orders to be ready to embark for home at an early date.

Fourth Battalion
1902—1914

After the close of the South African War the 4th Battalion remained at Harrismith under peace conditions, although their tour of home service was not due to end for several years.

On January 14, 1903, Lieut.-Colonel F. A. Fortescue, who had succeeded Colonel Herbert on October 15, 1902, joined and took over command.

In August 1903 the Battalion took part in manœuvres in Natal which seem to have been of a strenuous nature, as it is recorded that on the 17th and the 18th they marched 35 miles in 29 hours.

On June 1, 1904, the Battalion—strength: Officers, 17; Other Ranks, 773—left Harrismith for Durban, where they embarked in the s.s. *Sicilia* for England. They reached Southampton on the 28th and trained to Gosport.

On August 20 sanction was granted by H.R.H. the Prince of Wales, Colonel-in-Chief, for 'The Duke of York's March' to be played by the Regiment as the Inspection tune. This slow march had been in use in the Regiment for a long time, probably since the days when they were the Duke of York's Rifle Corps, but so far had had no official sanction.[1]

On July 15, 1904, the Battalion furnished a Guard of Honour and Band on the occasion of the opening of the Riflemen's Cottage Homes, Winchester, by H.R.H. Princess Christian of Schleswig-Holstein.

The following Battalion Order of April 16, 1905, refers to the earthquake in India, of which Dharmsala, where a Gurkha battalion was almost wiped out, was the centre :—

'The Lieutenant-Colonel Commanding wishes to inform all ranks of the 4th Battalion that a sum of £50 has been sent to the Brigade of Gurkhas, in the name of all ranks, towards the Widows' and Orphans' Relief Fund which has been opened in consequence of the severe losses of the Brigade in the recent earthquake. . . .'

The Order then goes on to tell the young soldiers of our traditional friendship with the Gurkhas and of its origin, and reminding them that the Gurkhas of all ranks had voluntarily subscribed to the Fund for the Widows and Orphans of those of our Regiment who fell in South Africa.

On May 1, 1905, the Battalion moved to Wool, in Dorset, for training. On June 7 they moved to Aldershot, where, next day, they took part in a Royal Review before H.M. King Edward VII and the King of Spain.

On July 1 they moved to Oxney Farm, Bordon, where the 5th and 6th Infantry Brigades were brought together

---

[1] At one time the Band of the 1st Battalion, if not others, used to play it before 'The Huntsman's Chorus' at the end of every programme. This practice of playing a succession of tunes before 'God Save the King' can be very wearisome. Under one C.O. the 1st Battalion Band played no less than three tunes—'The Duke of York's March,' 'The Huntsman's Chorus' (at that time our Regimental March), and then a melancholy, wailing thing called 'The Queen-Empress,' which I really think the C.O. and the Bandmaster must have composed between them, as I can thankfully say that I have never heard it since.—S. W. H.

for training under Major-General Sir Edward Hutton, K.C.M.G.

In September the Battalion took part in the 1st Army Corps manœuvres, returning to Gosport on the 30th, after five months under canvas.

On February 13, 1906, the new short Lee-Enfield rifle was issued to the Battalion. In July the Battalion went to Bordon to join the 3rd Division for training under Major-General Sir Edward Hutton, followed by Army Corps Manœuvres near Chichester.

On October 10, 1906, the Battalion moved to Colchester on change of station.

On July 25, 1907, H.R.H. the Prince of Wales, Colonel-in-Chief, inspected the Battalion. After parade H.R.H. lunched with the Officers; then inspected the Institutes, the Sergeants' Mess, and some of the Barrack rooms, saw a gymnastic display by the obstacle race team, which won at Aldershot two years in succession, and listened to bugle marches by the Buglers.

H.R.H. was pleased to issue a very complimentary Order to the Battalion, conveying his entire satisfaction with all that he saw.

On August 8 the Battalion moved to Ringwood, Hants, for brigade and divisional training and manœuvres. From September 12 to 21 they were in London to relieve the Guards of guard duties.

On November 13 8 Officers and 150 Other Ranks went to London to line the streets for the visit of the German Emperor and Empress.

The Battalion won the Army Association Football Cup for the season 1907–8, beating, in the final, the 2nd Battalion Lancashire Fusiliers by one goal to none. This was the first and so far the only time that this cup has been won by the Regiment.

On December 1, 1909, the Battalion—strength: Officers, 17; Other Ranks, 423—left Colchester and embarked on the s.s. *Dongola* at Southampton for India. They disembarked at Karachi on the 21st and arrived at Meerut on the 23rd.

The Battalion went to Chakrata for the hot weather of 1910.

Lieut.-Colonel the Hon. A. R. Montagu-Stuart-Wortley, D.S.O., succeeded to the command of the Battalion on October 15, 1910, on the completion of his period of command by Colonel O. S. Nugent, D.S.O., A.D.C.

On November 23, 1911, the Battalion trained to Delhi for the Coronation Durbar. They were camped near the famous ' Ridge,' and were brigaded with the 2nd Battalion 2nd Gurkha Rifles, the 2nd Battalion 9th Gurkha Rifles, and the 130th Baluchis (Jacob's Rifles). A detailed account of the duties performed at the Durbar assembly by both the 3rd and the 4th Battalions can be found in the *Chronicle* for 1912.

The Battalion trained to Rawal Pindi on December 19. They went into camp at Barakao for brigade training from February 12 to 17. On May 5 Headquarters and four companies left Rawal Pindi for Upper Topa, in the Murree Hills, for the hot weather.

In April 1913 Headquarters and half the Battalion moved to Gharial for the hot weather, returning to Rawal Pindi in November.

In November the Battalion was rearmed with new rifles of English manufacture—short magazine Lee-Enfield, Mark III.

In 1914 the whole Battalion went to Gharial for the hot weather, the first party leaving Rawal Pindi on April 15.

Lieut.-Colonel Stuart-Wortley was appointed to the

Staff without completing his period of command, and was succeeded by Lieut.-Colonel the Hon. C. J. Sackville-West on April 1.

The four-company system was adopted for work only from August 1, but did not come into use for administrative purposes till after the return of the Battalion to England.

On August 22 Lieut.-Colonel Sackville-West was appointed G.S.O. 1st Grade on the Staff of Sir James Willcocks, who commanded the Indian Corps about to sail for France.

The Battalion left Gharial for the Great War on October 8.

CHAPTER XVIII

Mounted Infantry

In the preceding pages it has been the endeavour of the writer to give some account of the services of our Regiment, in all the campaigns of the period under review in which our Battalions took part.

It would be impossible to recount in detail the services of individuals of the Regiment serving apart from their corps during all this period without extending the work beyond reasonable limits; but there is one sphere of action in which Officers and men of the Regiment served together in many campaigns, during the last quarter of the nineteenth century and the first few years of the twentieth, without some account of which a history of the Regiment during those years would be incomplete, and that is the Mounted Infantry.

It would be safe to say that, during the time in which Mounted Infantry was a regular feature in our wars, our Regiment contributed more Officers and men to its ranks than any other Corps. We are the only regiment which ever turned out a complete battalion of Mounted Infantry, and that great Rifleman, the late Lieut.-General Sir Edward Hutton, certainly did more for Mounted Infantry in raising, training, and leading it in the field than any other Officer in the British Army.

As Mounted Infantry had become practically extinct before the majority of the present generation of soldiers had joined the Army, it may be as well to give some short sketch of what it was and what were its functions.

It must be remembered that, at the time when Mounted Infantry first came into general use in our campaigns, the training of the Cavalryman for dismounted action was not taken very seriously. Certainly he was armed with a carbine and went through an annual course of musketry of a more or less perfunctory nature, but it is doubtful if he ever expected to use his carbine except on outpost duty. He followed James Pigg's motto, "Ar niver gets off." His equipment certainly did not help him. It was not till well on in the eighties that the sword began to be worn on the saddle; it was adopted by Army Order of November 1889, though it had been thus carried by the Americans in their Civil War more than twenty years earlier. It can be imagined that a man in knee-boots with a sabre dangling from his waist had his style somewhat cramped as a skirmisher.

The mounted Infantryman was an Infantry soldier who fought only on foot and used his horse merely as a means of locomotion. He was trained as an Infantryman, and the extra training required to make him a mounted Infantryman consisted of enough equitation to enable him to get about without damage to himself or his horse and the enlargement of his views by practice in mounted reconnaissance.

There was a good deal of heated controversy, at the time, as to whether the mounted Infantryman supplied a want or not. There was even in those days a school which preached that the days of shock action by mounted men were over, and the Cavalryman not unnaturally was inclined to look upon the mounted Infantryman as the thin end of the wedge which, driven home, would secure his abolition.

In a lecture delivered before the Royal United Service Institution in June 1886, Major Hutton laid down the object of Mounted Infantry under three headings, and this may be taken as the orthodox view and that adopted by the authorities when they sanctioned the establishment of a School of Mounted Infantry at Aldershot, which put a constant stream of Infantry soldiers of all ranks through a two—later three—months' course of Mounted Infantry duties.

These headings were :—

1. *To provide an improvised substitute for an expensive Cavalry in small and hastily organised expeditions.*

By sending a contingent of trained mounted Infantrymen out to the theatre of war and mounting them at once on the horse or pony of the country, which could be obtained fit for immediate work and, at the same time, was unsuited in size as a Regular Cavalry troop horse, a substitute could be found to take on mounted duties long before the Regular Cavalry horses could be got fit for service after a sea-voyage.

The Cavalryman's answer to this was that this object could be as well, and better, achieved by sending out a few dismounted Cavalrymen to be mounted on local remounts of whatever description, to stop the gap till the Cavalry who brought their own horses should be ready to take over.

The counter to this, in which there was some truth, but which could not be given openly, as being a matter of opinion and hopelessly controversial, was that the Infantryman who had been trained in peace and possibly served in war as a mounted Infantryman was a better man at the service of protection and information, in fact in all mounted duties except shock action, than the Regular Cavalry soldier, as then trained.

The truth was probably somewhere between the two extremes. The training of different Cavalry Regiments varied. Although the training of some of them was more in accordance with modern ideas than that of most of the Army, many were still trained much on the lines of heavy Cavalry in the Napoleonic Wars.

A very good instance of this use of Mounted Infantry is found in the Egyptian Expedition of 1882, when, as already related, on Sir Archibald Alison's arrival in Alexandria he authorised Captain Hutton to raise a corps of Mounted Infantry—they were less than a hundred strong to start with—from the men of two battalions, the South Staffordshire and our 3rd Battalion, who had served as Mounted Infantry in the Zulu and First Boer Wars. These men left their units one day and took the field the next on Arab horses supplied from the Khedive's stables. This little band did all the mounted duties of Intelligence and Security till the Regular Cavalry arrived. This lasted for some weeks, as the Mounted Infantry was raised from battalions which came from Mediterranean stations and the Regular Cavalry came all the way from England and India.

Even when the Regular Cavalry arrived and took the field, it was some time before their horses were fit for the hard work of which those of the Mounted Infantry, who were working with them, were already capable.

2. *To provide for a campaign on a large scale an efficient Auxiliary to our Cavalry.*

It was generally recognised, at the time of which we speak, that, in the event of the British Army going to take part, at full strength, in a big war, the numbers of the Regular Cavalry were barely sufficient to supply their due proportion of mounted troops for the Expeditionary Force. The question of finance prohibited any permanent addition to the Regular Cavalry in time of peace—the auxiliary forces at that time were intended solely for home defence—so there was no question of sending the Yeomanry abroad. To raise additional Cavalry regiments on the outbreak of war would take too long, owing to the time necessary to train both man and horse to take their place in the ranks of units whose prime object was mounted shock action. It would therefore be necessary to improvise mounted troops which could relieve the Regular Cavalry by taking over, as much as possible, any mounted duties which could be performed by troops whose components, man and horse, would be insufficiently trained for mounted combat—such as outposts, orderly duty, escorts, and to some extent reconnaissance. It was thought that a force of Mounted Infantry trained in peace to a reasonable standard of horsemanship and to some knowledge of the care of horses, mounted on animals obtained in or near the theatre of war or hastily purchased at home, which might be too small for Cavalry remounts and would require only to be so far trained as to be fairly docile conveyances for indifferent horsemen, would supply this want.

This aspect of the use of Mounted Infantry was much more popular with the Cavalry soldier than number one. It would relieve him of duties which, when not actually distasteful, took a very secondary place in his affections, and left him free to devote his whole energies to what he looked upon as his chief duty, and probably wished was his only one, the mounted combat.

3. *To provide a force of selected Infantry sufficiently mobile to act as such in conjunction with Cavalry.*

The advantage of giving increased fire-power to an independent force of Cavalry by a body of men highly trained in the use of the rifle, instead of leaving an unwilling and partially trained Cavalryman to do his own shooting, was beyond dispute, and was nowhere more popular than with the " Ar niver gets off " school.

There was one individual with whom the Mounted Infantry was not popular, and that was the Infantry

Commanding Officer, who saw himself deprived of the pick of his Officers and men on the outbreak of war.

With the Infantry generally, service with the Mounted Infantry was extremely popular. To those who were fond of horses it gave the opportunity of associating professionally with the animal they loved ; and in those days there were many horse-lovers who, except in India and a few other foreign stations, were, from financial reasons, unable to indulge their ruling passion. The Great Unknown, to whom the subalterns of the British Army should certainly erect a monument, who first convinced the authorities that hiring out Government horses as hunters was a business proposition, had not yet evolved his system. It gave those who went through the training a much better chance of seeing active service ; and in the field, or even on the training-area, it introduced them to a more interesting and broader view of war. It also brought them together with and taught them to work with Officers of other corps in a day when the regimental Officer was very much inclined to get into a groove and think it the only possible groove.

The argument which probably had most weight with the authorities, dominated as they must always be by the guardians of the public purse, in deciding to adopt the Mounted Infantry system, was that of finance. Leaving aside the balancing of the deficiencies of the Cavalryman as a foot-soldier against those of the Infantryman as a horseman, there remained the undoubted fact that a man who only had to be supplied with a horse, in peace time, for two or three months in twenty-four, was a very much cheaper article than one who had to be mounted year in, year out.

Thus the mounted Infantryman became a recognised feature of the British Army, and remained so for at least a quarter of a century, and he certainly pulled his weight.

It would be waste of ink to raise the question when use was first made of Mounted Infantry. The Dragoon Regiments have been quoted as the first Mounted Infantry. True, when originally raised, they were intended only to fight on foot, but they were not Mounted Infantry, as we use the words, because they were mounted all the year round.

The truth seems to be that, from time immemorial, commanders have put Infantry on to horses for a longer or shorter period, and this had occurred from time to time in the British Army, but what we may call the Mounted Infantry period in our Army began with the Zulu War of 1879.

The Zulu War of 1879 and Boer War of 1881

Two squadrons, as Mounted Infantry companies were first called, were formed under Captain and Local Lieut.-Colonel J. C. Russell, 12th Lancers, and Captain Percy Barrow, 19th Hussars. They did good work throughout the campaign, but, as our Regiment was not represented among them, we may pass on to the Boer War of 1881.

On the outbreak of war Major W. V. Brownlow, K.D.Gs., with a small number of the N.C.O.s and men of his regiment, which had only just left the country for India, were awaiting passage to England.

Sir George Colley, who was totally devoid of mounted troops, called upon him to raise a body of Mounted Infantry. They were made up to 120 of all ranks, a medley of Dragoons, Riflemen, and other Infantrymen.

The Infantry had most of them never been on a horse before. Their training consisted of the four weeks' march from Pietermaritzburg to Mount Prospect. At Laing's

Nek they were sent on an errand, the accomplishment of which was absolutely necessary to the success of the main attack, with what result has been already told. Lieutenant C. B. Pigott, in saving the life of a wounded man close to the Boer position, by putting him on his horse and himself retiring on foot under a heavy fire, performed the first of the many gallant acts for which this Officer was distinguished in his short career.

In spite of their unfortunate first experience, Brownlow's Mounted Infantry carried out all the mounted duties for Colley's force till the arrival of the 15th Hussars, just before the Majuba disaster ended the campaign.

On the outbreak of war a regiment of Mounted Infantry was raised in England by Major Percy Barrow, 19th Hussars, and Captain E. T. H. Hutton commanded the so-called squadron contributed by our Regiment.

This Regiment reached Durban on February 12 without horses or equipment, and all their horses but fifty had to be purchased locally; yet they left Durban, ready to take the field, on the 19th.

The work of the Mounted Infantry in Egypt in 1882 has been already related in the accounts of that campaign.

About January 1, 1884, a company of Mounted Infantry was formed at Abbassia, near Cairo, to which our 3rd Battalion contributed a section under Lieutenant P. Marling. The company left for Suakim in the middle of February and served with Sir Gerald Graham, taking part in the actions of El Teb and Tamaai, and returned to Abbassia in April.

Lieutenant Marling was awarded the Victoria Cross 'for conspicuous bravery at the Battle of Tamaai, on March 13, 1884, in risking his life to save that of Private Morley, Royal Sussex Regiment, who, having been shot, was lifted and placed in front of Lieutenant Marling on his horse. He fell off almost immediately, when Lieutenant Marling dismounted, and gave up his horse for the purpose of carrying Private Morley, the enemy pressing close on to them, until they succeeded in carrying him about eighty yards to a place of comparative safety.'

Rifleman Hunter also obtained the D.C.M. for assisting Lieutenant Marling.

The Nile, 1885

When, late in 1884—too late to be of any use—the British Government at last made up its mind to send an expedition to the relief of Gordon, a Camel Corps was organised composed of a Heavy and a Light Camel Regiment made up of Cavalrymen, a Guards Camel Regiment and a Mounted Infantry Camel Regiment. The Rifle Company of the Mounted Infantry Regiment was commanded by Captain R. S. Fetherstonhaugh, the subalterns being: K.R.R.C., Lieutenant W. Pitcairn Campbell and Lieutenant A. E. Miles; Rifle Brigade, Lieutenant Lord Hardinge and Lieutenant Maxwell Sherston.

The Rifle Company left Southampton on August 27, 1884, landed at Alexandria, and went on to Wady Halfa. There they took over their camels and rode the rest of the way to Korti.

Lord Wolseley's original intention had been to make the whole journey to Khartum by water, but on his arrival at Korti he decided that the time for this deliberate advance was not available if Gordon was to be relieved, and he decided to send a mounted column across the Bayuda Desert to Metammeh, where Gordon's steamers were awaiting them. It was the possibility of this necessity which had led Lord Wolseley to organise the Camel Corps.

As local supplies would be totally unprocurable during and after the crossing of the desert, and as it would be impossible, when in touch with the enemy, even to turn the camels out to graze, the column would have to be entirely self-supporting.

The amount of forage and the number of baggage camels required for a dash across the desert of well over 150 miles, carrying all their forage with them, was insufficient, and a depot had to be established at Gakdul Wells, a little over half-way.

A convoy was therefore dispatched under Brigadier-General Sir Herbert Stewart, K.C.B., on December 30, with an escort of all arms, of which the Mounted Infantry Camel Regiment (24 Officers, 359 Other Ranks) formed a part. They marched at 3 p.m., and by 7.30 a.m. on the 31st had covered 34 miles. Making short halts at the Wells of El Howeiya and Hambok, where only small quantities of indifferent water were found, they reached the gorge leading into Gakdul at 6.45 a.m. on January 2—98 miles from Korti.

The wells, or rather rock cisterns, of Gakdul were found to contain ample water for man and beast.

Sir Herbert Stewart, leaving the Guards Camel Regiment, 422 of all ranks, and a detachment of Royal Engineers to develop the water-supply, which was very difficult of access, started on his return march at 8 p.m. January 2, reaching Korti at noon on the 5th.

On January 7 another convoy of 1,000 camels, escorted by the Light Camel Regiment, left Korti for Gakdul.

On January 8 Sir Herbert Stewart left Korti with much the same force as before, reinforced by the Sussex Regiment (mounted on camels), 400 of all ranks, and a company of the Essex Regiment, also on camels. This time his orders were to establish a post at Metammeh, on the Nile. From there he was to send on Colonel Sir Charles Wilson, Lord Wolseley's chief Intelligence Officer, in whatever of the Egyptian steamers Captain Lord Charles Beresford, R.N., and his sailors could get into working order, to get in touch with Gordon. It was obvious that it would still be a long time before Wolseley would be in a position to relieve Khartum by force of arms, but he was in hopes that the arrival of the steamers with a few red-coats on board would bluff the Mahdi into raising the siege.

Sir Herbert Stewart, after dropping some detachments and picking up others at the wells on the line of route, reached Gakdul on the morning of the 12th.

Wolseley's information at this time was that the Mahdi was detaching 20,000 men to oppose the Desert Column; he did not know that Omdurman had already fallen and that a much larger force was thus liberated for operations against them.

On January 14 at 2 a.m. Stewart resumed his advance on Metammeh, with the following force :—

2 troops 19th Hussars (commanded by Major J. D. P. French) ;[1]
Naval Brigade, 1 Gardner gun, under Captain Lord Charles Beresford, R.N. ;
Camel Battery, 3 guns ;
Heavy Camel Regiment ;
Guards Camel Regiment ;
Mounted Infantry Camel Regiment ;
250 men of the Royal Sussex Regiment, on camels ;
A detachment of Royal Engineers and a proportion of Medical and Supply services.
Total, about 1,500 combatants of all ranks and 1,118 transport camels.

At 11.30 a.m., when the force was halted near a line of low hills that separated them from the walls of Abu Klea, the Cavalry reported that the enemy were in sight, and shortly afterwards that they were in position between the British force and the wells.

[1] Field-Marshal the Earl of Ypres.

The force advanced till they were within 3½ miles of the wells and bivouacked for the night.

The enemy had taken up a position, marked by a line of flags, across a broad sandy wady which was the direct way to the wells.

Next morning Stewart, leaving his baggage camels in zariba with a weak guard of the Royal Sussex Regiment, formed his force in a square and moved out to attack. The square was directed as if to turn the left of the enemy's position. This took it over a rather rough country which was awkward for camels and made it difficult for the square to keep closed up. To keep down the fire of the enemy's sharpshooters, which was causing casualties, a small number of Infantry were sent out from the square on foot. The detachment which covered the left front, that nearest the enemy, was commanded by Lieutenant W. P. Campbell, 1st K.R.R.C.

When the square was within 500 yards and our skirmishers within 200 yards of the line of flags, a halt was made to close up. At this moment a mass of about 5,000 Arabs rose up from concealment in the wady and charged for the left front corner of the square. Campbell's party had to sprint for it. Two hundred yards in five is not enough start for a soldier in fighting kit against a naked Arab to make it anything of a certainty, and one man was speared before he could reach the square.

When the dervishes rose up and charged, a Cavalry Officer who had been studying the Infantry drill-book drew his sword and called out, ' Form rallying square ' (the formation laid down for skirmishers to assume when attacked by Cavalry). If this had been done, not one of the skirmishers would have been alive two minutes later. Johnny Campbell saved the situation by shouting, ' No ! Run like hell ! ' ; the moral of which is that a difficult situation is more likely to be saved by presence of mind and common sense than by looking for a ready-made solution among the text-books.

As they approached the square, the heavy fire from the left front corner, which was held by the Mounted Infantry, caused the Arabs to swerve to their right, which brought them against the left rear and rear, held by the Heavies with the naval Gardner gun in the middle of them. This part of the square, which had been disordered by the hanging back of the camels inside the square, was not yet quite closed up. The Arabs broke into the square and a hand-to-hand fight ensued. Fortunately the slope of the ground enabled the front face and part of the right face, which were a good deal higher than the rear face, to turn round and shoot over the mêlée that was going on into the mass of the enemy. These soon wavered, and then fell back, and those who had got to close quarters were all dispatched, but not before they had inflicted heavy losses on the Heavies and Naval Detachment.

The enemy then gradually drew off, speeded by the carbine fire of the 19th Hussars, who followed them up and then went on to locate the wells.

The square moved slowly on, and about 5 p.m. the Hussars reported that the wells were close by and unoccupied. The square bivouacked near them, and the Transport joined the force there next morning.

The British losses were 9 Officers, 65 Other Ranks, killed; 9 Officers, 85 Other Ranks, wounded. Most of the casualties were among the Heavies and the Naval Detachment.

The enemy's losses were very heavy, 1,100 bodies being counted close round the square.

Leaving his wounded under guard of a detachment of the Royal Sussex Regiment, which had orders to entrench itself and hold the wells, Stewart resumed his march to the Nile about 4 p.m. on the 18th.

A very trying night march followed. The distance to be covered was only twenty-three miles, but such were the difficulties of the march owing to darkness and, for a good part of the way, thick bush—thorny acacia—that dawn (6 a.m.) found them still with five miles to go. A halt was then made to get the column closed up as it had become thoroughly disorganised during the night march.

At 7.30 a.m., as the force topped a ridge, it came in sight of the Nile and Metammeh with the enemy in great force ready to oppose their advance.

Seeing that he was not going to reach the river without a fight, Stewart laagered his transport and the men had breakfast.

While this was going on the enemy's sharpshooters, who got good cover in the long grass, opened a hot fire which caused a lot of casualties, and Sir Herbert himself received the wound from which he died nearly a month later.

Colonel Sir Charles Wilson, K.C.M.G., R.E., D.A.G. for Intelligence, succeeded to the command.

Half the Heavies, the 19th Hussars, the Royal Artillery, and Naval Detachment were left to guard the baggage, and, at 3 p.m., the square began its advance to the river under a hot fire. No skirmishers were sent out, as at Abu Klea they had, when running in, considerably masked the fire of the square. It was necessary, therefore, to halt now and then and reply to the enemy's fire to keep it under some control. At last the enemy made their charge in greater numbers and in better combination than at Abu Klea, but this time the fire from the square was unobstructed; its effect was tremendous, and only one Arab got within 100 yards of our ranks. The attack then melted away.

The advance then continued unopposed and the square reached the Nile half an hour after dark, and bivouacked for the night.

Next day—January 20—the village of Gubat, on a ridge overlooking the river at less than half a mile and two miles from Metammeh, was occupied.

The story of how Gordon's four steamers arrived next day with the latest news from Khartum, of Wilson's dash up-stream with them only to find that Khartum had fallen, of the adventures of his party on their return, need not be told here, as it does not affect our Mounted Infantry. The Regiment was represented by Lieutenant E. J. Montagu-Stuart-Wortley,[1] attached to the Intelligence Department, who, when Wilson's steamer was wrecked some forty miles above Gubat, on the return journey, on January 31, made an adventurous voyage in an open boat down to Gubat to report his situation.

Lieutenant Stuart-Wortley accompanied Lord Charles Beresford, who brought a steamer to the rescue and, after a very close call, lying the whole of one day at anchor within 500 yards of a hostile fort while the boiler, which had been holed by shell, was being repaired, brought Wilson and his party back to Gubat on the evening of February 4.

During Sir Charles Wilson's absence not much had occurred at Gubat, the enemy after their severe repulse of January 19 not being in condition to renew the attack. A large camel convoy was sent off to Gakdul on the 23rd and returned laden with supplies on the 31st.

On receipt of the news of the fight on the 19th and of Sir Herbert Stewart's wound, Lord Wolseley at once decided to send Sir Redvers Buller to take command of

[1] Major-General the Hon. E. J. Montagu-Stuart-Wortley, C.B., C.M.G., M.V.O., D.S.O.

the Desert Column, Sir Evelyn Wood succeeding him as Chief of the Staff.

On February 11 Buller reached Gubat.

The question now remained to be decided by the Government what was to be the next step. Whether preparations should be made for a campaign against the Mahdi when the hot weather should be over and the Nile have risen again, and if so, whether the first step should be the capture of Berber by a combined attack from downstream by the River Column, which was now advancing up the river from Korti, and from up-stream by the Desert Column, who would follow the river down from Gubat, or the Sudan be given up to the Mahdi and the whole force withdrawn to within the Egyptian frontier, wherever it should be decided that the frontier should be.

The Government eventually decided for evacuation, Gladstone thereby postponing the inevitable reconquest of the Sudan for a dozen years; just as, in 1881, he deferred the equally inevitable South African War for nearly twenty years.

Meanwhile Buller, on his arrival at Gubat, had quickly summed up the situation and decided that he could not remain there. He started to withdraw to Abu Klea on February 14, and this, as it turned out, was the first step in the evacuation. By March 16 the last troops of the Desert Column had reached Korti, without any more serious fighting, and the work of the Camel Corps was over.

The Officer Commanding the Mounted Infantry Regiment of the Camel Corps reported that ' the behaviour in action of the men of the Rifle Company has been a matter of special remark in the Desert Column.'

In the operations in Burma in 1891–2 a considerable number of the 4th Battalion served as Mounted Infantry.

They did a lot of hard work and suffered much from the climate, but had no serious fighting.

MASHONALAND, 1896

In May 1896 a battalion of four companies under command of Captain (temporary Lieut.-Colonel) E. A. H. Alderson, 2nd Royal West Kent Regiment, embarked for Cape Town to be ready for service in Rhodesia should they be required. Of the four companies one was a Rifle Company, under Captain A. V. Jenner, D.S.O., 4th Rifle Brigade, two sections of which were found from our Regiment and were commanded by Lieutenants G. S. St. Aubyn and C. L. E. Eustace.

On arrival at Cape Town on May 19 they were kept doing nothing for a month, and nothing was done about mounting them. Things were going well in Matabeleland, which so far had been the theatre of war. Early in June the Mashonas, whose supposed lack of any fighting instincts was thought to be such as to render any protection for the settlers in the country unnecessary, rose in rebellion and began to massacre every white man, woman, and child in the country.

Two companies of the Mounted Infantry Battalion were at once ordered to embark for Beira at the mouth of the Pungwe River in Portuguese East Africa, whence they were to get to Salisbury, the capital of Mashonaland, as quickly as possible. Wholly taken by surprise by the outbreak of the rebellion, the inhabitants of Salisbury went into laager in and around the gaol, the few men being formed into a local corps. They were perfectly safe against any attack by the Mashonas, but liable to be starved out if not relieved within a given time. The Rifle and Irish Companies (the latter under Captain Sir H. W. McMahon, Bart., Royal Welsh Fusiliers) were the lucky ones.

Remounts were immediately bought locally—rather a scratch lot and many in poor condition—and on June 26, less than a week after the receipt of the order, the troops embarked. Calling at Durban to take on more horses, they anchored off Beira on the morning of July 3.

Arrived at Beira, Alderson, after great transport difficulties—including a railway accident—by river and rail to Fontesvilla (40 miles), by rail Fontesvilla to Chimoio (118 miles), by march route to Umtali (73 miles), concentrated his force at Umtali ready to start on his march of another 155 miles to Salisbury by the evening of July 27.

His force now consisted of two companies Mounted Infantry, a company Royal Engineers, a detachment Royal Artillery with two 7-pounder guns, 50 men of the West Riding Regiment, and a few locally raised Mounted Scouts.

He set out on July 28. He had succeeded in commandeering forty-five wagons, about one-third drawn by oxen in very bad condition and two-thirds by mules.

On his way to Salisbury, Alderson had to secure his communications by beating up the kraals of any hostile chiefs in the neighbourhood of his line of march and establishing a series of small fortified posts. The first of these kraals to be attacked was Makoni's (see Plate 19), and as the whole campaign consisted of a series of similar operations it will be enough by describing this one to give an idea of the rest.

These kraals, in nearly every case, consisted of a number of Kaffir huts clustering over a rocky kopje, which was almost invariably honeycombed by a perfect warren of caves. The Mashona never put up much of a fight in defence of his kraal, but went to ground in the caves, where he was unassailable and, with a store of mealies laid by, could not be starved out in any reasonable time. These caves generally contained springs, giving a plentiful water-supply.

The only way to bring the rebels to subjection was to attack their kraals by surprise, so that they might have considerable casualties before they could get to ground, drive off their cattle, carry off their stores of mealies, and burn their kraals. This process, though slow, if continued long enough was bound to tire them out in the end.

On August 2 Alderson's force laagered about six miles in a straight line from Makoni's. At 2 a.m. next morning he marched with two companies Mounted

PLATE 19.
VIEW OF MAKONI'S KRAAL FROM THE N.N.W.

Infantry (with one Maxim), a detachment of Royal Engineers, two 7-pounder guns Royal Artillery, and a few locally raised Colonial troops. The force was guided by Mr. Ross, Native Commissioner of the District, who knew the ground. Not knowing the habits of the Mashonas, who, as it turned out, never made massed attacks in the open as did the Zulus and Sudanese, Alderson moved in a formation from which he could quickly form square. It was a fine moonlight night. After some anxious moments when Mr. Ross, miscalculating the distance, thought that they were farther from the kraal than they really were, and that they would not arrive within striking distance before daylight, the force arrived about a mile to the south-west of the kraal. It was still too dark to see anything of the enemy's position, but Alderson, from Ross's description of the ground, decided to divide his force and made two converging attacks from the south and north-west. He sent Jenner with the Rifle Company Mounted Infantry and forty Colonials to the south side, with orders to attack as soon as the guns opened, and himself with the rest of his force moved to a point about 800 yards north-west of the kraal.

The garrison, who did not expect to be attacked before midday—night marches on the part of the enemy not being calculated for in their school of military thought—were fairly caught napping. They were making a night of it, tom-tomming, singing, gorging looted beef, and swilling Kaffir beer. At 5.30 a.m., just as it was getting light, the guns opened. The first shot was a sighter at a mark on a rock face; the second set fire to some huts on the top of the hill.

The defences consisted of a few outlying piquets in sangars which lay between the points of assembly of the two halves of Alderson's force, and a stone wall enclosing the kraal where it was not protected by perpendicular rocks. The piquets ran in at the first shot, but the wall was immediately manned, and a hot but badly aimed fire was opened on our men as they advanced. The two attacks worked their way forward, rushing from cover to cover, till at about 7.30 they had two hundred yards of open ground between them and the wall. At this time, though a considerable number of the garrison had been seen hurriedly departing up a valley to the east, the wall was still stoutly held. It was in itself no great obstacle, and the two attacks fixing bayonets and rushing it simultaneously were too much for the Mashonas. Only one man remained to be bayonetted, the rest going to ground in the caves in haste, though their parting shots caused most of the casualties of the day.

It would have been a useless sacrifice of life to follow the enemy into the caves and there was no means of bolting them. There was nothing therefore to be done but burn the kraal, drive off the captured cattle, which had been rounded up close by, the surprise not having given the Mashonas time to drive them off into the hills, and march back to camp.

Makoni himself, who was the biggest chief in Mashonaland, had escaped, but his kraal had been destroyed, he had lost some 200 men, 355 head of cattle, and 210 goats and sheep, while only some 50 head got away. Alderson's losses were: killed, 1 Officer (Captain A. E. Haynes, R.E.) and 2 Other Ranks; wounded, 4 Other Ranks.

The same process was repeated all over the country within a fifty-mile radius of Salisbury till, early in November, most of the Mashonas had had enough of it, and it was considered that some 600 newly raised Mashonaland Police would be able to take care of those who were still in rebellion. The services of the Imperial troops were therefore dispensed with, fortunately before the rainy season began, which is unhealthy for man and horse, and the Mounted Infantry began their return journey to Beira early in December.

The losses in action during the campaign in the half company found by our Regiment had been: killed, 1 Rifleman; wounded, 1 Officer (Lieutenant C. L. E. Eustace), and 5 Other Ranks.

This campaign was the first in which Mounted Infantry trained in the Mounted Infantry School at Aldershot, founded in 1888 by Major Hutton, had taken part, and they fully justified its existence.

Colonel Baden-Powell, in his book ' The Campaign in Matabeleland, 1896,' says : ' The Mounted Infantry Corps from Aldershot was probably the finest of its kind that had ever taken the field. It was employed entirely in Mashonaland, where its doings in the field drew unqualified praise from Colonials and Dutch alike.'

South African War, 1899—1902

In the small wars of the last quarter of the nineteenth century South Africa had seen more of the use of Mounted Infantry than any other theatre, and in the war of 1899—1902 it reached its culminating point. The longer the war lasted, the more did it become one of mounted troops, to supply the demand for which the formation of Mounted Infantry units was the most obvious and quickest method.

At the time of the outbreak of the war, the Infantry Battalions of the permanent garrison had, most of them, a company of Mounted Infantry. The Mounted Infantry Company of our 1st Battalion was with Battalion Headquarters and was commanded by Captain E. Northey, a detachment under Lieutenant V. H. S. Scratchley being at Etshowe (Zululand). A Company from the 2nd Battalion joined Hildyard's Brigade of Buller's Force in Natal.

The 1st Battalion Company at Dundee took part in the Battle of Talana Hill, one section under Lieutenant F. M. Crum, who was badly wounded, having the misfortune to be involved in the erratic manœuvres of Lieut.-Colonel Möller, 18th Hussars, which ended in their being made prisoners of war.

A Battalion of Mounted Infantry was attached to each of the two Cavalry Brigades of the Expeditionary Force. To one of these the 4th Battalion contributed a Section under Captain E. J. Dewar, who was killed in action.

For the next two years the 4th Battalion furnished a constant stream of drafts for the Mounted Infantry, to which they must have contributed as much as any battalion in the British Army.

The numbers of Mounted Infantry found by our Regiment went on increasing till we attained the unique honour of being the only Regiment in the Army to find a complete Battalion of Mounted Infantry. This Battalion was numbered the 25th Mounted Infantry and was formed in September 1901.

It would be impossible, in reasonable compass, to follow the careers of our various Mounted Infantry Companies during two and a half years' fighting, or even that of this one Battalion, but an account of their great fight at Bakenlaagte cannot be omitted and must be taken as an example of their services throughout the war.

In September and October 1901, of the various columns which had been sweeping the Eastern Transvaal, that commanded by Colonel G. E. Benson, R.A., had caused the Boers most annoyance. Louis Botha, just returned from an unsuccessful attempt to raid Natal, determined to suppress it. His opportunity came when, towards the end of October, owing to other neighbouring columns having been withdrawn to refit, Benson was temporarily isolated.

These columns, which were engaged in trying to end the guerrilla war by rounding up the Boers still in the field, were generally composed of a mounted force with a proportion of Field Artillery, and, to enable them to keep the field, were accompanied by a train of ox-drawn or mule-drawn wagons with an Infantry escort; this train acted as a movable supply depot round which the mounted force could act against their extremely mobile enemy.

On October 20 Benson set out from Middelburg on the railway with the 3rd Mounted Infantry (501) men under Major Anley, Essex Regiment; 25th Mounted Infantry (462), under Captain Eustace, K.R.R.C.; 2nd Scottish Horse (434), under Major F. D. Murray, Black Watch; 2nd Buffs, 6 Companies (650), under Major Dauglish;

four guns 84th Battery R.F.A. and two pom-poms. The train consisted of 350 vehicles, of which 120 were ox-wagons. After rounding up a certain number of prisoners in the country between Middelburg and Bethel, Benson, aware of his own isolation and seeing signs of a concentration against him, decided to retire to Brugspruit on the railway.

On the 29th he laagered at Zwakfontein, thirty-five miles from Brugspruit.

At 4.30 a.m. on the 30th, on a misty morning, the ox-wagon convoy started under the escort of two companies 25th Mounted Infantry, one and a half companies of the Buffs, and two guns. The rest of the column followed an hour later. The advance and flank guards of the main column were formed by the 25th and 3rd Mounted Infantry; three and a half companies of the Buffs, the Scottish Horse, and two guns accompanied the convoy of transport other than ox-drawn; while the rearguard was made up of 180 men of the 3rd Mounted Infantry (K.O.Y.L.I., Dublin Fusiliers, and Loyal North Lancashire detachments), a company of the Buffs, and one pom-pom.

No sooner was the column under way than the Boers began to press the rearguard energetically, at the same time harassing the flanks and front. The country was bare, giving no cover except for a few ant-heaps, but sufficiently undulating to allow large bodies to move within a distance of a mile or so, completely unseen. Recent rain had made the going very heavy, the transport soon began to straggle, and by 9 a.m. the ox-wagon convoy had been so delayed in crossing a spruit that the two columns became one. From this hour till about 1 p.m. Major Anley (Essex Regiment), commanding 3rd Mounted Infantry, fought a skilful and successful rearguard action. The North Lancashire Company of the 3rd

Mounted Infantry formed the rear screen, with detachments of the Dublin Fusilier Company wide on the flanks. The K.O.Y.L.I. Company with the pom-pom were in support a thousand yards nearer the column. The Company of the Buffs marched with the tail of the column. A cold, driving rain came on from the south, helping the attackers to get closer unseen. Rifle and pom-pom fire, however, still kept them at a respectful range.

About 1 p.m. the rearguard halted to wait for two wagons which had stuck. At the same time the pressure on the rearguard by the enemy, who had an hour before been reinforced by Botha in person, became very much stronger. Anley therefore abandoned the wagons and ordered the retirement to continue.

As the rear screen reached the ridge marked A on Plate 20, the pom-pom jammed and was sent on into camp under a small escort, the rest of the K.O.Y.L.I. Company joining the rear screen.

Anley had already reported that the situation was getting serious, and on Ridge A he was joined by Benson himself, who brought with him a reinforcement of two squadrons of Scottish force. Benson arrived with the idea of rescuing the two wagons—he had so far never lost a wagon—but he quickly saw that it was not only the wagons but his whole rearguard that was imperilled. He therefore ordered the rearguard to withdraw to the ridge, afterwards known as Gun Hill, which formed a part of the line of defence he was taking up to cover his convoy which was parking at Nooitgedacht Farm. The rest of the line was already occupied as shown on Plate 20, chiefly by the 25th Mounted Infantry. Two guns and twenty men of the 25th Mounted Infantry under Sergeant Ashfield, detached from Captain Crum's Company, were already on Gun Hill.

When the order to retire from Ridge A was given, the

Infantry of the rearguard, a company of the Buffs (Lieutenant Greatwood), which had been marching at the rear of the transport but had been delayed by the broken-down wagons, had not yet got half-way to Gun Hill, while 30 men under Lieutenant Lynch were still short of but nearer Gun Hill.

On the order being given, the Scottish Horse and Mounted Infantry began to retire on Gun Hill, leaving a section apiece on Ridge A to cover their withdrawal.

This was the moment that Botha had chosen for his great stroke. Concealed by folds of the ground, he had collected some eight or nine hundred men opposite Ridge A, and these he ordered to charge.

Benson with the Scottish Horse and K.O.Y.L.I. Company, 3rd Mounted Infantry, made for Gun Hill; Anley with the North Lancashire Company for a ridge nearly a mile farther east. The Boers came on in one line, all within reach, joining in on the right and left, till they covered such a wide front as to overlap Anley's detachment on the east and Crum's on the west; but the weight of the attack was on Gun Hill.

On reaching Gun Hill the Scottish Horse and K.O.Y.L.I. quickly got into line to right and left of Sergeant Ashfield's party. They had no time to spare. The two detachments of the Buffs had no chance and were quickly overpowered. Their field of fire had been masked by the covering section left on Ridge A, who were now galloping in with the Boers right on their tails. The Boers came on till they reached dead ground in front of Gun Hill, when they dismounted and attacked on foot.

Then ensued the fiercest bit of fighting of the whole war. It was a fire fight at very close range, with the British hopelessly outnumbered. The guns very quickly lost every man of the detachment, killed or wounded.

In twenty-five minutes it was all over and the Boers were in possession of Gun Hill. The only possible reinforcement, two weak companies of the Buffs who turned back when close to camp, could not get up in time, though they lost 33 men in their advance, and their commander,

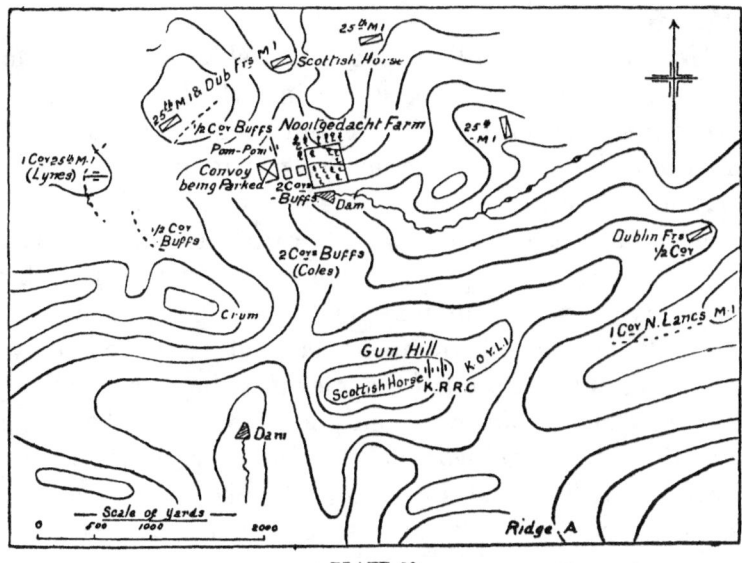

PLATE 20.

ACTION NEAR BAKENLAAGTE, OCTOBER 30, 1901.

Major Eales, who rode on ahead, was killed as he reached the firing-line. Benson himself was mortally wounded. Of 171 defenders of the hill only 17 were untouched. Of Sergeant Ashley's detachment of 20, 17 were killed or wounded, the 3 untouched being horse-holders. But the Boers got no farther.

They had lost nearly a hundred of their best men, and any attempt to advance down the far side of the hill was quickly stopped by artillery and rifle fire. Benson's last order, sent off after the Boers had captured the position, was to the guns in camp to shell the ridge, which they did so effectually as to drive the captors off it.

It was only after dark that they managed to withdraw the captured guns.

Meanwhile Crum's detachment had gallantly held its own and retained its position till he was ordered to withdraw after dark.

He held on to a hill with a saucer-shaped top, and for hours held off a vastly superior enemy who kept him under a constant and accurate rifle fire, but could never get nearer him than 250 yards. The enemy might have rushed his position at any time, but so well was his weakness concealed and so accurate was the fire of his Riflemen that the Boers were not equal to facing the certain losses they must have incurred in making Crum's position another Gun Hill!. Crum's detachment had not only the enemy's fire to contend with, but for some time they were severely shelled by one of our own pom-poms from near the laager. Rain and mist combined with the similarity of dress of the combatants, both sides wearing slouched hats and the Boers wearing cavalry cloaks, had made it extremely difficult to distinguish friend from foe throughout the day.

Lynes to the north of Crum and Anley to the east of Gun Hill had both been heavily attacked.

Botha, some of whose men had ridden sixty miles in twenty-four hours to take part in the attack, made preparations to rush the camp during the night, but either he changed his mind or else found his men had had enough, and he withdrew before dawn. Colonel Woolls-Sampson, who succeeded to the command on the death of Benson, dug himself in and remained unmolested till relieved two days later by several columns which had been sent to his rescue.

Somaliland

The writer, not long ago, heard the following story told, to illustrate the manner of the growth of the British Empire, by a speaker who replied at a public dinner to the toast of 'The Dominions Overseas.'

'A party of commercial travellers were sitting round after dinner, and, getting short of subjects for conversation, began comparing notes as to the circumstances in which they had first met their respective wives.

'One depressed-looking little man was sitting by himself, taking no part in the conversation, and when the others had all recounted their experiences, one of them turned to him and said : " And how did you first meet your wife, sir ? " " Well, y-you s-see, I d-didn't exactly m-meet her ; she o-o-o-overtook me." '

It was much in this way that the British Empire gradually found itself, without malice prepense, responsible for the protection of the tribes dwelling near the coast of that useless, troublesome, and extensive tract of semi-desert now known as British Somaliland.

It came as a legacy from the then defunct Egyptian sovereignty of the Sudan, and in February 1885 a British Protectorate was proclaimed over a part of the Somali coast. Up till 1898 the administration was under the Government of India and the small garrison was found from Aden ; then the Foreign Office took over from the Indian Government.

Except for a few very minor punitive expeditions, all went quietly till towards the end of 1900 ; but meanwhile a disturber of the peace had arisen in the shape of one Mahommed-bin-Abdullah Hassan (commonly known as the Mullah), who set himself up as a holy man, had gradually acquired a considerable following, and evidently aimed at combining the whole country against the Infidel interlopers.

Two expeditions, with some slight co-operation by the Abyssinians, were sent against the Mullah in 1901 and 1902 which inflicted very heavy losses on him and relieved him of many more camels, sheep, cattle, and horses than he had previously looted; but the withdrawal of the expeditionary force, or even the cessation of active operations, was both times soon followed by a renewal of his activities. In these two expeditions the troops employed were mostly locally raised.

On October 6, 1902, Captain and local Lieut.-Colonel E. J. E. Swayne, who commanded the expedition, fought a severe action against the Mullah in which, though he inflicted severe losses on the enemy, he had a very narrow escape, owing to a panic among his Somali troops, of having his whole force cut up. Though the Mullah had been hard hit, had lost all the camels he had looted from friendly tribes, and had been obliged to retire to recuperate in Italian territory, Colonel Swayne was obliged to report that he could not place sufficient reliance on his troops to continue offensive operations.

It was therefore decided largely to increase the force, the command being given to Brigadier-General W. H. Manning, Inspector-General of the King's African Rifles. Permission was obtained for the use of a base and for carrying on operations in Italian territory.

Among the reinforcements sent, there went from South Africa a company of Boer Mounted Infantry and a company of British Mounted Infantry, which latter was drawn entirely from our Regiment and was commanded by Captain G. C. Shakerley, his subalterns being Lieutenants H. H. R. White, G. J. Acland-Troyte, G. H. Barnett, and G. C. Kelly. Lieutenants T. G.

Dalby and H. W. M. Watson also took part in the campaign.

The war in Somaliland was, as far as the enemy was concerned, 'a one-man show.' If the Mullah could be captured or killed, the problem would be solved. Failing the achievement of this desirable object, the only alternative was to destroy his prestige, on which alone his power as a leader of fanatics rested. As soon as he sank from a leader of armies which believed him to be invincible to a hunted fugitive, nine-tenths of his followers would leave him, if they did not go over to the winning side.

The first of these objects was very difficult of attainment, owing to the enemy's extreme mobility. The second was a certainty if only he could be brought to battle. His superiority in mobility only applied to his armed forces. To keep these in the field he was dependent on large herds of camels, cattle, and sheep, whose rate of progress was very much slower. Deprived of these, his forces would dissolve. The only chance of bringing him to battle was to make him fight in their defence. If he fought, he would be beaten, and the bubble of his invincibility would be burst. If he did not fight, his flocks and herds, his only source of supply, would be lost, his forces would have to scatter, his prestige would be gone, and his followers would have to submit or starve. Operations against him on these lines could only be carried out with any hope of success during the dry season.

During the wet season the presence of rain-water pools would enable him to wander at will over this vast country, to scatter in every direction when pressed, and to concentrate against any point in our long line of communications which he might find himself strong enough to attack. In the dry season water is only obtainable at wells, often several days' march apart, and all movements are confined to well-defined routes.

The British plan of campaign was to hold a certain number of these watering-places, and then by the use of mobile columns force the Mullah either to fight in defence of his flocks and herds or leave them behind him—a process which, if continued long enough, must lead to his final extinction as a source of trouble to the Government.

The next campaign during the first half of 1903 only just failed of success, the Mullah having had a narrow escape when the rains began, which gave too much scope to his movements for there to be any hope of rounding him up before the next dry season.

Considerable reinforcements were now dispatched from India, and with them Major-General Sir C. C. Egerton,[1] a distinguished Indian Frontier soldier, came to take over command.

The next campaign was successful in so far that the Mullah, at the end of it, though still alive and free, was a fugitive and almost without a following, and nothing more was heard of him for some years.

General Egerton's 'crowning mercy,' from which the Mullah never recovered, was the action fought at Jidbali on January 10, 1904; where, having marked down the enemy's main force of from 6,000 to 8,000 men, and having concentrated a force of two brigades and over 1,000 mounted troops under Lieut.-Colonel Kenna, V.C., of which our Mounted Infantry Company formed a part—about 4,000 of all arms—within striking distance, Egerton made an early-morning march followed by a daylight attack which scattered the Mullah's force to the winds. The enemy's losses were very heavy; 668 bodies were counted in or near his position, and it was estimated that

[1] Field-Marshal Sir C. C. Egerton, G.C.B., D.S.O.

the mounted troops inflicted as many more casualties in the pursuit which Kenna carried on with his usual vigour for eighteen miles, till ammunition and horses were exhausted. The mounted troops had already taken a prominent part in the action by making a wide turning movement, followed by an effective flank attack.

The British lost 3 Officers killed and 9 wounded out of a total of 27 killed and 37 wounded of all ranks. Among the wounded (both severely) were Captain G. C. Shakerley, K.R.R.C., commanding No. 1 Corps, Mounted Infantry, and Lieutenant H. H. R. White, K.R.R.C., his Adjutant.

The remarks of Lieut.-Colonel P. A. Kenna,[1] V.C., D.S.O., commanding the Mounted Troops, on the equipment, organisation, training, etc., of Mounted Infantry ['Official History of the Operations in Somaliland, 1901–4,' Vol. II], though now, alas! only of academic interest, are well worth reading by students of military archæology. He particularly recommends, for the nether man, trousers with a buckle and strap at the knee, cut loose above the knee—in fact, easy Jodhpores—these articles when smartly made and without knee-buckles being too difficult of ingress and egress to be serviceable.

He complains that in this campaign Mounted Infantry entirely superseded Cavalry, though the whole of the British and Indian Cavalry was at the time available. The fact was that after the South African War the *arme blanche* was under something of a cloud, and it was only in the Great War in one or two theatres that it came into its own again.

In this campaign the weak spot in Mounted Infantry, the want of a hand-to-hand weapon for use in pursuit, was very much felt. Revolvers were tried, but were

---

[1] Brigadier-General P. A. Kenna, V.C., D.S.O., killed in action on the Gallipoli Peninsula, 1915.

found to be a greater source of danger to friends than to the enemy.

Most of the Mounted Infantry units sent to Somaliland were, in Colonel Kenna's opinion, insufficiently trained on arrival, though fortunately most of them got three months' training between landing and taking the field. He also deprecates the practice of sending out composite companies made up of detachments from different corps.

He gives the K.R.R.C. Company as an example of the advantage of an unmixed company which, coming straight from South Africa, was ready to take the field immediately on arrival in Somaliland.

He concludes his remarks by saying :—

'In spite of the many disadvantages mentioned, and which were chiefly in evidence when these Mounted Infantry landed, a high state of efficiency was eventually attained by them. In proof of this I may quote a few examples :—

'On April 18, 1903, every available man of British, Burgher (Boer), and Indian Mounted Infantry marched from Galadi to Gumbur, 48 miles through bush, in 12 hours, without a man or horse falling out ; no water *en route*, and intense heat during the last four or five hours.

'Between 4 p.m. 17th and 9 a.m. 19th December, 1903, 200 British and Indian Mounted Infantry, with Bikanirs (Camel Corps) and 200 Tribal Horse, marched from Badwein to Jidbali, 38 miles, engaged the enemy for 5 hours at the latter place, and then returned to Badwein ; the distance covered, apart from reconnoitring and 5 hours' desultory fighting, was 76 miles in 41 hours, without any water.

'Between 6 p.m. April 30, and 8 a.m. May 2, 1904, some 250 British and Indian Mounted Infantry, with 150 Bikanirs and 40 irregular (Somali) horsemen, marched from Biliyu to Kheman and back to Biliyu, thus covering 100 miles of waterless country in 38 hours on one gallon of water per man and none for horses. About one-third of these men and horses had done 60 miles in the two previous nights, and thus covered 160 miles in 3 days 14 hours. Not one of these horses was in more than moderate condition, having been in the field from six to twelve months.'

In 1909 the Mullah was again raiding the tribes in the British Protectorate. This time the British Government came to the conclusion that campaigns in the interior were costly and ineffective, that our occupation of isolated posts did not afford the friendly tribes the protection which was the only *raison d'être* of those posts, and that we might as well let the Mullah have the country, as he seemed to want it, and confine our administration to the coast towns.

APPENDIX I

PORTRAITS

IN this volume very little has been mentioned of the subjects of the four portraits which it contains, except incidentally of Buller as a Brigadier-General in the Sudan and as Commander-in-Chief in Natal. As regards the first three, the reason for this omission is that all their active service, except as very junior officers, was done away from the Regiment. Nevertheless no history of the Regiment for the last quarter of the nineteenth century and first few years of the twentieth would be complete without some account of them. The first three stand out as the most distinguished figures which our Regiment produced during that period. Colonel H. D. Browne was almost unknown, professionally, outside the Regiment and was so unfortunate as never to see a shot fired on active service. In the seventies, eighties, and nineties of the last century, especially in the two former decades, our Regiment cannot be said to have been fortunate in the average calibre of its Commanding Officers. A former Prime Minister is reported to have said that of his two Secretaries of State for War, one could never have passed into the Army, and the other, if he had, would certainly have been the victim of a ragging case. One often wonders, of many Commanding Officers of those days, how they ever got into the Army and, having got there, how they ever remained. The really first-rate Commanding Officers of that period could be counted on the fingers of one hand. It would take more than two hands to enumerate the thoroughly incompetent ones. In that small group of great Commanding Officers, since Hawley, I doubt if anyone who knew Donald Browne would hesitate to place him at the top of the list.

The following brief sketches of the careers of these four are adapted from longer articles which have appeared from time to time in our *Chronicle*.

Redvers Buller was born on December 7, 1839, and joined the Rifle Depot at Winchester in July 1858. Next year he joined the 2nd Battalion at Benares, and with it sailed for

China in February 1860. He took part in the expedition to Pekin and returned to England with the Battalion in February 1862. In December of the same year, on promotion to Lieutenant, he joined the 4th Battalion under Hawley at Quebec. So far he had been chiefly known for his argumentative nature, great personal strength, and fondness for sport. He had not shown any particular keenness for his profession. No one could serve long under Hawley without soon putting soldiering before every other interest. Seven years under that great soldier, including some months as his Acting Adjutant, entirely changed Buller's view of life. The 4th Battalion returned to England in the summer of 1869, but in May 1870 Buller was posted as a Captain to the 1st Battalion, which was just starting on the Red River Expedition. There he attracted the favourable notice of the leader of the expedition, Colonel Wolseley. He left his Battalion to join the Staff College in the end of 1871, and never did regimental duty again with the Regiment.

Before he had completed his course at the Staff College he was one of the band of remarkably able men which Wolseley took out with him to the Ashanti Expedition. There he was at the head of Wolseley's Intelligence Department. That General's appreciation of his subordinate may be given in his own words. 'First and foremost among them as one whose stern determination of character nothing could ruffle, whose resource in difficulty was not surpassed by anyone I ever knew, was Redvers Buller. Endowed with a mind fruitful in expedients, he inspired general confidence, and thoroughly deserved it. Had a thunder-bolt burst at his feet he would have merely brushed from his Rifle jacket the earth it had thrown upon him, without any break in the sentence he happened to be uttering at the moment.' Buller got his brevet Majority for this campaign.

After Ashanti, Buller did a tour of duty as D.A.A.G. at the War Office. Early in 1878 he went to South Africa for special duty under General Thesiger, better known as Lord Chelmsford. After a month or two on the Staff he was appointed to the command of the Frontier Light Horse. He soon had this very mixed crew in such good order that they would 'eat out of his hand.' By the end of the campaign he was as famous throughout South Africa for his military skill as for his absolute fearlessness.

No sooner were the Kaffirs accounted for than the Zulu War broke out. In this war Buller added to his reputation, and for his gallantry at Inhlobana Mountain was awarded the Victoria Cross ; by the end of it he was a full Colonel, A.D.C. to the Queen, and was looked upon as one of the coming men.

Another tour of Staff duty at home followed, but Buller was soon back in South Africa, only to arrive after the armistice which followed Majuba.

His services in Egypt, 1882, the Eastern Sudan, 1884, and the Nile Expedition, 1885, have already been referred to in this work and need not be repeated, but his services in those campaigns, especially his skilful withdrawal of the Desert Column from Metammeh to Korti, placed him in the front rank and marked him as the obvious successor to Lord Wolseley as Adjutant-General, the office which in those days corresponded most nearly to that of C.I.G.S.

For about a year in 1886–7 Buller had a spell of civil employment in Ireland, firstly in the reorganisation of the Constabulary, in which he was in his right place and eminently successful ; secondly as Under-Secretary for Ireland, in which he was less so, not from any failing on his part, but that, though a convinced Unionist, his sense of justice and shrewd common sense caused him to see that there was a good deal to be said on the tenant's side in the land question ; hence he could not hope to please either political party.

From October 1887 to October 1890 Buller was Quartermaster-General, his great achievement in that office being the reorganisation of the Army Service Corps. In October 1890 he succeeded Lord Wolseley as Adjutant-General. On the retirement of the Duke of Cambridge, Buller, but for his loyalty to his old chief, might have been Commander-in-Chief, but the story is too long to tell here.

A Major-General in 1884, he became Lieut.-General in 1891. His term as Adjutant-General expired in 1899. In this office he had shown the same ability that he had hitherto displayed in everything he had undertaken. During his régime the Army made a marked advance in its training, though the system under which he laboured, without a properly organised General Staff, prevented his work from having its full effect.

After a year in command at Aldershot, he embarked for the South African War. He was in his sixtieth year, and after some fifteen years on an office stool he was not the man he had been. He himself accepted the command with reluctance. His most ardent admirers cannot say that in the campaign on the Tugela he showed his old qualities of self-reliance and decision. True, his task was an impossible one, and the succession of disasters at the beginning of the war on all the fronts was enough to shake any ordinary man, but he was no ordinary man, and we may say with confidence that they would not have shaken the man of fifteen years before.

After the relief of Ladysmith and the ensuing pause in the operations he came out like a giant refreshed, and his campaign in Northern Natal was conducted more in the way that would have been expected of him ; but his work was over, and shortly after his junction with Lord Roberts his force was broken up and he came home to resume his command at Aldershot. He did not retain it long, and soon retired to spend the few remaining years of his life on his estate at Downes in Devonshire.

He died in 1908. To the end he kept up his interest in his old Regiment. He inaugurated our Veterans' Association, and attended the first dinner in 1907 and that of the following year.

How great a soldier Redvers Buller was is a question which can never now be answered. He was one of those unlucky ones who did not get his great chance till some of his powers had gone from him. Of all the attributes which go to make a great commander he had one in the fullest measure which he never lost, one which has not been given to all great commanders, and that is the unstinted devotion of all who served under him, and more especially of the men in the ranks.

Francis Grenfell was born on April 29, 1841. He was gazetted as an Ensign to the 60th Rifles in August 1859, and after a few months at the Depot joined the 1st Battalion on its return home after the Mutiny. He was a young man of varied tastes—played the violin, was a clever caricaturist, a good boxer, and a devoted patron of the old-time prize-ring. Being essentially a *bon camarade*, he very soon gained popularity among his brother Officers. Promotion in the Regiment was then very slow and he did not get his promotion to Captain till October 1871. Soldiering at that time had no great attraction for him and he was on the point of retiring when he was invited to accompany General Sir A. Cunyngehame to South Africa as A.D.C.

He was just in time to withdraw his application for retirement, which had already gone in, and this proved the turning-point in his career, which from then on was one continued success.

For his services in the Kaffir War of 1878 Grenfell was mentioned in dispatches and received a brevet Majority. Both in that and in the Zulu War which followed it he served as D.A.A.G. at Headquarters, and at the end of the latter campaign became a brevet Lieut.-Colonel.

Having returned to England meanwhile, he was again in South Africa in 1881 as A.Q.M.G. to Sir Evelyn Wood, but only after the armistice which followed Majuba.

He served under Sir Garnet Wolseley in Egypt in 1882, being rewarded with the appointment of A.D.C. to the Queen, carrying with it the brevet rank of Colonel. In the Nile Expedition of 1884-5 he was employed on the line of communication. In 1886, after commanding a Division of the Egyptian Frontier Field Force at Sir Frederick Stephenson's fight at Ginnis in December 1885, he received the K.C.B.

In April 1886 he succeeded Sir Evelyn Wood as Sirdar of the Egyptian Army. While holding this command he fought the battle of Toski against the Dervish invaders on the Nile frontier and completely defeated them. This was in 1889, and the same year he was promoted Major-General.

Grenfell was Commander-in-Chief in Egypt during the reconquest of the Sudan under Kitchener, his successor as Sirdar.

In 1899 he went to Malta as Governor. Affairs at the time in that island were in a disturbed condition owing to racial and religious agitation. Grenfell with his combination of firmness, tact, and sound common sense was the very man that was required. His years of governorship in Malta were probably the most valuable of his career. When the South African War broke out, Buller asked that his old comrade-in-arms should accompany him as second in command, but he could not be spared. In 1902 he was raised to the Peerage as Baron Grenfell.

From 1904 to 1907 Grenfell commanded the forces in Ireland, which was his last active appointment, but in 1908 he was promoted to the rank of Field-Marshal. The last years of his life were devoted to his duties in the House of Lords, to the care of the interests of the Regiment as senior Colonel Commandant, to the Riflemen's Aid Society, and most of all to the Church Lads' Brigade. He died in 1925.

Lord Grenfell's career was one of unbroken success. He may not have been a man of the highest abilities, but whatever he did he did well. Probably he had not the stimulus either of personal ambition or consuming energy—his greatness may have been somewhat thrust upon him—but his exceptional tact and good temper, his knowledge of the world, and above all his vast common sense carried him through where many more brilliant men would have failed. He was witty in conversation, had great personal charm, and was regarded with the same respect and affection outside the Regiment as in it.

'Curly' Hutton—no one knew him by any other name—was born on December 6, 1848, and joined the 4th Battalion in 1867, so having the privilege of serving for his first six years under Hawley. He was Adjutant of the Battalion from 1874 to 1877, and was on the point of beginning his course at the Staff College when he was ordered out to Zululand with the 3rd Battalion. There he served as A.D.C. to Major-General Crealock, was present at the action at Ginginhlovo and was mentioned in dispatches. Returning to the Staff College at the end of the war, he was back again with Barrow's Mounted Infantry in 1881, but not in time for any fighting. He then completed his course at the Staff College and was for a short time employed in the Intelligence Department at the War Office. In 1882 he went out to Egypt as A.D.C. to Sir Archibald Alison, and, as has been already related, raised a corps of Mounted Infantry the day after landing at Alexandria, which did all the mounted duties for the force pending the arrival of the Regular Cavalry. Having resumed his duties as A.D.C., he had his horse shot under him at Tel-el-Kebir, was mentioned in dispatches and promoted to brevet Major.

In the 1884-5 campaign he served on the Staff and raised a battalion of Mounted Infantry, but a breakdown in health prevented him from getting to the front. After a last spell of regimental duty he was appointed D.A.A.G. at Aldershot in 1887, which post he held till 1892. One man's work was never enough for Curly, and in 1888 he started the Mounted Infantry School. It was due to him more than to any other man that Mounted Infantry became a recognised branch of the Army and so remained for the next twenty years.

In 1892 he was appointed A.D.C. to Queen Victoria, with the brevet rank of Colonel.

In 1893 he went to Australia to command and reorganise the local forces in New South Wales. Returning in 1897, after a short spell on the Staff in Ireland, he went to Canada on a similar errand to that in New South Wales. In the South African War he achieved the desire of his heart in commanding a force of some 7,000 Mounted Infantry, Regulars and Colonials, in Lord Roberts's advance on Pretoria and his further advance along the Delagoa Bay Railway. He afterwards held an independent command in the Eastern Transvaal. For these services he was promoted Major-General in December 1901 and received the K.C.M.G.

In January 1902 he was back in Australia as the first Commandant of the Commonwealth Military Forces. Returning home in the end of 1904, he commanded the temporarily mobilised 3rd Division in the summer of 1906. He was promoted Lieutenant-General in 1907 and retired the following year. In 1912 he received the K.C.B. In the Great War he organised and for a few months commanded the 21st Division in the New Army, but had to resign on account of ill-health.

Of Curly Hutton's two great works, the raising, organising, training, and commanding of Mounted Infantry and the reorganisation of our Colonial Forces in Australia and Canada, the first had become ancient history before the Great War, though it may fairly be said that the Army still benefited by the wider view of war which his training had imparted to so many Infantry Officers. His work in the Dominions bore more direct fruit, and it was largely due to the seed that he had sown that the prophecy which he made at a public dinner at Melbourne shortly before he left Australia had such a fulfilment. 'I venture to guarantee,' he had said, 'that if Australia takes part in a great Imperial conflict, which may threaten the existence of the Empire, your contingent will not be unworthy of the past traditions of the best forces of the British Empire.'

The Australians themselves have ever gratefully acknowledged the work that he did for them. In a speech in the House of Representatives of the Commonwealth of Australia, delivered on August 7, 1923, Mr. Borden, in reporting to the

House the death of General Hutton, said : ' It is to him that Australia is indebted for the organisation and the system of training which enabled her to put the Australian Imperial Force into the field at the beginning of the late war.' At a memorial service held in Sydney in August 1923, Archbishop Wright described him as ' one to whom Australia owes a debt that can never be forgotten,' and went on to say : ' When we to-day thank God for the glorious deeds of arms by which the sons of Australia helped to save the Empire, it is our duty and privilege to offer our thanks to God for the whole-hearted devoted service of Sir Edward Hutton that made this record possible.'

Curly Hutton could never be idle, and the last few years of his life had innumerable interests and occupations, not the least of which were the duties of Colonel Commandant in the Regiment and of Vice-Chairman of the Riflemen's Aid Society. He was chiefly, one may say entirely, responsible for the move of the Headquarters of the Society from Winchester to London, which has so greatly increased its usefulness. He died in August 1923. He was certainly a very remarkable character. His energy was superhuman. His great kindness of heart and loyalty to those who had ever worked for him made him beloved by his subordinates. His intolerance of any opinion which did not fit in with his own, which he was most persistent in supporting, must have made him difficult both as a colleague and as a subordinate, but one inevitably found that in all parts of the Empire those who had the worst official quarrels with him always retained a warm corner for him in their hearts.

Henry Donald Browne was born on August 9, 1843, and was gazetted to the 60th Rifles as an Ensign on June 16, 1863.

He joined the 4th Battalion in Canada and served in it till he was promoted to be Captain on March 27, 1874. He was Adjutant of the Battalion from May 17, 1871, till his promotion. That he had been Hawley's Adjutant was, in after-life, the thing of all others of which he was proud. Promoted into the 1st Battalion, he served in it as a Captain and Major till he got command of the 3rd Battalion at Gibraltar on April 16, 1890. On completion of his four years in command he went on half-pay, but was almost immediately brought back to the command of the Rifle Depot, which he held till May 1899, when he retired.

His nearest approach to active service was when in 1881 he took out a draft to the 3rd Battalion in Natal, only to arrive when the fighting was over. For some time he acted as A.D.C. to his old 4th Battalion comrade, Redvers Buller. He was only a few years junior to his General in the Regiment and they had always been the greatest friends. In Canada the 4th Battalion had had a pack of hounds which Donald Browne hunted, while Buller was one of his Whips. Never having had very good health, he did not live many years after his retirement and died on January 8, 1907. An uneventful career; but there were only two elements wanting to take Donald Browne to the top of his profession—luck and good health. Like his master, Hawley, he was a thinking soldier, in advance of his age. His magnetic personality and thorough knowledge of his profession made him the outstanding figure in his Battalion. His opinion on any subject under discussion was accepted by his brother Officers without demur.

Remarkably good-looking, he was always perfectly turned out. With a beautiful seat on a horse, he was always well mounted. He had some considerable knowledge of art and was himself a clever caricaturist. His kindliness and charm were the same to the last-joined subaltern as to his equals in rank, but he had a dignity, and when he cared to use it a sternness, which forbade any liberties. To the writer he has always been his ideal of a soldier and a gentleman.

APPENDIX II

As could only be expected of a Rifle Regiment, the K.R.R.C. has always had a reputation for good shooting.

The best evidence for this in old days is Marshal Soult's famous letter of September 1, 1813, given in the second volume of our *Annals*, in which he complains that he will find it difficult to maintain the supply of Officers if the 5th Battalion of the 60th Regiment continue to pick them off.

The 1st Battalion at Delhi had an unpleasant reputation among the mutineers for the accuracy of their shooting.

The 4th Battalion in Hawley's day had the name of being the best shooting battalion in the Army, but owing to varying conditions and perhaps also owing to the uneven way in which markers in different corps felt their responsibilities, the results of the annual course were never looked upon as a very satisfactory test. It was not till the institution of the competitions organised by the Army Rifle Association that the shooting of different units of the Army could be compared by reliable figures.

The remarkable series of successes given below, especially those of the 1st Battalion in the Company Match, will challenge comparison with those of any other Regiment in the Service.

ARMY CHAMPIONSHIP (*At Home*)
Gold Jewel

1892. Sergeant-Bugler J. Williams, 1st K.R.R.C., at Depot.

Silver Jewel

1910. C.S.I.M. F. Walton, 2nd K.R.R.C.
1913. Lieutenant W. A. C. Saunders-Knox-Gore, 1st K.R.R.C.

QUEEN VICTORIA CUP

Winners (Home)	*Winners (Abroad)*
1910. 2nd K.R.R.C.	1909. 2nd K.R.R.C.
1911. 2nd K.R.R.C.	
1912. 2nd K.R.R.C.	

YOUNG SOLDIERS' CUP

Winners

1894. 3rd K.R.R.C.
1895. 3rd K.R.R.C.
1897. 4th K.R.R.C.
1899. 4th K.R.R.C.
1903. 4th K.R.R.C.

THE COMPANY MATCH

Winners (Home)

1898. D Company, 4th K.R.R.C.
1909. F Company, 1st K.R.R.C.
1910. H Company, 1st K.R.R.C.
1911. H Company, 2nd K.R.R.C.
1912. B Company, 1st K.R.R.C.

Winners (Abroad)

1905. D Company, 1st K.R.R.C.
1906. E Company, 1st K.R.R.C.
1907. A Company, 1st K.R.R.C.
1913. A Company, 4th K.R.R.C.

THE ARMY SIXTY CUP

Winner

1910. Lieutenant C. F. Lee, 2nd K.R.R.C.

The following are the placings in the Company Match. The entries in this competition are, of course, enormous—most of the companies in the Army entering a team—and the prize list a long one; all those given below are 'in the money.'

COMPANY MATCH (*Abroad*)

1905

1st Battalion: 1st, 3rd, 9th, 14th.
2nd Battalion: 17th, 53rd.
3rd Battalion: 15th, 27th, 29th, 31st, 62nd, 69th.

1906

1st Battalion: 1st, 2nd, 3rd, 4th, 5th, 6th, 8th, 36th.

MARKSMANSHIP

1907
1st Battalion : 1st, 2nd, 5th, 7th, 8th, 10th, 11th, 17th.

1908
1st Battalion : 3rd, 4th, 7th, 8th, 14th, 24th, 34th, 62nd.

1913
4th Battalion : 1st, 2nd, 16th, 22nd, 37th, 41st.
3rd Battalion : 18th, 24th, 30th, 43rd.

COMPANY MATCH (*Home*)

1909
1st Battalion ; 1st, 2nd, 3rd, 8th.

1910
1st Battalion : 1st, 2nd, 4th, 10th, 29th.

1911
1st Battalion : 4th, 11th, 26th, 32nd, 34th, 43rd, 45th.
2nd Battalion : 1st, 7th, 9th, 16th, 40th, 57th.

1912
1st Battalion : 1st, 3rd, 4th, 8th, 14th, 20th, 35th.
2nd Battalion : 10th, 11th, 25th, 27th, 33rd, 34th.

INDEX

A

Abadie, R.N., 310
Abbasiyeh, 92, 305, 338
Abbotabad, 124, 312
Abdin Barracks, 95
Abdurrahman, Amir, subdues Hazaras, 50 ; accepts throne of Afghanistan, 58 ; takes over his capital, 59
Abu Klea, battle of, 341–344 ; withdrawal to, 346
Abyssinians, 360
Acland-Troyte, G. J., 360
Acton Homes, occupied by Boers, 204
Adams, Captain, Guides Cavalry, leads charge, 132
Adams, Major F. J. S., A.Q.M.G., Kandahar, 63
Addington, H. R., 160
Aden, 1
Afghanistan, Amir of, 314
Afghan War, 39–70
Afridis, some of, help Orakzais, 119
Agadir, 318
Agra, 137, 314, 315
Ahmad Khel, battle of, 52–55
Aios Giorgios, 307
Aios Miron, 307
Akserai, Lepel Griffin meets Abdurrahman at, 58
Aldershot, 1, 2, 111, 113, 114, 147, 155, 166, 309, 322, 327, 351
Alderson, Lieut.-General Sir E. A. H., in Mashonaland, 347–351
Alexandria, 71, 72, 74, 110, 163, 305, 308, 309, 339
Algar, J. S. H., 137, 138, 151, 153
Ali Musjid, British Mission stopped at, 40
Alison, Sir Archibald, commands advanced force, Egyptian Expedition, 73; operations of, at Alexandria, 75–77 ; reaches Ismailia and moves forward, 86 ; at Tel-el-Kebir, 89 ; in Alexandria, 334
Allahabad, 139
Alleman's Nek, taken, 285

Allen, Sergeant, in *Warren Hastings*, 175, 179
Allfrey, H., 7
Allgood, G. G. H., killed at polo, 139
Allgood, W. H. L., 144, 150
Almorah, 314
Aloe Knoll, on Spion Kop, 226
Aman-ul-Mulk, Mehtar of Chitral, 127
Amersfoort, 288, 290
Anderson, W. S., 31, 71, 100
Anley, Major, Essex Regiment, at Bakenlaagte, 353–358
Arabi, rebels against Khedive, 72 ; advances against Kassassin and is beaten, 87, 88 ; defeated at Tel-el-Kebir, 90–92
Archer, F. W., 31, 92, 96
Arghandab Valley, 62–65
Arrowsmith, Rifleman, in *Warren Hastings*, 174, 180
Arzu, action at, 56, 57
Ascot, 112
Ash, 319
Ashanti, expedition to, 165
Ashburnham, Sir Cromer, succeeds to command of 3rd Batt., 16 ; at Ingogo, 20–24 ; to Malta with 3rd Batt., 31 ; in temporary command of 2nd Batt., 38, 42 ; rejoins 3rd Batt. at Cyprus, 71 ; occupies Mallaha Junction, 76 ; A.D.C. to the Queen, 77 ; appointed to command a Brigade, 88 ; commands 4th Brigade at Tel-el-Kebir, 89 ; with 3rd Batt. to Suakim, 100 ; completes period of command, 163
Ashfield, Sergeant, at Bakenlaagte, 356, 357
Assam, 140, 142
Astell, G., 7, 151
Atkinson, G. M., 324
Attock, detachment at, 36
Aylmer, L., 150
Ayub Khan, defeats Burrows at Maiwand, 58 ; at Kandahar, 63, 66

INDEX

B

Baden-Powell, Lord, 351
Badfontein, 293, 303
Badwein, 364
Baio, 124
Bakenlaagte, action near, 353–358
Baker, Fort, occupied, 101
Baker, G. C. B., 7, 31, 100
Baker, Major-General T., in Roberts's march, 60–68
Baker, Valentine, defeat of, 99
Bala Hissar, 48
Balfour, C. E., 160
Balmoral (Transvaal), 302
Banks, H. D., 42, 151
Bapam, action at, 143
Barakao, 329
Barberton, 293, 297
Bareilly, 313, 314
Barnett, G. H., in Somaliland, 360
Barnett, R. C., 182, 195, 196
Barnett, W., 309
Barrow, Major Percy, 337, 338
Barter, Brigadier-General R., 40, 49
Barton, Major-General, at Colenso, 216, 217; at Chieveley, 222; activities of, 241; in Relief of Ladysmith, 246–260
Bastion Hill, capture of, 224
Bayley, Lieutenant, in *Warren Hastings*, 175
Baynes, G. S., 42, 158
Bayuda Desert, 339
Beauclerk, C. E. de V., 160
Beaumont, F. M., 31, 71, 100, 182
Beaumont, R., in Chin Hills, 144, 145; wounded at Twin Peaks, 228
Beginderlyn, 290
Beith, 200, 282
Beira, 347, 348, 351
Belfast (Transvaal), 288, 291
Belturbet, detachment at, 156
Bemba's Kop, 5
Benha, 94
Bennet, Mr., British Consul, Réunion, 173, 177
Bennet's Drift, 152
Benson, G. E., at Bakenlaagte, 353–357
Beresford, Lord Charles, in Nile Expedition, 341–345
Bergendal Farm, attack on, 292, 293
Bermuda, 321
Bester's Station, Boers attack, 204
Bester's Valley, 268
Bethel, 354

Bethune, General, 213, 242, 280, 282, 283
Bewicke-Copley, R. C. A., at Colenso, 218; at Twin Peaks, 227; at Horse-Shoe Hill, 254; commands detachment, 288; exchanges, 300; commands 1st Batt., 302; commands Column, 303; completes period of command, 305
Biddulph, Major-General M. A. S., 40
Biggarsberg, 187, 200, 280, 281, 282, 283
Biggleswade, 319
Biliyu, 364
Birch, Lieutenant, 162
Bircham, A. H., 7
Blackdown, 319, 320
Blacklock, C. A., 150
Blackwood-Price, J. N., 42, 151
Black Mountain, expedition to, 116
Blesboklaagte Pass, 200
Blewitt, A., 140, 160
Blockhouse, Fort, 147
Blood, Sir Bindon, 301, 302
Blood River, Zululand, 6
Blore, H. R., 159, 182, 195, 277
Bloy's Farm, 247, 248, 249, 250
Blundell-Hollinshead-Blundell, D. H., at Twin Peaks, 228; at Wynne's Hill, 254, 255
Blyde River, 298
Boaz Island, 322
Boers, annexation unpopular with, 3; Dingaan defeated by, 3
Boer War, 1881, 14–35, 151–153
Bolan Pass, Stewart marches through, 41
Bombay, 115, 146, 151
Bordon, 327
Botha, General C., 284, 285, 287
Botha, General Louis, commands on Tugela, 214; determination of, 230, 232; effect of his return, 238; recommends retirement, 250; in Eastern Transvaal, 291, 295, 297; at Bakenlaagte, 353–358
Botha's Pass, invasion by, 187; attack on, 284
Botong, 145
Boultbee, C. A. T., 182, 195, 196
Bowen, R. S., 162; killed in action, 273, 275, 277
Bower, R. L., 31, 71, 100
Boyle, C., 164
Boyle, M. C., 26
Brakfontein, 226, 229, 235, 237
Bridle Drift, failure to find, 216

380 INDEX

Bright, Quartermaster-Sergeant, 146
Brind, Sir James, 37
Briscoe, H. W., wounded at Twin Peaks, 228
British Empire, growth of, 359
Brocklehurst, Major-General J. F., 281, 289, 294, 295
Brown, Rifleman, in *Warren Hastings*, 174
Browne, H. D., command of 3rd Batt., 163; completes period of command, 165; note on, 373, 374
Browne, Sir Sam, 41
Browning, F. A., 158
Brownlow, Sir Charles, order by, 37
Brownlow, J. R., 150, 160
Brownlow, Lieut.-Colonel (72nd), killed at Kandahar, 68
Brownlow, Lieut.-Colonel (Indian Army), 120
Brownlow, Major (K.D.G's), 17, 20, 337, 338
Brugspruit, 354
Brungshe, Chin Hills, 144
Buchanan-Riddell, H. E., 26, 42, 100, 158, 210
Buchanan-Riddell, R. G., command of 3rd Batt., 166; exchanges, 181; at Colenso, 218; at Twin Peaks, 227–231, 300, 320
Buddhist Road, discovered in Malakhand Pass, 132
Buffalo River, 5, 187, 194, 283
Buller, Sir Redvers, reconnoitres Egyptian position, 89; commands a Brigade in Suakim Expedition, 100; at Tamaai, 107, 108; leaves for South Africa, 211; his plan, 212; problem before, 213; fails at Colenso, 214–218, 266, 267; next effort, 220–233; attempt of, at Vaal Krantz, 234–240; plans fresh attempt at Colenso, 240–242; success at last, 243–260, 279; clears Northern Natal, 280–286; advances into the Transvaal, 287; orders from Lord Roberts, 288; in Eastern Transvaal, 289–298; in Nile Expedition, 345, 346; note on, 366–369
Bulwana, 202
Bulwer, E., D.A.G., Horse Guards, 155
Buner, 124
Bunerwals, show signs of unrest, 116
Burger's Pass, 298
Burgers, President, annexation accepted by, 3

Burma, 4th Batt. in, 139–146; Mounted Infantry in, 346, 347
Burn-Murdoch, Colonel (Royal Dragoons), 234, 240, 242, 250, 259, 281
Burrows, Brigadier-General G. R. S., defeated at Maiwand, 58
Busby, issued to 3rd Batt., 1; issued to 2nd Batt., 158
Buys, Stephanas, 303
Byron, W. G., 42, 69, 151, 154

C

CACHAR, retreat on, 142
Cæsar's Camp, guns on, 264; attack on, 267–276
Cairo, 73, 92, 94, 96, 305, 308, 338
Cambridge, H. R. H. Duke of, inspects 3rd and 4th Batt., 147, 165; inspects 2nd Batt., 153, 154; in Malta, 160; cable from, to 1st Batt., 178
Campbell, Sir W. Pitcairn, with 1st Batt., 182; at Talana Hill, 191–195; at Wagon Hill, 272–275; commands 3rd Batt., 300; mention by Lord Roberts, 301; commands a Column, 302; assumes command 3rd Batt., 320; completes period of command, 321; in Camel Corps, 339; at Abu Klea, 342
Campbell, Captain (Central India Horse), wounded, 127
Campbellpore, 123
Candia, 306, 307, 323
Canea, 306, 307, 323
Canning, C. S. G., 100
Cape Colony, Dutch of, 185; disloyalty in, 211, 212
Cape Town, 150, 161, 166, 167, 211, 212, 305, 320
Cardwell, Lord, introduction of Short Service by, 1
Carleton, Lieut.-Colonel, in retreat from Dundee, 201; at Nicholson's Nek, 207
Carlisle Fort, 113
Carolina, 289, 293
Carolina Commando, garrison of Twin Peaks, 227–230
Carr, Rifleman, in *Warren Hastings*, 174, 180
Cathcart, R., killed in action, 254
Cavagnari, Sir Louis, murder of, 47
Ceylon, 309, 310

INDEX 381

Chagru Kotal, 122
Chakrata, 137, 138, 325, 329
Chalmer, R., appointed Brigade Major, 50 ; command of 4th Batt., 139 ; with Manipur Expedition, 140
Chaplin, C. S., 158, 308, 323, 325
Charasia, Roberts's victory at, 48
Charlestown, 286
Charley, J., 42, 154, 163
Chatham, 3rd Batt. to, 1
Chaton, Sous Officier, Réunion, 173
Chelmsford, Lord, commanding the Forces in South Africa, 5 ; defeats Zulus at Ulundi, 10 ; relieves Etshowe, 10 ; superseded by Sir Garnet Wolseley, 13
Cherat, 125, 137
Chester-Master, R., 160, 161
Chichester, 328
Chieveley, 220, 241, 250, 251
Chilibagh, 119
Chimoio, 348
Chin Hills, operations in, 144, 145
Chindwin River, 142
Chitral, expedition for relief of, 126–134
Chittagong, 145
Christian, H. W., 159, 160
Cingolo, Boer position on, 242 ; orders for attack of, 243, 244 ; capture of, 245 ; guns on, 246
Clarke, C. A. G., in Manipur Expedition, 140
Clarke, General Sir C. Mansfield, in Zululand, 13
Clery, General, 212, 213, 217, 220, 240, 281, 285, 287, 288, 302
Clump Hill, Naval guns on, 249 ; East Surrey on, 250
Cobbold, R. P., in Manipur Expedition, 140
Coke, Talbot, General, 222, 224, 226, 251–260
Colchester, 2, 328, 329
Colenso, repulse at, 214–218, 266, 267 ; demonstration against, 220 ; fresh try against, 240 ; crossing at, 251 ; bridges broken at, 257
Colenso Kopjes, 214, 216, 251, 253, 256
Collett, Brigadier-General, in Manipur Expedition, 143
Colley, Major-General Sir George Pomeroy, succeeds Wolseley, 15 ; repulsed at Laing's Nek, 16–18 ;

in action at Ingogo River, 20–24 ; his failure, 20–24 ; grave of, 284 ; shortage of mounted troops, 337, 338
Collins, J. J., 39, 44, 69
Columbo, 310
Connaught, H.R.H. Duke of, commands Guards Brigade at Tel-el-Kebir, 89 ; visits 2nd Batt., 320 ; at Malta, 324
Connaught, H.R.H. Prince Arthur of, visits 2nd Batt., 320
Connell, Rifleman, in *Warren Hastings*, 176, 180
Corbett, Rifleman, receives V.C., 96
Cork, 147, 320, 321
Cork Harbour, 113, 135
Cornish (Medical Officer), 27
Cossins, H. W., murder of, 142
Coulon, Monsieur, at Réunion, 173
Couper, R. G. H., 151
Cowley, Captain, at Manipur, 142
Coxhead, Lieut.-Colonel J. A., 201, 202
Cramer, C. P., embarks with 3rd Batt., 7 ; commands escort to Ketchwayo, 13 ; to Malta with 3rd Batt., 31 ; to Egypt with 3rd Batt., 71 ; to command of 1st Batt., 114 ; wounded, 121 ; retires, 123
Crane, E. J., 140, 146
Crawley, A. P., 7
Cretans, 306
Crete, 305, 323
Creusot guns, 185, 237
Crocodile River, 293
Croft, Rifleman, in *Warren Hastings*, 175, 180
Crofton, Morgan, Colonel, 161, 253
Crondall, 319
Cronje, A. P., at Rietfontein, 206
Crosbie, J. G., 96, 100
Crowley, Sergeant John, drowned, 112
Crow's Nest, *see* Wagon Hill, attack on
Crum, F. M., with 1st Batt., 182 ; wounded, 196 ; temporary command, 2nd Batt., 316 ; with Mounted Infantry in South Africa, 352, 356, 358
Cumberland, L. B., in *Warren Hastings*, 167
Cundycleugh Pass, 278
Curteis, J., 160
Curzon, Lord, 312
Cyprus, 71, 163, 305

D

Dagshai, 137, 325
Dalby, T. G., in Somaliland, 361
Dalmanutha, 291, 292, 303
Dalstroom, 301
Danner, Rifleman, in *Warren Hastings*, 175
Dannhauser, Buller reaches, 283
Dannhauser Road, patrols on, 198
Danvers, Sergeant, rewarded for distinguished conduct, 113
Dargai, Malakhand Pass, 130
Dartnell, Colonel J. G., guides Column, 200
Dauglish, Major (The Buffs), at Bakenlaagte, 353
Davidson, A., 42, 50, 151
Davidson, J. H., 182, 195
Davis, Major-General John, in Suakim Expedition, 100
De Aar, 302
Deane, Colonel B. M., at Laing's Nek, 17
Dehra Dun, 311
Delagoa Bay, 297, 303
De la Rue, Colonel, 323
Delhi, 36, 37, 312, 314, 325, 329
Denison, E. B., 314
Denniss, 2nd Lieutenant G. B. B., at Wagon Hill, 274
Deolali, 115, 166
Dewar, E. J., with Mounted Infantry in Manipur, 140; killed in action, 352
Dhar, 121
Dharmsala, earthquake at, 327
Diamond, Rifleman, in *Warren Hastings*, 175
Digby Jones, Lieutenant R. J. T., at Wagon Hill, 269–274
Dingaan, defeated by Boers, 3
Dir, 127, 133
Dir, Khan of, troops of, capture Sher Afzul, 133
Diwaas, 200
Diyathlawa, 310
Dobbin, Lieutenant, in *Warren Hastings*, 168–181
Donegal, trouble in, 156, 157
Doornkop, 216, 237
Dost Muhammed, Amir of Afghanistan, 39
Douglas, Lieut.-Colonel W., 301
Douglas-Pennant, F., 150
Dover, 147

Downe, Sergeant, in *Warren Hastings*, 175, 176, 179
Drakensberg Mountains, passes of, 185, 281
Dubba, Sudanese camp at, 105
Dublin, 113, 135, 157
Dukhteran Hill (Kandahar), 65
Dundas, J. D., 111, 112
Dundee, protection of, 184; force at, 186; threatened, 187; retreat from, 196–203; wounded from, 264; Boers evacuate, 282; Mounted Infantry at, 352
Dundonald, Lord, commands Mounted Brigade, 213; at Colenso, 217; seizes Potgieter's Drift, 222; success of, 223; captures Bastion Hill, 224; command of Mounted Brigade, 234; takes Hussar Hill, 243; captures Cingolo, 245; turning movement by, 246, 247; enters Ladysmith, 259, 279; in Northern Natal, 281–283; in Eastern Transvaal, 289–296
Dunfanaghy, 156, 157
Dunn, John, in Zululand, 13
Dunn, Mr., Bandmaster, 2nd Batt., 315
Du Pré, W. B., 160
Durban, 7, 14, 150, 152, 153, 166, 181, 204, 212, 213, 309, 326, 338, 348
Durband (Black Mountain), 117, 124
Durband Kotal (Miranzai), 120
Durnford, Port, 13
Dwane, C., 316
Dwane, J., 161, 167, 310, 316

E

Eales, Major (The Buffs), killed in action, 357
Eckford, Lieutenant, 162
Edwards, Colour-Sergeant, 195
Edwards, F. W. L., 150
Egerton, Field Marshal Sir C. C., wounded, 121; in Somaliland, 362
Egerton, Major-General G. G., order by, 325
Egypt, 163, 307
Egyptian Campaign, 1882, 72–95; Mounted Infantry in, 338
Elands Spruit, 293
Elandsfontein, 293
Elandslaagte, action at, 199, 205; cavalry reach, 280; 2nd Division at, 281

INDEX

Elles, Major-General Sir W. K., commands Black Mountain Expedition, 116
El Teb, *see* Teb.
Enniskillen, 156, 157
Erasmus, General, task of, 187; advance of, 194; contact with, 196; nearing Ladysmith, 206
Ermelo, 288, 290
Estcourt, 153, 213
Etshowe, surrounded by Zulus, 6; relieved, 10; detachment, 1st Batt. at, 181, 352
Eustace, C. L. E., in Manipur Expedition, 140; in Chin Hills, 145; to South Africa, 161; death of, 308; in Mashonaland, 347, 351; at Bakenlaagte, 353
Evans, A. P., 150, 307
Eversley, 319
Ewshott, 319
Eyre, C. D., 307

F

FALAM (Chin Hills), 144, 145
Farmer, G. L. McL., 42, 43, 151, 158, 159
Fatehgarh, 37
Feilden, J. H. G., 159, 160
Fermoy, 135, 147
Ferozepore, 137
Fetherstonhaugh, R. S. R., rejoins 3rd Batt., 12; command of 3rd Batt., 165; finishes command, 166; commands Rifle Company, Mounted Infantry Camel Regiment, 339
Finch, S. A. G., 150
Fitz Gerald, F., 42, 151
Fitzpatrick, farewell to, 38
Foljambe, H. F., 160
Fontesvilla, 348
Football, 4th Batt. wins Army Cup, 328
Forestier-Walker, M. C. B., to India with 4th Batt., 135; in Chin Hills, 145; returns with 4th Batt., 146; to Malta, 160; command of 1st Batt., 166; in *Warren Hastings* 167–181; appointed to Staff, 181
Forman, 2nd Lieutenant, in *Warren Hastings*, 175
Forster, O., 42
Forster, W., 87
Fortescue, Major H., letter from, 148
Fortescue, F. A., 160, 326

Foster, J. L., killed in action, 210
Fowke, Lieut.-General Sir George, in raid on Boer gun, 266
Foxstangways, Captain, 162
France, policy of, affected by Arabi's rebellion, 72; in Crete, 306
Fraser, E. L., 71, 100
Fraser, Major-General Keith, 158
French (Lord Ypres), at Elandslaagte, 205; at Lombard's Kop, 206, 207; escapes from Ladysmith, 212, 263; in Cape Colony, 213; in Eastern Transvaal, 290–297; in Nile Expedition, 341
French fleet, leaves Alexandria, 74
French-Brewster, H. G., killed in action, 228, 231
Frere, 213, 220, 222
Frere, Sir Bartle, High Commissioner in South Africa, 4; prepares for war, 5
Fuzzy Wuzzies, break a British Square, 107

G

GAFFNEY, Quartermaster-Sergeant, receives D.C.M., 96
Gakdul Wells, 340, 345
Galadi, 364
Gandamak, treaty of, 41
Gansvlei Spruit, 285
Garrett, J. R., killed in action, 21, 23
Gatacre, General, 133, 212, 213
Gawari Ghat, 317
Geluk, 291
German Emperor, visits Malta, 324; visits London, 328
Gharial, 123, 313, 329, 330
Ghazni, Afghans retire on, 46; Stewart reaches, 54; Roberts reaches, 61
Ghezireh, 95
Ghilzais, peaceable attitude of, 46
Ghlo, cavalry action at, 44
Ghora Dhaka, 123, 124
Ghustang, 122
Gibraltar, 158, 159, 163, 164
Gilgit, relief of Chitral from, 127
Ginginhlovo, action at, 8, 9
Gladstone, W. E., abandons Sudan, 346
Glencoe, Symons occupies, 182, 184, 185; Yule advances on, 199
Godwaan Station, 297
Gogra, 121
Golightly, R., 42, 151

384 INDEX

Good Hope, Cape of, 160
Gordon, C. A. B., 111
Gordon Pasha, Governor of the Sudan, 97; at Khartum, 339–345
Gore-Browne, H., to South Africa, 161; in *Warren Hastings*, 167–181; commands 1st Batt., 203; at Wagon Hill, 270; exchanges to 2nd Batt., 300; takes over 2nd Batt., 310; completes period of command, 313
Gore-Browne, Lady Muriel, in *Warren Hastings*, 167
Gosling, C., 159, 161, 167–181, 325
Gosport, 147, 165, 309, 326, 328
Gough, General Sir Hubert, commands Battalion of Mounted Infantry, 287
Gough, General Sir Hugh, commands Cavalry in Roberts's march, 59–68
Graham, Major-General Sir Gerald, in command at Nefisha, 81; commands 2nd Brigade at Tel-el-Kebir, 89; commands expedition to Suakim, 100; at El Teb, 102; asks for trouble at Tamaai, 107; at Suakim, 338
Graham, Brigadier-General T., in Manipur Expedition, 140, 141
Grant, R. J., killed in action, 228, 231
Greaves, General Sir George, A.G. in India, 152
Greece, war with Turkey, 306; Crete handed over to, 307
Green, H. C. R., 150, 160, 161, 310
Green, Lieutenant, 162
Green Hill (Spion Kop), 224, 225
Green Hill (Vaal Krantz), 235, 237
Green Hill (Colenso), 242, 243, 244, 245, 247, 248, 250
Greer, C. R., at Ingogo, 20, 21
Grenfell, F. O., 150, 314
Grenfell, Lord, letter from, 28; Governor of Malta, 305; visits 2nd Batt., 320; note on, 369–371
Greylingstaad, 288, 302
Greytown, 14, 242
Grierson, Lieut.-General Sir James, 319
Griffin, Lepel, interview of, with Abdurrahman, 58
Grimwood, F., murder of, 142
Grimwood, G. G., 140, 160, 161, 206–209, 265, 300
Griqualand East, 15
Grisley, Rifleman, in *Warren Hastings*, 174, 180

Grubelaar Mountain, 251
Gubat, 345
Gulistan, 122, 123
Gulistan Karez, 43
Gumbur, 364
Gundigan, 65
Gundi Mulla Sahibdad, 66
Gunning, R. H., Adjutant, 3rd Batt., 7; in Chin Hills, 144; exchanges, 166; commands wing of 1st Batt., 166; command of 1st Batt., 181; marches with 1st Batt., 182; at Talana Hill, 190–196, 300
Gun Hill (Chieveley), 244, 245, 249
Gun Hill (Ladysmith), 265, 266
Gun Hill (Bakenlaagte), 356, 357
Guns, manned by Riflemen, 15, 20, 22
Gwada, 121, 122
Gwajha Pass, road over, 43

H

HABIBULLAH, Amir, 314
Haines, Sir Frederick, C.-in-C. in India, 152
Haka, Chin Hills, 144
Hambok, 340
Hambro, W. J., with 1st Batt., 182; killed in action, 196
Hamilton, General Sir Ian, at Lombard's Kop, 206–209; in Ladysmith, 262; at Wagon Hill, 271–275; in Eastern Transvaal, 294–296
Hamilton, W. H. P., commands Cavagnari's escort, 47
Hamley, General Sir Edward, commands 2nd Division, E.E.F., 79; ordered to Ismailia, 85; at Tel-el-Kebir, 89
Hammersley, F., wounded, 191
Hammond, Brigadier-General A. G., Brigadier Isazai F.F., 124
Hangu, 119, 120
Hankey, G. F. B., 160
Hardinge, Sir A. E., 38
Hardinge, Lord, in Camel Corps, 339
Hardinge of Penshurst, Lord, 325
Hare, S. W., 317, 319
Haripur, 116, 119, 124
Harker, T. H., 310, 314
Harris, A. F. W., 161, 309
Harris, Lieut.-Colonel, East Surrey Regt., at Wynne's Hill, 255
Harrismith, 150, 326
Hart, General, 216, 217, 245–260, 288

INDEX

Hart's Hill, attack on, 255–257
Hartley Row, 319
Hasan Abdal, 41, 119, 124
Hashim Ali, causes Isazai Expedition, 124
Hatchell, G., 112, 113
Hatting's Farm, 233
Hatting Spruit, 196, 283
Haulbowline, 113
Hawley, C. F., 182
Hawley, finishes period of command, 135; present at inspection of 3rd and 4th Batts., 147; D. A. G. at Horse Guards, 153
Haworth, W. S. S., died of wounds, 23
Hay, Colonel J., letter from, 311
Haynes, Captain A. E., killed in action, 351
Haynes, E. C., Paymaster, 3rd Batt., 7
Hazaras, bring supplies to Stewart, 50
Hazara Expedition, 115–117
Healey, Serjeant, 146
Heidelberg, 287, 288, 303
Height 360, proposed attack on, 238
Helmets, issued to 1st Batt., 111; Wolseley pattern issued, 313
Helmund River, reconnaissance towards, 44
Helpmakaar, 200, 282
Helpmakaar Ridge, 264, 265
Helvetia, 293
Henderson, Lieut.-General Sir David, in raids on Boer guns, 266, 298
Henderson, K. G., 137, 154
Henley, R., 26, 31
Henniker, F. B. M., 316
Herat, garrison of Kandahar leave for, 44
Herbert, E. W., 100, 147, 150, 160, 326
Herbert-Stepney, C. C., 150
Hewett, Admiral, occupies Suez, 78; takes over defence of Suakim, 99
Heytesbury (Wilts), 317
Hicks Pasha, force of, wiped out, 98
Hildyard, General, at Colenso, 216, 217; at Vaal Krantz, 240; Relief of Ladysmith, 245–260; commands 5th Division, 281; in Northern Natal, 282–287; to Wakkerstroom, 286; on L. of C., 287
Hill, Lieut.-Colonel L., letter from, 311
Hills, Major-General Sir James, commands 3rd Division in Afghanistan, 57
Hinxman, R. W., 135
Hlangwani, occupation of, essential, 214, 240, 241; attack on, 216, 217; Boers on, 242; shelled, 243; occupied, 248; Boer rearguard on, 249; garrison of, 250; 2nd Division at, 251
Hodgson, Corporal, in *Warren Hastings*, 175, 180
Holland, Commander G. E., of *Warren Hastings*, 166–181
Holmes, Quartermaster-Sergeant, 146
Holmes, W., 42
Hope, C., 42
Hope, J. A., 159, 160
Hopton, Major-General E., 159
Horse-shoe Hill, 251, 252, 253; attack on, 254–256
Hoshangabad, 115
Hoti Mardan, 116, 129
Howard, General Sir Francis, Brigade Commander, 206; in Ladysmith, 262, 265; commands 8th Brigade, 281; operations of, 286; in Eastern Transvaal, 294, 296
Howard-Vyse, H. G. L., 27, 31, 71; killed in action, 77
Howarth, Sergeant, in *Warren Hastings*, 175, 179
Howeiya, El, 340
Howes, Rifleman, in *Warren Hastings*, 174, 180
Huddleston, Sub-Lieutenant, in *Warren Hastings*, 175
Hughes, Brigadier-General, in Afghanistan, 46–57
Hull, strike duty at, 318
Hunter, General Sir Archibald, raids Boer gun, 266; commands 10th Division, 281; Prinsloo surrenders to, 288
Hunter, A. J., 150
Hunter, Rifleman, gets D.C.M., 339
Hussar Hill, 243, 248, 250
Hutton, E. T. H., embarks with 3rd Batt., 7; raises Mounted Infantry at Alexandria, 75, 334; in action near Alexandria, 75–77; in Eastern Transvaal, 297; commands 3rd Division, 328; work of, for Mounted Infantry, 331; lecture by, 332–335; to Natal with Mounted Infantry, 338; good results of Mounted Infantry School of, 351; note on, 371–373

I

IMPATI Mountain, overlooking Dundee, 198, 199
India, 1st Batt. embark for, 115
Indian Ocean, H.M.S. *Crocodile* breaks down in, 115
Indumeni, 199
Indus River, heat in valley of, 117; crossed, 124
Ingogo River, action at, 20–24; 3rd Batt. camp at, 283; 4th Division at, 286
Inkwella Mountain, 26, 27
Inman, E. M. L., killed in action, 18
Intintanyoni Mountain, Boers occupy, 205
Intombi Spruit, neutral camp at, 264
Inyezane River, 9
Irby, L. P., 159, 160
Ireland, J., 7, 31
Isandhlwana, British defeat in Zululand at, 3, 6; effect of defeat at, on British troops, 12
Isazai Field Force, 123–125
Ismailia, Wolseley's intention to advance from, 73
Italy, in Crete, 306

J

JACOBABAD, 43
Jagers De, Field Cornet, at Wagon Hill, 274
Jagers De Drift, Boers at, 186; crossed, 187
Jalala, near Malakhand Pass, 129
Jandol, Umra Khan's Headquarters at, 127
Jani-ka-Sang, 116; cholera at, 125
Jan Murad, Stewart halts at, 50
Jelf, R. G., 182
Jenner, A. V., in Mashonaland, 347, 350
Jhansi, 115
Jidbali, action at, 362, 364
Johannesburg Police, at Bergendal, 292
Johnson, H. C., 203, 305, 307
Johnstone, R., 182, 195, 196
Jones, Captain E. P. (R.N.), commands Naval Guns, 213
Jones, Colour-Sergeant, in *Warren Hastings*, 175, 179
Jones, C. B., Rifleman, in *Warren Hastings*, 180
Jones, T., Rifleman, in *Warren Hastings*, 176, 180

Joubert, General P., Boer C.-in-C., 185; moves, 187; declines to sanction retirement, 250; sanctions neutral camp, 264
Joubert's Farm, Buller at, 285
Jubbulpore, 315, 317
Julian, Major O. R. A., at Talana Hill, 195; at Lombard's Kop, 210; at Wagon Hill, 277
Jullundur, 134, 166
Junction Hill, 264, 269

K

KABUL, Russian Mission to, 39; British Resident to be received at, 41; Residency attacked in, 47; Roberts starts his march from, 60
Kabul River, 124
Kaffir Drift, 226, 227
Kafiristan, 126
Kafr-ed-Dawar, Arabi's army at, 74; orders for attack on, 79; bravery of Rifleman Corbett at, 96
Kahan, capital of Mari country, reached, 69
Kakul, 312
Kalat-i-Ghilzai, Stewart moves on, 44; occupies, 46; reaches on his march North, 56; Roberts halts at, 62
Kaley, Rifleman, in *Warren Hastings*, 176, 180
Kambula, Wood defeats Zulus at, 10
Kandahar, Stewart's march on, 41–44; cholera epidemic at, 47; Stewart marches from, 49; siege of, raised, 62; Battle of, 66–69
Kanhow, Chin Hills, 144
Karachi, 325, 329
Karez Hill, 65, 66
Kashmir, 126; shooting in, 139
Kasr-el-Nil Barracks, 96
Kassassin, projected seizure of, 81; Arabi's attack on, 87, 88
Kays, W. S., to Ashanti, 165; wounded, 229; temporary command 1st Batt., 301; commands a Column, 302; temporary command 3rd Batt., 303; command of 2nd Batt., 313; completes period of command, 316
Kelly, G. C., 310, 360
Kelly, Lieut.-Colonel, relieves Chitral, 127, 133
Kendat, Burma, 142

INDEX

Kenna, Brigadier-General P. A., in Somaliland, 362–364
Kennedy, Colonel, 1
Kennedy, W. H., 31, 71, 100
Kensington Barracks, 154
Ketchwayo, Zulu King, 4; truculent attitude of, 4; captured by Major Marter, 13
Khandwah, 115
Khanna Plain, Royal Review on, 314
Khanki River, 121, 123
Khar, in Swat Valley, 132
Khartum, 97, 308
Kheman, 364
Khojak Pass, road over, 43
Khushab, 44
Khushk-i-Nakhud, action at, 46
Kilkenny, 166
Killick, G. L. B., 31, 100
Kilworth Camp, 147, 321
Kimberley, besieged, 212, 219
H.M. King Edward VII, proclamation of, 312; funeral of, 317; visit of, to Cork, 321; sees water-polo, 322; visits Malta, 324; holds review, 327
H.M. King George V, visits Cairo, 308; telegram from, 309; visits India, 314; coronation of, 317; inspects 2nd Batt., 320; inspects 3rd Batt., 322; inspects 4th Batt., 328
Kingstown, 156, 158
Kinloch, A. A., commands Brigade, Chitral Relief Force, 128–133; command of 4th Batt., 139; of 2nd Batt., 155; to Dunfanaghy, 156; services of, 157, 158
Kinloch, H. A., 312
Kinsale, 113
Kirkpatrick, Major W. J., in *Warren Hastings*, 166–181
Kitchener, Field-Marshal Lord, Chief of Staff, South Africa, 219
Kitchener, F. W., 252, 290
Kitchener's Hill, plan for attack on, 258
Klip River (Natal), 259, 261, 262, 265
Klip River (Transvaal), 285
Klipfontein, 290
Klipstapel, 290
Knox, Major (18th Hussars), good work of, 198; at Wagon Hill, 274
Knox, Colonel W. G., in Ladysmith, 262
Kock, General, task of, 187; defeat of, 204, 205

Kohat, 119
Kohima, 142
Kohistan, 126
Kohkaran, 65
Komati Poort, advance on, 287
Kordofan, attempt to reconquer, 98
Korti, 339, 340, 346
Kotal-i-Babawali, in Afghan position at Battle of Kandahar, 65–68
Kranspan, 290
Kromdrai, 287
Kruger, President, ultimatum by, 184–186; at Nelspruit, 293; goes to Europe, 297
Kruger's Post, 298
Kudetse, 307
Kuldana, 312, 313
Kuram Valley, 48, 57
Kurkora Kotal, cavalry action near, 44
Kushalgarh, 119, 123
Kushi, Roberts reaches, 48

L

LADYSMITH, 2nd Batt. passes, 153; occupied, 184; force at, 186; retreat on, 200–203; White reaches, 204; situation at, 211; plans for reduction of, 220; unsuccessful operations for relief of, 211–240; successful, 241–260; relieved, 259; replenishing of, 260; siege begins, 261; raids from, 266; sickness in, 267, 278; food shortage in, 267, 278; great attack on, 268–278; relief of, 279; Boers retreat from, 280; garrison of, unfit, 280; 2nd Division returns to, 282; 4th Division leaves, 283
Laffan's Plain, Royal Review on, 147
Laing's Nek, Boer position on, 15; British repulse at, 16–18; Dundonald reconnoitres, 283; turning of, 284; evacuated, 285, 286; Mounted Infantry at, 337
Lainson, A. J., 144, 161
Lakenvley, 291, 293
Lakka, 120
Lambton, Hon. Hedworth, at Lombard's Kop, 209
Landkhwar, 129
Laurenco Marques, 297
Law, F. T. A., 7
Lee, C. F., wins Army Sixty Cup, 376
Legard, A. D., 182
Legh, H. C., 42

388 INDEX

Leicester Post, 264, 265
Leith, A. R., 309
Lennox Hill, *see* Talana Hill
Letterkenny, 156
Limerick, 113
Limit Hill, 264
Lisbon, 316
Lloyd, T. P., 42, 151
Lockhart, General Sir William, 116, 118, 125
Logar Valley, 58
Lombard's Kop, 202, 206–210
London, 154
Londonderry, 156, 158
Long, W. J., 145
Long Hill, Boers on, 206
Longmoor, 319
Lord, N., 159
Lovell, Bandmaster, 323
Lovett, H. R., 151
Low, Lieut.-General Sir Robert, commands Chitral Relief Force, 128–133
Lowari Pass, 127
Lowe, General Sir Drury, 84, 85
Luneberg, 6
Lushai, 145
Lydenburg, 293, 294, 295, 297, 298
Lynes, W. P., at Bakenlaagte, 358
Lyons, Major-General, 155
Lysley, W. du V., 12
Lysons, D., 42
Lyttleton, General Hon. Sir Neville, to Natal, 212 ; at Colenso, 216, 217 ; at Potgieter's Drift, 223 ; relieves pressure on Spion Kop, 226–230 ; address to 3rd Batt., 231 ; at Vaal Krantz, 236–239 ; commands 2nd Division, 240 ; in operations for relief of Ladysmith, 243–260 ; commands 4th Division, 281 ; on L. of C., 287 ; in Eastern Transvaal, 289, 295, 298, 301

M

MacCall, H. B., 123, 166
McCann, Surgeon, at Ingogo, 22
McGregor, Captain (R.E.), killed in action, 21
MacGregor, Brigadier-General C. M., commands Brigade in Roberts's march, 60 ; commands Expedition to Mari country, 69, 70
McGrigor, C. R. R., with 3rd Batt., 31, 71, 100 ; vacates command, 3rd Batt., 308 ; command of 3rd Batt., 321 ; to Staff, 323

Maclachlan, A. C., killed in Great War, 126
Maclachlan, L. C., killed at polo, 125
Maclachlan, N. C., accidental death of, 126
Maclachlan, Brigadier-General R. C., attached to 2nd Batt., 162 ; wounded, 277 ; killed in Great War, 126
McLoughlin, Colour-Sergeant, wounded, 228
Machadodorp, 293, 301
Mackworth, Brevet-Major D., at Wagon Hill, 270, 271, 275, 277
McMahon, Sir H. W., in Mashonaland, 347
McNally, T. C., 203
McNamara, Rifleman, in *Warren Hastings*, 169, 174, 180
Macpherson, Sir Herbert, 37, 60–68, 90, 94
McQue, Sergeant, gallantry of, 164
Magersfontein, defeat at, 214, 267
Magfar, danger to Fresh Water Canal at, 80 ; dam at, 81
Mahdi, The, rising of, 97 ; besieges Khartum, 341–346
Mahommed-bin-Abdullah Hassan, *see* Mullah
Mahsama, Egyptian camp at, captured, 84
Maiden Castle, 271, 272, 277
Maiwand, British defeat at, 58 ; avenged at Kandahar, 69
Majendie, B. J., 167, 182
Majuba, 26–30, 338
Makins, G., 161, 309
Makoni, defeat of, 348–351
Malakhand Pass, storming of, 127–132
Mallaha Junction, occupied by 3rd Batt., 76
Malta, 71, 159, 305, 323–325
Mamuzai Bazar, 123
Manipur, Expedition to, 140–143, 145
Manning, Brigadier-General W. H., in Somaliland, 360
Marchwood, 2, 111, 153
Margala, quarantine camp at, 125
Mari country, Expedition to, 69, 70
Mariut, Lake, 75
Markham, C. J., 140, 305
Marling, P. S., at Ingogo, 20 ; to Malta, 31 ; to Egypt, 71 ; with Mounted Infantry to Suakim, 100 ; with Mounted Infantry in Cairo, 338 ; wins V.C., 339

INDEX

Marsden, H. S., joins 1st Batt., 182; killed in action, 210
Marsham, H. S., 42, 151
Marter, Major (K.D.G's), captures Ketchwayo, 13
Martin, G. H., 182, 195, 196, 307
Masbury Camp, 317
Mashaki, 51
Mashonas, 347–352
Mashonaland, Expedition to, 347–352
Massowa, black troops raised at, 99
Massy, Brigadier-General, 48
Mastan, 121–123
Matabeleland, 347, 351
Mauchberg, 296
Mauritius, 166, 181
Mazra, Ayub retires to, 62
Meerut, 37, 137, 138, 139, 151, 325, 329
Meerzight, 289
Mehemet Ali, conquers Sudan, 97
Mehtar, the (of Chitral), 126
Mends, H. R., 147, 151
Metammeh, 339, 344, 345
Metcalfe, Lieut.-Colonel C. T. E., raids Boer howitzer, 266
Methuen, Field-Marshal Lord, task of, 212; defeats Boers, 213; defeat of, 267
Meux, Sir Hedworth, *see* Lambton.
Meyer, Lukas, force of, 185; defeat of, 187–195
Michell, C., 7
Middelburg, 288, 301, 353, 354
Middle Hill, 264, 265, 270, 273
Middlepunt, 293
Miles, A. E., 12, 31, 339
Miller-Wallnut, Major, at Wagon Hill, 274
Minto, Lord, 315
Miranzai Expedition, 118–123
Mir Asghar, 122
Mitchell, Sergeant-Major, drowned, 112
Modderspruit Station, 205, 251, 282
Mohammed Ahmed, *see* Mahdi
Moharrem Bey Railway Station, 3rd Batt. occupy, 75
Möller, Colonel, 352
Moncrieff, Captain (R.N.), death of, 99
Monte Cristo, Boer position at, 242; attack on, 245–248; East Surrey Regt. on, 250; British troops visible on, 278
Montgomery, B., 42
Montgomery, H. P., 36, 37, 39

Moor de Kraal, 243, 245
Morah Pass, 129, 132
Morland, T. L. N., 160
Morley, Private, rescue of, 338
Morris, A., 7, 12, 138, 139
Mott, S. F., 160, 161
Mount Alice, 222, 227, 233
Mount Prospect, Colley reaches, 15; camp at, 15–31; graves at, 284; Mounted Infantry march to, 337
Mounted Infantry, at Laing's Nek, 16–18; at Ingogo, 20–24; raised at Alexandria, 75; in action at Ramleh, 75; in action at Tel-el-Mahuta, 82–84; in action near Kassassin, 87; in Suakim Expedition, 102–106; found by 4th Batt., 139; pursuit by, at Bapham, 143; drafts for, 148, 154; Company of, 2nd Batt., 161; Company to Rhodesia, 165; Company of 1st Batt., 181; disposition of, 186; at Dundee, 187–194; at Lombard's Kop, 207; object of, 331–337; in Nile Expedition, 339–346; in Burma, 346, 347; in Mashonaland, 347–352; in South Africa, 352–358; in Somaliland, 360–364
Mounted Infantry Hill, 264
Mullah, The, 359–365
Müller's Pass, 204
Multan, 40, 41
Munger's Drift, 235, 236
Mure, G. A. S., 150
Murghan, 65
Murray, Major F. D., at Bakenlaagte, 353
Murree Hills, 36, 123, 312, 313, 329
Myengyan, 139, 140, 144, 145, 146
Myer's Farm, 282
Myers, W. J., joins 3rd Batt., 12; killed in action, 203, 210
Mynors, A. C. B., with 3rd Batt., 7; death of, 12

N

NAAU POORT, 212
Naoshera, 127
Napier, Field-Marshal Lord, 96
Natal, 4, 151, 181, 183–187, 211, 212, 277, 280–285, 326
Natal Native Contingent, 5, 8
Natal Naval Volunteers, in Cæsar's Camp, 269

390 INDEX

Naval Brigade, at Lombard's Kop, 209; at Wagon Hill, 269, 274
Nefisha, 79, 81
Nelspruit, 293
Nelthorpe, 259
Nevill, H. J., 12
Newara Eliya, 310
Newby, Lance-Corporal, in *Warren Hastings*, 174, 180
Newcastle (Natal), 15, 24, 152, 153, 187, 283
Newdigate, Major-General H. R. L., 159
Nicholson, H. B., 160
Nicholson, John, statue of, 314
Nicholson's Nek, disaster at, 207
Nile Expedition, 339–346
Nivengal, Chin Hills, 145
Nolan, Colour-Sergeant, 146
Nooitgedacht, 293
Nooitgedacht Farm, 356
Norcott, Colonel C. H. B., 240
North West Frontier, campaigns on, 115–134
Northey, E., to the Cape, 160; to Mounted Infantry, 161; with 1st Batt., 182, 301, 302; command of 1st Batt., 309; with Mounted Infantry in South Africa, 352
Northey, F. V., with 3rd Batt., 7, 8; mortally wounded, 9
Nugent, O. S. W., with 1st Batt., 182; at Talana Hill, 195, 196; commands 4th Batt., 329
Nuttall, Brigadier-General, 66, 68

O

OBSERVATION HILL, 265, 272
O'Brien, A. V., 7
O'Connell, M., killed in action, 23
Oghi, 124
Ogilvy, W. L. K., 7, 12, 16, 26, 71, 100, 101, 156, 163
Olivier's Huek Pass, 204
Omdurman, fall of, 341
Onderbroek Spruit, 249, 251, 255, 256
Orakzais, outbreak of, 118
Orange, J. E., 31, 71
Orange Free State, 184, 211
Orde-Powlett, W. G. A., 159
Orleans, duc d', 138
O'Shea, T., 146, 150
Osman Digna, raises Eastern Sudan, 99; attack on, at Tamaai, 105–108
Oxley, R. S., 140, 308, 309, 323

P

PAARDEBERG, success at, 279
Paarde Kop, 287
Paarde Plats, 295
Paine, A. I., 160, 161
Palel, 143
Palliser, Brigadier-General, in Stewart's march, 50–56
Palmfontein, 294
Panjkora River, crossed, 127–133
Park, Major C. W., at Wagon Hill, 274, 275
Parkhouse Camp, 309
Parkhurst, 113, 147, 164
Parkinson, Rifleman, in *Warren Hastings*, 176, 180
Parnell, Major-General Hon. H., 160
Pat Durband, 120
Pearce-Serocold, 208, 310, 319
Pearson, Colonel, at Etshowe, 6
Pearson, Fort, 5, 7
Pechell, C. A. K., 159, 160
Pechell, M. K., in *Warren Hastings*, 167; rejoins 1st Batt., 182; killed at Talana Hill, 195, 196
Peiwar Kotal, 40
Pemberton, W. L., 1, 7, 12, 16, 27
Penn Symons, Major-General Sir W., at Glencoe, 182; views of, 186; at Dundee, 187–195
Pepworth Hill, 206, 207, 209
Peshawar, 41, 125, 137, 138
Peshin, 49
Peter's Farm, 282
Piat, Mr., in Réunion, 173
Pickersgill, Rifleman, in *Warren Hastings*, 176, 180
Pieter's Hill, 246, 258
Pieter's Hoek, 249, 250
Pietermaritzburg, 14, 31, 152, 153, 181, 204
Pigg, James, quoted, 332
Pigott, C. B., on Majuba Day, 27; with 3rd Batt., 31; severely wounded, 86; gallantry of, 338
Pilgrim's Rest, 295, 297, 298
Pilkington, T. E. M. S., 26, 31, 158
Picquet Hill, 224
Pir Paimal, 66–68
Pixley, A. D., wounded, 23
Pöe, C. V., 150
Pointe Des Galets, 170, 171, 172
Pokoko, 140
Pole-Carew, Major-General R., 291, 293, 297

INDEX 391

Polo, home of, 140; Infantry Tournament, 2nd Batt., winners of, 313
Pomeroy, 282
Pompeii, sentry at, 177
Porter, H. C. M., 150
Porter, M. L., 150, 160, 162
Port Louis, 173, 181
Port Said, 71
Portsdown Forts, 316
Portsmouth, 2, 111, 153, 164, 316
Portuguese East Africa, 347
Potchefstrom, besieged, 16
Potgieter's Drift, route to Ladysmith by, 213, 221; Dundonald seizes, 222; crossed, 223, 235, 241
Pratt, M., 305
Pratt-Barlow, E. A., 150
Prendergast, G. N., 100; in *Warren Hastings*, 167–181
Pretoria, 3, 14, 293
Prevost, G. H., 140
Priaulx, G. K., 313
Price-Davies, L. A. E., 161
Primrose, Major-General, in Kandahar, 49
Prinsloo, General, surrender of, 288
Pungwe River, 347
Pur, 138

Q

H.M. QUEEN MARY, visits Cairo, 308; visits India, 314; coronation of, 317
Queenstown, 113, 135, 148, 166, 320
Quetta, 40, 41, 43, 47
Quinton, Mr., Chief Commissioner of Assam, murder of, 142

R

RAIKES, F. H., killed in action, 277
Rangeworthy Heights, 225, 233
Rangoon, 145, 146
Ration Post, 265
Rawal Pindi, 36, 115, 116, 123, 124, 125, 310, 312, 313, 314, 329
Rawson, Lieutenant (R.N.), steers Wolseley's night march on Tel-el-Kebir, 90
Reade, R. E., 182
Ree, Lough, boating accident on, 112
Regent's Park, camp in, 317
Regiments :
  Artillery : at Ahmad Khel, 52, 54; at Mahuta, 81–86; at Tel-el-Kebir, 89–92; in Miranzai, 120, 121; at Malakhand, 130; at Dundee, 189–199; at Lombard's Kop, 206, 208, 209; at Colenso, 216, 217; at Potgieter's Drift, 226; at Vaal Krantz, 235–237; in Relief of Ladysmith, 243–253; in Siege of Ladysmith, 264–268; in Northern Natal, 289; at Bergendal, 292; at Mauchberg, 296; at Bakenlaagte, 354, 356, 358
  Baluchis, 130th, 329
  Bedfordshire, 128–132
  Bengal Cavalry, 3rd, in Roberts's march, 59–65
  Bengal Lancers, 11th, 116; 19th, 51–56, 120
  Bengal Infantry, 15th, 120; 19th, 116, 120; 27th, 120, 121; 29th, 120
  Bethune's Mounted Infantry, 213, 226
  Bikanir Camel Corps, in Somaliland, 364
  Blackwatch, The, at Tel-el-Kebir, 90–92; in Suakim Expedition, 101–107
  Bombay Cavalry, 3rd, 68
  Bombay Infantry, 1st, 4th, 19th, 28th, 66
  Buffs, The, 7, 9, 353–357
  Camel Corps, The, 339–346
  Camel Regt., Heavy, 339–344
  Camel Regt., Light, 339
  Camel Regt., Guards, 339–341
  Camel Regt., Mounted Infantry, 339–346
  Cameron Highlanders, at Tel-el-Kebir, 90–92
  Central India Horse, in Roberts's march, 59, 60
  Connaught Rangers, 240
  Devons, 1st Batt., 207, 262, 275, 276, 297, 298
  Devons, 2nd Batt., 237–240, 254
  Dogras, 37th, at Malakhand, 128–132
  Dragoon Guards, 5th, 204, 207, 275
  Dragoons, Royal, 213
  Dublin Fusiliers, Royal, 186–194, 201, 206, 262, 354–357
  D.C.L.I., 76, 80, 83, 88, 92, 319
  Durham L.I., 212, 226, 236–238, 250, 255, 257
  East Surrey, 248, 250, 254, 255, 258

Regiments—cont.:
  Eighty-third Foot, 18
  Essex, 340
  Eton College Rifle Volunteers, 203
  Fifty-seventh Foot, 7, 9
  Fifth-eighth Foot, 15, 17, 18, 26, 27
  Fifty-ninth Foot, 51–56
  Fusiliers, Royal, 66
  Fusiliers, Royal Irish, 89, 101, 189–192, 200, 201, 207, 262
  Fusiliers, Royal Scots, 15
  Gharwal Rifles, 39th, 312
  Gloucester, 207, 262
  Gordon Highlanders, 1st Batt., 90–92, 101, 130; 2nd Batt., 18, 24, 26–28, 60–68, 152, 206, 262, 269–274, 295–297
  Guides, The, at Malakhand, 130–132
  Guides Cavalry, charge by, 132, 133
  Gurkha Rifles, present from, 310; losses of, in earthquake, 327
  Gurkhas, 2nd, 36, 37, 60–68, 311, 314, 329; 3rd, 37, 51–56; 4th, 60, 62, 120, 143; 5th, 60, 119–122; 9th, 329
  H.L.I., 2nd Batt., at Tel-el-Kebir, 90–92
  Household Cavalry, 78, 80, 81, 86
  Hussars, 10th, 101; 13th, 213, 221, 288; 14th, 280; 15th, 18, 24, 152; 18th, 186–201, 207, 273, 285, 289; 19th, 81, 101, 207, 273–275, 289, 341–344
  Imperial Light Horse, 204, 207, 213, 259, 269–274
  Inniskilling Dragoons, 18
  Inniskilling Fusiliers, 292
  Kashmir Rifles, 4th, in Chitral, 127
  K.O.S.B., 2nd Batt., 130
  K.O.Y.L.I., Mounted Infantry of, 353–357
  K.O.Y.L.I., detachment of, 124
  K.R.R.C., ceases to be 60th, 30
    1st Batt., to Winchester, 111; to Aldershot, 112; to Dublin, 113; to India, 115; Hazara and Samana, 115–123; Isazai Expedition, 124, 125; Chitral Relief Expedition, 128–134; to Mauritius, 166; wrecked in *Warren Hastings*, 167–181; marches North, 182; at Dundee, 186; at Talana Hill, 189–196; in retreat from Dundee, 200–203; at Lombard's Kop, 206–210; in Ladysmith, 262–265; at Wagon Hill, 269–277; in 8th Brigade, 281; with Howard, 286; with Buller in Eastern Transvaal, 289–296; with Lyttleton, 301; to De Aar, 302; to Malta, Egypt, and Crete, 305; to Khartum, 308; to Gosport and Aldershot, 309
    2nd Batt., reaches Durban from India, 18; inspected by Colley, 24; detailed for Afghan War, 40; leaves Multan, 42; reaches Kandahar, 44; marches with Stewart, 49; in Roberts's march, 60–68; with MacGregor to Mari country, 69, 70; to South Africa, 151; to England, 153; to Shorncliffe, 155; to Enniskillen, 156; to Dublin, 157; to Gibraltar, 158; to Malta, 159; to the Cape, 160; to Calcutta, 161; in Natal, 186; reaches Ladysmith, 204; at Rietfontein, 205, 206; at Lombard's Kop, 206–210; in Ladysmith, 262, 265; at Wagon Hill, 269–277; in 8th Brigade, 281; with Howard, 286; to Ceylon, 309; to Rawal Pindi, 310; to Delhi, 312; to Bareilly, 313; to Jubbulpore, 315; to Shorncliffe, 317; to Blackdown, 319
    3rd Batt., returns from Aden, 1; embarks for South Africa, 7; at Ginginhlovo, 9; joins Clarke's Column, 13; to Natal, 14; in Griqualand East, 15; at Laing's Nek, 16–18; at Ingogo, 20–24; on Majuba day, 26–30; reaches Malta, 71; at Alexandria, 75; at Ismailia, 80; at Mahuta, 83–85; action near Kassassin, 87, 88; at Tel-el-Kebir, 90–92; at Cairo, 95; in Suakim Expedition, 101–108; to Egypt, 110; joint inspection with 4th Batt., 147; to Cyprus, 163; to Parkhurst, 164; to Shorncliffe, 165; to

INDEX

Regiments—*cont.*:
  Aldershot, 166; reaches Durban, 212; at Colenso, 218; captures Twin Peaks, 227–233; at Vaal Krantz, 236–238; occupies Moorde Kraal, 243; at Bloy's Farm, 250; crosses Tugela, 251; at Colenso Kopjes, 252; attack on Horseshoe Hill, Wynne's Hill, 254–258; reaches Dundee, 283; at Standerton, 287; to Heidelberg, 288; on Column and L. of C., 302, 303; to Cork, 320; to Bermuda, 321; to Aldershot, 322; to Crete and Malta, 323; to Umballa and Dagshai, 325; to Meerut and Chakrata, 326
  4th Batt., at Portland, 135; to India, 136; to Chakrata, 137; to Meerut, 138; to Burma, 139; to Manipur Expedition, 140–143; to Gosport, 147; to South Africa, 150; in South Africa, 304; to Harrismith, 326; to Colchester, 328; to Meerut and Chakrata, 329
Lancashire Fusiliers, 328
Lancashire, Loyal North, 353–357
Lancaster, Royal, 253, 254
Lancashire, South, 253
Lancers, 5th, 201, 202, 207, 273–275, 289; 9th, in Roberts's march, 59; 17th, 148
Leicestershire, 186, 189, 202, 206, 262, 281, 286
Liverpool, 206, 262, 281, 286, 291
Madras Infantry, 12th (Burma), 143
Manchester Regt., 120, 122, 207, 262, 265, 269, 271
Marines, Royal, 75, 77, 80, 82–84, 88, 101–106
Middlesex, 167–181
Middlesex Rifle Militia, draft of, to 1st Batt., 111
M.I., Composite Regiment, 244, 287
M.I., 3rd, at Bakenlaagte, 353–358
M.I., 25th, at Bakenlaagte, 353–358
Natal Carbineers, 186, 204, 213, 259, 266
Ninety-first Foot, 7, 9
Ninety-fourth Foot, 14
Ninety-seventh Foot, 18

Ninety-ninth Foot, 7, 9
Oxfordshire and Buckinghamshire L.I., 319
Pioneer, 23rd (Punjab), in Roberts's march, 60
Punjab Cavalry, 1st, 49–56; 2nd, 51–54; 3rd, 59; 5th, 120
Punjab Infantry, 1st (Coke's Rifles), 36, 37, 119, 121; 2nd, 120, 121; 6th, 120; 19th, 51–56; 24th, 60; 25th, 40, 49–54, 60; 27th, 116; 29th, 118
Queen's, The, 245, 255, 277
Rifle Brigade, 1st Batt., 212; at Potgieter's Drift, 226; at Vaal Krantz, 236, 237, 250; at Hart's Hill, 255, 257; 2nd Batt., 113, 155; at Lombard's Kop, 207; in Ladysmith, 262, 265, 266; at Wagon Hill, 273; at Bergendal, 292, 314; 3rd Batt., 312
Rifle Reserve Battalion, 242, 253, 255
Rifles, Royal Irish, 113, 155, 314, 315
Rifles, Scottish, 1st Batt., 315; 2nd Batt., 212, 218, 226, 236, 237, 250–252, 256, 258
Scinde Horse, 3rd, 68
Scottish Horse, 353–357
Seventy-second Highlanders, in Roberts's march, 60–68
Sikh Infantry, 2nd, 51–54, 60–68; 3rd, 60–62, 120
Sikh Pioneers, relieve Chitral, 127
Sikhs, 4th, at Malakhand, 130–132; 14th, 127; 15th, 40, 51–54, 60–65, 128
Sixty-sixth Foot, 66
Somerset L.I., 251
South African Light Horse, 213, 222, 224, 244, 284, 285, 289
Staffordshire, South, 71, 75
Strathcona's Horse, 288, 289, 296, 302
Sussex, Royal, 307, 340–343
Thorneycroft's M.I., 213, 224, 244, 250, 256, 286, 288, 302
West Riding, 348
York and Lancaster Regiment, 81, 82, 101–107, 166–181
Yorks, West, 245
Rethymo, 323
Réunion Island, *Warren Hastings*, wrecked on, 170–181
Rhanikhet, 314, 326

Rhodes, J. E., 309
Rhodesia, Mounted Infantry in, 165, 347
Rickman, A. T., 160
Rietfontein, action at, 201, 205, 206
Rifle, Martini-Henry, 1, 3, 115, 135; Snider, 1; Lee-Metford, 114, 115, 124, 125, 164; Short L.E., 308, 315, 322, 328; L.E. Mark III, 319, 329
Rigaud, G., 36
Riley, T., 316
Ringwood (Hants), 328
Ritchie, Rev. G. M., 22
Robat, 62
Robeck, C. de, 42
Roberts, Hon. Aileen, letter from, 149
Roberts, F. H. S., death of, 217
Roberts, Lord, in Afghanistan, 40–70; defeats Afghans at Charasia, 48; repels attack at Sherpur, 49; appointed to command Kabul-Kandahar Force, 59; march of, to Kandahar, 64; defeats Ayub Khan, 66–69; inspects 1st Batt., 115; cable to, 148; C.-in-C. in South Africa, 219; enters Free State, 278; success at Paardeberg, 279; campaign in Free State, 280, 281, 282; advance on Komati Poort, 287; in Eastern Transvaal, 291–294; despatch of, 300; visits 2nd Batt., 320
Robertson, Field-Marshal Sir W., attempt on life of, 134
Robertson, Surgeon-Major, in Chitral, 127
Robinson, Lance-Corporal, in *Warren Hastings*, 175
Roe, Colonel P. B., 1
Roe, Private (Y. and L. Regt.), in *Warren Hastings*, 176, 177
Rooderkop, 303
Rorke's Drift, 5
Ross, C. E., 100
Ross, General, 57
Ross, Mr., Native Commissioner, Mashonaland, 349, 350
Royal Irish Constabulary, 112, 157
Rundall, Captain F. M., 143
Rush, Colour-Sergeant, at Talana, 195
Rushmoor Bottom, 111
Rushmoor Green, 155
Russell, Sir Baker, 83, 85, 87, 155, 156

Russell, Colonel C. J., 337
Russia, danger of war with, 39, 111; in Crete, 306
Russian Infantry, march of, 323
Rutter, Lieutenant, 162
Ruyston, Colonel, 207
Ryder, D. G. R., 7, 17, 20, 31

S

SABI RIVER, 297, 298
Sackville-West, C. J., 140, 144, 330
Saidabad, 57
St. Aubyn, E. G., 150
St. Aubyn, E. S., 71
St. Aubyn, G. S., 347
St. George's, 322
St. John, Lieut.-Colonel, 63
St. John's River, 14
St. Vincent, 6
Salahiyeh, 87, 88
Salisbury (Mashonaland), 347, 348, 351
Salisbury Plain, 147
Salmon, W. H., 100
Samana Ridge, 118
Sand Spruit, *see* Talana Hill
Sangar, 120–122
Saragarahi, attack on, 122
Saugor, 315
Saumarez, De, L. W., 160, 161, 309
Saunders-Knox-Gore, W. A. C., wins Silver Jewel, A.R.A., 375
Saxe-Weimar, H.S.H. Prince Edward of, 153, 154
Schalk Burgher, 227, 269
Schleswig-Holstein, Prince Christian Victor of, death of, 149
Schleswig-Holstein, H.R.H. Princess Christian of, 327
Scratchley, V. H. S., 352
Scudamore-Stanhope, E. T., 31, 71, 100
Senapati, 140, 142
Sewell, C. F., 160
Seymour, Admiral Sir Beauchamp, bombards Alexandria, 74; conference with Wolseley, 79
Seymour, C. H. N., 161
Seymour, G. Culme, 310
Shahjui, action near, 49
Shakerley, G. C., 150, 159, 160, 309, 360–363
Shakespear, Captain, 145
Shakot Pass, 129, 132
Shalez, action at, 56, 57
Shandur Pass, 127

INDEX

Shekabad, 57
Shepstone, Sir Theophilus, mission of, to Pretoria, 3
Sher Afzul, besieges Chitral, 126–133
Sher Ali Khan, Amir of Afghanistan, 39 ; abdicates, 41
Sher Dahan Pass, 61
Sherpur, attack on, 49
Sherston, Maxwell, 339
Shifaldara, 121
Ships :
  Aboukir, H.M.S., 307
  Arabia, S.S., 316
  Agincourt, H.M.S., 71
  Assistance, H.M.S., 156
  Avoca, S.S., 161
  Boadicea, H.M.S., 7
  Bokhara, S.S., 100
  Braemar Castle, S.S., 309
  Canning, R.I.M.S., 146
  Carysfort, H.M.S., 79
  Clive, R.I.M.S., 181
  Clive, S.S., 310
  Crocodile, H.M.S., 115
  Danube, S.S., 7
  Dilwara, S.S., 305, 322
  Dominion, S.S., 320
  Dongola, S.S., 329
  Dryad, H.M.S., 105
  Dublin Castle, S.S., 7, 153
  Euphrates, H.M.S., 80, 151, 152
  Himalaya, H.M.S., 158
  Immortalite, H.M.S., 164
  Irrawaddy, R.I.M.S., 146
  Jumna, H.M.S., 155
  Kensington, S.S., 322
  Lalpoora, S.S., 170–172
  Malabar, H.M.S., 146
  Mohawk, S.S., 310
  Northumberland, H.M.S., 71
  Nurani, S.S., 162
  Orient, S.S., 309
  Orion, H.M.S., 79
  Orontes, H.M.S., 31, 100, 110
  Osiris, S.S., 100
  Plassey, S.S., 317
  Purnea, S.S., 161
  Rewa, S.S., 325
  Roslin Castle, S.S., 150
  Sardinia, S.S., 305
  Serapis, H.M.S., 115, 135, 136
  Servia, S.S., 166, 212
  Shah, H.M.S., 7
  Sicilia, S.S., 323, 326
  Sladen, R.I.M.S., 140
  Tenedos, H.M.S., 7
  Utopia, S.S., 105, 163
  Victoria, S.S., 159, 160
  Warren Hastings, R.I.M.S., wreck of, 166–181 ; ship's bell of, 313
Shorncliffe, 1, 155, 156, 317
Shutargardan Pass, 40, 48
Sibi, 69
Simpson, W. H., murder of, 142
Sinkat, siege of, 99, 100
Skene, Lieut.-Colonel, murder of, 142
Skiets Drift, 223, 235
Skylos, 307
Slade, Colonel C. G., 155
Slade-Wallace, 158, 164
Smith, C. Holled, 12, 16, 26, 28, 30
Smith, K. S., 150
Smith's Farm, *see* Talana Hill, battle of
Smith's Nek, *see* Talana Hill, battle of
Smith-Dorrien, General Sir Horace, 294
Smuts, General, 297
Snow, Lieut.-General Sir T. D'O., 318
Soames, A. A., 150
Soltau-Symons, G. A. J., 160
Somaliland, expedition to, 359–365
Soult, Marshal, remarks on 5th Batt., 375
South African Republic, independence of, proclaimed, 14
South African Republics, war declared by, 182 ; forces of, 183
South African War, 183–304, 352–358
Southampton, 309, 317, 322, 326, 329, 339
Spain, King of, 327
Spion Kop, 222–233
Spitz Kop, 297
Spottiswoode, J., 160
Springfield, 222, 240, 252
Standerton, 285, 287
Steele, Rifleman, in *Warren Hastings*, 176, 180
Steward, Sergeant Isaac, drowned, 112
Stewart, Field-Marshal Sir D., in Afghanistan, 40–70; defeats Afghans at Ahmad Khel, 52–55
Stewart, Sir Herbert, 101–104, 108, 340–345
Stewart, Major-General R. C., 145, 146
Stirling, R. G., 182
Stopford, Sir Frederick, 165
Stormberg, reverse at, 214
Stuart, W. D., 140, 143, 145

396 INDEX

Stuart-Wortley, A. R. M., 167, 182, 195, 196, 329
Stuart-Wortley, E. J. M., 151, 158, 242, 317, 345
Suakim, 99, 101, 105, 108, 338
Suda Bay, 323
Sudan, The, rising in, 96–100 ; given up, 346
Sudanese, tactics of, 349
Suez, 96
Suez Canal, danger to, 72 ; covered by advance from Ismailia, 73 ; Wolseley's move to, 79
Sugar Loaf, *see* Twin Peaks
Sukkar, 42
Sunday's River, 201, 282
Surprise Hill, raid on, 266
Swart Kopjes, 292–294
Swat Valley, 127–133
Swayne, Lieut.-Colonel E. J. E., 360
Swindon, 147
Sym, Major-General Sir John, 120
Symons, *see* Penn Symons

T

TABANYAMA, 281
Talana Hill, memorial service for, 147 ; battle of, 187–196 ; Mounted Infantry at, 352
Talbot Coke, *see* Coke
Tamaai, 105, 106–108, 338
Tamanieb, 110
Tammu, 140
Tashon, 144, 145
Taylor, Colour-Sergeant, at Talana Hill, 195
Taylor, J., in *Warren Hastings*, 167 ; with 1st Batt., 182 ; killed in action, 196
Taylor, Rifleman, in *Warren Hastings*, 175
Tchaka, Zulu national hero, 2
Teb, El, action at, 102–105, 338
Tel-el-Kebir, Wolseley's foresight, 73 ; battle of, 90–94
Tel-el-Mahuta, dam at, 81 ; action at, 82–84
Terry, A., 16, 113, 114, 138
Tewfik, Khedive of Egypt, 72, 94
Tewfik, Bey, heroism of, 100
Tewkesbury, Lord, 151, 158
Thackwell, Colonel W., 75, 76
Thana, 133
Thayetmyo, 139, 143, 146
Thesiger, General, *see* Chelmsford

Thistlethwayte, E. W., 23, 158, 228, 303
Thompson, Colour-Sergeant James, drowned, 112
Thompson, Rifleman, at Lombard's Kop, 210
Thorneycroft, 213, 232
Three Tree Hill, 224, 233
Thurlow, E. H., 12, 26–28
Thynne, U. O., 160
Tilden, W., 151
Tillard, Major, 56
Tipnor, 111, 153
Tlang Tlang, 144
Tod, Lieutenant N. M., attached 2nd Batt., 162 ; killed in action, 273, 275, 277
Tokar, 99, 101, 105
Tolmie, T. C., 71, 95
Tournay Barracks, 147
Townshend, Major-General Sir C. V., at Chitral, 127
Transvaal, threatened by Zulus, 3 ; annexed, 14 ; beleaguered garrisons in, 15 ; outbreak in, 151 ; invasion of, 284
Trickhardt's Drift, 223, 233
Trinkitat, 99, 101, 105
Trotman, G. H., 42
Tsalai, 118, 121
Tufnell, A., 7
Tugela River, 5, 213, 221, 223, 233, 235, 236
Tundla, 115
Tunnel Hill, 275
Turkey, inaction of Sultan of, 72 ; war with Greece, 306
Turner, Lieut.-Colonel A. H., 120
Turner, Colour-Sergeant, 146
Turnour, K., 7, 123, 159, 160
Twin Peaks, capture of, 227–233
Twyfelaar, 290
Tyler, Bandmaster, in *Warren Hastings*, 175 ; at Talana Hill, 195 ; at Lombard's Kop, 210 ; at Wagon Hill, 277, 278 ; awarded D.C.M., 301

U

ULUNDI, 5
Umballa, 115, 312, 325
Umbulwana, 264
Umra Khan, at Chitral, 127–133
Umtali, 348
Upper Topa, 329
Utrecht, 283

INDEX

V

VAAL RIVER, 287, 290
Vaal Krantz, 222, 234–240
Val, 288
Valetta, 324
Van Reenen's Pass, 280
Van Tonder's Pass, 200
Van Wyk's Hill, 284
Van Wyk's Vlei, 290
Venter's Spruit, 221
Vermaak's Kraal, 282
Vernon, H. A., 310
Vernon, R. J., 140
Vertnek Mountain, 250
Queen Victoria, proclaimed Empress of India, 37 ; holds Review in Windsor Park, 112 ; inspects 1st Batt., 113 ; Jubilee of, 113 ; Diamond Jubilee of, 147, 156 ; funeral of, 150 ; inspects 3rd Batt., 165 ; cable to 1st Batt., 178
Viljoen, General, 187
Villiers, de, Commandant, at Wagon Hill, 274
Vlakfontein, 303
Vlaklaagte, 288
Volksrust, 285–287
Vryheid, 283, 287

W

WAAIKRAAL, 291
Wady Halfa, 339
Wagon Hill, 264 ; attack on, 267–277
Wagon Point, *see* Wagon Hill
Wake, H., at Wynne's Hill, 255
Wakkerstroom, 286, 287
Wales, H.R.H. Prince Albert Victor of, attached to 3rd Batt., 163
Wali Sher Ali, 58
Wallace, Brigadier-General A., 316
Walsh, H. H. A., 140
Walton, C.S.I.M. F., wins Silver Jewel, A.R.A., 375
Ward, E. F., 160, 161, 309
Ward, H. A. H., 71
Warren, Sir Charles, 220, 221, 223–226, 232, 245–260, 281
Warter, Major, at Arzu, 56
Warwick Camp, 322
Waschbank River, 200, 201, 282
Waterval Boven, 303
Waterval Onder, 293
Watson, H. W. M., 361
Watson, J. K. (Sen.), 1
Watson, J. K. (Jun.), 144

Weinarshoek, 294
Wells (Somerset), 317
Wheatley, Colour-Sergeant, 146
Whitaker, G. T., 163
White, Fort, 144, 145
White, Sir George, commands in Natal, 184, 211 ; influenced by political situation, 185 ; orders from, 200 ; at Rietfontein, 201 ; arrives in Ladysmith, 204 ; energetic action of, 205–209 ; Buller's instructions to, 214 ; his message to, 218 ; attacked, 220 ; report from, 251 ; attempt at pursuit by, 259 ; in siege of Ladysmith, 261–279
White, H. H. R., 360–363
Wickham, Major, brilliant action of, 203
Widdrington, B. F., 310
Wilkins, J., 24, 30, 71, 95, 100, 104
Wilkinson, Brigadier-General, 85
Wilkinson, E. O. H., 7, 23
Willan, F. G., 309
Willcocks, General Sir James, 330
Williams, Sergeant-Bugler J., wins Gold Jewel, A.R.A., 375
Williamson, C., 36, 135
Willis, General, 82, 87, 88, 89
Wilson, Sir C., in Nile Expedition, 340–345
Wilson, R. C., 151
Winchester, 2, 111, 153, 327
Windham, Lieutenant, in *Warren Hastings*, 165–181
Windsor, Royal Review at, 112
Wingate, 2nd Lieutenant, 162
Wingfield, C. J. T. R., 150
Wiseman Clarke, Major-General S. M., 157
Witbank, 290
Witklip, 294
Wolseley, Viscount, arrives in Zululand, 13 ; C.-in-C. Egyptian Expedition, 72–95 ; compliments 3rd Batt., 165 ; Army Order by, 179–181 ; in Nile Expedition, 339–345
Wood, Sir Evelyn, defeats Zulus at Kambula, 310 ; second in command to Colley, 18–24 ; succeeds to command, 30 ; commands at Alexandria, 85 ; raises new Egyptian army, 98 ; commands at Aldershot, 114 ; at manœuvres, 147 ; inspects 2nd Batt., 152 ; in Nile Expedition, 346

Woodgate, Major-General, 222, 224, 225, 232
Wool (Dorset), 309, 327
Woolls-Sampson, Colonel, 358
Woolwich, 2
Wooton, Rifleman, in *Warren Hastings*, 174, 180
Wylie, Fort, 214
Wynberg, 161, 166
Wynn, A., 159, 160
Wynne, Colonel A. S., 235–237
Wynne-Finch, G., 150
Wynne's Hill, 251–256

Y

YAKUB KHAN, Amir, 41, 45, 47, 48, 49
Young, Corporal, in *Warren Hastings*, 175, 176, 180
Young, Lieutenant (Royal Scots Fusiliers), 20
Yule, Major-General, at Talana Hill, 189–191; retreats from Dundee, 196–203

Z

ZAGAZIG, 94
Zandspruit, 287
Zuiker Bosch Bridge, 302
Zuiker Bosch River, 288, 303
Zululand, 2–13, 181, 185, 186
Zulus, history of, 2–5; tactics of, 2, 349; attack, 9
Zulu War, 2–13; Mounted Infantry in, 337
Zwagershoek, 294
Zwakfunein, 354
Zwartkop, 235, 236

www.ingramcontent.com/pod-product-compliance
Lightning Source LLC
Chambersburg PA
CBHW050324230426
43663CB00010B/1729